6.50

COMMENTARY
on
THE EPISTLE OF PAUL
TO THE ROMANS

by
CORNELIUS R. STAM
President, BEREAN BIBLE SOCIETY
Editor, BEREAN SEARCHLIGHT
Radio Teacher, BIBLE TIME

BEREAN BIBLE SOCIETY
7609 W. Belmont Avenue
Chicago, Illinois 60635

Copyright, 1981
by
CORNELIUS R. STAM

PRINTED IN U.S.A.

**WORZALLA PUBLISHING CO.
STEVENS POINT, WISCONSIN**

IN GRATEFUL ACKNOWLEDGMENT

Heartfelt thanks are due the many friends who helped in the preparation of this volume.

Virginia (Mrs. A. S.) Bengtson transcribed all the basic copy from 69 magnetic tapes containing my radio messages on *Romans*—a difficult and painstaking task most carefully done. From this manuscript I then proceeded to make additions and corrections so as to provide more complete and refined copy for Pastor Ricky Kurth and Brother Chuck Milkevitch, who typeset the entire book by *Linocomp*.

Pastor Richard Jordan offered many valuable suggestions and he, Pastor Kurth and Brother Milkevitch joined me in numerous proofreadings. Pastor Russell Miller also read much of the copy and offered many excellent suggestions. Ruth Stam, my dear wife, spent many hours listening as I read passage after passage to her aloud. She caught many a "slip in the type" and her criticisms and suggestions were most valuable.

The frontispiece is from a watercolor by Bernadette (Mrs. Russell) Miller. We are grateful indeed for this contribution by a truly gifted artist.

Preoccupied as I was with the writing of this volume, the members of the *Berean Bible Society* staff also did much to encourage and help by relieving me of many responsibilities. The heavy load of daily correspondence devolved largely upon Pastor Jordan and his secretary, Rosemary (Mrs. W.) Cummings.

Sincere thanks go also to many *Searchlight* readers who sent books, booklets and personal suggestions to help me in this undertaking. It has been heartwarming indeed to find so many friends *concerned* about our work on this great epistle. And those from whom I requested technical information responded most graciously and helpfully. Also, we are deeply grateful to those who helped supply the financial needs involved.

Most of all, we are profoundly grateful to God for supplying needed mental and physical strength (Eccl. 12:12), along with some degree of insight into the profound truths contained in the *Epistle to the Romans*.

Finally, while we thank God for each person who had any part in the completion of this volume, it must not be assumed from the above acknowledgments that all of those mentioned concur in all the author's conclusions.

CONTENTS

PAGE

Preface ix

Introduction: The Importance of the Romans Epistle — The Author — The Church at Rome — Time of Writing — Basic Outline xiii

CHAPTER I—Romans 1:1-17

Paul And the Believers at Rome: His Apostleship And Message — Paul's Apostleship — Paul's Message — A Prophesied Gospel? — Faithful And Beloved Saints — Beloved of God — Saints by Calling — Grace And Peace — Thanksgiving And Prayer — Paul's Defense of His Gentile Apostleship — "The Jew First" — Is the Jew First Today? — No Difference — The Righteousness of God — The Paradox of Grace — The Power of the Gospel — Something to be Proud Of — From Faith to Faith — Conclusion 20

CHAPTER II—Romans 1:18-32

The Wrath of God And the Guilt of Man: God's Wrath Revealed Against the Suppression of Truth — The Guilt of Man — How the Heathen Got That Way — Pagan Idolatry Reveals the Depths of Man's Philosophical Stupidity — The Gentiles Given Up — An Abandoned Race — The World No Better Today — The Fool! 42

CHAPTER III—Romans 2:1—3:20

Jew And Gentile Pronounced Guilty Before God: Moralizers No Better — God No Respecter of Persons — Jew And Gentile Both Under the Judgment of God — An Argument From Logic — The Justice of the Judgment to Come — God Will Judge the Secrets of Men — God Will Judge the Secrets of Men By Jesus Christ — God Will Judge the Secrets of Men According to the Gospel Committed to Paul — The Jew And the Law of Moses — The Jew Condemned By the Law — Circumcision And the Law — "What Advantage, Then, Hath the Jew?" — Advantage Turned Into Disadvantage — Does Sin Glorify God? — All Under Sin — Every Mouth Stopped — All the World Guilty Before God — No Justification By the Works of the Law 58

CHAPTER IV—Romans 3:21—5:5

But Now!—Righteousness Through Christ: The Righteousness of God Without the Law — Justification by Faith

Establishes the Law — Two Examples From Jewish History — The Case of Abraham — The Case of David — A Contradiction? — Righteousness Imputed Entirely Apart From Circumcision — Righteousness Imputed Entirely Apart From the Law — "That It Might Be By Grace" — The Father of Us All — The Mother of Us All — Genuine Faith vs. Intellectual Assent — If We Believe — The Direct Results of the Death of Christ For Us And of Justification by Faith — In the Believer's Personal Experience — Peace With God — Access to God — Rejoicing In Hope of the Glory of God — Rejoicing In Tribulations Also — The Love of God Shed Abroad In Our Hearts 85

CHAPTER V—Romans 5:6-21

Christ's Death For Us Dispensationally Considered: The Answer to Man's Helplessness, His Sinfulness And His Willfulness — The Personal Aspect — The Historical Perspective — From Adam to Moses — The Reign of Death Through Adam — From Moses to Christ — The Reign of Sin Through the Law — The Present Dispensation — The Reign of Grace Through Christ — The Unpardonable Sin 124

CHAPTER VI—Romans 6:1-23

Shall We Continue In Sin? Crucified, Buried and Raised with Christ — A Pivotal Passage — Crucified with Christ —Buried And Raised with Christ — Bury That Corpse! — Alive From the Dead — Whose Slave Am I? 139

CHAPTER VII—Romans 7:1—8:4

Another Husband: Correspondent Death — Who Is the Husband? — Double Death — The Law And Sin — Paul's Struggle With the Old Self — Out of Romans 7 Into Romans 8? — Five Important Laws — The Moral Law of God — The Law of Indwelling Sin — The Law of the Renewed Mind — The Law of Sin And Death — The Law of the Spirit, Life In Christ — Who's Who? — Further Lessons From Romans 7:14-25 — No Condemnation to Those Who Are In Christ Jesus — Romans 8:1 And the Authorized Version 158

CHAPTER VIII—Romans 8:5-39

Life In the Spirit: The Christian Walk — Sonship — A Position as Grown Sons — Present Suffering And the Glory to Come — The Spirit's Help — The Called According to His Purpose — Who Can Be Against Us? — Who Shall Separate Us? 184

Contents

CHAPTER IX—Romans 9:1-33

The Opening of the Dispensational Section of Romans: Paul's Sorrow Over His Unbelieving Kinsmen — Israel's Place of Privilege — The Basic Theme of Chapters 9-11 — A Theological Battleground — They Are Not All Israel Which Are Of Israel — Is There Unrighteousness With God? — The Potter And the Clay — The Future Jewish Remnant — God's Present Work Among the Gentiles 215

CHAPTER X—Romans 10:1-21

Israel's Failure Under the Law: Her Unbelief And Resistance to Grace — Zealously Religious, But Lost — Christ the End of the Law for Righteousness — The Righteousness of the Law vs. the Righteousness of Faith — By Works After All? — Two Twosomes — There Is No Difference — There Is No Difference For All Have Sinned And Come Short of the Glory of God — There Is No Difference For the Same Lord Over All Is Rich Unto All That Call Upon Him — Whosoever Shall Call — The Quotation By Peter — The Quotation By Paul — God's Patience With Israel 237

CHAPTER XI—Romans 11:1-36

Israel And the Gentiles In the Program of God: Israel's Present Condition — Not Completely Abandoned — An Introductory Word — The Believing Remnant — Unbelieving Israel Judicially Blinded — Israel's Fall And Recovery — The Diminishing of Them — The Blessing of the Gentiles Today — The Olive Tree, The Root, And The Branches — Be Not Highminded — Prophecy And the Mystery — The Scriptural Motive For Jewish Missionary Work 259

CHAPTER XII—Romans 12:1-21

The Opening of the Practical Section of Romans: Your Reasonable Service — The One Body And the Functions of Its Members — The Christian's Responsibility With Regard To Himself And Others 289

CHAPTER XIII—Romans 13:1-14

The Christian And His Government, His Neighbor And His Lord: Subjection To the Powers That Be — Should a Christian Go To War? — One Exception — The Christian, His Neighbor And His Lord — The Christian And His Neighbor — Time To Wake Up — Our Night And Day —

Let Us Not Sleep — *High Time* To Awaken — Awake And Arise 307

CHAPTER XIV—Romans 14:1—15:7

The Christian And Matters of Conscience: Diets And Days — Each One To Give an Account of Himself To God — Walking In Love — Closing Appeal 322

CHAPTER XV—Romans 15:8-33

Paul's Ministry To the Gentiles And To the Jews: Two "Ministers" — The Ministry of Christ To Israel And the Ministry of Paul To the Gentiles — Paul's Apostolic Objectives — The Poor Saints At Jerusalem 336

CHAPTER XVI—Romans 16:1-27

The Three Postscripts: Affectionate Greetings — The Holy Kiss And Divisive Brethren — More Greetings! From the Corinthian Saints — The Final Postscript — The Distinctiveness of Paul's Message — The Unity of Paul's Message — Finis 351

Appendix I: A Consideration of Romans 8:1b As Found In the Authorized Version 369

Appendix II: A Brief Consideration of Divine Election And Human Responsibility: The Lord Jesus Christ — The Bible — Personal Salvation — The Doctrine of Election — Election And Foreknowledge — The Question of Limited Redemption — Human Responsibility — Conclusion 372

PREFACE

Imperfectly indeed does this volume convey the profound message of the *Epistle of Paul to the Romans*. Yet we make no apology for publishing it, for we are sure that it contains many precious and enlightening truths *not* found in the great majority of commentaries, simply because most commentators, great men of God among them, do not, or did not, understand the "mystery" revealed through Paul. This is evident from at least two important facts:

1. While the "mystery" is the very *theme* of Paul's great message (Rom. 16:25), most commentators seldom even *mention* the word, much less expound or proclaim this great body of truth.

2. The vast majority of living Bible commentators are still operating under *the wrong commission*, the commission given by our Lord *on earth* to His eleven apostles. *They* call this "*the* Great Commission," seemingly unaware that *from His glory in heaven*, the Lord *later* gave *another* and *different* commission to the Apostle Paul—and to us (II Cor. 5:14-21; cf., Gal. 2:2-9).

Technically this commentary finds its origin in notes from *Studies in Romans*, which the author conducted at *Milwaukee Bible Institute* during the first five years of its existence, while he served as its Dean and Instructor in various Bible subjects. These notes were later used as the basis for a series of radio messages on *Romans*, and the radio messages, in turn, as the basis for this volume.

In writing this book we have had average-type readers in mind, feeling that if we could make its message clear to them perhaps the intellectuals might also be able to understand.

For numerous reasons we have adhered to the *King James Version* of the Bible in the text of this volume. Indeed, the fact that 47 godly men, so evidently and eminently qualified for their task, were the instruments in God's hand to produce this translation, has often constrained us to exercise great caution in criticizing its renderings. Much more might be said along this line, were this the place for such a discussion.

Where the exact meanings of particular words are of vital importance we have sought to bring this out, but we have exercised restraint here also, lest we inadvertently violate God's wise counsel: *"Strive not about words to no profit, but to the subverting of the hearers"* (II Tim. 2:14; cf., I Tim. 6:4). Indeed, in the author's study of the Word of God for more than fifty years, it has been his earnest and unceasing prayer that he might be given the Spirit's aid in understanding the *sense* of Scripture.

Mention should here be made about our use of the italics in the Scripture text. While not altering the wording in any way, we have used italics for emphasis rather than to indicate which words were supplied by the translators. Wherever the latter in any way affects the sense of any passage we state this in our comments.

We are well aware that this volume will probably call forth more criticism than any of our previous writings— simply because *Romans* deals with more subjects which have been warmly debated through the years than any other book of the Bible.

While for years the author has gained much light and blessing from the writings of others, the readers of this volume will by no means find it filled with quotations from "authorities." Research is indeed essential to the writing of any serious commentary, but there is always the danger that an author may spend so much time reading that he has little time left to *think*. It is no mere cliché that meditation has become a lost art. Then too, many "authoritative" definitions and conclusions are sadly lacking in actual *authority*. Thank God, He has given us valuable tools for further research where the meaning of His Word is concerned.

Whatever the mental and physical rigors involved in producing this volume, it has been sheer delight, spiritually, to study the great *Epistle of Paul to the Romans* in depth and then to commit to writing the light received.

And now, as we send this commentary to press it is our most earnest prayer that God will graciously use it to lead many a reader into a clearer understanding, not only of the

Romans epistle itself, but also of the most glorious message ever sent by God to man, the message which Paul here calls, *"my gospel, and the preaching of Jesus Christ according to the revelation of the mystery, which was kept secret since the world began, but now is made manifest..."* (Rom. 16:25,26).

CORNELIUS R. STAM

Chicago, Illinois
January 5, 1981

INTRODUCTION

THE IMPORTANCE OF THE ROMANS EPISTLE

Paul's *Epistle to the Romans* is one of the most profound, yet one of the most enlightening books of the Bible—indeed, of all literature. Nowhere else in the Bible do we find the great doctrines of the Christian faith set forth so completely or systematically.

The longest of Paul's letters, it has to do basically with the nature of God, the sin of man, and the believer's justification before the bar of God, revealing the righteousness of God (1:17) for those who deserve the wrath of God (1:18). It deals with man's alienation from God, the believer's reconciliation to God, and then applies this in a practical way.

It deals also with such great theological subjects as election, predestination, sanctification, law, grace, faith, the believer's identification with Christ and God's program for Israel and the nations.

These are all subjects that vitally affect us, subjects we ought to understand as fully as the renewed mind is enabled to understand the things of God.

In the canon of Scripture Romans is first among Paul's epistles, not because it was written first, but because logically it takes first place, presenting the great foundation truths of the gospel, revealing God's wrath against sin and the basis upon which alone He can declare the sinner righteous.

The *Epistle to the Romans* falls naturally into three basic sections: (1) *Doctrinal*, Chapters 1-8, (2) *Dispensational*, Chapters 9-11, and (3) *Practical*, Chapters 12-16.

THE AUTHOR

Paul, the human author of *Romans*, was ideally qualified

to write this epistle. A man of profound intellectual acumen, and of brilliant achievement, he was at the same time the chief of sinners, saved by grace, the foremost example of what had been accomplished through the death and resurrection of Christ. Moreover, in his background there was the Jewish legalism, the Greek culture and the Roman stature that suited him so well to make known a God-given message for *all mankind.*

The theological confusion in the Church today is basically the result of her rebellion against the authority of Paul as the divinely-appointed apostle for the present "dispensation of the grace of God."

On every hand Paul is referred to merely as one of the apostles, sometimes even as one of the twelve, though the record of Scripture proves that he could not possibly have qualified as one of the twelve (Matt. 19:28, cf. Acts 9:1).[1]

The Scriptures teach beyond the shadow of a doubt that Paul's apostleship and message were absolutely unique and separate from that of the twelve or of any who had preceded him. This is what Christendom as a whole has ignored or refused to accept, thus confusing God's prophesied kingdom program with the "mystery" committed to Paul for us in this present dispensation.

The Scriptures emphasize not only the Apostle's repeated use of the first person pronoun, "I," "me," "my," but also the *unique character* of his apostleship and message. Ignore this fact and confusion must inevitably result; accept it and a hundred seeming contradictions in Scripture disappear.

Surely no one even superficially acquainted with the Book of Acts or the epistles of Paul will question the fact that some time *after* our Lord's commission to the eleven and His ascension to heaven, *Paul* was sent forth, as an apostle of Christ, to proclaim to all mankind *"the gospel of the grace of God"* (Acts 20:24).

The Apostle opens and closes his *Epistle to the Romans* with the declaration that his message is for *"all nations"*

---

1. See the author's book, *Things That Differ*, Pp. 122-125.

(Rom. 1:5; 16:26). Whereas the twelve never got beyond their own nation in carrying out their commission to proclaim Christ as King, we have the record of Paul's extensive apostolic journeys among the Gentiles. It is written of Paul that during his stay at Ephesus *"all they which dwelt in Asia* [a province of Asia Minor] *heard the word of the Lord Jesus"* (Acts 19:10). To the Romans he writes, *"from Jerusalem, and round about unto Illyricum, I have fully preached the gospel of Christ"* (Rom. 15:19), and mentions his plans to go to Spain (15:24), plans which may well have been accomplished between his two Roman imprisonments. Even of his helpers it was said, *"These that have turned the world upside down are come hither also"* (Acts 17:6).

All this casts its light upon the *Epistle to the Romans* and the Apostle's purpose in writing it. With the new dispensation being ushered in, a comprehensive treatise on the nature of God, the fall of man and God's great plan for the justification of sinners was needed.

THE CHURCH AT ROME

There may well have been several local churches at Rome, like that referred to in 16:3-5, but the Apostle addresses his epistle to "all" the believers there, i.e., the entire "called out" assembly (1:7).

The "Church of Rome" today, of course, ascribes the founding of the early church there to the ministry of Peter, but there is not one scintilla of evidence in Scripture to bear this out, so we will not go into detail about it, especially since the Scriptures clearly state in Gal. 2:9 that Peter and the Judaean leaders publicly and solemnly agreed that they would thenceforth confine their ministry to Israel, acknowledging Paul as God's appointed apostle to the Gentiles.

There are also some who argue that since Paul had not even been to Rome at the time he wrote his epistle, it must be that believers from the Jerusalem Church had gotten as far as Rome under their "great commission."

We do not accept this as valid for the following reasons:

1. While indeed there were some "strangers of Rome" present at Pentecost, there is no indication that there was any substantial number of these, or that those present were even converted, much less that they started a church at Rome. On the other hand we read that later, in the great persecution in Jerusalem, "they were all scattered abroad throughout *the regions of Judaea and Samaria, except the apostles*" (Acts 8:1). Then, with regard to these same people, we read still later:

"Now they which were scattered abroad upon the persecution that arose about Stephen travelled *as far as Phenice, and Cyprus, and Antioch*, preaching the Word to none but unto the Jews only.

"And some of them were men of Cyprus and Cyrene, which, when they were come to Antioch, spake unto the Grecians,[2] preaching the Lord Jesus" (Acts 11:19,20).

When the Church at Jerusalem heard of this they sent Barnabas to look into it and *he* went to Tarsus to find *Saul*, and under Saul the church at Antioch became the base of operations for the evangelization of the *Gentiles* with "the gospel of the grace of God" (Acts 11:25,26; 14:26,27).

2. It was *from Antioch* that Paul went by revelation to Jerusalem to communicate to the leaders there "that gospel" which he had been preaching among the Gentiles (Gal. 2:2), with the result that they, through "James, Cephas [Peter] and John," *promised to confine their ministry thenceforth to Israel*, recognizing Paul as the apostle to the Gentiles.

Even *at that "council"* the Circumcision "apostles and elders" wrote concerning those who had gone out from them to impose their message and program upon the Gentiles:

". . .we have heard that certain which went out from us have troubled you with words, subverting your souls, saying, Ye must be circumcised and keep the law: TO WHOM WE GAVE NO SUCH COMMANDMENT" (Acts 15:24).

How, then, could the great church at Rome have been established by converts of the kingdom believers at Jeru-

---

2. Greeks, Gentiles. See Acts 15:1-29.

salem? Doubtless the Roman believers had been won to Christ through those whom Paul had sent forth with "the gospel of the grace of God."

3. If the believers at Rome were converts of kingdom believers who had returned or come to Rome from Jerusalem after Pentecost, how is it that we do not find even one similar case in any other Gentile city? Did converts from Pentecost go all the way to Rome and found a church, or churches, there, but *not* to Corinth, Ephesus, Thessalonica, etc.? In these cities the Apostle Paul went first to *the Jewish synagogues*, and when he preached the gospel in these synagogues it was evidently new to his hearers.

It might at first appear from Acts 18:24-28 that the case of Apollos argues against the above, but not so. Apollos, a Jew from Alexandria, knew "only the baptism of John" (Ver. 25), who had preached that Christ *was to come* (19:4), and he had only "begun" to speak boldly *in the synagogue* when Aquila and Priscilla found him (18:26). It is evident, therefore, that he had not established any Christian church at Ephesus.

4. Three days after Paul arrived at Rome, he "called together" the "chief" Jews there. This phraseology already indicates considerable prestige on Paul's part. These men then asked Paul to explain the doctrine he preached, "for," they said, *"as concerning this sect, we know that everywhere it is spoken against"* (Acts 28:22).

Why this interest in *Paul* and *his* message if the church, or churches, at Rome had been founded by some of *their own number* who had returned or come to Rome from Jerusalem?

The phrase, "everywhere [this sect] is spoken against," reminds us of the charge made against Paul by the Jews when he stood before Felix (Acts 24:5).

By now it was not Peter and his associates who were everywhere opposed; it was *Paul*. Even a casual reading of the *Acts* makes this clear. At Acts 8:1 we find the Messianic believers being driven from Jerusalem, but by Acts 15 most of them, evidently, have already returned, for by this time the church there is so strong that Messiah's followers can hold their own "council" right *in Jerusalem*, without any great opposition. Thus, by the time we reach Acts 28, it is no longer the message of the twelve, but the message of Paul that is meeting with bitter opposition on every hand.

We do not deny that some Jews who had returned to Jerusalem may have, even *must* have, told their Roman brethren what had happened there, and how the crucified King was evidently actually alive, but by this time even Peter had learned much of Paul's message and had endorsed it (Gal. 2:1-9; cf. Acts 15:11), so that now Paul was the dominant figure in the religious world.

5. Though there were, of course, some Jewish brethren in the Church at Rome, it was made up predominantly of Gentiles in the flesh. In Rom. 1:13 the Apostle tells how often he had purposed to go to Rome that he might have fruit among them *"even as among other Gentiles,"* and in 11:13 we have his declaration:

"I speak to you Gentiles, inasmuch as I am the apostle of the Gentiles; I magnify mine office."

6. The attitude of the Roman believers toward Paul bears witness to the argument that he, through his emissaries, had founded the church there. Here we quote from the noted French theologian, Godet, in his *Introduction* to the Romans epistle.

"A still more significant fact is related in the first part of Acts 28. On hearing of St. Paul's approach, the brethren who reside at Rome haste to meet him, and receive him with an affection that raises his courage. Does not this prove that they already loved and venerated him as their spiritual father, and that consequently their Christianity proceeded directly or indirectly from the churches founded by Paul in Greece and Asia, rather than from the Judeo-Christian church at Jerusalem?"

7. The above is further emphasized by the fact that Romans 16 clearly indicates that he already had many dear, personal friends at Rome. In this chapter he mentions more than twenty-five of these, plus some households! Some of

these had come to know Christ directly through his ministry and had since travelled to Rome.

TIME OF WRITING

The great offering from the Gentile churches to "the poor saints at Jerusalem" had now been completed, and Paul was on his way with others to deliver it to the leaders there. This is clear from Rom. 15:25,26:

> "But now I go unto Jerusalem to minister unto the saints.
>
> "For it hath pleased them of Macedonia and Achaia to make a certain contribution for the poor saints which are at Jerusalem."

We know from I Cor. 16:3-5 that this journey was to take him through Corinth, and it was evidently from here that he wrote the *Epistle to the Romans*. Greetings the Apostle sends to Rome from *Corinthian* believers appear to bear this out.

For example, in Rom. 16:23 he sends greetings from Gaius, his host, and I Cor. 1:14 indicates that Gaius was from Corinth. Then, in the same verse, he also sends greetings from Erastus, the treasurer of the city, and II Tim. 4:20 later indicates that Erastus had been living *at Corinth*.

Evidently the epistle was personally delivered to the Roman Christians by Phebe, a Corinthian woman [3] who had business at Rome (Rom. 16:1,2). Thus God, in His grace, entrusted the most valuable of all the sacred manuscripts to the frail hand of a woman—protected, of course, by *His* almighty hand.

---

3. From Cenchrea, Corinth's eastern harbor.

Chapter I — Romans 1:1-17
PAUL AND THE BELIEVERS AT ROME
HIS APOSTLESHIP AND MESSAGE

"Paul, a servant of Jesus Christ, called to be an apostle, separated unto the gospel of God,

"(Which He had promised afore by His prophets in the holy Scriptures),

"Concerning His Son, Jesus Christ our Lord, which was made of the seed of David according to the flesh;

"And declared to be the Son of God with power, according to the spirit of holiness, by the resurrection from the dead:

"By whom we have received grace and apostleship, for obedience to the faith among all nations, for His name."

—Rom. 1:1-5

PAUL'S APOSTLESHIP

As we open our Bibles to the *Epistle to the Romans* the very first word strikes our attention. It is a name: *Paul*, the author of the book. He introduces himself directly as *"Paul, a servant*[1] *of Jesus Christ, called to be an apostle."*

But who is this Paul? Can it be that he is actually *an apostle of Jesus Christ!?* Had not our Lord appointed a full complement of twelve apostles to rule with Him over the twelve tribes of Israel? And when Judas turned traitor, had not the twelve immediately sought the mind of God for the right man to fill his place? And was not Matthias divinely chosen to bring the number up to twelve again? Who can deny this, when the Scripture Record clearly states that "the lot fell upon Matthias, and he was numbered with the eleven apostles....and *they were all filled with the Holy Ghost*" (Acts 1:26; 2:4).

---

1. Lit., *bondman, slave.*

How, then, shall we explain the appearance of *another* apostle some time later? If after reading the four records of our Lord's earthly ministry we should turn next in our Bibles to the *Epistle to the Romans*, this would indeed be hard to understand.

Ah, but *Acts*, "the book between," explains! It is this book, indeed, that relates the appointment of Matthias to bring the number of Messiah's apostles up to twelve again, so that later there may be no question that Paul's apostleship is unique, and separate from that of the twelve. Acts relates the raising up of this "other apostle," and explains the reason for this action on God's part.

That Paul was *not* God's choice for Judas' place is clear, not only from Acts 2:4 above, but from the fact that Paul could in no way have qualified to take Judas' place. Matt. 19:28, Luke 22:28-30 and Acts 1:21,22 indicate that the twelve who were to reign with Him must be men who had *consistently* "followed," "companied with" and "continued with" Christ *all through His earthly ministry*, beginning with His baptism by John (the *first* day of His ministry) until "that same day" that He ascended to heaven (the *last* day of His ministry on earth).

Paul had not thus faithfully followed Christ; indeed, at the time of his conversion, after Pentecost, he had been our Lord's bitterest enemy on earth. How, then, could he have qualified as one of the twelve?[2]

Acts further supplies the answer to the question of Paul's apostleship, relating how the message of the twelve and their offer of the kingdom at Pentecost was rejected and how, as a result, the establishment of the kingdom was postponed (by a divinely-planned postponement) and held in abeyance until a future time.

Acts shows how, when all was ready for the prophesied judgment of God to fall upon Israel and the world for their rejection of Christ, God did a wonderful thing: He *saved* the

---

2. This subject is discussed at length in the author's book, *Things That Differ*, Pp. 122-125; also in his *Acts, Dispensationally Considered*, Vol. I, Pp. 61-67.

chief of sinners, the flaming leader of the rebellion against Christ, and sent him forth to all nations to proclaim *"the gospel of the grace of God"* (Acts 20:24), based upon the redemptive work of Christ at Calvary. Thus was ushered in *a new dispensation, "the dispensation of the grace of God"* (Eph. 3:2,3).

Now, in the light of Acts, we can begin to understand the introduction to Romans:

"Paul, a servant [slave][3] of Jesus Christ, called to be an apostle, separated unto the gospel of God" (Rom. 1:1).

God had known how bitter an enemy Saul of Tarsus would be to His anointed Son and, in the counsels of the Trinity, had chosen *him* to become the herald and the living example (cf. Gal. 1:15,16) of His mercy, love and grace. How precious, now, become the words of *this* man, in such passages as Rom. 5:20,21, Eph. 2:4-7 and I Tim. 1:12-16!

PAUL'S MESSAGE

If we bring Verses 1 and 3 together—Verse 2 is a parenthesis—we see that the Apostle Paul was called to proclaim *"the gospel [good news] of God, concerning His Son, Jesus Christ our Lord."* He was "separated" to the proclamation of this message.

Paul was always talking about *Christ*; his epistles are filled with *Christ*; *Christ*, in his ministry and message, was everything. At least a dozen times it is *stated* either *of* Paul, or *by* him, that he "preached *Christ*," and this fact is clearly evident as we read the latter part of the Acts and the epistles written by his hand.

This stands in striking contrast to much of modern evangelism, which is man-centered rather than Christ-centered. The late Dr. A. W. Tozer was right when he said:

"The flaw in current evangelism lies in its humanistic approach.... It is frankly fascinated by the great, noisy,

---

3. How touching! He *had been* the bitter persecutor of any who dared profess the name of Christ.

aggressive world with its big names, its hero worship, its wealth and pageantry....

"This concept of Christianity is a radical error, and because it touches the souls of men it is a dangerous, even deadly error....At bottom it is little more than weak humanism allied with weak Christianity to give it ecclesiastical respectability . . . . Invariably it begins with man and his needs, and then looks around for God" (As quoted by DeVern F. Fromke in *The Ultimate Intention*, P. 187).

We do well to take note of this as we begin our studies in *Romans*, for the gospel Paul proclaimed was *God's* good news about *Christ* and His glorious triumph in defeating Satan, overcoming death, nailing the Law to the cross and providing for sinners salvation full and free.

This is why the Apostle calls his message *"the good news of the glory of Christ"* (II Cor. 4:4) and *"the good news of the glory[4] of the blessed God"* (I Tim. 1:11). To enter intelligently into the truth of this good news brings to the human heart the greatest blessing it can possibly experience.

A PROPHESIED GOSPEL?

Verse 2, the parenthesis, presents a problem for many, for it states that Paul's gospel was "promised afore by [God's] prophets in the holy Scriptures."

To some this is evidence that either (1) Paul preached "the gospel of the kingdom" during his early ministry, or that (2) "the gospel of the grace of God" was prophesied in the Old Testament Scriptures.

Those who hold these views generally draw a contrast between "the gospel...promised before," referred to in the *opening* verses of Romans, and what Paul calls "my gospel ...the mystery...kept secret since the world began," referred to in the *closing* verses of the epistle.

This view fascinates many, but it will not stand the Berean test for various reasons:

---

4. Both passages are thus rendered in the *Received Text*.

1. There is no evidence that Paul ever preached "the gospel of the kingdom." He proved to his *Jewish* hearers that Jesus was the Christ: so would we, for how can a Jew trust Christ as his Savior if he does not believe that He was the true Messiah?

But even in Paul's *first recorded address* at the synagogue in Pisidian Antioch, the *climax* of his message, that which all the rest led up to, was *justification by grace, through faith in Christ, apart from the Law* (See Acts 13:38,39).

2. "The gospel of the grace of God" was *not* prophesied in the Old Testament Scriptures. Paul states clearly that "the dispensation of the grace of God" had been "a mystery," kept secret until it was made known to him "by revelation" (Eph. 3:2,3).

3. The essence of Paul's good news in Romans had *not* been prophesied in the Old Testament Scriptures. Where in the Old Testament do we read about God's righteousness imputed through the death of Christ, or of justification without the deeds of the Law [5] or of Jews and Gentiles placed on the same level before God, or of the believer's baptism into Christ, or of the one joint-body? All this is dealt with in the *Epistle to the Romans*.

4. In both his earlier and later epistles the Apostle consistently speaks of *"my gospel," "the gospel which I preached unto you," "that gospel which I preach among the Gentiles,"* etc. Never is there any indication that he had preached *two gospels*, one earlier and the other later. Indeed, in Acts 20:24, looking backward as well as forward, he expresses the desire:

" . . .that I might *finish my course* with joy, and the ministry which I *have received* of the Lord Jesus, to testify the gospel of the grace of God."

This statement, made toward the close of his ministry,

---

5. More is sometimes read into Rom. 4:6,7 than it says. David, *in the case of his sin with Bathsheba*, "describes" the blessedness of the man to whom the Lord imputes righteousness apart from works, but if David had taught the people of Israel that they did not need to obey the ceremonial law he would have been stoned to death for blasphemy.

about his *whole* ministry, past and future, could hardly state more clearly the fact that the Apostle had been commissioned to proclaim *one* gospel, the full content of which was, indeed, *gradually* unfolded to him. (See Acts 26:16; II Cor. 12:1).

5. "The gospel" here in Rom. 1:1-5 which, in the minds of some, refers to Paul's *earlier* message, is *stated* to be the same basic message as that which he still preached just before his martyrdom at Rome. Note carefully:

Rom. 1:1-4: "...the gospel of God...concerning His Son, Jesus Christ our Lord, which was made of THE SEED OF DAVID according to the flesh [this is how Christ *had* been known], and DECLARED TO BE THE SON OF GOD WITH POWER...BY THE RESURRECTION FROM THE DEAD."

II Tim. 2:7,8: "Consider what I say, and the Lord give thee understanding in all things. Remember that Jesus Christ, of THE SEED OF DAVID, was RAISED FROM THE DEAD ACCORDING TO MY GOSPEL."

In both passages it is clear that Jesus Christ "of the seed of David" (as He *had been* known), was preached by Paul in a fuller light. Whereas Peter, at Pentecost, had proclaimed Christ as raised from the dead to sit on the throne of His father, David (Acts 2:29-31), Paul was given further light on the resurrection, proclaiming Christ as raised with respect to "our justification" (Rom. 4:25), and declaring that,

"Even when we were dead in sins [God] hath quickened us together with Christ (by grace ye are saved),

"And *hath raised us up together,* and made us sit together in heavenly places in Christ Jesus" (Eph. 2:5,6).

6. At both the beginning and the end of the *Epistle to the Romans* Paul declares that his gospel is God's message, to be received in the "obedience of faith"[6] among "all nations" (Rom. 1:5; 16:26). Obviously "the gospel of the kingdom" and "the gospel of the grace of God" were not *both* to be proclaimed by the same apostle for the "obedience of faith among all nations" in so short a span of time.

---

6. The Greek is identical in both passages.

The "gospel" which he refers to in both the opening and the closing of his epistle, therefore, is that *one* message which he calls *"my gospel...the preaching of Jesus Christ according to the revelation of the mystery," "the gospel of the grace of God."*

Why, then, does the Apostle say that his gospel had also been "promised before" by the prophets in the holy Scriptures"?

In the light of the Word of God as a whole, and especially of the *Epistle to the Romans* itself, it is clear that Paul here refers *not* to the *contents* of his gospel but simply to the fact that God had predicted that He had wonderful good news in store for mankind. This is complemented by I Cor. 2:9,10. Referring here to Isa. 64:4, the Apostle says:

"But as it is written, Eye hath not seen, nor ear heard, neither have entered into the heart of man, the things which God hath prepared for them that love Him.

"But God hath revealed them unto us by His Spirit...."

Wonderful news for mankind, glorious blessings for His own! And this good news, and these blessings, God has now revealed to us by His Spirit, in His Word. We shall seek to enter more fully into an appreciation of this good news and these precious blessings as we continue our studies in the *Epistle to the Romans*.

FAITHFUL AND BELOVED SAINTS

"Among whom are ye also the called of Jesus Christ.

"To all that be in Rome, beloved of God, called to be saints: Grace to you and peace from God our Father, and the Lord Jesus Christ.

"First, I thank my God through Jesus Christ for you all, that your faith is spoken of throughout the whole world.

"For God is my witness, whom I serve with my spirit in the gospel of His Son, that without ceasing I make mention of you always in my prayers;

"Making request, if by any means now at length I might have a prosperous journey by the will of God to come unto you.

"For I long to see you, that I may impart unto you some spiritual gift, to the end ye may be established;

"That is, that I may be comforted together with you, by the mutual faith both of you and me."

—Rom. 1:6-12

BELOVED OF GOD
SAINTS BY CALLING

"The called of Jesus Christ...beloved of God, called to be saints."

What a blessed position to occupy! But how widely misunderstood, for many religious people have been led to believe that all the saints are in heaven!

The Church of Rome has arrogated to herself the elevation of certain individuals to sainthood. In Roman Catholic doctrine a saint is *"one whose holiness of life and heroic virtue have been confirmed and recognized by the Church's official processes of beatification and canonization."*[7]

Thus, according to the Church of Rome, no one can be a saint until canonized by the Church, generally hundreds of years after death.

Actually, a saint (Gr., *hagios*) is not one who has attained to anything, but rather one who has been *set apart by God as sacred to Himself*. That this is so of every sincere believer in Christ is confirmed by the overwhelming testimony of Scripture regarding saints (e.g., Acts 9:13; 26:10; Rom. 12:13; 15:25,26; 16:2; Eph. 3:8; Phil. 4:22). Thus believers in Christ, with all their failures and sins, are still "the beloved of God," His own sacred possession,[8] and He would have us enter into the joy of this precious truth. Our peculiar characteristic should be that *we are His*.

As to the word "called" (Gr., *kleetos*), in Vers. 6,7, too many commentaries declare without reservation that this

---

7. *The Catholic Dictionary*, Macmillan, P. 444.

8. God loves all men; indeed He loves them so deeply that He gave His Son to die for them (John 3:16; Heb. 2:9), but His own are "the beloved of God" in a special sense, just as a man might love his friends and neighbors—even his enemies, but his wife is "his beloved" in a special sense.

word is *always* used of an *"effectual calling,"* and means *chosen,* or *elected.* This is incorrect. Indeed, in Matt. 22:14 we have our Lord's words: *"many are called, but few are chosen"!* This should teach us not to make sweeping statements that cannot be substantiated by Scripture, or to blindly accept what some Greek scholar may carelessly affirm.

We do not deny that election is involved in Rom. 1:6,7, but *here* the word "called" rather indicates that the believers at Rome had not arrogated sainthood *to themselves*; they were saints by *a divine calling,* just as Paul had not presumptuously appointed himself an apostle, but had been *called* to that position *by God.* As the believers at Rome responded to God's call they became the *"beloved of God, saints by calling."*

GRACE AND PEACE

Much misunderstanding has surrounded the words, *"Grace to you and peace from God our Father, and the Lord Jesus Christ"* (Ver. 7).

For many years the author considered this a beautiful, spiritual salutation. Actually, however, it is much more than this. It is an *official proclamation* by the apostle of grace, from the rejected Father and His rejected Son. This is why it is found among the opening words of every one of Paul's epistles signed by his name.

But why is this proclamation sent by the Father and the Son, but *not* by the Holy Spirit? Two familiar Old Testament passages provide the answer.

Psalm 2 depicts the nations and *the* nation, Israel, waging war "against the Lord, and against His Anointed" (i.e., against the *Father* and the *Son*), and declares that:

"He that sitteth in the heavens shall laugh: the Lord shall have them in derision.

"Then shall He speak unto them in His wrath, and vex them in His sore displeasure" (Vers. 4,5).

In Psalm 110 we have a similar passage. Here the Father says to the Son:

"...Sit Thou at My right hand, until I make Thine enemies Thy footstool" (Ver. 1).

Thus man's declaration of war on God and His Christ was to be—and will be—visited with severe judgment. God will make a counter-declaration of war on a Christ-rejecting world in the Great Tribulation to come.

At Pentecost Peter declared that the last days had arrived —they *had begun*—and that as God was "pouring out" His Spirit upon His own, He would pour out judgment upon His enemies (Acts 2:16-20). In grace, however, God interrupted the prophesied program just as the stage was all set for the judgment to fall. The Spirit was indeed poured out, but the wrath—*not yet*. Rather, when Israel's cup of iniquity was full, God reached down in wondrous grace to *save* Saul of Tarsus, the flaming leader of the rebellion against Christ, and sent him forth as a special envoy to all nations, an apostle of *grace*, to offer peace to His enemies everywhere through faith in Christ.

This is why we read in II Cor. 5:19:

"...God was in Christ,[9] reconciling the world unto Himself, not imputing their trespasses unto them; and hath committed unto us the word of reconciliation."[10]

And thus it is, too, that Paul opens all of his epistles except that to the Hebrews[11] with the wonderful proclamation: *"Grace be to you and peace."* This blessed message is ours too. We, like Paul, are ambassadors of *grace and peace*, and we too proclaim this gracious offer from God the Father and His rejected Son *by* the Spirit, who indwells us, and on the authority of the Word, of which He is the Author. Thus the Spirit works on earth to reveal to men the gracious attitude of the Father and the Son toward a world of sinners.

After this "dispensation of the grace of God" has run its course, God will resume His prophetic program. Recalling His ambassadors (I Thes. 4:16-18), He will wage war on His

---

9. I.e., at Calvary.

10. The reader should carefully read and meditate on the remainder of this amazing passage: Verses 20,21.

11. Hebrews was purposely written anonymously.

enemies, pouring out the bowls of His wrath upon the earth (I Thes. 5:1-3; cf. Rev. 16:1).

As the believer looks about him he knows that the world is headed straight for that awful day, speeding toward the day of judgment at an ever-faster pace. How urgent, then, is our responsibility to reach the lost with the blessed message of *"grace and peace,"* while there is time, *"redeeming the time, because the days are evil"* (Eph. 5:16).

THANKSGIVING AND PRAYER

The Apostle's statement in Verse 8 is significant: *"Your faith is spoken of throughout the whole world"*—the "world" of Paul's day, of course.

Think of it! Paul had never even visited Rome to encourage and establish the believers there, yet their faith in Christ was such that it excited world-wide attention and discussion!

As faith honors and pleases God, it also caused Paul's heart to overflow with thanksgiving and loving prayer for these dear saints (Vers. 8,9). Christians sometimes lightly say to each other, "I'll pray for you," but Paul could remind these believers of his faithful service to God and could swear to them in His name that he prayed for them "without ceasing," i.e., that he never stopped praying for them.

With special earnestness the Apostle prayed that "now at last" (after many disappointments, Ver. 13) he might have "a prosperous [successful] journey" to them, for he longed to see them and be with them (Ver. 10,11).

"I long to see you." How large and affectionate was the Apostle's heart! He did not desire to go to Rome merely to see the world's capital, [12] or to fulfill some personal gratification; he "longed" to see *them*. Here we should ponder over such passages as Phil. 1:8, I Thes. 3:6 and II Tim. 1:4, to get an insight into the heart of the apostle of grace.

---

12. From the above passage, from Acts 23:11, and from all that we know about Paul, it is evident that the phrase, "I must also see Rome," in Acts 19:21, does *not* imply a desire merely to "see the sights" at Rome.

Also, it was more than a desire for Christian companionship that drew the Apostle's heart to Rome. It was rather a longing that he might impart to them the blessings of his God-given message and establish them further in the faith (Ver. 11). Many of them were still experiencing a "first love." Their faith was aflame with excitement, but now the Apostle would lead them further into the truth, that their faith might be more firmly grounded and they might stand unshakeable.

As this was realized, by the grace of God, both they and he would reap the benefits. As always, the teacher would be as richly blessed as the pupils. This he stresses with a threefold emphasis in Ver. 12:

"...that *I* may be comforted [encouraged] *together with you*, by the *mutual* faith *both of you and me.*"

So confident was the Apostle that God would use him to impart spiritual blessings to them that he could say—and by divine inspiration:

"And I am sure that when I come unto you, I shall come in the fullness of the blessing of the gospel of Christ" (Rom. 15:29).

The Roman Christians, then, had much to look forward to: Paul bringing blessing to them, and they to him!

PAUL'S DEFENSE OF HIS GENTILE APOSTLESHIP

"Now I would not have you ignorant, brethren, that oftentimes I purposed to come unto you (but was let hitherto), that I might have some fruit among you also, even as among other Gentiles.

"I am debtor both to the Greeks, and to the Barbarians; both to the wise, and to the unwise.

"So, as much as in me is, I am ready to preach the gospel to you that are at Rome also.

"For I am not ashamed of the gospel of Christ: for it is the power of God unto salvation to every one that believeth; to the Jew first, and also to the Greek.

"For therein is the righteousness of God revealed, from faith to faith: as it is written, The just shall live by faith."

—Rom. 1:13-17

God would not have His people ignorant—especially not with respect to His revealed program. Six times in Paul's epistles we find him saying, *"I would not have you to be ignorant."* Five of these are related in some way with his great message, *"the mystery,"* and three of *these* have to do with one particular aspect of the mystery: God's *program* for the present dispensation. Sad to say, however, those matters of which God says, *"I would not have you to be ignorant,"* these are the very matters of which God's people are most apt to be ignorant.

To what truth, then, does the Apostle refer in *this* passage when he says, *"I would not have you ignorant"*? We believe he refers to the validity of his ministry among the Gentiles.

"THE JEW FIRST"

The above passage is familiar to all Bible students, and Verse 16 is most familiar of all—*and* most widely misunderstood. From this verse the argument is drawn that the Jew is first in God's program for evangelism during the present dispensation. Indeed, *"the Jew first"* is the watchword of many a Jewish missionary organization.

The author has many Jewish friends and a very special place in his heart for the Jew, but here we must all be objective and see what this passage, in context, *actually says*.

We know that the Jew *was* first in God's program. Most of the so-called Old Testament has to do with Israel. Most of the so-called New Testament has to do with Israel. From both Old and New Testaments it is clear that Israel is God's chosen nation and that He has great things in store for her.

When Messiah's kingdom was proclaimed on earth by John the Baptist, Christ and the twelve, it was proclaimed to *Israel alone*. In our Lord's first "great commission" to the twelve He instructed them *not* to go to the Gentiles, nor even to the Samaritans, saying:

"But go rather to the lost sheep of the house of Israel" (Matt. 10:5,6).

Concerning Himself He said:

"I am not sent but unto the lost sheep of the house of Israel" (Matt. 15:24).

Was this because He hated, or did not sufficiently love, the Gentiles? No, it was because He understood the covenants and prophecies of the Old Testament Scriptures. He knew from Gen. 22:17,18 and a hundred other Old Testament passages that it was God's purpose to bless the nations *through Israel*.

This explains why, when a Gentile woman came to our Lord for help, He said:

"Let the children first be filled..." (Mark 7:27).

It explains too, why, even after His resurrection, He commanded His apostles that "repentance and remission of sins should be preached in His name among all nations, *beginning at Jerusalem*" (Luke 24:47).

In early Acts we find the twelve doing just this. In Acts 3:25,26 Peter declares to the "men of Israel":

"Ye are the children of the prophets, and of the covenant which God made with our fathers, saying unto Abraham, *And in thy seed shall all the kindreds of the earth be blessed.*

"*UNTO YOU FIRST* God, having raised up His Son Jesus, sent Him to bless you, in turning away every one of you from his iniquities."

Paul confirmed Peter's declaration some years later when he said to the Jews in Pisidian Antioch:

"...It was necessary that the Word of God should *FIRST* have been spoken to you..." (Acts 13:46).

Why was this *necessary*? Simply because according to all covenant and prophecy, and according to the words of the Lord Jesus Christ, the Gentiles were to be—and one day *will* be—blessed *through redeemed Israel*, with Christ as King.

As we have seen, however, Israel rejected the King and His kingdom even after our Lord's resurrection and the coming of the Holy Spirit in miraculous power. It was then that God *saved* Saul, the rebel leader, and sent him forth to proclaim *"the gospel of the grace of God"* to all men everywhere.

IS THE JEW FIRST TODAY?

All this has an important bearing on Romans 1:16. Some, who love the Jew—as does this writer—have construed this passage to mean that the gospel of the grace of God should *now* be sent to the Jew first. This is an error in the very nature of the case, and in the light of the context.

First, "the dispensation of the grace of God" is to *no one first*. It is infinite, as our Lord's payment for sin was infinite. Thus it is to be offered to all alike, *"for there is no difference...for the same Lord over all is rich unto all that call upon Him"* (Rom. 10:12).

But let us go back to Rom. 1:16 and consider it in the light of both the immediate and the more remote context.

As we have seen, the church at Rome was composed primarily of *Gentiles* (Rom. 11:13). Thus the Apostle writes in 1:13, above:

"Now I would not have you ignorant, brethren, that oftentimes I purposed to come unto you (but was let [hindered] hitherto), *that I might have some fruit AMONG YOU also, EVEN AS AMONG OTHER GENTILES.*"

Paul did not wish the believers at Rome to be ignorant of the fact that his was basically an apostleship *to the Gentiles* and that he had often made plans to include those at Rome too, but these plans had been hindered. Thus, pressing home his Gentile apostleship, he continues:

"I am debtor both to the Greeks, and to the Barbarians; both to the wise, and to the unwise" (Ver. 14).

Mark well, he does not even mention the Jews here, but only the "Greeks" and the "Barbarians."[13] This is not because he did not feel himself a debtor to the Jews. This he had fully demonstrated. It was rather because, though a Hebrew, he felt himself a debtor *"to the Gentiles also."* God had sent him forth with a message of grace for all, and he felt himself obligated to proclaim it to all: Gentiles as well as Jews. Indeed, when he finally arrived at Rome *in chains*, he

---

13. The two classes of Gentiles.

wrote from his prison to other Gentile believers as "the prisoner of Jesus Christ *for you Gentiles*" (Eph. 3:1).

Thus he says here, "I am debtor," and goes on to declare that he is prepared to pay his debt, to discharge his obligation:

"So, *as much as in me is*, I am ready to preach the gospel to you that are at Rome also" (Ver. 15).

It is in the light of all this that we must read Verse 16:

"For I am not ashamed of the gospel of Christ, for it is the power of God unto salvation to every one that believeth; to the Jew first, and also to the Greek." [14]

The Jew, as a nation, had rejected Christ, but Paul was not ashamed of Him: neither was he ashamed of the good news he proclaimed about Him. This good news, [15] he says, "is the power of God unto salvation to *every one that believeth*, to the Jew first, and *also* to the Greek."

It should be observed in the light of all the above that the emphasis here is *not* on the words *"the Jew first"*; it *had gone* to the Jew first. Thus the emphasis is rather on the words, *"also to the Greek."*

Paul considered himself a *"debtor,"* and he was *"ready,"* with all that was in him, to discharge this debt, for he had that with which to discharge it! He was *"not ashamed"* over inability to pay, for the great message he bore was, and still is, *"the power of God unto salvation to EVERY ONE THAT BELIEVETH."*

NO DIFFERENCE

If Rom. 1:16 teaches that "the gospel of the grace of God" is to go to the Jew first, it is a flat contradiction to the Apostle's letter to the Romans as a whole, and particularly to his glad declaration in Rom. 10:12,13:

---

14. Here he uses the term "Greek" because the Roman Gentiles were not "Barbarians" or illiterate.

15. Note that here, as in 1:1, he uses a *general* term, not the distinctive designation, *"the gospel of the grace of God."* This is doubtless because *"the gospel of the kingdom"* had gone to the Jew, and now he was bearing *"the gospel of the grace of God"* to both Jew and Gentile. Both messages were indeed good news about Christ.

"FOR THERE IS *NO DIFFERENCE* BETWEEN THE JEW AND THE GREEK, FOR THE SAME LORD OVER ALL IS RICH UNTO ALL THAT CALL UPON HIM.

"FOR WHOSOEVER SHALL CALL UPON THE NAME OF THE LORD SHALL BE SAVED."

Do these facts discourage Jewish missionary work? By no means! We Gentile believers should recognize our debt to the Jews and do more to bring the wondrous message of grace to them. This we will consider at length when we come to Rom. 11:30,31, where the Apostle gives us the true basis for missionary work among God's ancient people.

Meantime, our Jewish friends must also face an important "fact of life": During the present dispensation of grace they have no priority on God. They, like we, must approach God as poor, lost sinners, trusting for salvation in Christ, who died for our sins.

THE RIGHTEOUSNESS OF GOD

"For therein is the righteousness of God revealed" (Ver. 17).

The *Epistle to the Romans* has much to say about the *righteousness* of God. In fact, this is its basic theme; all else revolves around this.

Regrettably, "righteousness" is to many a weighty theological term about which the ordinary person need not trouble himself. On the contrary, every man and woman, yes, every boy and girl who has come to the age of discretion, ought to understand what the Bible teaches about the righteousness of God.

"Righteousness" is an old English word for *rightness*. God does only and always that which is *right*. He does not— He *cannot*—ever do anything that is *not right*.

Thus, God does not *merely forgive* sinners and accept them into His favor because He loves or pities them, for this would not be *right*; it would not be *just*. In giving the Law, Moses said:

"If there be a controversy between men, and they come unto judgment, that the judges may judge them; then they shall justify the righteous, and condemn the wicked" (Deut. 25:1).

Indeed, Prov. 17:15 declares:

"He that justifieth the wicked, and he that condemneth the just, even they both are abomination to the Lord."

Bildad, though a "miserable comforter," reiterated this basic principle when he said to Job:

"Behold, God will not cast away a perfect man, neither will He help the evildoers" (Job 8:20).

And Job acknowledged this to be so for, exasperated, he replied:

"I know it is so of a truth, but how should man be just with God?" (Job 9:2).

Yes, here is the problem: How can God, who does only what is right, *justify sinners* and pronounce them *righteous?* How? The *Epistle to the Romans* explains how! Its message of grace is God's answer to this vexing question.

THE PARADOX OF GRACE

In "the gospel of the grace of God" we find a striking paradox: God Himself *condemning the righteous and justifying the wicked; forsaking the perfect and helping evildoers.*

Behold the spotless Lamb on Calvary as He cries, *"My God, My God, why hast Thou forsaken Me?"* Judas kisses Him in base betrayal; wicked men spit in His face, mock Him, smite Him, scourge Him, crown Him with thorns and nail Him to a tree! *And God, the Judge of all, does nothing to stop them!* Indeed, He Himself unsheathes His sword and smites the *one* Person in all history who could truly say, *"I delight to do Thy will, O God."*

And this is not all, for on the other hand God *saves* Saul of Tarsus, Christ's bitterest enemy, "a blasphemer, and a persecutor, and injurious," his hands dripping, as it were, with the blood of martyrs. To *him* God shows *"grace... exceeding abundant"* and *"all longsuffering"* (I Tim. 1:13-16).

Indeed, He *sends him forth* to proclaim openly to all men that:

"To him that worketh *not*, but believeth on *Him that justifieth the ungodly*, his faith is *counted for righteousness*" (Rom. 4:5).

How can all this be *right?* The answer is that the One who died in agony and disgrace at Calvary was *God Himself*, manifested in the flesh. There, at Calvary, *"GOD was in Christ, reconciling the world unto Himself, not imputing their trespasses unto them"* (II Cor. 5:19). It was the Judge Himself, stepping down from the throne to the cross to represent the sinner and pay for him the full penalty of his sins.

And who will say this is injustice? *Injustice?* It is *perfect* justice and more. It is *grace!*

Under the terms of the Law we find God *"showing mercy unto thousands of them that love Me and keep My commandments"* (Ex. 20:6). But grace is infinitely more: it is the riches of God's mercy and love to "the children of *disobedience*...the children of *wrath*" (Eph. 2:2-7), paying the penalty for their sins *Himself* in strictest accord with perfect and infinite *righteousness!*

THE POWER OF THE GOSPEL

Why is the gospel of Christ "the power of God unto salvation"? Wherein lies its mighty power to save? The answer is: *In the cross.* Here is where God dealt justly with sin. The Apostle states this very clearly in I Cor. 1:

"For Christ sent me not to baptize, but to preach the gospel; not with wisdom of words LEST THE CROSS OF CHRIST SHOULD BE MADE OF NONE EFFECT.

"For THE PREACHING OF THE CROSS is to them that perish foolishness, but unto us which are saved it is THE POWER OF GOD" (Vers. 17,18).

"But we preach CHRIST CRUCIFIED, unto the Jews a stumblingblock, and unto the Greeks foolishness;

"But unto them which are called, both Jews and Greeks, Christ THE POWER OF GOD AND THE WISDOM OF GOD" (Vers. 23,24).

Thus the Apostle could say in Rom. 1:16,17:

"I am not ashamed of the gospel of Christ, FOR it is the power of God unto salvation to every one that believeth... FOR therein is the righteousness of God revealed...."

SOMETHING TO BE PROUD OF

Actually the words, "I am not ashamed," carry much greater force in the original. Paul was *proud* of the gospel he proclaimed because it revealed the *righteousness* of God. Does the reader say, "I thought that the *love* of God was revealed in the gospel"? We reply that indeed the love of God *is* revealed in the gospel, and the Apostle was deeply *grateful* for this. But what made him *proud* of the gospel was the fact that it reveals God *dealing justly with sin*.

"I am not ashamed of the gospel of Christ... for therein is the righteousness of God revealed."

God has not lowered His standards of righteousness or "let down the bars," so to speak. The Apostle protests against any such thought:

"Do we then make void the law through faith? God forbid; yea, we establish the law" (Rom. 3:31).

The good news Paul was sent to proclaim, then, was the story of the glorious, all-sufficient work of Christ in the sinner's behalf. This was what made him so proud of it. This was the *one* thing he boasted of everywhere he went, as in Gal. 6:14:

"...God forbid that I should glory [Lit., boast], save in the cross of our Lord Jesus Christ...."

May this be *our* motto too, for we should indeed be proud that we can say to sinners everywhere: "Your sins have been *paid for* by the Lord Jesus Christ. You may be saved by grace through faith."

FROM FAITH TO FAITH

We must not close this passage without commenting on the words *"from faith to faith,"* in Ver. 17. "The righteousness of God," he says, is revealed in the gospel, *"from faith to faith*, as it is written, The just shall live by faith."

Many commentators have a problem with this phrase. Most of the commentaries this writer has access to explain that the words "from faith to faith" here evidently mean *from one degree of faith to another*. This, however, would have no logical connection with the words that immediately precede or follow. Paul's gospel *reveals* the righteousness of God *"from faith to faith,"* as it is written, *"The just shall live by faith."*

We feel that this confusion has come about because so few understand the phrase *"the faith of Christ,"* used seven times in Paul's epistles. In these seven passages faith is spoken of, not objectively, but *subjectively*.

Objectively, faith is simply *trust in another*, or in what another has said or done. But *subjectively* faith is the *character* which constitutes one *worthy of trust*. *Objectively* faith is associated with what one *does*; *subjectively* it concerns what he *is*. One might say, "If I have faith in you, you had better keep faith with me." Any English dictionary will give these two definitions of the word "faith," and the same is true of the Greek equivalent, *pistis*.[16] The Scriptures also speak of *"the faith,"* i.e., that which is *to be believed* (I Cor. 16:13), but for the present we confine our discussion to *faith* in its twofold significance as shown above.

In Rom. 3:22, Gal. 2:16, Gal. 3:22 and Phil. 3:9 we find "the faith *of* Christ" and the believer's faith *in* Christ mentioned in the same verses, showing the one as complementary to the other. How sad, then, to find modern versions of the Bible changing that precious phrase *"the faith of Christ"* to "faith *in* Christ." [17]

Does not the above cast clear light on the phrase, *"from faith to faith"* in Rom. 1:17? In the gospel which Paul

---

16. Even the word *faithful* is used in this twofold way. Abraham was *"faithful,"* i.e., *full of faith* (Gal. 3:9), trusting in a *"faithful"* God (I Cor. 10:13), i.e., One who can be fully depended upon.

17. For a more comprehensive discussion of this subject see the author's booklet, *The Faith of Christ*.

proclaimed *"the righteousness of God [is] revealed from faith to faith,"* i.e., from *His faith* (subjective) to *our faith* (objective). *His* trustworthiness is revealed as an appeal to our trust. This interpretation *does* fit logically with the words that precede and follow. Paul's gospel reveals the righteousness of God *"from faith to faith, as it is written, The just shall live by faith,"* i.e., on the principle of faith, faith in the One who always keeps faith with us.

CONCLUSION

To briefly review Rom. 1:16,17 in closing:

1. Paul was *proud* of the gospel of Christ. Why?

2. *Because* "it is *the power of God* unto salvation." And *why* is it "the power of God unto salvation"?

3. *Because* "therein is the *righteousness [rightness]* of God revealed,"

4. *"From faith to faith,"* His "faith" (fidelity), appealing to us to *have faith* in Him.

> My faith has found a resting place,
>   Not in device or creed;
> I trust the ever-living One;
>   His wounds for me shall plead.
>
> I need no other argument,
>   I need no other plea.
> It is enough that Jesus died,
>   And that He died for me.
>
> —L. H. Edmunds

Chapter II — Romans 1:18-32
THE WRATH OF GOD
AND THE GUILT OF MAN

GOD'S WRATH REVEALED AGAINST
THE SUPPRESSION OF TRUTH

"For the wrath of God is revealed from heaven against all ungodliness and unrighteousness of men, who hold[1] the truth in unrighteousness."

—Rom. 1:18

It is impossible to appreciate the grace of God, except against the background of man's sin and God's wrath against sin.

It should be noted, moreover, that the above passage does not warn against the wrath *to come*; it is rather concerned with wrath *now being* revealed from heaven. "For the wrath of God *is* [not "will be"] revealed from heaven."

Before we explain *how* God's wrath is being revealed, let us first consider *why*.

God's wrath is revealed *"against all ungodliness,"* says the Apostle. Ungodliness, it should be noted, is not the breaking of laws or the commission of wicked acts, though it often leads to these. Ungodliness is simply a disregard for God and His claims. An ungodly person is one in whose life God has no welcome part. Many who fit into this category would be insulted if called *ungodly*, yet they would be embarrassed if called *godly!*

It is ungodliness that causes men to suppress the truth as they do, *in unrighteousness*. All about us we see man's unrighteous suppression of the truth and God's righteous wrath revealed against it.

---

1. Lit., hold down, suppress.

Men of learning, closing their eyes to the most obvious facts, deny or ignore God's record of creation, teaching instead the *theory* of evolution. But as they teach that man is steadily rising to higher levels, conditions in their institutions of learning and among those whom they influence provide increasing evidence of the moral and spiritual fall of man taught in the Bible.

TV commercials advertise intoxicating liquors as though they brought nothing but pleasure and satisfaction, but they never mention the results of drunkenness. They boast the finest products but throw a veil over the *finished* product. They never show pictures of intoxicated men and women making fools of themselves, or mention how alcoholics often deprive their families of food and clothing, become involved in crime and ruin their own bodies.

The communications media promote all kinds of sin and immorality in the name of pleasure and fun, but fail to mention the results of their "fun": broken homes, broken hearts and wrecked lives.

Thus they "suppress the truth in unrighteousness," and *this* springs from *ungodliness*. Indeed, those who practice and promote sin suppress the truth in *their own hearts* as they try to convince themselves that continuance in sin will not adversely affect *them*. Strangely, however, one of the outstanding examples of the suppression of truth in unrighteousness is the promotion of the "gospel" of good works for salvation, as we shall see further on in our studies.

But while men suppress the truth, they cannot escape the consequences of their folly, for God reveals His wrath against sin every day as the fruits of their conduct continue to take their toll. And God's wrath against their ungodliness and unrighteousness is as just as their sin is inexcusable.

THE GUILT OF MAN

"Because that which may be known of God is manifest in them; for God hath showed it unto them.

> "For the invisible things of Him from the creation of the world [2] are clearly seen, being understood by the things that are made, [3] even His eternal power and Godhead; so that they are without excuse."
>
> —Rom. 1:19,20

Getting down to the root of the matter, the Apostle exposes the *nature* of man's ungodliness.

The phrase, "that which may be known of God," [4] does not include *all* that may be known about God, for this is *not* "manifest in them" (I Cor. 2:9,11). He evidently refers to *"His eternal power and Godhead [deity]"* (Ver. 20). This fact man knows instinctively as he observes God's vast creation.

Man's suppression of the truth is unrighteous *"because* that which may be known of God" (i.e., His eternal power and deity) "is manifest *in* them, for *God hath showed it unto them"* (Ver. 19). Built into the very nature of man is an instinctive knowledge of the God who created him. Indeed, even *"the devils...believe, and tremble"* (Jas. 2:19).

These "invisible things," says the Apostle, are "clearly seen" from "the creation of the world...being understood by the things that are made...*so that they are without excuse"* (Ver. 20).

> "The heavens declare the glory of God; and the firmament showeth His handiwork.
>
> "Day unto day uttereth speech, and night unto night showeth knowledge" (Psa. 19:1,2).

Man observes the wonders of nature every day and must be wilfully blind if he does not conclude that all this has behind it a great Mastermind. This is particularly true in the day in which we live. Man, now aided by the telescope, can look far out into outer space and see literally billions of great stars and planets in constellations, galaxies and uni-

---

2. Lit., *harmonious arrangement*, probably including the entire universe here.

3. In the Greek, the phrase "things that are made" is one word: *poyeema*, from which our word "poem" is derived. It occurs here and in Eph. 2:10, where it is rendered "workmanship." Rom. 1:20 refers to the poem of *creation*, Eph. 2:10 to the poem of *redemption*.

4. Lit., "the knowable of God."

verses billions of light years away. The stronger his lenses, the more of these giant heavenly bodies he sees. As far as he can tell, this vast creation is limitless, infinite. Likewise, aided by the microscope, he can observe hundreds of tiny organisms on the space of a pinhead, organisms which the naked eye could not even begin to see. And here too, the stronger his lenses the more of these infinitesimal objects are brought into view. Thus where the *small* things are concerned, the creation must also appear to man to be limitless, infinite.

Meantime, with the naked eye man daily observes beautiful flowers and breathtaking sunsets, mighty oceans and tiny rivulets, the star-studded heavens and the little birds that fly above him.

Should not these wonders of creation move man to worship the Creator? Would it not be the most wilful folly to assert that all this, so intricately and perfectly designed, so harmonious in its movement, *has no Designer, no Creator!* How *guilty* before God, then, must that man be who declares that the universe, and man himself, came into being merely by "natural causes"!

The atheistic evolutionist claims that all this just somehow came about, but in this he is like a man, shipwrecked on an island, searching to see if there are not others beside himself inhabiting the island. Coming upon a shining object, he picks it up. It looks for all the world like a watch! It has a beautiful case that appears to be gold. Its face is covered with what looks and feels like glass on one side, through which he can see two hands, or arms, projected from the center, encircled by numbers from 1 to 12. Indeed, on the face he can clearly read a word: E-L-G-I-N. He even puts it to his ear and hears it tick. But foolishly he says: "This looks like a watch we have in the United States but, of course, that cannot be, for there is no one here. This object must have evolved somehow, perhaps from stones lying about. All its parts must just have come together by 'natural causes,' for there is no one here who could have put them together."

"Nonsense!" you say. "Such a man should rather say: 'Look! Here is a watch! Somebody's been here—and it's ticking! He must be here *now*, not far away! Hello! Hello! Where *are* you?!' "

Speaking of God and creation on Mars' Hill, Paul declared the divine intent:

"That they should seek the Lord; if haply they might feel after Him, and find Him, *though He be not far from every one of us*" (Acts 17:27).

As evolutionists view God's creation and hear it tick, as it were, they should conclude that indeed "He is not far from every one of us," but instead they act as though He does not exist. It is in the light of this wilful ignorance, this refusal to heed overwhelming evidence, that the Apostle declares: *"They are without excuse"* (Ver. 20).

Thus the natural man, entirely apart from the Law of Moses, is guilty of *moral wrong*—and, apart from the redeeming work of Christ, stands under the condemnation of a just and holy God.

HOW THE HEATHEN GOT THAT WAY

"Because that when they knew God, they glorified Him not as God, neither were thankful; but became vain in their imaginations, and their foolish heart was darkened.

"Professing themselves to be wise, they became fools."

—Rom. 1:21,22

With the word *"Because,"* the Apostle proceeds to present further evidence that ungodliness is *unrighteous* (Ver. 18); that it is *not right*; that it is *indefensible*.

Speaking historically, he points out that when mankind "knew God" (in the sense of Vers. 19,20), they did not render to Him the honor and thanks that were His due.

As they beheld the beauties and wonders of nature, and saw the sun and rain producing healthful and luscious food for their sustenance, they should have fallen to their knees in *worship*, humbly thanking God for His loving care for them. They should have acknowledged His infinite greatness and their nothingness. David showed such an attitude when he said:

"When I consider Thy heavens, the work of Thy fingers, the moon and the stars, which Thou hast ordained;

"What is man that Thou art mindful of him...?" (Psa. 8:3,4).

But mankind as a whole did not regard God with such reverence and gratitude. Rather they *"became vain in their imaginations [reasonings], and their foolish heart was darkened."* This is an apt description of human philosophy and its results. *"The fear of the Lord is the beginning of wisdom"* (Psa. 111:10). Turn off this light, and darkness will inevitably result. Thus, *"professing themselves to be wise"* (not always directly, but usually by implication), *"they became fools."*[5] The word "fools" is emphatic in the Greek, and expresses the low estimate that God has of the world's intellectuals.

In Eph. 4:17,18 the Apostle exhorts believers not to "walk," or conduct themselves, as the unregenerate Gentiles do,

"...in THE VANITY OF THEIR MIND,

"Having THE UNDERSTANDING DARKENED, being alienated from the life of God through THE IGNORANCE THAT IS IN THEM, because of THE BLINDNESS OF THEIR HEART."

This is not a flattering picture of the Gentile intellect, but enlightened believers recognize it as accurate. In I Cor. 3:19 we read that *"the wisdom of this world is foolishness with God,"* and if *God* pronounces it foolishness we may be assured that it *is foolishness*. Little wonder that so many of the plans devised by the world's great leaders, so many of the measures taken, *turn out wrong*. Let unregenerate men, then, boast of their superior intelligence; *God* calls them moronic, stupid, and in this passage He proceeds methodically to prove it.

---

5. Gr., *moraino*, from which our word "moron" is derived.

PAGAN IDOLATRY
REVEALS THE DEPTHS OF
MAN'S PHILOSOPHICAL STUPIDITY

"And [they] changed the glory of the uncorruptible God into an image made like to corruptible man, and to birds, and fourfooted beasts, and creeping things."

—Rom. 1:23

See where, and to what depths, human philosophy soon led mankind!

They did not, in their worship, *exchange* the glory of God for something else. They *"changed"* it; they corrupted it. Instead of reverently *worshipping* the immortal, incorruptible God, they began to make for themselves gold and silver representations of what *they* considered Him to be. And as they did so, their conception of Him grew more and more degraded. See the downward trend in Verse 23, where we go from (1) *God* to (2) *corruptible man*, to (3) *birds*, to (4) *quadrupeds*, and even to (5) *reptiles!*

It is significant that the Egyptians, with all their intellectual superiority (Acts 7:22)[6] yet worshipped the hawk, the bull, the cow, the cat, the frog, the baboon, the jackal, the crocodile and other beasts and reptiles. Later even Israel took part in these iniquities (Psa. 106:19,20; Acts 7:40-43), though it appears that, disciplined by their captivity in Babylon (the seat of the world's idolatry), they had their fill of idol worship and never again practiced it, at least *in that form.*

When one contemplates the infinite majesty of the eternal God, *any* idolatry must be considered a hideous insult, a vile indignity. It is not strange, then, that Paul said to the philosophers at Mars' Hill:

"Forasmuch, then, as we are the offspring of God, we ought not to think that the Godhead is like unto gold or silver, or stone, graven by art and man's device" (Acts 17:29).

---

6. The Egyptians knew secrets about embalming, engineering and astronomy which our greatest minds have not been able to penetrate. See the author's book, *Satan in Derision,* Pp. 9,10.

The only *true* representation of God is *Christ* (John 1:18; Col. 1:15; 2:9; Heb. 1:3), and when unregenerate man makes images to represent *his* conception of God, he invariably belittles and degrades Him, and the surest way to self-degradation is to degrade the object of one's worship.

Does the reader object that all this has little relevance today? We reply that it has profound relevance. Nearly half of the world's population today is steeped in pagan idol worship, and bound by superstition and fear. Add to these the millions who bow down to images in the name of Christianity—who are also bound by superstition and fear—and the number is greatly increased. Moreover, paganism is growing, here in America, at an alarming rate, with so-called "Christians" giving Buddhism, Hinduism, and a dozen other pagan religions favorable consideration.

Make no mistake about it: Idolatry is the devil's masterpiece. The so-called "Christian" cults are nothing compared to pagan idolatry, demon worship, much of which is morally vile and all of which is spiritually degrading.

THE GENTILES GIVEN UP

"Wherefore God also gave them up to uncleanness through the lusts of their own hearts, to dishonor their own bodies between themselves:

"Who changed the truth of God into a lie, and worshipped and served the creature more than the Creator, who is blessed forever. Amen.

"For this cause God gave them up unto vile affections: for even their women did change the natural use into that which is against nature.

"And likewise also the men, leaving the natural use of the woman, burned in their lust one toward another; men with men working that which is unseemly, and receiving in themselves that recompense of their error which was meet.

"And even as they did not like to retain God in their knowledge, God gave them over to a reprobate mind, to do those things which are not convenient;

"Being filled with all unrighteousness, fornication, wickedness, covetousness, maliciousness; full of envy, murder, debate, deceit, malignity; whisperers,

"Backbiters, haters of God, despiteful, proud, boasters, inventors of evil things, disobedient to parents,

"Without understanding, covenantbreakers, without natural affection, implacable, unmerciful:

"Who, knowing the judgment of God, that they which commit such things are worthy of death, not only do the same, but have pleasure in them that do them."
—Rom. 1:24-32

Three times in Romans 1 (Vers. 24,26,28) we read that God "gave up"[7] the Gentile world. This occurred at the Tower of Babel with the confusion of tongues and the scattering of the race over "the face of all the earth" (Gen. 11:6-9). The confusion of tongues at Babel was followed by the call of Abraham and the covenant concerning his seed, Israel (Gen. 12:1-4). Some two millenniums later, however, Israel too was given up "for a season" and likewise scattered over all the earth (Rom. 10:21; 11:15-25; cf. Jas. 1:1; Jer. 31:10). Now, with both given up and scattered there was only a world of poor, lost sinners left, and the foundation laid for God's offer of reconciliation by grace to all men everywhere (Rom. 11:32; cf. II Cor. 5:14-21).[8]

It is important to observe here that the very phrase, "God *gave them up*," is a refutation of the teaching that God does *not* love, or that Christ did *not* die for, the non-elect. This phrase clearly implies that the Holy Spirit strove with them earnestly and for a prolonged period of time and *then* finally ceased working with them further. We have a similar passage in Gen. 6:3, where God says of those who lived in "the days of Noah":

"My Spirit shall not always strive with man, for that he also is flesh; yet his days shall be an hundred and twenty years."

Does not this passage, along with I Pet. 3:20 and II Pet. 2:5, also clearly imply that God's Spirit *had* striven with them, earnestly and long, and that even then *"the longsuffering of God waited"* for 120 *more* years, *"while the ark was a*

---

7. The three occurrences are identical in the Greek: *paredoken*.
8. See the author's book, *Things That Differ*, Pp. 58,84,94,95,168,237.

preparing" and Noah, *"a preacher of righteousness,"* warned them of the judgment to come?

How, then, can theologians teach, as some do, that God "elected some *not* to be saved"? How can they say, as one does: "If God's grace can be *successfully* resisted then *God* can be overcome and your god is no greater than the fictitious, failing, faltering, fainting, feeble god of...."? The extreme Calvinists, who have so much to say about "irresistible grace," ought to give equal time to what the Bible says about *"resistible grace,"* as seen above, for there is overwhelming evidence in the Sacred Record that the grace of God *has been* resisted again and again, and is constantly resisted by unbelievers.

Finally, the phrase, *"God gave them up,"* proves that God did not *wish* them to perish. How then can theologians say, without qualification, "God is sovereign and does what He pleases." In Ezek. 33:11 God *swears*: *"As I live...I have no pleasure in the death of the wicked: but that the wicked turn from his way and live."*

God does *not* always do what He pleases, but He always does what is *right*. As we consider the giving up of the Gentile world it will be evident that God did not wish them to perish, that they brought this righteous judgment upon themselves.

Does all this mean that God is defeated in the case of those who perish? No, He is "blessed forever" (Ver. 25); it is rather they who are defeated as we shall presently see.

AN ABANDONED RACE

The Gentiles, having sunk to the depths of spiritual decline, were now judicially abandoned to "the lusts of their own heart," as *"God...gave them up to uncleanness...to dishonor their own bodies between themselves."*

As they had *"changed* the glory of...God" and "the truth of God"[9] (Vers. 23,25), so now they *"changed"* natural human

---

9. It has been well said that "You can *make* the Bible teach anything."

functions into "that which is *against* nature" (Ver. 26). Worshipping and serving the creature more than the Creator, they wallowed in almost unbelievable immorality, bringing upon themselves all its consequent trouble, wretchedness and despair.

All their professions of intellectualism were now hollow indeed. As they had degraded God, they were now degrading *themselves*, given up to passions they could not control.

It should be observed that the words "to dishonor their own bodies between themselves," do not apply merely to *illicit* sex behavior, but to sex *perversion*. Note the words "natural," "against nature" and "men with men," in Vers. 26,27:

"For even their women did change the natural use into that which is against nature;

"And likewise also the men, leaving the natural use of the woman, burned in their lust one toward another; men with men working that which is unseemly [indecent, shameless] . . . ."

Such is the depravity of the human heart when abandoned by God. And this was not merely the *unfortunate lot* of the Gentiles; it was their *just due*.

It should be noted, however, that God did not give them up because of their sins. Rather He gave them up *to* their sins because they had rejected the truth—and Him. Surrounded by overwhelming evidence of the eternal power and deity of God, they had clearly demonstrated that they did not wish Him to have any part in their lives.

THE GENTILE WORLD NO BETTER TODAY

The Gentile world has not improved since the day when God first "gave them up!" Paul exhorted the believers of his day not to walk as the unregenerate Gentiles:

"Who, being past feeling, have given themselves over unto lasciviousness [excess, wantonness], to work all uncleanness with greediness" (Eph. 4:19). [10]

---

10. Note, the same sequence as in Romans 1, for this passage immediately follows that concerning the *deep spiritual ignorance* of the Gentiles.

Neither was any lasting change brought about by the Reformation under Luther and Calvin, nor later through the Great Awakening under the Wesleys and Whitefield. Even in our own day multitudes *"work all uncleanness with greediness."* Our American newspapers and magazines are filled with it, as are our radio and television broadcasts. Indeed, often illicit sex and sex perversion are openly justified and even promoted by the communications media. Homosexual intercourse between consenting parties has even been *legalized* in some European countries, and here in America adultery and promiscuity are subsidized in many ways. Though spiritual revivals under Luther, Wesley, Darby, Scofield and others had a temporary beneficial effect on those in enlightened nations, the unregenerate heart always reverts to paganism and immorality, so that even today America is widely known for its sex-madness.

But while men may change the glory of God and the Word of God in their *thinking* and their *philosophies*, they cannot change *Him!* How refreshing to hear Paul exclaim, right in the midst of this sad catalog of human depravity, that *"the Creator...is blessed for ever. Amen"* (Ver. 25). Also, in the midst of all the pagan wickedness of his day there were some who had *"turned to God from idols, to serve the living and true God, and to wait for His Son from heaven"* (I Thes. 1:9,10), and so it still is today.

It is not without significance that in this passage on human depravity the women are first mentioned; then the men. Here *the law of first mention* takes us back to Eden, where it was Eve who first partook of the forbidden fruit; then Adam, who should have restrained his wife from partaking. Satan was "subtle," we read, and knew that he could most readily seduce *both* our parents by *first* seducing Eve. Throughout history Satan, in his subtlety, has often used women to lead men astray, even though the man by nature is the more aggressive.

"Even their women"! Sad phrase! The sex whose fairest ornament is modesty, stoops to lewdness, and helps to drag down the other sex. How important, then, for Christian

women to keep morally pure and to be always modest in appearance (I Tim. 2:9). [11]

When the women in any society become morally corrupt, that society soon collapses. Look at Babylon, look at Greece, look at Rome! Cicero says of homosexuality among the Greeks that their poets, their philosophers and their great men not only practiced it but gloried in it, but behind all this was the influence of their immoral women.

It was because of this sin that the land of Canaan "spued out" its inhabitants (Lev. 18:28). It was because of this sin that God *"rained upon Sodom and upon Gomorrah brimstone and fire,"* and *"turning the cities of Sodom and Gomorrah into ashes, condemned them with an overthrow, making them an example unto those that after should live ungodly"* (Gen. 19:24; II Pet. 2:6). It is because of the homosexuals in Sodom (Gen. 19:5-9) that this sin came to be known as *sodomy*, but those who practice this wickedness today should reflect that Sodom now lies, utterly destroyed, at the shores of the Dead Sea, "an example" of God's fury against moral uncleanness. God calls this sin "an abomination" (Lev. 18:22) that will not go unpunished. Indeed, here in Rom. 1:27 we read of those participating in such depravity "receiving [12] *in themselves* that recompense of their error which [is] meet." Statistics bear witness to this fact on every hand, as a rising rate of disease, insanity and suicide follow in the wake of growing immorality.

THE FOOL!

"They did not like [desire] to retain God in their knowledge."

—Rom. 1:28

God has a name for those who no longer wish to retain Him in their thoughts. As the Lord *"looked down from*

---

11. Many Christian women need to consider this more seriously in the light of the Word, for too often they conform themselves to the world by wearing immodest apparel, displeasing God as they incite unwholesome thinking among men. David rightly condemned himself for his sin with Bathsheba, but what was Bathsheba doing bathing herself where she could be observed by the king?

12. Gr., *apolambano*, to receive back one's due.

heaven upon the children of men" (Psa. 14:2), He exclaimed, *"The fool!*[13] *He has said in his heart, No God"* [14] (Ver. 1).

And must not God say the same as He "looks down from heaven" upon today's world? What place does *He* have in politics, education, society, business—even religion?

Politics? You can't put *God* into politics! *Education?* Man's *mind* is the highest court of appeal. One's *faith* must not sway his thinking! *Social relationships?* Bringing *God* in here would spoil everything! We have to have *some* fun! *Business?* Why, "business is business!" How often this defense is raised by businessmen when confronted with moral or spiritual considerations! And *religion?* In how many churches do pastor and people meet with open Bibles to prayerfully study about *God?* The truth is that the vast majority of our religious organizations are given over to form and ritual rather than the worship and study of *God.* Many, indeed, worship the "God" they have conjured up in their own minds, but how many worship the God of the Bible? And so in today's world, even in the religious world, the attitude is still the same: *"No God!"*

Since the pagan world no longer wished to retain God in its thinking, *He* "gave *them* over to a reprobate mind, to do those things which are not convenient [becoming]" (Ver. 28). Thus, in Vers. 29-31 we have a list of the sins in which men wished to continue *without divine interference,* the sins that prevail so widely in our modern world, even in enlightened America. Who can read this catalog of wickedness and deny that it is a true portrayal of mankind without God?

Since some of the words here used in our *King James Version* have by now changed their meanings, we will clarify these before commenting further: "covetousness" = *greed, always wanting more;* "debate"=*strife;* "deceit"=*craft, guile;* "whisperers"=*gossips;* "backbiters"=*slanderers;* "despite-

---

13. The Hebrew is emphatic.
14. The words "There is," in KJV, are in italics, and we believe were erroneously supplied by the translators. This passage has nothing to do with speculative atheism for, as we have seen, *all* men *know* that there *is* a God, but the natural man does not wish to give God a place in his mind or his heart. He says in his *heart: "No God."* This is exactly what Rom. 1:28 teaches.

ful"=*insolent, insulting*; "proud"=*arrogant*; "without understanding"=*without discernment*; "implacable"=*refusing to be persuaded*.

The reader will do well to study the entire list carefully, for these are the sins to which God abandoned those who no longer wished to retain Him in their knowledge. We comment only briefly on this passage.

Note the words *"filled with"* and *"full of,"* in Ver. 29. They are now *given over* to wickedness; they are *living in sin* as a way of life. The word "fornication," so early in the list, brings to mind II Pet. 2:14: *"Having eyes full of adultery, and that cannot cease from sin."* Those indulging in this sin should remember God's warning in Heb. 13:4: *"Marriage is honorable in all* [i.e., *completely honorable*], *and the bed undefiled:* BUT WHOREMONGERS AND ADULTERERS GOD WILL JUDGE."

"Covetousness," or greed, too, has all but taken over the civilized world. With an increased abundance of material wealth everybody, it seems, keeps wanting more. This has affected the Church too, for many live in affluence while the cause of Christ suffers.

"Whisperers" and *"backbiters,"* or gossips and slanderers, also abound in our day, recklessly ruining reputations, lives and homes.

"Haters of God" and *"inventors of evil things."* Compare these with Ver. 32 and note the sense of defiance.

"Disobedient to parents." Who would have thought that this sin, so lightly considered in our day, would be found in a catalog along with fornication, murder, haters of God, etc.? Ah, but disobedience to parents is a grievous sin in God's sight, reflecting as it does the general lack of respect for age and experience. And it is the more grievous because so often it reflects the parents' failure to "train up a child in the way he should go." Significantly, disobedience to parents is included in the Apostle's list of evils that will bring the present dispensation of the grace of God to a close (II Tim. 3:2). How important, then, for Christian parents to care-

fully *train* their children to be obedient, and for Christian young people to heed the divine admonition: *"Children, obey your parents"* (Eph. 6:1; Col. 3:20).

"Without natural affection." Sad words! Yet we see this characteristic spreading among us, as men abandon their God-appointed responsibilities in the home, and women, who should be known for compassion and "natural affection," join in the clamor for "equal rights" with men.

And the whole appalling list closes with the charge:

"Who, knowing the judgment of God, that they which commit such things are worthy of death, not only do the same, but have pleasure in them that do them" (Ver. 32).

Fools indeed! They *know* in their hearts that God will judge them. They have *seen* the present results of wicked living and know that *God will not tolerate it.* Yet they have sunk to such depths of immorality that they not only practice these sins, but have pleasure in those who join them.

> Sin, like a venomous disease,
>   Infects our vital blood;
> The only hope is sovereign grace,
>   And the physician, God.
>
> Madness by nature reigns within;
>   The passions burn and rage,
> 'Til God's own Son, with skill divine,
>   The inward fires assuage.
>
> We lick the dust, we grasp the wind,
>   And solid good despise;
> Such is the folly of the mind
>   'Til Jesus makes us wise.
>
>   —Isaac Watts

Chapter III — Romans 2:1—3:20
JEW AND GENTILE PRONOUNCED GUILTY BEFORE GOD

MORALIZERS NO BETTER

"Therefore thou art inexcusable, O man, whosoever thou art that judgest: for wherein thou judgest another, thou condemnest thyself, for thou that judgest doest the same things.

"But we are sure that the judgment of God is according to truth against them which commit such things.

"And thinkest thou this, O man, that judgest them which do such things, and doest the same, that thou shalt escape the judgment of God?

"Or despisest thou the riches of His goodness and forbearance and longsuffering; not knowing that the goodness of God leadeth thee to repentance?

"But after thy hardness, and impenitent heart, treasurest up unto thyself wrath against the day of wrath and revelation of the righteous judgment of God."

—Rom. 2:1-5

God probes ever deeper, here, into the sinful heart of man. The unsaved do not want to face up to their sinful condition, but they would be better off if they did.

If a man has early evidence of cancer and the physician merely tries to encourage him by telling him to ignore it, that man will die of his disease. A wise and good physician will say, "You have cancer and it will be wise to do something about it without delay."

Thus God faithfully lays bare our sinful condition, but only so that He might save us from it. This is where most philosophies and the Bible clash head-on. Most philosophies deny or disregard man's sinful nature. They contend that man is basically good, while the Word of God and general observation bear witness that man is basically *bad* by nature. Thus human philosophies *offer no salvation from sin and its penalties*. Only the gospel of the grace of God does this.

How did the heathen become what they are today: idol-worshipping, superstitious, wicked, fear-ridden? As we have seen, this was the result of their having *rejected God*. And it is in direct proportion to our departure from God and His Word here in America that crime, superstition and fear have so greatly increased.

It would have been difficult to believe, half a century ago, that our young people would be dancing to the wild, exotic "music" of pagan lands, or that our stores would be selling the twisted, hideous paintings of pagan "art." When we wonder why the lovely melodies of yesteryear have given way to the screaming noise and din of our juke boxes; when we wonder why the truly beautiful paintings of a few decades ago have been so largely replaced by grotesque, meaningless nothings; why in so many ways we are reverting to paganism, we should read Romans 1, and learn that it is because God and His Word have been increasingly ignored.

Romans 1 does not say that the heathen are poor, unfortunate people, longing for better things. It says that *"they are without excuse."* And America is not reverting to paganism because we are unfortunate—we have been blessed above all nations—but because increasingly we are rejecting His Word and will. And if we continue to slight Him and ignore His Word we will, like the pagan world, be *"without excuse."*

Now, in Chapter 2, the Apostle, by inspiration, deals with the self-righteous moralizer who looks down upon those who live in open sin, and says, *"Shame on them!"*

In Paul's day, as in ours, there were many who preached virtue but practiced vice. Moral and refined, such people are apt to forget that God looks upon the heart and sees all its desperate wickedness. He also sees our "downsitting" and our "uprising," and knows what we do in secret. And He, "who knoweth the heart," says, *"Thou that judgest doest the same things"* (Ver. 1). He knows that many a criticism is but a cover-up for a guilty conscience.

Note; He does not say here, "You do things that are *just as bad.*" He says, "Thou that judgest doest the *same things.*" How prone man is to condemn in others *the very things* he does himself!

"But we are sure," says the Apostle, "that the judgment of God is according to truth against them which commit such things" (Ver. 2), and the surest way to condemn ourselves is to sit in judgment upon those who commit sins of which we ourselves are guilty. You may seek to cover *your* sins by pointing to your neighbor's, but,

"Thinkest thou this, O man, that judgest them which do such things, and doest the same, *that thou shalt escape the judgment of God?*

"Or despisest thou the riches of His goodness and forbearance and longsuffering, not knowing that the goodness of God leadeth thee to repentance?" (Vers. 3,4).

Alas, the self-righteous moralizer, blessed by God in that *he* has been protected from actively committing gross, open sin, too often fails to *thank* God and to repent of the sins that fill *his heart,* but rather covers his guilt by standing off and criticizing others. But God knows us better than our friends do. This is why His Word searches us out so deeply:

"For the Word of God is quick [living] and powerful, and sharper than any two-edged sword, piercing even to the dividing asunder of soul and spirit, and of the joints and the marrow, and is a discerner of the thoughts and intents [motives] of the heart.

"Neither is there any creature that is not manifest in His sight; but all things are naked and opened unto the eyes of Him with whom we have to do" (Heb. 4:12,13).

Thus the Apostle says of the moralizer, "You should be thanking God for His mercy and be repenting of *your* sins,

"But after thy hardness and impenitent heart, [thou] treasurest up unto thyself wrath against the day of wrath and revelation of the righteous judgment of God" (Ver. 5).

Thus He reminds Mr. "Better-Than-Others" that "the goodness of God" should lead us to repentance, and that when even self-righteous moralizers "harden" their hearts and remain "impenitent," they only store up to themselves wrath to be visited upon *them* in "the day of wrath."

GOD NO RESPECTER OF PERSONS

"Who will render to every man according to his deeds:

"To them who by patient continuance in well doing seek for glory and honor and immortality, eternal life:

"But unto them that are contentious, and do not obey the truth, but obey unrighteousness, indignation and wrath.

"Tribulation and anguish upon every soul of man that doeth evil, of the Jew first, and also of the Gentile:

"But glory, honor and peace to every man that worketh good, to the Jew first, and also to the Gentile:

"For there is no respect of persons with God."

—Rom. 2:6-11

Consistently in the Epistles of Paul we are taught salvation by grace, through faith, apart from works. Is this *one* passage inconsistent with the rest? Does the Apostle here contradict himself?

No, for before explaining God's plan of salvation by grace, he must first show the *basic principles* of divine justice, for God does only that which is *right*. God *will* reward the good with eternal life—if there are any who *are* truly good. That there are none to claim this reward does not alter the basic principle. Let the Apostle teach one lesson at a time. *Here* he says simply: "God is just; He will reward the good and punish the evil." *Then, later* he goes on to say: *"There is none righteous . . . .there is none that doeth good . . ."* (3:10-12).

The Apostle here, in Rom. 2, is doing just what the author did one Sunday morning with a class of boys in a "modernistic" church.

We asked the boys: "How can we get to heaven?" *"Be good!"* they all answered in chorus. "That's right," we said, and then: "Have *you* been good?" "Yes," they all responded. "Always?" we asked. Then they hesitated. Looking at one boy, we asked, "Have you ever told a lie?" Bowing his head he nodded that he had. Then we asked another, "Have you ever stolen anything?" "Oh, no!" he answered very innocently, but he had hardly gotten the words out of his mouth when some of the others reminded him that just yesterday he had been caught red-handed with Joe's "shooter"! That opened the way for a message on salvation by grace.

So Paul *first* sets forth the basic principle that God rewards the good and punishes the evil. *Then* he demonstrates that there is not one truly, consistently good person on the face of the earth and that this is why *we need a Savior*. This demonstrated, he proceeds to present a message of salvation in which both the righteousness and the love of God are gloriously revealed.

This is how our Lord dealt with the rich young ruler (Luke 18:18-23). The ruler had asked, *"Good Master, what shall I do to inherit eternal life?"* and our Lord, already pressing the important lesson home, replied: *"Why callest thou Me good? none is good, save one, that is God. Thou knowest the commandments . . ."* (i.e., he knew what he ought to do to inherit eternal life). What, perhaps, he did *not* know was that now there was an even higher standard than the Ten Commandments. Thus, as he objected, *"All these have I kept from my youth up,"* our Lord simply added the even loftier requirement for entering into the kingdom. *"Yet lackest thou one thing,"* He said, *"Sell all that thou hast, and distribute unto the poor . . . ."* This was to be the way of life in the coming reign of Christ.

Our Lord was showing the rich young ruler that (as he knew in his heart) he had *broken* the Law and that, clinging to his riches while others were poverty-stricken, he was not even good enough to enter the prophesied kingdom on earth! *He needed a Savior.*

In Vers. 9,10 we find both the Jew and the Gentile subject to God's just judgment according to their works, *"For there is no respect of persons with God"* (Ver. 11). Yet, where both punishment and reward are concerned, he adds the words, "to the Jew *first*, and *also* to the Gentile." Why? Simply because the Jew, having a great spiritual advantage over the Gentile, was therefore the more responsible.

The revenues provided for the kings of Israel and Judah made them exceedingly rich, in order that they might rule with equity; that there might be no danger of their being bribed or intimidated. *They* were always far more wealthy than any of their subjects, thus they never needed to be "respecters of persons." How blessed, then, to reflect that God is infinitely above the greatest of men and need not— nor does He ever—pay respect to persons. His absolute justice is the basis for our complete confidence in Him. If He "smuggled" any man into heaven without having justly dealt with his sins, all in heaven might well exclaim, *"What! You here? How can this be?"* But God justly takes every man before the bar of justice, to pronounce him *guilty. Then* He steps down from His position to pay the debt of sin Himself, and as this payment is received in faith, the sinner is declared *righteous!* (See Rom. 3:25,26).

JEW AND GENTILE
BOTH UNDER THE JUDGMENT OF GOD

"For as many as have sinned without law shall also perish without law: and as many as have sinned in the law shall be judged by the law;

"(For not the hearers of the law are just before God, but the doers of the law shall be justified.

"For when the Gentiles, which have not the law, do by nature the things contained in the law, these, having not the law, are a law unto themselves:

"Which show the work of the law written in their hearts, their conscience also bearing witness, and their thoughts the meanwhile accusing or else excusing one another;)

"In the day when God shall judge the secrets of men by Jesus Christ according to my gospel."
—Rom. 2:12-16

Why does the Apostle say that those who have sinned

without the Law [1] shall *perish*, while those who have sinned in the Law shall be *judged*?

First it should be observed that entirely apart from the Law, *sin kills*. We see this on every hand in the natural realm. Envy, hate, vice, profligate living, etc., dissipate the human frame and destroy it. *"Sin, when it is finished, bringeth forth death,"* entirely apart from the Law. But not only does sin destroy the body; it destroys the soul as well.

This is not to deny that God will judge *all men*, for Ver. 16, Acts 17:31 and other passages clearly indicate that He will. The subject here is the possession or non-possession of the Law of Moses, and the Apostle shows that even without the Law the heathen would perish, and *then* he goes on to explain on what basis they will be *judged*. Those who have sinned, then, without the Law, will *perish*, but not because they rejected or disregarded the Law, for the Law was not given to them. But those who have sinned "in," or under, the Law will be *judged* by the Law.

Thus we read, *"there is no respect of persons with God, for as many as have sinned without law shall also perish without law; and as many as have sinned in* [or *under*] *the law shall be judged by the law"* (Vers. 11,12).

AN ARGUMENT FROM LOGIC

And now he inserts a parenthesis: Vers. 13-15. In it he explains why, apart from God's grace in Christ, Jews and Gentiles alike stand condemned before God.

As to the Law, he says, the Law is of no advantage if its subjects do not *obey it*. In John 8 we read about the woman taken in the act of adultery. She was a Jewess and had the Law, but that did not help her. Rather, the scribes and Pharisees were about to have her stoned *according to the Law*. Thus her advantage as a possessor of the divine revelation now turned out to be a *disadvantage*, "for, not the *hearers* of the Law are just before God, but the *doers* of the

---

1. The reader should understand that the use of the definite article in English differs widely from its use in Greek—and in other languages. In this case it is clear that *the* Law of Moses is referred to (See Vers. 13,14).

Law shall be justified" (Rom. 2:13). Note, the Apostle does not say that any man *can* obey the Law; he simply states what would happen *if he did*. He is speaking logically rather than predicting what will happen to those who might obey or disobey the Law.

The Gentiles know, entirely apart from the Law, that it is *wrong* to lie and steal and kill and commit adultery. Few of them have even heard of Moses and the Law, yet they have their own moral codes, be they ever so primitive. How, then, do they know that these things are morally *wrong*? The answer is that, first, God created them with this knowledge for *He* is holy and righteous. Second, at the fall, *conscience*, a sense of blameworthiness for sin, came into operation.

This is indirectly referred to in Ver. 15, where the Apostle states that they "show *the work of the law* written in their hearts." Note: he does not say that the Law is written in their hearts (Cf. Jer. 31:31-33), but that "the *work* of the Law" is written in their hearts. What, then, is the work of the Law? *to condemn!* *"For by the Law is the knowledge of sin"* (Rom. 3:20). *"The Law worketh wrath"* (4:15). Its ministry is *"the ministry of condemnation"* (II Cor. 3:9).

Thus the Gentiles, who did not possess the Law, showed "the work of the law written in their hearts." They *knew*, apart from the Law, that their stealing, lying, killing and immorality were wrong, "their consciences also bearing witness, and their thoughts the meanwhile *accusing* or else *excusing* one another" (Ver. 15). Note: not "congratulating," but either "accusing" or else "excusing." Both indicate guilt, which causes the sinner either to accuse himself or to make excuses.

THE JUSTICE OF THE JUDGMENT TO COME

Now let us bring together the two verses that precede and follow the parenthesis:

> "For as many as have sinned without [the] law shall also perish without [the] law: and as many as have sinned in the law shall be judged by the law"

"In the day when God shall judge the secrets of men by Jesus Christ according to my gospel" (Vers. 12,16).

Three important facts are emphasized in Verse 16:

1. God will judge the secrets of men.

2. He will do so *by* Jesus Christ; Christ will be the actual Judge.

3. He will do so *according to the gospel committed to Paul*.

GOD WILL JUDGE THE SECRETS OF MEN

Unsaved people, rather than confessing their sins to God and trusting Christ as their Savior, seek to *hide* their sins—yes, *from God*. But He sees their hearts, and if they persist in their rejection of Christ their sins will all be brought to light in the day of judgment. On the throne will be a Judge with "eyes like a flame of fire," before whom no secret will remain hidden.

"Neither is there any creature that is not manifest in His sight, but all things are naked and opened unto the eyes of Him with whom we have to do" (Heb. 4:13).

"For God shall bring every work into judgment . . . whether it be good or whether it be evil" (Eccl. 12:14).

GOD WILL JUDGE THE SECRETS OF MEN BY JESUS CHRIST

Verse 16 has sometimes been interpreted to teach that the judgment of the unsaved by Jesus Christ was part of Paul's gospel, but this is incorrect. Why would the Apostle designate this fact as part of *his* gospel when it had been made known long before? When our Lord ministered among His own on earth, He said:

"For the Father judgeth no man, but *hath committed all judgment unto the Son*" (John 5:22).

"*And hath given Him authority to execute judgment also, because He is the Son of man*" (John 5:27).

At Athens Paul indicated that God had ordained Christ to

this position *before* His resurrection from the dead—doubtless *long before:*

> "Because He hath appointed a day, in the which He will judge the world in righteousness *by that Man whom He hath ordained*; whereof He hath given assurance unto all men, in that He hath raised Him from the dead" (Acts 17:31).

Thus, the truth that Christ would be the Judge of all was not part of Paul's special message.

GOD WILL JUDGE THE SECRETS OF MEN ACCORDING TO THE GOSPEL COMMITTED TO PAUL

But how, it may be asked, can it be just to judge men of bygone ages on the basis of a message which they have never heard? If it is true that Paul's gospel was "kept secret since the world began" (Rom. 16:25), until made known to him by the glorified Lord, how can it be just to judge men of all ages according to *his* gospel?

The answer is that in the Pauline revelation we have the very "*secret* of the gospel" (Eph. 6:19), i.e., the secret of all God's good news down through the ages.

For example, we know from Heb. 10:4 that *"it is not possible that the blood of bulls and of goats should take away sins."* Yet God *required* from both Cain and Abel the offering of a blood sacrifice for acceptance with Him. How then was Abel actually saved? God has given us the answer in the epistles of Paul. Only *instrumentally* did Abel's sacrifice save him, for *essentially* it was by grace, through faith. Abel was justified because he took God at His word and approached Him in the way *He* had prescribed. This is the *"obedience of faith."*

> "*BY FAITH* Abel offered unto God a more excellent sacrifice than Cain, by which he obtained witness that he was righteous, God testifying of His gifts; and by it he, being dead, yet speaketh" (Heb. 11:4).

But how could God *require* sacrifices for sin, which in themselves had no saving value, and then accept men for offering them? The answer is that Christ was to die for sin and that on *this basis* God could justly accept those who approached Him in the way that *He* had prescribed. It was because of our Lord's death that God could justly offer *anyone* salvation on *any* terms, though this was not manifested until Paul.

Now that the glorious secret of God's good news has been made known, no works, religious or otherwise, can be required for salvation. In fact, works for salvation are now *forbidden*. Salvation is now *"to him that worketh NOT, BUT believeth"* (Rom. 4:5).

This is why the Apostle declares;

"BUT NOW the righteousness of God without the law is manifested" (Rom. 3:21).

This is why he says of Christ:

"Whom God hath set forth to be a propitiation [satisfaction] through faith in His blood, to declare *His righteousness* for the remission of sins that are past, [2] through the forbearance of God.

"To declare, I say, AT THIS TIME, *His righteousness*: that He might be just, and the Justifier of him which believeth in Jesus" (Rom. 3:25,26).

There is abundant evidence in Scripture that, as we have said, the unsaved will appear before the judgment of the Great White Throne. When these are condemned, it will not be only because they were sinners. The very Judge on the throne will be *the One who died to save sinners!* When mere professors of the Mosaic dispensation, for example, appear before that throne, they will not be condemned for imperfections in the sacrifices they offered or technicalities in the Mosaic Law which they failed to observe. Ah no. Their being "judged by the law" will entail factors more basic than this. They will be judged because their sacrifices and religious works were not brought in *faith*, but rather were deeds of *self*-righteousness and rebellion against the very God they professed to serve. Thus the works for which men will be judged in that day will merely be the fruit, or evidence, of their *unbelief*, whether "good works" or bad works.

---

2. I.e., of past generations. See Heb. 9:15.

Suppose God, in that day, should judge those who have "sinned under the Law" *merely* for breaking the Law. What, then, about David? Did he not break the Law by both adultery and murder? Conversely, what about the self-righteous Pharisees who boasted in their observance of the Law, while breaking it on every hand? Indeed, no one has ever perfectly obeyed the Law but our Lord Jesus Christ. Thus the only sense in which the Law will enter into the judgment of the unsaved who lived during the Mosaic dispensation is that man's response to the revealed will of God is ever the evidence of his faith or lack of it. This is an important element of the revelation committed to Paul, and it is what he teaches in Rom. 2:11-16.

Thus, the judgment of the Great White Throne will be presided over *by the One who died for our sins* and will proceed on the basis of the good news proclaimed by Paul, that through the death of Christ for sin, salvation is, and always has been, *essentially* by grace, through faith; that never in any age has salvation been denied to one person who has taken God at His Word and has approached Him by faith in the way that *He* has prescribed.

Only the *unsaved* will be judged at the Great White Throne. This will be discussed later on in this volume.

THE JEW AND THE LAW OF MOSES

"Behold, thou art called a Jew, and restest in the law, and makest thy boast of God,

"And knowest His will, and approvest the things that are more excellent, being instructed out of the law;

"And art confident that thou thyself art a guide of the blind, a light of them which are in darkness,

"An instructor of the foolish, a teacher of babes, which hast the form of knowledge and of the truth in the law.

"Thou therefore which teachest another, teachest thou not thyself? thou that preachest a man should not steal, dost thou steal?

"Thou that sayest a man should not commit adultery, dost thou commit adultery? thou that abhorrest idols, dost thou commit sacrilege?

"Thou that makest thy boast of the law, through breaking the law dishonorest thou God?

"For the name of God is blasphemed among the Gentiles through you, as it is written.

"For circumcision verily profiteth if thou keep the law, but if thou be a breaker of the law, thy circumcision is made uncircumcision.

"Therefore if the uncircumcision keep the righteousness of the law, shall not his uncircumcision be counted for circumcision?

"And shall not uncircumcision, which is by nature, if it fulfil the law, judge thee, who by the letter and circumcision dost transgress the law?

"For he is not a Jew, which is one outwardly; neither is that circumcision which is outward in the flesh:

"But he is a Jew, which is one inwardly; and circumcision is that of the heart, in the spirit, and not in the letter; whose praise is not of men, but of God."

—Rom. 2:17-29

THE JEW CONDEMNED BY THE LAW

It is amazing that before presenting God's wonderful plan of salvation in his *Epistle to the Romans*, Paul must take the better part of three chapters to show men that they are sinners and need a Savior.

One would think that he could simply *say* this in a few verses, for what is more evident than the sinful, fallen condition of mankind? Read the newspapers, listen to the news broadcasts; they have mostly to do with *sin*. And every class is included: the rich, the poor; the educated, the illiterate; the religious, the Godless—all are proven every day to be sinners. But such is the pride of the human heart that a man can look about him and see the whole world tainted with sin, yet does not see *himself* as a sinner! He will deny being a sinner, excusing himself, justifying himself, sometimes even congratulating himself, utterly closing his eyes to his own wretched condition and his desperate need of a Savior. The whole world is soiled with sin—*but not he!* So Paul, by the Spirit, writes one whole chapter and parts of two others to *prove* to men that they *are* sinners and must be *saved* from its penalty or perish.

In 1:18-32 he deals with the uncivilized heathen, openly wallowing in gross wickedness. In 2:1-16 he proves that the pagan moralizers, the cultured Greeks, are equally sinful and guilty. But there is still another segment of humanity who place themselves—as God has placed them—in a still different category: *the Jews, the chosen seed of Abraham.* Paul deals with these in 2:17—3:8.

By the term *Jew*, we refer to *all* the children of Israel, for while the term applied only to those of the tribe of Judah, or of Judah and Benjamin for some time after the apostasy of the ten tribes, it began again to refer to those of *all the twelve tribes*, after the return from the Assyrian and Babylonian captivities (See Acts 2:5 cf. 2:22,36; 26:7; Rom. 3:1,2). Thus once again, God's ancient people came to be known as *Hebrews* by race, *Israelites* by nationality and *Jews* by religion.

The Jew rightly felt—and still feels—himself privileged of God above all men, because God gave to *him* the Law, the written revelation of His will. So the Apostle here deals with the Jew, not to single him out as worse than others, but to show him that he too is a sinner and needs a Savior—in fact that he is the living demonstration of the fact that *all* are sinners and need to be saved.

Our Lord had already demonstrated this fact in His dealings with the Pharisee, Nicodemus. In John 2:24,25 we read that Jesus did not "commit Himself" to the many who had superficially believed on Him because of the miracles He had performed. The passage explains: *"He knew all men, and needed not that any should testify [to Him] of man; for He knew what was in man."* And then Chapter 3 continues with the words: *"There was a man...."*

Here God selects the very highest specimen of manhood: educated, cultured, refined, genuinely sincere, devoutly religious—a Pharisee, a ruler of the Jews. Coming to Jesus by night, Nicodemus frankly acknowledged Him to be "a teacher come from God," but Jesus lost no time pointing out to the venerable Pharisee that *he needed to be "born again."* Merely knowing the truth does not entitle one to eternal life; Nicodemus needed to be *"born of the Spirit."*

While our Lord, however, dealt with Nicodemus from the standpoint of his need of a new *life* of another kind, the Apostle here deals with the Jew's *condemnation* under sin and his need of *justification*.

The Apostle's tact and grace are seen in his approach to this matter.

He says, *"Behold, thou art called a Jew...."* He could have said, *"You call yourself a Jew,"* but as one of their kinsmen he could appreciate their deep feelings about being God's chosen people. He could have said, "You teach others, but you don't teach yourself," and "You preach that a man should not steal, but *you* steal," etc., but in each case he *asks*, rather, *"Do* you? Do you fail to teach yourself, do *you* steal, do you commit adultery and sacrilege, do you dishonor God by breaking the Law?" It is only after thus tactfully putting these questions to them that he goes on to quote the Scriptures on the subject, saying:

"For the name of God is blasphemed among the Gentiles through you, as it is written" (Ver. 24).

Perhaps the reader has noticed in this passage the recurrence of such words as rest, boast, know, approve, instructed, confident, a guide, a light, an instructor, a teacher, having the form, etc. But one important word is conspicuously absent in this catalog of Jewish virtues: the word *do*. What good to rest in the Law, to boast in it, to approve it, teach it, preach it, etc., if one does not *obey* it and *do* what it says? Thus, by their disobedience to the Law of Moses, the Jews gave the Gentiles cause (though not *just* cause) to blaspheme the name of God. This is no less so with the Church today, for the Church has departed so far from the message committed to Paul for us that, confused and divided, she gives the world cause to blaspheme the name of God.

CIRCUMCISION AND THE LAW

In the remainder of Chapter 2 the Apostle deals with the

Jew and circumcision. to show his kinsmen according to the flesh in another way that they are sinners and need a Savior.

Circumcision was the token of the covenant God made with Abraham, the rite that separated Israel from the wicked and licentious Gentiles. It spoke of separation to God and death to the flesh and its passions. Under Moses it became part of the Law. This is why circumcision and the Law are so often referred to together (e.g., Acts 15:1,5; Gal. 5:3). Thus the Apostle says:

"For circumcision verily profiteth if thou keep the law: but if thou be a breaker of the law, thy circumcision is made uncircumcision" (Ver. 25).

This is self-evident, and it explains why Paul wrote to the Galatians, who were tempted to submit to this religious rite:

"I testify again to every man that is circumcised [3] that he is a debtor to do *the whole law*" (Gal. 5:3).

What good to possess the sign without that which it is supposed to signify? Surely the mere *possession* of the Law, or the mere submission to circumcision did not entitle one to special favor from God. And conversely:

". . .if the uncircumcision keep the righteousness of the law, shall not his uncircumcision be counted for circumcision?" (Ver. 26).

Of course there were no Gentiles who perfectly kept the Law, but some did accept it as God's revealed will and earnestly *sought* to obey it. This did not save them, but it did place them in a position where God could reveal Himself to them further. We have an example of this in the case of Cornelius the centurion.

In Acts 10:34,35 we have Peter saying to Cornelius and his household:

"Of a truth I perceive that God is no respecter of persons, but in every nation he that feareth Him and worketh righteousness is accepted with Him."

Peter did not mean that such were saved, for Acts 11:14 clearly indicates that Peter was sent to tell them how to be

---

3. As a religious ceremony, of course.

saved. What he meant, therefore, was that such God-fearing Gentiles were "accepted" by God along with the chosen race, the Circumcision, because they were sincerely trying to do what circumcision taught—and what those of the circumcision so largely failed to do. Thus the Apostle continues:

> "And shall not uncircumcision, which is by nature, if it fulfil the law, judge thee, who by the letter and circumcision dost transgress the law?
>
> "For he is not a Jew, which is one outwardly; neither is that circumcision which is outward in the flesh:
>
> "But he is a Jew, which is one inwardly; and circumcision is that of the heart, in the spirit and not in the letter; whose praise is not of men, but of God" (Vers. 27-29).

He does not mean here that the Gentiles could perfectly fulfil the Law, but that when Gentiles sought in heart to obey the Law they condemned those who boasted that they possessed the Law, but failed to sincerely obey it.

So God here teaches a twofold lesson: (1) The Law cannot save sinners; it can only condemn them (cf. 3:19,20). (2) Religious rites cannot save. External conformity to the rite of circumcision did not meet the true design of the requirement. In a word: Religion cannot save. Cain was religious, but lost. He brought a beautiful offering to God, but God rejected it not only because it was the wrong sacrifice, but also because it was brought in pride rather than in faith. It was no acknowledgment of sin or of the need of salvation or of faith. Millions of religious people today are likewise lost, for they have placed their trust in the Church, their character, their good works, etc., rather than in the Lord Jesus Christ as the One who "died for our sins."

The last two verses of Chapter 2 bring to mind the words of Paul in Phil. 3:3:

> "For we are the circumcision, which worship God in the Spirit, and rejoice in Christ Jesus, and have no confidence in the flesh."

It does not follow from this that God has abrogated His promises to national Israel, or that these promises have been transferred to the Church today. Rather these verses teach that the outward form of religion is not acceptable to God and that He is pleased only with an inward work, the work of the Holy Spirit.

"WHAT ADVANTAGE THEN HATH THE JEW?"

"What advantage then hath the Jew? or what profit is there of circumcision?

"Much every way: chiefly, because that unto them were committed the oracles of God.

"For what if some did not believe? shall their unbelief make the faith of God without effect?

"God forbid: yea, let God be true, but every man a liar, as it is written, That Thou mightest be justified in Thy sayings, and mightest overcome when Thou art judged.

"But if our unrighteousness commend the righteousness of God, what shall we say? Is God unrighteous who taketh vengeance? (I speak as a man).

"God forbid: for then how shall God judge the world?

"For if the truth of God hath more abounded through my lie unto His glory; why yet am I also judged as a sinner?

"And not rather, (as we be slanderously reported, and as some affirm that we say), Let us do evil, that good may come? whose damnation is just."
—Rom. 3:1-8

Having demonstrated that without Christ the Jew as well as the Gentile stands guilty before God, the Apostle asks the next natural question:

"What advantage then hath the Jew? or what profit is there of circumcision?" (Ver. 1).

And he answers: *"Much every way..."* (Ver. 2).

The Jew could, indeed, insist that he belonged to the chosen race. Paul says of *"my kinsmen according to the flesh"*:

"Who are Israelites; to whom pertaineth the adoption, and the glory, and the covenants, and the giving of the law, and the service of God, and the promises;

"Whose are the fathers, and of whom, as concerning the flesh, Christ came, who is over all, God blessed forever. Amen" (Rom. 9:4,5).

But the Apostle goes on to say in Rom. 3:2 that Israel was in a place of advantage "*chiefly* because that unto them were committed the oracles of God" (Ver. 2).

It is generally held that Paul here refers to the written Word of God. This is true, but it is only part of the truth.

The Hebrew word consistently rendered "oracles" in the *King James Version* of the Bible is the word *d'veer*. It is *never* translated by *any other word* than "oracles." Similarly, the Greek word *logion*, though the diminutive of *logos*, or *word*, is *never* translated "word," but *always* "oracles."

What, then, does this word "oracles" mean in Scripture? Consulting an English dictionary will not help us to find the meanings of Greek and Hebrew words. Nor will Greek legends or a study of the oracle of Delphi help us here. We must find the meaning of the word *as used in the Bible*. And this is not difficult, for *in Scripture* these words refer to the *Word—and worship* of God. Thus in Rom. 9:4 *"the giving of the law, and the service [worship] of God"* stand together. In the Old Testament, indeed, the word *d'veer* is used exclusively of the Holiest place in the tabernacle and temple (I Ki. 6:16; Psa. 28:2; *et al*) where, however, the Word was housed. In the New Testament the word *logion* differs from *logos* in that it denotes a *response*, rather than merely a *word*. The translators of the *King James Version* evidently saw all this clearly.

When God gave Moses the Law (His Word to Israel),[4] He also said: *"And let them make Me a sanctuary, that I may dwell among them"* (Ex. 25:8). This sanctuary was to be the God-appointed place where His people could approach Him through their priests.

Thus at Mt. Sinai Moses received *two* things from God: the *Law—and a blueprint for the tabernacle* (Heb. 8:5).

The first and chief article of furniture in this tabernacle

---

4. More than the Law, of course, was included in the Scriptures committed to Israel, but the Law was given auspiciously as *His Word to them*.

was a *coffin* for the law (See Ex. 25:8-16)[5] and it was from a "mercy seat" upon this coffin that God met with His people (Vers. 21,22).

We believe, therefore, that the word "oracles" in Rom. 3:2 refers to *the Word and worship* of God, His priceless gifts to Israel alone before their casting away "for a season" (Rom. 11:15,25-27). Thus the oracles of pagan religions were—and their modern counterparts are—merely corrupted reflections of the true, for at these oracles petitions or inquiries are made and answers received from heathen "deities."

The most precious treasures in all the world, the Word and worship of God, are now the exclusive possession of the members of the Body of Christ. By "a new and living way," we may now approach God; all of us, and whenever need arises. Moreover we approach Him, not before a "mercy seat," as did Israel, but before the *"throne of grace"* (Heb. 4:16). His Word, too, has been enlarged and greatly enhanced since it was Israel's peculiar possession, especially in that it now contains the mighty message committed by the glorified Lord to Paul—*"the mystery."*

ADVANTAGE TURNED INTO DISADVANTAGE

Verse 3 clearly indicates that *unbelievers* receive no benefit from the Law. While the Law, like all Scripture, is a great blessing in itself, the advantage of possessing it becomes a *dis*advantage through unbelief and sin. We have already seen this in the case of the Jewess taken in adultery. The very Law that so favored her above the Gentiles now condemned and cursed her. This was equally true of the unbelieving but self-righteous Jew.

Yet, *"shall their unbelief make the faith of God*[6] *without effect?"* (Ver. 3). Will He not make good His Word to those

---

5. The word rendered "ark" here is translated "coffin" in Gen. 50:26, a word more easily understood than "ark." This is not the same word as that used in Gen. 6 of Noah's "ark," however. See the author's book, *Satan in Derision*, pp. 132-134.

6. Note: Not "faith *in* God." Nor does *He* exercise faith *in us!* Rather, He *keeps faith with us.* The word is here used subjectively of *God's fidelity, His worthiness to be believed.*

who *do* believe? What if some approach Him in mere religious formality, but not in faith, shall their unbelief have any effect upon His fidelity? (See Num. 23:19).

"God forbid: yea, let God be true, but every man a liar; as it is written, That Thou mightest be justified in Thy sayings, and mightest overcome when Thou art judged" (Ver. 4).

This quotation, of course, comes from David's confession in Psa. 51:4. Here God uses it to justify Himself in condemning not only the uncivilized heathen and the civilized moralizers, but even His favored nation *Israel*.

What a lesson to those who trust in the Law! To such God says: "You have already broken the Law. On this basis I can only condemn you." Salvation must be by grace; justification must be based on the death of Christ for our sins.

Nor is it enough to *try* to keep the Law and look to God to forgive where we have failed. If I commit a crime, can the judge acquit me on the basis that I have *sometimes* obeyed the law?

DOES SIN GLORIFY GOD?

The Universalists come perilously close to deserving the condemnation of Vers. 5-8, for they openly teach from Isa. 45:7 that God is the author of sin. At John 4:27-45 the notes in the *Concordant* (Universalist) *Version* refer to "the blessed results when grace grows in the fertile field of sin,"[7] and they go on to state that "sin is...indirectly essential to the satisfaction of [God's] love. Love cannot be lavished on those who are deserving." The Universalists teach that God created sin to bring glory to Himself, but the fact is rather that He *overrules* and *turns* sin to His own glory; a very different thing.

The "evil" of Isa. 45:7 is not *sin*, for it does not stand opposed to "good," in this verse, but to *"peace."* Thus it refers to trouble and calamity rather than to sin. Also, does

---
7. But God's Word says, *"Sin when it is finished bringeth forth death"* (Jas. 1:15).

not God lavish His love upon His Son? Is *He* not deserving of it?[8]

If the Universalists were right, God *would* be unrighteous for "taking vengeance" (Ver. 5), and the sinner *would* be justified in complaining, *"Why yet am I also judged as a sinner?"* (Ver. 7). Nor have the Universalists adequately answered the challenge, *"Let us do evil that good may come"* (Ver. 8). The Apostle does not even reply to those who "slanderously affirm" that *he* teaches these things. Rather he cuts them off with the severe rebuke: *"whose damnation is just"* (Ver. 8).

ALL UNDER SIN

"What then? are we better than they? No, in no wise, for we have before proved both Jews and Gentiles, that they are all under sin.

"As it is written, There is none righteous, no, not one;

"There is none that understandeth, there is none that seeketh after God.

"They are all gone out of the way, they are together become unprofitable; there is none that doeth good, no, not one.

"Their throat is an open sepulchre; with their tongues they have used deceit; the poison of asps is under their lips:

"Whose mouth is full of cursing and bitterness:

"Their feet are swift to shed blood:

"Destruction and misery are in their ways:

"And the way of peace have they not known.

"There is no fear of God before their eyes."

—Rom. 3:9-18

Thus the Apostle presses home the fact that the Jew, by nature, is no better than the Gentile. Indeed, in Vers. 10-18 he uses the Jews' own Scriptures to emphasize this fact conclusively.

In Vers. 10-12 the Apostle quotes from Psa. 14, the famous

---

8. For a comprehensive study of this subject see the author's book, *Man, His Nature and Destiny*, Chapter X.

passage which so many people erroneously apply to the atheist, while actually it applies to "the fool" who gives God no place in his life. We have dealt with this passage under Rom. 1:28.

As God "looked down from heaven upon the children of men" (Psa. 14:2), He exclaimed: *"The fool hath said in his heart, No God"* (Ver. 1). And as He scoured the earth, as it were, His judgment could only be:

"There is *none* righteous, *no, not* one. There is *none* that understandeth [i.e., the seriousness of his condition, and his need], there is *none* that seeketh after God" (Rom. 3:10,11).

Man, in his guilty state, foolishly follows Adam, *hiding from God* rather than *hastening to Him* to seek forgiveness.

Then, quoting from other Old Testament passages, the Apostle goes on in Vers. 13-18 to *describe* man's depraved condition. Note the progress of evil. It proceeds from the heart (cf. Mark 7:21-23), through the throat, the tongue and the lips, until the whole mouth is filled with "cursing and bitterness" (Vers. 13,14). This is followed in Vers. 15-18 by a list of the sins that have raged in the world all through its history.

EVERY MOUTH STOPPED
ALL THE WORLD GUILTY BEFORE GOD

"Now we know that what things soever the law saith, it saith to them who are under the law; that every mouth may be stopped and all the world may become[9] guilty before God."

—Rom. 3:19

The Apostle, having shown the deep depravity of man's very nature, and the consequent universality of sin, now proceeds to demonstrate the impossibility of justification before God by the works of the Law.

First, it should be noted that the Law was *not* given to the Gentiles, nor does Paul cite it against them. The Law was given *"to them who are under the law,"* i.e., to Israel. The

---

9. I.e., may be *shown to be* guilty.

Apostle emphasizes this fact to keep the Jew from evading the force of his argument that, apart from Christ, *all men*, without exception, stand guilty before God. It was not difficult to prove the Gentiles guilty, but the Jew—had he not been specially favored *by God?* Hence the Apostle exposes Jewish guilt by the very Law in which the Jew boasted.

Thus "every mouth" is "stopped" and "all the world" is brought in "guilty before God." Where sin and grace are concerned, God shows no partiality to the Jew (cf. 3:9).

How then does the condemnation of *Israel* by the Law bring *"all the world"* in guilty before God? In two ways:

1. Since mankind as such had already been proved to be "without excuse" (1:20), the *additional* condemnation of Israel by the Law confirmed, without question, that *all* are guilty before God.

2. God's covenant with Israel in Ex. 19:5,6 affected the Gentiles too. The only way in which a Gentile could approach God, in Old Testament times, was *through Israel* (Isa. 56:6,7). As Gentiles became proselytes they were included among God's "covenant people" but, as we have seen, under this covenant they could *actually* be His people *only* if they obeyed His voice indeed and kept the Law (Ex. 19:5,6; Rom. 2:25). This *neither Jew nor Gentile* could perfectly do, hence any Gentile would, if he *merely* became a proselyte, still stand guilty before God, for now the very Law he embraced would condemn him.

The acknowledgment of our guilt before God is one of the first steps to salvation. There is one thing that God, the Judge of all, insists upon: the sinner must stop saying things in his own defense. It is not sin that keeps men out of heaven; it is rather their *attitude.* God, in love, has made full provision for sin, paying the penalty Himself, but He has made no provision for a self-righteous attitude.

Sometimes the defendant in court comes to the place where his attorney says to him, "It will be to your advantage to plead guilty and throw yourself on the mercy of the court."

This is exactly our position. God can see through all our illegitimate arguments in our own defense. They bear no weight with Him. But if we confess our sin and throw ourselves upon His mercy He will graciously forgive and justify us through Christ. To be justified before God we *must* come as Charlotte Elliot came: *"Just as I am, without one plea, but that Thy blood was shed for me."*

NO JUSTIFICATION BY THE WORKS OF THE LAW

"Therefore by the deeds of the law there shall no flesh be justified in His sight; for by the law is the knowledge of sin."

—Rom. 3:20

We come now to the second step in the great logical argument of the *Epistle to the Romans*. Before proceeding with a discussion of this passage we should show all the steps in their sequence, connected as they are by the word *"therefore."*

"*Therefore* thou art inexcusable..." (2:1).

"*Therefore* by the deeds of the Law there shall no flesh be justified in His sight" (3:20).

"*Therefore* we conclude that a man is justified by faith, without the deeds of the law" (3:28).

"*Therefore*, being justified by faith, we have peace with God through our Lord Jesus Christ" (5:1).

"There is *therefore* now no condemnation to them which are in Christ Jesus..." (8:1).

"I beseech you *therefore*, brethren, by the mercies of God, that ye present your bodies a living sacrifice, holy, acceptable unto God, which is your reasonable service" (12:1).

In Rom. 3:20 the Apostle reiterates what the Old Testament Scriptures state or imply again and again (Psa. 130:3; 143:2; *et al*), but here he uses it in a progressive argument to show man, and especially the Jew, his need of Christ.

It is important to observe that the word "knowledge," in Ver. 20, is not the simple word *gnosis*, generally rendered "knowledge," but *epignosis*, denoting thorough or conclusive knowledge. [10]

Man does not need the Law to tell him he is a sinner; he knew that the first time he was old enough to tell a lie, or to steal something not his. One could see it in his face and read it in his demeanor! We have seen from Rom. 2:15 that man's *conscience* tells him he is a sinner. But the Jew had—and now those in enlightened nations also have—the Law to confirm this fact. Conscience accuses men of sin and the Law adds its dreadful confirmation in writing.

The process may be likened to that involving a man who, ignoring "reduced speed" signs, repeatedly drives through the main street of a small, unincorporated town at 80 miles an hour. He *knows* this is wrong, for it endangers the lives of the town's inhabitants, especially the children. But this knowledge becomes a more serious matter when the people of the town incorporate, set up a legal structure, and hire a law officer, who then waits to confront the speeder at the other side of town. This time, not merely his conscience but the law accuses him, and condemns him to pay the appropriate penalty. Thus the Law confirms the accusations of conscience and, remember, Gentiles in enlightened lands today are not exactly in the position of the heathen of Rom. 2:14, for they *do* have the Law, the divine standard of righteousness, in the Bible.

It should be noted here, however, that "the *knowledge* of sin" is not the same as the *conviction* of sin. All men have the knowledge of sin, but all are not under conviction about their sins, else men would rush to hear the gospel. The Law adds its testimony to that of conscience, that we *might be* brought under conviction, as the Holy Spirit uses His Word.

How completely all this destroys any hope of salvation by works!

Many religious people persist in believing that the Law was given to show us "how to be good." But this is the

---

10. The prefix *epi* is a superimposition, indicating something more, further, greater, deeper, higher, etc.

opposite of the truth, for the Law, while condemning the sinner, does *not* show him *how* to be good. Paul, the apostle of grace, rather does this by divine inspiration.

Not only Rom. 3:20, but other passages of Scripture clearly indicate that the Law was *not* given to help us to be good, but rather to show us *that we are bad and need a Savior*. Rom. 5:20: it *"entered that the offence might abound."* Rom. 7:13: *"that sin by the commandment might become exceeding sinful"* (cf. Gal. 3:19).

"Therefore by the deeds of the law there shall no flesh be justified in His sight, for by the law is the knowledge of sin" (Rom. 3:20; cf. Acts 13:39).

Be our sins ever so great or so many, Christ's death is sufficient; but how can the keeping of a few of God's laws avail to justify us when we have already broken so many?

> Let Jews and Gentiles stop their mouths,
>   Without a murmuring word,
> And the whole race of Adam stand
>   Guilty before the Lord.
>
> In vain we ask God's righteous Law
>   To justify us now,
> Since to convict and to condemn
>   Is all the Law can do.
>
> Jesus, how glorious is Thy grace!
>   When in Thy name we trust,
> Our faith receives a righteousness
>   That makes the sinner just!
>
> —Isaac Watts

Chapter IV — Romans 3:21—4:25
BUT NOW!
RIGHTEOUSNESS THROUGH CHRIST

THE RIGHTEOUSNESS OF GOD WITHOUT THE LAW

"But now the righteousness of God without the law is manifested, being witnessed by the law and the prophets:

"Even the righteousness of God, which is by faith of Jesus Christ, unto all and upon all them that believe: for there is no difference:

"For all have sinned and come short of the glory of God;

"Being justified freely by His grace, through the redemption that is in Christ Jesus:

"Whom God hath set forth to be a propitiation through faith in His blood, to declare His righteousness for the remission of sins that are past, through the forbearance of God;

"To declare, I say, at this time, His righteousness; that He might be just and the justifier of him which believeth in Jesus.

"Where is boasting then? It is excluded. By what law? of works? Nay: but by the law of faith.

"Therefore we conclude that a man is justified by faith, without the deeds of the law."

—Rom. 3:21-28

"But now!" Precious words coming, as they do, after all the world has been brought in guilty before God. Some hold that these words merely indicate a logical step forward, but not so. They also indicate a *dispensational* change. This is confirmed by the emphatic phrase, "I say, *at this time*," in Ver. 26. For 1500 years God had kept Israel under the Law to demonstrate *historically* that "by the deeds of the law there shall no flesh be justified in His sight," *but now* the

righteousness of God *without the Law* was being manifested (Vers. 19-21).

"The righteousness of God" is, obviously, *His* righteousness. We are aware that some translators render this phrase "*a* righteousness of God," but this leaves us wondering why, in the absence of the definite article in the Greek, an *in*definite article should necessarily be called for. We believe that here, as in many other cases, the definite article must be supplied in the English to express what the Greek says, for in this passage, certainly, the Apostle is comparing divine righteousness with human "righteousness."

Mark well, he says that this righteousness, graciously imputed to the believer, is now *"manifested."* The principle of righteousness apart from the Law had always been in operation, but it had not yet been "manifested" or "testified."[1] Several other passages of Scripture help to make this clear. Before citing these passages, however, we should first ask *when* this *bestowed righteousness* was first manifested. Was it manifested through John the Baptist, or through Christ on earth and His twelve apostles, or at Pentecost? No, not even at Pentecost. Let us be Bereans and see.

Our Lord on earth was "made *under the law*" (Gal. 4:4) and taught His disciples to be subject to the Law (Matt. 23:1-3). Under His commission to the eleven He further taught them to teach obedience to the Law (Matt. 28:20). Certainly no revelation had yet been given to the effect that the Law had been done away. Even at Pentecost, the disciples remained under the Law and practically lived in the Jewish temple (Acts 2:46; 3:1,11).

It was not until the raising up of Paul that the imputation of the righteousness of God "without the law" was revealed. No one before Paul had ever risen to proclaim what Paul says in Rom. 3:21: *"But now the righteousness of God without the law is manifested."* And note again how he insists upon this fact as he adds to the words *"But now"* the words "I say,

---

1. See Chapter I of the author's book, *Things That Differ*.

at this time" (Ver. 26). Indeed, all through his epistles he stresses the fact that with his apostleship a new dispensation was ushered in:

Gal. 3:23: "But before faith came, [2] we were kept under the law, shut up unto the faith which should afterward be revealed."

I Tim. 2:6,7: "Who gave Himself a ransom for all, to be testified in due time.

"Whereunto I am ordained a preacher, and an apostle (I speak the truth in Christ, and lie not), a teacher of the Gentiles in faith and verity."

II Tim. 1:10,11: "But is now made manifest by the appearing of our Savior Jesus Christ, [3] who hath abolished death, and hath brought life and immortality to light through the gospel: [4]

"Whereunto I am appointed a preacher, and an apostle, and a teacher of the Gentiles."

Tit. 1:2,3: "In hope of eternal life, which God, that cannot lie, promised before the world began; [5]

"But hath in due times manifested His Word through preaching which is committed unto me, according to the commandment of God our Savior."

These are but four of many passages on this important subject. Indeed, as long as Christian leaders refuse to recognize Paul as God's special apostle for the present dispensation of grace, theological confusion and division will continue to grip the Church.

But the Apostle goes on to say in Ver. 21 that this righteousness without the Law is "witnessed [6] by the law and the prophets." What does this mean? That it was proclaimed in the Law and by the prophets? Hardly, for then how could he say that it had just "now" been manifested? The answer is evidently that no Scripture in either the Law or the prophets could be adduced to nullify the validity of

---

2. I.e., the proclamation of justification *by faith alone*, committed to him.

3. Note carefully: it was *now* made manifest *by* the appearing of Christ, not *at* the appearing of Christ. The time element affects not the death of Christ, but the revelation of what that death had accomplished.

4. Clearly *Paul's* gospel (See next verse and Acts 20:24; Rom. 16:25).

5. Cf. II Tim. 1:1; Eph. 1:4-11.

6. Not merely *observed*. The word is *martureo*, to *bear witness*, to *testify*.

this plan of justification, for here was righteousness indeed, the full *payment* of sin's penalty by Christ! Little wonder Paul expressed pride that the power of this gospel lay in the fact that *"therein is the righteousness of God revealed"* (Rom. 1:16,17).

In Ver. 22 the Apostle proceeds to show that this righteousness of God is assured to believers by the *"faith of Christ."* This phrase is used seven times in Paul's epistles, but it is sad that so few believers, even Bible commentators, understand its significance. The "faith *of* Christ," like the "faith of God," in Ver. 3, is *subjective* in nature, referring to what one *is* rather than to what he does. It has nothing to do with faith in Christ [7] but with *His worthiness to be trusted*; His fidelity and His ability to fulfil His promises. The One to whom our sins were imputed at Calvary possesses all the righteousness of God, and when we trust Him for salvation we may be fully assured that all His righteousness is indeed imputed to us. He was "made...sin for us...*that we might be made the righteousness of God in Him"* (II Cor. 5:21). Thus our faith *in* Christ is based upon the faith *of* Christ (See especially Gal. 2:16, where our faith *in* Christ and the faith *of* Christ are also brought together).

The words, *"unto all and upon all them that believe,"* (Ver. 22), indicate that this righteousness is *proffered to* all, but is *conferred upon*, or *imputed to, only such as believe*. It is difficult for some to quite take in the blessed fact that since Christ paid the full penalty for our sins, we may receive the righteousness of God by faith alone, i.e., by simply *believing* God's Word as to salvation through Christ. This, however, is God's way, the *only* way in which the sinner may be justified (Gal. 2:16).

In this connection there is a beautiful comparison between Rom. 3:22,23 and Rom. 10:12:

Rom. 3:22,23: "...for there is *no difference, for all have sinned, and come short of the glory of God."*

---

[7]. Our faith *in* Christ is referred to in the latter part of this same verse. (See the author's booklet, *The Faith of Christ.*)

Rom. 10:12: *"For there is no difference between the Jew and the Greek, for the same Lord over all is rich unto all that call upon Him."*

It should be further observed from Vers. 22,23, that "there is no difference" *in this*, that *"all have sinned, and come [8] short of the glory of God."* This fact is fully established in Rom. 1:18—3:20. There may be differences in the nature or the degree of men's sins, but not in the basic fact that *"all have sinned,"* and continually *"come short of the glory of God."*

Those who, in God's mercy, have been sheltered from the grosser forms of sin sometimes feel that they are *not* sinners. These should consider the fact that as it takes only one murder to make a man a murderer, one robbery to make him a robber; as his setting just one house afire makes him an arsonist, so just one sin constitutes him a sinner by choice in addition to the fact that he is a sinner by nature.

The Apostle now returns to his basic argument: *"the righteousness of God...unto all, and upon all them that believe."* Those who do believe, he affirms, are *"justified freely by [God's] grace, through the redemption that is in Christ Jesus"* (Ver. 24).

Grace! How sadly misunderstood and underrated! Something for nothing, unmerited favor, *GRACE: G*od's *R*iches *A*t *C*hrist's *E*xpense, and many other definitions have been given for the word "grace," but most of them seriously fail to convey the significance of this precious word. The Greek *charis*, at least in this context, has in it the idea of *delight*, as when a grandparent, for example, delights in that precious grandchild, and seeks opportunities to make him happy. The marvel of *God's* grace, however, is that *He* delights in saving *sinners* and filling their lives with blessing (Eph. 2:1-7). W. E. Vine well defines the Bible usage of this word in his *Expository Dictionary of New Testament Words*:

> "Charis has various meanings, (*a*) objective, that which bestows or occasions pleasure, delight, or causes favorable regard....(*b*) subjective (1) on the part of the

---

8. Not *have* come, but *do* come short (present tense). All *have* sinned and *do* come short of the glory of God.

bestower, the friendly disposition from which the kindly act proceeds . . . .(2) on the part of the receiver, a sense of the favor bestowed, a feeling of gratitude . . . ."

The thought here in Rom. 3:24, then, is that God *delights* to save sinners. He *Himself* has made full provision to save them and now invites them to come and be "justified freely through the redemption that is in Christ Jesus" (Cf., II Cor. 5:18-21 here).

The word *"freely,"* in this passage, adds emphasis to the fact that justification is *by grace*. The Greek *dorean*, rendered "freely" here, is also used in John 15:25, where we read of Christ: "They hated Me *without a cause.*" As men hated Christ *without a cause* (except in their own evil hearts), so God justifies believers *"without a cause"* (except in His own heart of love). God loves sinners, and delights to do them good, not because of any good thing in them, but because *"God is love"* (I John 4:16) and judgment is "His strange work" (Isa. 28:21).

The Apostle takes up almost three chapters in Romans writing about sin. He does this to prepare us to receive salvation by grace, for righteousness can be imputed to us in no other way than by God's *grace, "through the redemption that is in Christ Jesus"* (Ver. 24).

Those who "go about to establish their own righteousness" (Rom. 10:3), or seek to "justify themselves" (Luke 10:29; 16:15), will be "judged. . .every man according to their works" (Rev. 20:13), and will justly suffer the consequences (Rev. 20:15). How much better to follow the example of those of John the Baptist's day who "justified *God*" (Luke 7:29), saying, "He is right," and acknowledging *His* appraisal of their condition, for in no other way is salvation possible. Thus the Apostle goes on to say with regard to Christ:

"Whom God hath set forth to be a propitiation [i.e., a satisfaction] [9] through faith in His blood, to declare His righteousness for the remission of sins that are past, through the forbearance of God.

---

9. The word is taken from the mercy seat on the ark, or coffin of the covenant, sprinkled with the blood of atonement.

"To declare, I say, at this time, His righteousness, that He might be just, and the justifier of Him which believeth in Jesus" (Vers. 25,26).

Ah, God has now "set forth" Christ! i.e., *prominently*. Blessed truth! No longer is it "the sin question" that determines a man's destiny. Now it is rather "the Son question." God has made full provision for sin and now invites us to receive "the *gift* of righteousness" (Rom. 5:17) by faith in Christ, who died for our sins. Thus the Apostle John, writing years later, declares:

"He that believeth on Him is not condemned, but he that believeth not is condemned already, because he hath not believed in the name of the only begotten Son of God" (John 3:18).

The Apostle Paul, in pointing out that God has set forth Christ and His shed blood as the just satisfaction for sin, indicates that this avails also for the *"sins that are past."* He does not refer here to the sins of *our* past, but to those of past *history* (See Heb. 9:15). "The forbearance of God" withheld judgment in those days because He had purposed that Christ's blood should be the full satisfaction for sin.

Do we wonder how, in the light of Ex. 19:5 and Gal. 3:10, men under the Law could possibly be saved; men like Moses, David and Daniel? Paul tells us how. They were justified because Christ's righteousness was imputed to them as it is to us, only this was not yet revealed to them. But this has "now," "at this time," been "manifested" and "testified" in "the gospel of the grace of God."

Thus the Apostle emphasizes both the dispensational aspect of these truths and the fact that we sinners *must* be justified by Christ's righteousness alone, since we have no righteousness of our own to offer (Rom. 3:25,26; cf. Phil. 3:9).

We must remember that justification is not acquittal; it does not declare us innocent of sin. Rather God justly condemns the sinner, but He *justifies* the *believing* sinner, declaring him righteous *in Christ*. How much more than acquittal! The process:

1. The sinner pronounced guilty (Rom. 3:19).
2. The sinner's sins imputed to Christ (Rom. 3:24).
3. Christ's righteousness imputed to the sinner (Rom. 4:5).

What joy has filled the hearts of those who have embraced this blessed truth! How many have been moved to proclaim it, expound it, write beautiful hymns about it and lead others into the joy of it! This truth has been the source of the author's confidence and joy for more than fifty-five years.

What a vast difference between Peter, at Pentecost, demanding repentance and baptism for the remission of sins (Acts 2:38), and Paul now gladly proclaiming imputed righteousness, the righteousness of Christ, for the remission of sins!

Thus God can be—and is—*"just and the justifier of him which believeth in Jesus"* (Ver. 26). The believing sinner's justification has been *righteously* accomplished. No principle of justice has been abandoned, so that the words *"believeth in Jesus"* bring the declaration to an abrupt and appropriate close.

When our Lord, still on earth, commissioned His eleven apostles to go into all the world and preach "the gospel" [10] He said, *"He that believeth and is baptized shall be saved"* (Mark 16:16). But here in the glorious message committed to Paul by the ascended Lord, the words "and is baptized" are conspicuously absent and, indeed, purposely omitted. Now, while maintaining absolute justice, God fully justifies those who simply, but sincerely, *"believe in Jesus."*

It is an interesting fact that in Paul's first recorded sermon, delivered in the synagogue at Antioch of Pisidia, he declared:

"Be it known unto you therefore, men and brethren, that through this man is preached unto you the forgiveness of sins;

"And *by Him all that believe are justified from all things*, from which ye could not be justified by the law of Moses" (Acts 13:38,39).

"Where is boasting then?" The Apostle's reply could not be more to the point: *"It is excluded"* (Ver. 27). God knows the evil and sorrow that have resulted from human pride, and He does not tolerate it in His redemptive plan. He gives

---

10. Obviously, the gospel they *had been* preaching: "the gospel of the kingdom" (Matt. 9:35; Luke 9:2; cf. Matt. 24:14).

man no part whatsoever in salvation but to receive it as a gift—*"lest any man should boast"* (Eph. 2:8,9). The joy of salvation and of heaven springs not from the pride of human accomplishment, but from sheer gratitude.

But on what principle is boasting excluded from God's method of justifying sinners? Am I not to receive credit for *anything* in this whole transaction? The Apostle deals with this in Ver. 27. *"By what law,"* he asks, is boasting excluded? By the law "of works?" and he answers, *"Nay, but by the law of faith."*

Two immutable, inexorable *laws* are enunciated in Rom. 11:6. One has to do with *grace*, received by simple *faith*; the other with *works*, involving human *effort*:

"And if by grace, then is it no more of works: otherwise grace is no more grace. But if it be of works, then is it no more grace: otherwise work is no more work."

There are the two alternatives! If salvation is *earned* by good works, then it is *not* the gift of God's grace to be received by faith alone. Conversely, if it is the gift of God's grace, it *cannot* be attained by good works, for grace and works for salvation are mutually exclusive.

"Therefore we conclude that a man is justified by faith, without the deeds of the law" (Ver. 28).

This is the third step in Paul's great logical argument in the *Epistle to the Romans*.

JUSTIFICATION BY FAITH ESTABLISHES THE LAW

"Is He the God of the Jews only? is He not also of the Gentiles? Yes, of the Gentiles also:

"Seeing it is one God, which shall justify the circumcision by faith, and uncircumcision through faith.

"Do we then make void the law through faith? God forbid. Yea, we establish the law."

—Rom. 3:29-31

Can *God* be the God of *Gentiles?*—Gentiles, whom He

had long ago given up to "vile affections" and "a reprobate mind" (Rom. 1:24,26,28)? This was difficult for the Jew to accept. To us the rite of circumcision may appear strange and even repulsive, but for the Jew it held great significance and importance. It was a token of the covenant God had made with Abraham, *separating* him and his seed from the Gentiles. Later, circumcision was incorporated into the Mosaic Law. Any uncircumcised male among Abraham's seed was to be "cut off from his people" (Gen. 17:14).

But Paul has already *"proved"* that *"both Jews and Gentiles...are all under sin"* (Rom. 3:9), and therefore "cut off," entirely apart from circumcision or the lack of it. He has also shown that *"through the redemption that is in Christ Jesus,"* all who believe are *"justified freely by [God's] grace"* (Rom. 3:22-24). Thus the "one God" justifies both believing Jews and believing Gentiles through Christ's work of redemption.

Theologians have long struggled over the reason why believing Jews are said to be justified "*by* faith," but believing Gentiles "*through* faith" (Ver. 30). [11] We believe that the solution lies in the original status of each. The Jews, belonging to the covenant race, were to be justified *by* (out of) faith. Faith *should be* the natural outcome of their favored relationship to God, but the "far off" Gentiles must come *through* (by way of) faith; *both* justified by "one God" upon believing.

While the Jews were justified "out of" faith, it is also evident that they were justified *by way of* works, while the Gentiles were justified directly "by way of" faith. For the Jew, sacrifices, etc., were (instrumentally) the *means* of his justification; he came "by way of" works, whereas the Gentile comes directly "by way of" faith for *his* justification.

But if both Jews and Gentiles are justified on the basis of faith, does not this "make void the law?" Why was the Law given to the Jew in the first place if *both* Jew and Gentile can be justified by faith *apart from the Law*? The answer is

---

11. *"by"* (Gr., *ek*, "out of"); *"through"* (Gr., *dia*, "by way of").

that the Law was given to the Jew not to justify him, but to prove him guilty *along with the Gentiles* (Ver. 19).

Thus the Apostle demonstrates the fact that his good news of justification by grace, through faith alone, by no means makes the Law void; rather it establishes the Law (See notes on 3:21).

TWO EXAMPLES
FROM JEWISH HISTORY

Realizing the difficulty of inducing the Jew to accept the principle of justification by faith alone, the Apostle now commences to demonstrate his point by referring to the Jews' own Scriptures regarding two outstanding personalities from their own history: *Abraham and David.*

"What shall we say then that Abraham, our father as pertaining to the flesh, hath found?

"For if Abraham were justified by works, he hath whereof to glory; but not before God.

"For what saith the Scripture? Abraham believed God, and it was counted unto him for righteousness.

"Now to him that worketh is the reward not reckoned of grace, but of debt.

"But to him that worketh not, but believeth on him that justifieth the ungodly, his faith is counted for righteousness.

"Even as David also describeth the blessedness of the man unto whom God imputeth righteousness without works.

"Saying, Blessed are they whose iniquities are forgiven, and whose sins are covered.

"Blessed is the man to whom the Lord will not impute sin."

—Rom. 4:1-8

As we know, the latter great section of the Bible, the so-called "New Testament," opens by presenting Messiah as *"the son of David, the son of Abraham"* (Matt. 1:1). This is the basis for *"the gospel of the kingdom,"* which is the subject of the four records of our Lord's earthly ministry, for there Christ is proclaimed as the rightful heir to the two great covenants made with these patriarchs.

The *Abrahamic Covenant* promised a *"land"* and a *"great nation"* to dwell upon it (Gen. 12:1-3; 13:14-18), while the *Davidic Covenant* promised a *kingdom* and an everlasting *King* as its ruler (II Sam. 7:16; Psa. 89:34-36). Thus in the four "Gospels" we have a *King* who is to reign as head of a *kingdom* over a *nation* in a *land*—the land of Canaan.

However, the Sacred Record relates how Israel rejected the King and His kingdom. As a result the nation was driven out of the land covenanted to her. The establishment of this kingdom was—and is now—held in abeyance until a future time, after the present dispensation of grace shall have been brought to a close (Rom. 11:25-27).

Now, here in Romans 4, we find Paul referring to these same two great patriarchs, but *not* in connection with the covenants God made with them. Rather the Apostle now uses them to demonstrate the validity of his God-given message. He uses them, not to proclaim the gospel of the kingdom, but to proclaim the gospel of the grace of God.

First he turns to Abraham—and with good reason.

THE CASE OF ABRAHAM

The author once asked a class of boys: "Who is the most honored, most respected, most loved man of all history?" With one accord they answered: *"Jesus!"* How wrong they were! The Lord Jesus Christ *should* indeed be loved and honored by all, but alas, millions despise Him and many even hate Him, while His name is taken in vain on every hand.

Without doubt, the most honored, most respected, most loved man of all history is—*Abraham*. Even today Abraham is venerated as the "father" of:

More than 15,000,000 Jews,

More than 550,000,000 Mohammedans,[12] and

More than 1,000,000,000 professing Christians.

---

12. The great disparity between the total number of Jews in the world today and the total number of Mohammedans is explained by such passages as Deut. 28:63 and Rom. 11:12.

Thus, as God chose *Paul* to demonstrate His *grace* to *sinners* (I Tim. 1:15,16), so He chose *Abraham* to demonstrate *justification by faith* (Rom. 4:1-5; cf. Gal. 3:6,7).

Writing as a Hebrew, the Apostle calls Abraham *"our father as pertaining to the flesh,"* and declares that *"if Abraham were justified by works* [a purely hypothetical case], *he hath whereof to glory,* 13 but not before God" (Rom. 4:1,2). *"No flesh"* will ever *"glory in His presence"* (I Cor. 1:29; Eph. 2:8,9). Thus the Apostle continues:

"For what saith the Scripture? Abraham believed God, and it was counted unto him for righteousness" (Ver. 3).

Having purposed (as Abraham did not yet know) that Christ would die as the satisfaction for man's sin, God said of Abraham, as it were: "He *believes* Me. I will honor his faith and count him righteous" (I.e., *in Christ*). Thus Abraham's justification was not the result of his *doing* anything; it was rather the result of his simple faith in God and His Word. Otherwise it would not have been "of grace," but "of debt."

It should be carefully noted in connection with Gen. 15:6, the passage which the Apostle quotes here, that this passage does *not* say that Abraham looked forward in faith to a coming Christ to be saved.[14] The whole passage (Gen. 15:2-6) clearly indicates that Abraham believed God as to the innumerable seed that should spring from him through Isaac. His implicit faith in God's word as to this showed that he *believed God*. We *now* know that Abraham's justification was based upon the then future death of Christ for his sins (Rom. 3:25), but Abraham, not yet knowing this, simply believed *what God said to him* and God *"counted it to him for righteousness."*

The passage in Genesis does not even say that God *told Abraham* that his faith was counted to him for righteous-

---

13. Gr., *echei kauchema*: "He has ground for boasting."
14. Those who teach this also generally interpret Gal. 3:8 to mean that the gospel of the grace of God was preached to Abraham, *even though* this very verse clearly states *what "gospel"* (good news) was there preached to Abraham.

ness. This was later written *about* him, and Paul here uses it as evidence for justification by faith.

Thus the works of the Law required in Old Testament times were accepted only as they expressed *faith*. It is a precious fact, however, that while God did not yet reveal to those of ancient times the significance of their sacrifices, we can *now* look back with Paul at these sacrifices—and *all* the types, physical and historical, and exclaim: "Truly the cross was not an accident, nor the dispensation of grace an afterthought. God had them in mind all the while. This was indeed His secret, eternal purpose, "hid from ages and from generations," but made known in due time through Paul, the chief of sinners *saved by grace!*

And now the Apostle applies the lesson to those of his day—and of ours:

"...to him that worketh is the reward not reckoned of grace, but of debt.

"But to him that worketh not, but believeth on Him that justifieth the ungodly, his faith is counted [15] for righteousness" (Rom. 4:4,5).

Mark well, God now does not merely pronounce works for salvation *unnecessary*; He *forbids* them. Justification is not merely *not* "to him that worketh"; it is "to him that *worketh not, but believeth.*" To be justified before God we must come to the end of ourselves, and "lay our deadly doing down," receiving "the gift of righteousness" in simple faith, through Christ, who died for us. *After* we have received salvation as "the gift of God" He will let us toil as slaves for Him and for others, but in this dispensation of grace He utterly rejects works for salvation, *"lest any man should boast"* (Eph. 2:8,9).

How many will miss heaven because they refuse to come to God in *His* way! How many remain unsaved because they keep *"going about to establish their own righteousness"* (Rom. 10:1,3)! How much better to heed the truth of Romans 4:5 and join Paul in praising God:

---

15. The Greek *logizomai* occurs eleven times in this chapter, variously translated "count," "reckon," and "impute" (Vers. 3,4,5,6,8,9,10,11,22,23,24).

"Who hath saved us, and called us with an holy calling, not according to our works, but according to His own purpose and [His own] grace, which was given us in Christ Jesus before the world began" (II Tim. 1:9).

THE CASE OF DAVID

David too is called upon to testify to Paul's basic contention as to justification by faith, apart from works. It must not be supposed, however, that David knew about "the dispensation of the grace of God" any more than Abraham did. The words are:

"...David also *describeth* the *blessedness* of the man unto whom God imputeth righteousness without works" (Rom. 4:6).

The Apostle goes on, in Vers. 7,8, to quote from Psalm 32, evidently written by David after he had experienced God's forgiveness in connection with his sin involving Bathsheba and her husband, Uriah.

The reader will do well to pause here to read in detail David's touching description of that blessedness in Psa. 32. First we have the theme of his song, followed by an account of his persistent effort to "cover things up," while in discipline the Lord's hand is "heavy" upon him "day and night," so that his bones "wax old" and his "moisture" (Lit., *freshness*) is turned to "the drought of summer" (Vers. 3,4). Finally He confesses all to the Lord, who readily forgives "the iniquity" of his "sin" (Ver. 5; cf. II Sam. 12:13). Then David "pulls out all the stops," as it were, in praise to God for His goodness.

It should be noted here that whereas Paul cites Abraham to show that justification is *obtained* by faith, without works, he cites David to demonstrate that the sinner, once justified, cannot be condemned to perdition by the Law. David "describes" this,

"Saying, Blessed are they whose iniquities are forgiven, and whose sins are covered.

"Blessed is the man to whom the Lord *will not*[16] impute sin" (Rom. 4:7,8).

---

16. The divine Author thus interprets His own words in Psa. 32:2.

Abraham lived *before the Law was given*, while David lived *under the Law*. Both are witnesses to justification by faith, without works, but unlike Abraham, David describes the blessedness of the justified man, whom the Law cannot condemn. When he sins God will discipline him to restore him to fellowship (Psa. 51:12), but will not cast him away. The case of Abraham is a purely *positive* one, while the case of David is ultimately *negative*: "Blessed is the man to whom the Lord *will not* impute sin."

We repeat that David could not have understood the "how and why" of all this, but he did know that God had forgiven him even though the Law condemned him, and he "described" the blessedness of this knowledge.

There is a third distinction between Abraham and David here. Every Jew knew Abraham as "the father of *circumcision*," while with David it was *the Law* that was mainly involved. Thus the Apostle goes on to deal with circumcision (Vers. 9-12) and the Law (Vers. 13-25) in the remainder of this chapter as they relate to justification by faith.

A CONTRADICTION?

Before proceeding with the remainder of this chapter we must deal briefly with a seeming contradiction between Rom. 4:3-5 and James 2:24.

In Rom. 4:3-5 Paul clearly declares that men are justified by faith alone, *without works*, but James 2:24 states with equal clarity:

"Ye see then how that by works a man is justified, and not by faith only."

Are these statements actually contradictory, or only apparently so? Let us see.

It has been explained that the recurrence of the words "ye see," in James' argument, indicates that he refers to proof *before men* that those who profess justifying faith actually have it. But Abraham did not offer Isaac *before men*, nor does this argument explain how men *are justified* by works,

Romans 4:1-8

as James 2:24 states. Surely both Romans 4 and James 2 refer to justification *by God*, but one says that this is received by faith only while the other says it is gained *"by works, and not by faith only."*

We believe that the answer to this seeming contradiction is a dispensational one, and with this in view let us note several background comparisons:

The writer in the first place is *Paul*; in the second place it is *James*. *Paul* addresses *Gentiles* (Rom. 11:13), while *James* writes to *"the twelve tribes [of Israel] which are scattered abroad"* (Jas. 1:1). *Paul* deals with Abraham *before* his circumcision; *James* deals with him *after* his circumcision (as the father of the Hebrew race). *Paul* quotes from *Gen. 15:6* to prove his point; *James* cites *Gen. 22:1-18*. *Paul* mentions only Abraham's acceptance of the *good news* concerning his seed (Gen. 15:4-6); *James* deals with his faith in a severe *test* (Gen. 22:16-18). These are significant differences.

With these differences in view we quote from one of our former writings:

"Faith [will] most assuredly approach God in God's way at any time, and to seek to gain acceptance with Him in any other way would, of course, be *unbelief* and self-will. Thus, while works never did or could save *as such*, they did once save as *expressions of faith*."

"When God says, 'Offer an animal in sacrifice and I will accept you,' what will faith do? Faith will offer an animal in sacrifice, of course. Abel did this and was accepted, not because the blood of beasts can take away sins, but because he approached God in *God's* way. This is 'the obedience of faith.'

"In the case of Cain we have a clear indication that God is not satisfied with mere works as such, for Cain offered a more attractive-looking sacrifice than Abel, but was rejected because he did not bring the sacrifice which God had required (Gen. 4:5).

"When God says, 'Build an ark and I will save you and yours from the flood,' what will faith do? Faith will build an ark, of course. And when Noah did this he showed his faith in God and 'became an heir of the righteousness which is by faith.'

"When God says, 'Obey My voice indeed and you will be Mine,' what will faith do? Faith will try earnestly to obey. You say: But they could not obey perfectly, therefore would be rejected by God. We reply that we have already proved that works in themselves cannot save. It was only as Israelites recognized the Law *as the Word of God* to them and *therefore* sought to obey it that they were saved. *Such* an effort to keep the Law represented 'the obedience of faith.'

"When God says, 'Repent and be baptized for the remission of sins,' what will faith do? Just one thing: repent and be baptized. We know that oceans of water cannot wash away one sin, yet when John the Baptist and Peter preached repentance and baptism for remission, not one of their hearers would have interpreted their words to mean: 'Trust in the death of Christ for salvation.' Indeed, when God required water baptism for salvation the *only* way to manifest faith was to be baptized, and those who refused to do so were condemned for their unbelief:

" 'But the Pharisees and lawyers REJECTED THE COUNSEL OF GOD AGAINST THEMSELVES, BEING NOT BAPTIZED OF HIM' (Luke 7:30).

"But when God says, *'BUT NOW the righteousness of God without the law is manifested'* (Rom. 3:21); *'To him that worketh not, but believeth on Him that justifieth the ungodly, his faith is counted for righteousness'* (Rom. 4:5) ....what will faith do? Faith will say, 'This is the most wonderful offer ever made by God to man. I cannot refuse it. I will trust Christ as my Savior and accept salvation as the free gift of God's grace' " (*Things That Differ*, Pp. 22,42,43).

This we believe is the answer to the seeming contradiction between Romans 4:5 and James 2:24. The Epistle of James will fit into God's dispensational plan just where it is found in the canon of Scripture: after the Pauline dispensation. When "the dispensation of the grace of God" has run its course God will again begin dealing with "the twelve tribes of Israel," now "scattered abroad." In that day the "gospel of the kingdom" will again be proclaimed (Matt. 24:14) and works will again be included in the terms of salvation as they were when our Lord was on earth (Mark 1:4; Luke 7:29,30; 18:18-22; *et al*). Does this mean that works will be efficacious in themselves? No. They will avail only as the expression and evidence of faith as, indeed, James clearly teaches (Jas. 2:18-26). [17]

RIGHTEOUSNESS IMPUTED
ENTIRELY APART FROM CIRCUMCISION

In Rom. 4:1-8 the Apostle uses Abraham and David to demonstrate the validity of his argument for justification by faith, apart from works. Now, from Verse 9 to the end of the chapter he presses this truth home, demonstrating further that righteousness is imputed to believers entirely apart from circumcision and entirely apart from the Law.

"Cometh this blessedness then upon the Circumcision only, or upon the Uncircumcision also? [18] for we say that faith was reckoned to Abraham for righteousness.

"How was it then reckoned? when he was in circumcision, or in uncircumcision? Not in circumcision, but in uncircumcision.

"And he received the sign of circumcision, a seal of the righteousness of the faith which he had yet being uncircumcised: that he might be the father of all them that believe, though they be not circumcised; that righteousness might be imputed unto them also.

"And the father of circumcision to them who are not of the Circumcision only, but who also walk in the steps of that faith of our father Abraham, which he had being yet uncircumcised."

—Romans 4:9-12

"Cometh this blessedness"—the double blessedness of righteousness imputed and sins *not* imputed—"upon the Circumcision only, or upon the Uncircumcision also"? This

---

17. For a more comprehensive study of this subject see the author's chapter on "The Principles and Dispensations of God," in his book, *Things That Differ* (Pp. 21-45).

18. The Jew and the Gentile are often called "the Circumcision" and "the Uncircumcision" in Scripture.

was a natural question for the Jew to raise seeing that the Apostle had just said that "faith was reckoned to *Abraham* for righteousness," and Abraham was the father of *the Hebrew race*—of which, indeed, David also was a member.

To answer this question, Paul asks another:

"How was [faith] then reckoned [to Abraham]? when he was in circumcision, or in uncircumcision?" and the answer is obvious: *"Not in circumcision, but in uncircumcision"* (Ver. 10).

In Verse 3 the Apostle quotes Gen. 15:6 in connection with an incident that took place some years *before* Abraham's circumcision. Indeed, Abraham was originally justified considerably *before that* when, as a poor, blind, idol-worshipping pagan, God spoke to him saying:

"Get thee out of thy country, and from thy kindred, and from thy father's house, unto a land that I will show thee:

"And I will make thee a great nation, and I will bless thee, and make thy name great; and thou shalt be a blessing:

"And I will bless them that bless thee, and curse him that curseth thee: and in thee shall all families of the earth be blessed" (Gen. 12:1-3).

This command Abraham,[19] after some hesitation (Gen. 11:31,32, cf. 12:1,4,5), obeyed "by faith," and it is clear from Heb. 11:8-10,39 that he "obtained a good report *through faith" as expressed by his departure from the Ur of the Chaldees and his reliance upon God's promise of "a better country."*

Thus the covenant of circumcision had nothing whatever to do with Abraham's justification before God. He was justified *by faith alone*.

"And he received the sign of circumcision, a seal of the righteousness of *the faith which he had yet being uncircumcised;* that he might be the father of *all them that believe,* though they be not circumcised; that righteousness might be imputed unto them also" (Rom. 4:11).

Circumcision did not justify Abraham. It was merely a

---

19. Then still called *Abram*; his name is changed to *Abraham* at Gen. 17:5. Paul consistently refers to him as *Abraham*, however.

"sign," a token; *"a seal of the righteousness of the faith which he had yet being uncircumcised"* (Ver. 11). Thus he became "the father of *all them that believe, though they be not circumcised"* (Ver. 11).

On the same basis he became "the father of circumcision," *not* to those who merely submitted to the religious *rite* of circumcision, but *"who also walk in the steps of that faith"* which Abraham had, "being yet uncircumcised," i.e., he became the father of those Jews who truly believe (Ver. 12). Such have the reality of which circumcision was but the outward sign.

"Know ye therefore that they which are of faith, the same are the children of Abraham" (Gal. 3:7).

How clearly all this teaches us that justification, or imputed righteousness, never did rest upon the mere performance of any physical rite, whether circumcision, or the sacrifices of the Law, or water baptism, but on faith alone. Especially is this so since the raising up of Paul to proclaim the all-sufficient, finished work of redemption wrought by Christ at Calvary. *Now* faith in God must, in the nature of the case, involve *faith in what He has said about justification through the finished work of Christ* (Rom. 3:25; I Cor. 15:1-3; II Cor. 5:21; etc.).

How clearly, too, this proves that the blessedness of righteousness imputed and sins *not* imputed *is* for both Jews and Gentiles *who approach God in faith*, believing what He says about Christ, and coming to Him through Christ (Rom. 3:21-27).

Finally, this passage teaches, by clear implication, that those who insist upon justifying themselves, *"going about to establish their own righteousness,"* are not, even if Jews,[20] recognized *by God* as the true children of Abraham, since Abraham is "the father of all them *that believe"* (Rom. 4:11). Indeed, we have already seen in our studies in Romans 2 that:

---

20. Indeed, Paul uses this phrase with regard to *unsaved Israel* (Rom. 10:1-3).

"...he is not a Jew which is one outwardly; neither is that circumcision, which is outward in the flesh" (Ver. 28).

Conversely, the Apostle says of *all believers in Christ*:

"For we are the Circumcision, which worship God in the spirit, and rejoice in Christ Jesus, and have no confidence in the flesh" (Phil. 3:3).

RIGHTEOUSNESS IMPUTED ENTIRELY APART FROM THE LAW

"THAT IT MIGHT BE BY GRACE"

As the Apostle has shown that righteousness is imputed to believers *entirely apart from circumcision,* he now proceeds to demonstrate that it is imputed *entirely apart from the Law.* This would interest Romans as well as Jews, for among the Romans law was held in such high regard that the echo of the Roman Code, as well as that of the Law of Moses, can be heard in our British and American courts of justice.

"For the promise, that he should be the heir of the world, was not to Abraham, or to his seed, through the law, but through the righteousness of faith.

"For if they which are of the law be heirs, faith is made void, and the promise made of none effect:

"Because the law worketh wrath; for where no law is, there is no transgression.

"Therefore it is of faith that it might be by grace; to the end the promise might be sure to all the seed; not to that only which is of the law, but to that also which is of the faith of Abraham; who is the father of us all."

—Rom. 4:13-16

It should be carefully noted that God does not hold the great men of Scripture up to us because of their moral goodness. Almost invariably their records are spoiled by failure and sin. But God bids us behold their *faith* and observe how He blessed them for *believing Him.* We have already seen this from Vers. 1-5 above, and it is emphasized with great force in Hebrews 11. Here we find many variables, but *one constant*: *"By faith....by faith....by faith."*

Many of the sins and shortcomings of these "heroes of faith" are omitted from Heb. 11, for God's purpose in this chapter is to show how He honored *their faith*. Indeed, this great chapter opens and closes with the declaration that those listed all *"obtained a good report through faith"* (Vers. 2,39). It is amazing what God will do for men if they will simply *believe* Him and trust Christ for salvation.

We have seen that unquestionably the one person in all Scripture who stands out as the great example of *faith* is Abraham. The writer's edition of the *Encyclopaedia Britannica* states a fact that many other secular volumes echo: that "the outstanding characteristic of Abraham's life was his implicit and childlike faith in God. In the Scriptures he is constantly held up as the great example of faith."

Thus the Apostle Paul, in proceeding to show how justification is *not* obtained by the Law, continues to use Abraham as a living demonstration of this fact.

"The promise that he should be heir of the world," [21] Paul argues, *"was not to Abraham or to his seed through the law, but through the righteousness of faith"* (Ver. 13). Neither Abraham nor his seed *earned* this honor, nor was it conferred upon them "through the law." It was simply *promised* to them. In fact, the Law was not even given until hundreds of years later.

"For," he goes on, *"if they which are of the law be heirs, faith is made void, and the promise made of none effect"* (Ver. 14).

What is the purpose of a promise if it is not to be believed and relied upon? And a legal contract immediately makes any oral promises "of none effect." This should be self-evident, but many still need to learn it. In Gal. 3:18, again referring to Abraham, Paul presses this truth home:

"If the inheritance be of the law, it is no more of promise, but God gave it to Abraham by promise."

And the lesson to us is clear from the same passage:

---

21. Cf. Ver. 17; Psa. 2:8; Isa. 60:1-3.

"But that no man is justified by the law in the sight of God, it is evident, for ["What saith the Scripture?"], The just shall live by faith. [22]

"And the law is not of faith: but ["What saith the Scripture?"], The man that doeth them shall live in them" [23] (Ver. 11,12).

How could the Law *justify* a *sinner*? Obviously the Law must *condemn* the sinner. *"The law worketh wrath."* Indeed there would be no *transgression* if there were no law to transgress (Rom. 4:15). Every criminal knows that "the law worketh wrath," and every sinner should know it. The Scriptures abound with testimony to this effect:

Gal. 3:19: *"It [the Law] was added because of transgressions."*

Rom. 3:19: *"That every mouth may be stopped, and all the world may become guilty before God."*

Rom. 5:20: It entered *"that the offence might abound."*

Rom. 7:13: *"That sin, by the commandment, might become exceeding sinful."*

Col. 2:14: Its decrees are said to be *"against us"* and *"contrary to us."*

Gal. 3:10: *"As many as are of the works of the law are under the curse."*

II Cor. 3:9: It is called *"the ministration of condemnation."*

II Cor. 3:7: It is called *"the ministration of death."*

I Cor. 15:56: *"The sting of death is sin, and the strength of sin is the law."*

Yet, with all this testimony from the Word of God, men *will* continue to seek to *gain* salvation by the works of the Law, approaching God on *their* terms—which He will never accept. He will not *sell* justification at *any* price, certainly not for a few paltry "good" works, offered by men whose entire lives have been corrupted by sin.

---

22. Hab. 2:4.
23. Lev. 18:5.

THE FATHER OF US ALL

It is to our infinite *advantage* to receive justification by faith alone, for Ver. 16 goes on to say:

"Therefore it is of *faith*, that it might be by *grace;* to the end the promise might be *sure* . . . ."

This also the Apostle stresses in his Galatians epistle:

"But the Scripture hath concluded all under sin, that the promise, *by faith of Jesus Christ*[24] might be given to them that *believe*" (Gal. 3:22).

All Abraham's seed, both that which is "of the law"[25] and that which is "of the faith of Abraham," will share in the promise made to Abraham, but this has its lesson for us today.

If justification were by the works of the Law rather than by grace, through faith, how could we be *sure* of it? If I had to do so much as lift up my little finger, much less obey the Law completely all my life, how could I ever be sure? Indeed, in such a case I *could* be sure of *condemnation*. This is why so many religious people live their lives in fear; fear that they will not be acceptable to God in the end.

"Therefore it is *of faith*, that it might be *by grace*, to the end the promise might be *sure* . . ." (Ver. 16).

Depend upon the Law; toil to *earn* justification, and you will never be sure of acceptance with God. But rest in His promise and your security could not be more complete.

What a blessing that God has made salvation accessible through the easiest, simplest, freest of channels! There is no toil in faith, no effort, and therefore no merit, no boasting —*and* His Word is a sure foundation to rest upon.

It is in view of the above that Ver. 16 calls Abraham *"the father of us all,"* i.e., the father of all who simply take God at His Word.

---

24. Subjective: His fidelity. See Pp. 39-41.

25. *"Of the law"*: In the Greek the article appears in Ver. 16, but not in Ver. 14. Ver. 14 refers to those who are "of law," i.e., who approach God on the basis of law, while Ver. 16 refers to those living under the dispensation of the Law.

THE MOTHER OF US ALL

Here a brief digression may be permitted. Has the reader ever asked himself who is *"the mother of us all"*? One woman in Scripture is so called, and who but Abraham's wife, *Sarah* (Gal. 4:26-31)! The Bible narrative is an absorbing one.

Abraham is promised a son. His wife is barren, however, and both are getting older. They begin to get anxious; at least Sarah does, so Sarah says to Abraham, in effect: "I must not stand in your way. Take Hagar, my slave girl, to wife and it may be that I can still have a son—*through her*." (See Gen. 16:1,2). Abraham did as Sarah suggested and Hagar did bear a son, Ishmael. But God said, as it were: "No, this is not the son I promised. You do not need to help Me fulfil My promise" (See Gen. 17:18-21).

It was not until Abraham was one hundred years old, and Sarah ninety, that *Sarah* bore Abraham a son, Isaac, as God had promised, and the Scripture portrays them laughing together with pure delight. Thus Abraham called his son, Isaac (Heb., *laughter*) according to the Word of God, and Sarah said:

"God hath made me to laugh, so that all that hear will laugh with me.

"And Sarah said, Who would have said unto Abraham, that Sarah should have given children suck? for I have born him a son in his old age" (Gen. 21:6,7).

Now, in Gal. 4 Paul uses this example, declaring that Hagar, the slave girl, speaks to us of the Law and its bondage and represents Jerusalem of that day, "in bondage with her children" (Ver. 25), while Sarah speaks of *grace*, and represents *"Jerusalem which is above, [which] is free, which is the mother of us all"* (Ver. 26).

Ah, many people, religious people, think that the Law produces greater results than grace. *How wrong they are!*

"For it is written, Rejoice thou barren, that bearest not; break forth and cry, thou that travailest not: for the desolate hath many more children than she which hath an husband!" (Gal. 4:27).

So here Abraham's wife, Sarah, represents *grace*, as Abraham represents *faith* in Scripture. Hagar, the slave girl, could only bring forth the son of a slave, but Sarah, the free woman, brought forth *the son of promise!*

"So then, brethren, we are not children of the bondwoman, but of the free" (Gal. 4:31).

GENUINE FAITH vs INTELLECTUAL ASSENT

Romans 4:17-22 might, at first sight, appear to teach that it was the strength, the firmness of Abraham's faith that gained him justification before God, but let us see:

"(As it is written, I have made thee a father of many nations), before Him whom he believed, even God, who quickeneth the dead, and calleth those things which be not as though they were.

"Who against hope believed in hope, that he might become the father of many nations; according to that which was spoken, So shall thy seed be.

"And being not weak in faith, he considered not his own body, now dead, when he was about an hundred years old, neither yet the deadness of Sarah's womb:

"He staggered not at the promise of God through unbelief, but was strong in faith, giving glory to God;

"And being fully persuaded that, what He had promised, He was able also to perform.

"And therefore it was imputed to him for righteousness."

—Rom. 4:17-22

"Before God" Abraham was "the father of believers" (Vers. 16,17), and God *"quickeneth the dead, and calleth those things which be not as though they were"* (Rom. 4:17). *This* was the God whom Abraham had come to know and in whom he had placed his faith. Thus the difference between one-hundred-year-old Abraham's laughter at the promise of Isaac's birth, and that of his barren, ninety-year-old wife, Sarah, should be carefully noted. Indeed laughter is mentioned *three* times in this connection—most significantly:

1. "Abraham *fell upon his face* [before God] *and laughed*" (Gen. 17:17); *the laughter of faith and wonder* that a child

should be born to a man of an hundred years of age, with a barren wife of 90!

2. *"Sarah laughed within herself"* (Gen. 18:12); *the laughter of unbelief.* "And the Lord said...wherefore did Sarah laugh?...Is anything too hard for the Lord?" (18:13,14).

3. Abraham *and* Sarah laughed (Gen. 21:3,6,7): "Abraham called the name of his son...Isaac [laughter]....And Sarah said, *God hath made me to laugh, so that all that hear will laugh with me....Who would have said unto Abraham that Sarah should have given children suck? for I have born him a son in his old age."*

Clearly Sarah, after being rebuked for inwardly ridiculing God's promise, took the rebuke deeply to heart, for we read in Heb. 11:11:

"Through faith also Sarah herself received strength to conceive [26] *seed, and was delivered of a child when she was past age, because she judged Him faithful who had promised."*

But *before* all this Abraham had *believed God "who quickeneth the dead, and calleth those things which be not as though they were"* (Rom. 4:17). Why should he take into consideration the deadness of his own body or that of Sarah's womb? What did *that* have to do with it! *God had promised!* Thus we read of Abraham:

"Who against hope believed in hope" (Ver. 18). Mark well, he did not merely believe without any rational ground for hope; he believed when all the outward circumstances militated "*against* hope." Himself one hundred years of age, and Sarah ninety, he "believed in hope," [27] i.e., he believed, eagerly anticipating the fulfillment of the promise. Thus the passage goes on:

"And being not weak in faith, he CONSIDERED NOT his own body, now dead, when he was about an hundred years old, neither yet the deadness of Sarah's womb:

---

26. Or, "to *bear*" Gr., *katabolee*, "to cast down." Elsewhere (10 times) rendered "foundation." In this connection note the remainder of Heb. 11:11.

27. The "hope" of Scripture is not a wish that may or may not be fulfilled. It is rather an eager anticipation of what will assuredly come to pass (See Heb. 6:19).

"He staggered not at the promise of God through unbelief; but was strong in faith, giving glory to God" (Vers. 19,20).

Note: Abraham believed in God as the One *"who quickeneth the dead"* (Ver. 17), and *"against hope, believed, in hope"* (Ver. 18). *"Being not weak in faith"* (Ver. 19), *"he staggered not at the promise of God through unbelief, but was strong in faith"* (Ver. 20).

In all this, we read, he gave glory to God (Ver. 20).

If we, then, would truly glorify God, we must learn that what pleases and honors Him most is *faith, taking Him at His Word.* Faith is merely the hand that *receives* what God offers, rather than spurning it. It is no glory to me if I believe God; rather my faith glorifies *Him.* The hand receives food, and the body is strengthened—by the food, not by my hand. It receives medicine and the body recovers—by the medicine, not by the power of my hand to restore.

But what made Abraham *"strong in faith"*? Was it some virtue in himself? No, he had known God for some time by now and was *"fully persuaded that what He had promised He was able also to perform."* It is as simple as that.

Thus the words, *"And therefore it was imputed to him for righteousness,"* in Ver. 22, do not imply that Abraham was justified because his faith was so strong. Rather God records all these tests to prove that Abraham *really did believe God*; that his faith was a heart trust, rather than mere intellectual assent.

Faith was not the *ground* of Abraham's justification; it was merely the *condition.* *God's Word* was the *ground* upon which his faith *rested.* Here an illustration might help:

Let us imagine two men of about equal weight, sitting on identical chairs. One seems fidgety and fearful that the chair might collapse, while the other rests comfortably. But each, in faith, has placed his weight upon the chair—and this is what matters. It is not the strength of our faith, but the *object* of our faith that is the deciding factor. If the chair is strong enough it will hold you no matter how weak your faith in it may be.

Thus the important thing is to place our trust in Christ, who died for our sins. The neo-evangelicals keep telling their hearers to "*make a commitment* to Christ" to be saved, but this is salvation by works, *and it is false doctrine*. We must rather recognize how desperate is our case and *commit ourselves* to Christ and His saving power, resting in His finished work of redemption, as *He* rests in it:

"For he that is entered into His rest, he also hath ceased from his own works, as God did from His" (Heb. 4:10).

God sent His Son into the world to pay the price of sin. When the Son had finished the work He was given to do, He returned to His home and sat down with His Father. Thus when we truly *commit ourselves* to Him who died for us, we enter into His rest and cease from our own works as He ceased from His.

IF WE BELIEVE

"Now it was not written for his sake alone, that it was imputed to him;

"But for us also, to whom it shall be imputed, if we believe on Him that raised up Jesus our Lord from the dead;

"Who was delivered for our offences, and was raised again for our justification."

—Rom. 4:23-25

The volume of "Old Testament" Scripture relating to Abraham's justification by faith was not written "for his sake alone," i.e., to ascribe importance to him, "but *for us also*" (Ver. 24).

"For whatsoever things were written aforetime were written for our learning, that we through patience and comfort of the Scriptures might have hope" (Rom. 15:4).

And in this particular case, the case of Abraham, what was written about him was "for us also, to whom it [righteousness] shall be imputed *if we believe*[28] on Him that raised up Jesus our Lord from the dead" (Ver. 24).

---

28. The phrase, "if we believe," is also found in I Thes. 4:14 in connection with the resurrection of Christ, but there it has to do with His resurrection as the basis of our comfort when bereaved of loved ones in Christ.

But why does the Apostle say that we must believe in the *resurrection* of Christ to be justified? Why not in *His death for our sins?* The answer follows in Ver. 25. To be sure we must believe in the death of Christ to be justified (Rom. 5:9), but we must believe in His death as a *sufficient* and *finished* work. It is not enough to believe in the "perpetual sacrifice" of the Church of Rome, in which our Lord is "offered" repeatedly in "the Sacrifice of the Mass." Nor is it enough to believe that "He lives" by the influence of the teachings He left behind, as liberals do. It is deplorable to see neo-evangelicals joining hands with such unbelievers to "win souls for Christ." The whole truth is vividly set before us in Ver. 25:

"Who was delivered [29] for our offences, and was raised again for our justification."

His death made full satisfaction for our sins, and His resurrection proved that full satisfaction had been made. As James McKendrick once said: "His death was the payment for our sins; His resurrection the receipt."

This is where Christianity differs from all the religions of the world. It proclaims *an accomplished redemption* and points to the evidence in the resurrection of Christ, confirmed "by many infallible proofs."

The great lesson of this chapter, then, is that justification before God is not obtained by the performance of any religious rite, nor by the observance of the Law, but by faith alone in the One who died for our sins and rose again.

THE DIRECT RESULTS OF THE DEATH OF CHRIST FOR US AND OF JUSTIFICATION BY FAITH

IN THE BELIEVER'S PERSONAL EXPERIENCE

"Therefore being justified by faith, we have peace with God through our Lord Jesus Christ.

---

29. Gr., *paradidomi*, to "deliver over" as a last necessity. Rom. 8:32 gives the sense: *"He...spared not His own Son, but delivered Him up for us all."* God could easily have spun a thousand worlds into space, but these could be no satisfaction for *sin*. This required the agony and death of His Son at Calvary, where He bore a load of sin "that would have sunk a world to hell."

> "By whom also we have access by faith into this grace wherein we stand, and rejoice in hope of the glory of God.
>
> "And not only so, but we glory in tribulations also: knowing that tribulation worketh patience;
>
> "And patience, experience; and experience, hope:
>
> "And hope maketh not ashamed, because the love of God is shed abroad in our hearts by the Holy Ghost, which is given unto us."
>
> —Rom. 5:1-5

We come now to the fourth major step in Paul's great theological argument.[30] *"Therefore being justified by faith..."* (Rom. 5:1).

Having proved that justification cannot be obtained by character, position, Law observance, or the performance of religious rites, but only by faith in the crucified, risen, living Savior, the Lord Jesus Christ, the Apostle now proceeds: *"Therefore being justified by faith,* we have"—*five* most precious blessings:

1. Peace with God (Ver. 1).

2. Access to God (Ver. 2).

3. Rejoicing in hope of the glory of God (Ver. 2).

4. Rejoicing in tribulations also (Ver. 3).

5. The love of God...shed abroad in our hearts (Ver. 5).

It should be carefully noted that *all* these blessings come to us *"through our Lord Jesus Christ,"* since He purchased them for us with His blood (4:25; 5:1). Is it strange, then, that we should read in John 3:35,36:

> "The Father loveth the Son, and hath given all things into His hand.
>
> "He that believeth on the Son hath everlasting life, and he that believeth not the Son shall not see life, but the wrath of God abideth on him."

God is concerned with our attitude toward His beloved Son. In the end it is our attitude toward the Lord Jesus Christ that will either save us for all eternity or cast us

---

30. See P. 82.

forever out of God's presence. All the ritual and mystery and eloquence of modern religion mean nothing to God. He will have His Son proclaimed, trusted, loved and honored (Col. 1:18).

With this in mind let us now consider the five precious blessings bestowed upon those who have been "justified by faith."

PEACE WITH GOD

"Therefore being justified by faith we have peace with God through our Lord Jesus Christ" (Ver. 1).

"Being justified by faith," our sins imputed to Christ and His righteousness imputed to us, the barrier of sin removed, we are now *at "peace with God—through our Lord Jesus Christ."* What a blessed relationship! Those who are forever trying to *make* their peace with God are to be pitied, for God Himself has made provision for this through Christ, and we are to receive it by faith. *"For He is our peace"* (Eph. 2:14), *"having made peace through the blood of His cross"* (Col. 1:20).

Before our justification by faith in Christ's finished work, we could only look forward to the judgment of God upon our sins. We were among those *"who through fear of death were all their lifetime subject to bondage"* (Heb. 2:15). But now by grace, through faith, we stand justified before the bar of God. It is true that believers sometimes fail to *enjoy* their status before God, but this does not change God's Word about it, nor the *fact* of their relationship to Him.

ACCESS TO GOD

"By whom also we have access by faith into this grace wherein we stand..." (Ver. 2).

The believer's access to God is one of the most precious truths of the Bible.

When the Law was given the people "stood afar off" and were warned repeatedly that they should not come near to Mt. Sinai, where God spoke to Moses, "lest they die." Later, when the tabernacle was built, a thick "veil" separated the people, even the priests, from God's presence: *"The Holy Ghost this signifying, that the way into the holiest of all* [God's actual presence] *was not yet made manifest..."* (Heb. 9:8).

But now, under grace, the believer is given *free access* into God's presence. Indeed, in Heb. 4:16 we are urged to come confidently to the throne of grace, not when it is convenient for God, but in *our* "time of need." Furthermore, the "mercy seat" of the Old Testament tabernacle has now become a "*throne* of *grace*." And as a throne surpasses a seat, or chair, in glory, so does grace far surpass mercy.

Some, failing to distinguish between standing and state, affirm that access to the throne of grace has nothing to do with the members of the Body of Christ since they are already seated in the heavenlies in Christ (Eph. 2:6).

This is a mistake, for the very epistle that has *most* to say about our position in the heavenlies *also* says:

"For through Him [the Lord Jesus Christ] we both have access by one Spirit unto the Father" (Eph. 2:18).

Indeed, Rom. 5:2 thus distinguishes between our position and our privilege, for it says that "we have *access by faith* into *this grace wherein we stand*."

Every believer falls far short of *occupying* his position in the heavenlies in Christ and of *appropriating* his "all spiritual blessings" there but, thank God, we have free access to enter into these blessings "by faith" at any time.

It would take some doing for this writer to obtain even one fifteen-minute audience with the President of the United States, a finite human being who will soon pass away. Indeed *no one* has free access to him *at all times*; not his wife or children, not the Secretary of State, not his most intimate adviser. *No one* has free access at *all* times. But *we* are bidden, as we have seen, to approach *God* and *talk with Him while He listens*—at *our* convenience. Moreover, *we* are soon confused when two or more people talk to us at once, but He who manages the universe, from the mightiest heavenly body to the tiniest part of an atom, who rules over men and angels, is *infinite* and *omniscient*. He can give *individual attention* to a million suppliants at the same time!

So God, the God of the universe, says to the humblest believer: "Come. Come with your sorrow and grief; come with your questions and problems; come with your anxiety and fear; come with your troubles and woes, and I will help you."

He does not necessarily give us all we ask for; He does better than this. He gives us what is *best* for us (Rom. 8:26-28), and we may *rest* in this fact.

"Be careful [anxious] for nothing; but in everything by prayer and supplication, with thanksgiving, let your requests be made known unto God.

"And the peace of God, which passeth all understanding, shall keep your hearts and minds through Christ Jesus" (Phil. 4:6,7).

"Now unto Him that is able to do exceeding abundantly above all that we ask or think, according to the power that worketh in us,

"Unto Him be glory in the Church by Christ Jesus, throughout all ages, world without end. Amen." (Eph. 3:20,21).

REJOICING IN HOPE OF THE GLORY OF GOD

". . .and rejoice in hope of the glory of God" (Ver. 2).

The reader will recall that the shepherds at Bethlehem were "sore afraid" when "the glory of the Lord shone round about them" (Luke 2:9). This was a natural reaction, *"for all have sinned and come short of the glory of God"* (Rom. 3:23).

How often we sin and make fools of ourselves! Even animals do not do this, but man, originally created in the image of God, does so. It has been said that only man can be ridiculous because only man can be dignified.

When man fell from his exalted position through sin God cursed the soil and said:

"In the sweat of thy face shalt thou eat bread, till thou return unto the ground; for out of it wast thou taken: for dust thou art, and unto dust shalt thou return" (Gen. 3:19).

Ever since that dreadful day, man's life has been one of continuous struggle and humiliation. Everything tends to go wrong rather than right and at the end comes death, the greatest humiliation of all.

Modern man either denies or ignores sin and the Fall, but their effects are manifest on every hand. How much wiser to acknowledge our depraved condition, trust Christ as our Savior, and *"rejoice"* with Paul *"in hope* [31] *of the glory of God"!*

Rejoicing in hope of the glory of God is another direct result of justification by faith. In Rom. 8:30 the Apostle declares that "whom He [God] justified, *them He also glorified,"* and in Col. 1:27 he speaks of "Christ in you" as *"the hope of glory."* By suffering humiliation, shame and death for us, our Lord became "the Captain of our salvation," *"bringing many sons unto glory"* (Heb. 2:10). For many centuries the blessed process has been going on. Already our great "Captain" has brought many sons to glory—not through *their* suffering and blood, but through *His!*—and the reader should ask himself whether he has joined the glad procession. If not, only judgment, shame and remorse lie ahead, but those who have been justified by faith may rejoice with Paul and all believers *"in hope of the glory of God."*

Best of all, "in that day" our blessed Lord will be *"glorified in His saints and . . . admired in all them that believe"* (II Thes. 1:10). Those who shook their heads and said *"Shame! Shame!"* as He hung on Calvary's cross, will someday exclaim *"What glory!"* as they behold the redeemed of all ages and see *what* "the death of the cross" accomplished!

REJOICING IN TRIBULATIONS ALSO

"And not only so, but we glory in tribulations also: knowing that tribulation worketh patience;

"And patience, experience; and experience, hope" (Rom. 5:3,4).

It should be noted here that the word rendered "glory" in Ver. 3 is *not* the same Greek word as that rendered "glory" in

---

31. Eager anticipation. See footnote 27.

Ver. 2, where "the glory of God" is referred to. Rather it is the same Greek word as that rendered "rejoice" in Ver. 2. This is confirmed by the use of the word "also" in Ver. 3. We "rejoice in hope of the glory of God," and we "rejoice in tribulations also." This word "rejoice" is sometimes translated "boast" and sometimes "glory" in the *Authorized Version*. It means to *exult*, or *rejoice triumphantly*.

It is natural to rejoice in anticipation of the revelation of the glory of God, but the believer rejoices—or should rejoice—*"in tribulations also."*

How so? Because he knows that tribulation produces patience; and patience, experience; and experience, hope.

Has the reader prayed for more patience? There is only one way to get it—through tribulations. *"Tribulation worketh patience."*

And patience produces *experience*. When the author was a young pastor he yearned for the experience that seemed to mean so much to older men of God. Their words seemed to carry greater weight and their hearers gave them more respectful and favorable attention. But one does not gain experience by wishing or even praying for it. Experience comes only from the *patient* endurance of *tribulation*. Thus James says, *"Let patience have her perfect work"* (Jas. 1:4).

And *hope!*—the *eager anticipation* of better things to come! This is the natural consequence of the *experience* that comes from the *patience* derived from enduring *tribulations*. There is no other way to gain this "hope."

Had Abraham been asked to give up Isaac earlier in his life as a man of God, it would doubtless have been too much for him to accept. But by the time God required him to offer up his beloved and only son in sacrifice, Abraham had gained a great deal of experience. He had been through many a test of faith and had learned that God does not desert those who trust in Him. Thus, when the really great test came, all his questions and misgivings were committed to God, and *"he that had received the promises* [32] *offered up his only begotten*

---

32. The promises about his seed becoming a blessing to all nations.

son, of whom it was said, That in Isaac shall thy seed be called; accounting that God was able to raise him up, even from the dead; from whence also he received him in a figure" (Heb. 11:17-19). Abraham did not despair or lose hope. Rather, all the while he still looked forward with eager anticipation to the fulfillment of God's promises made so long before.

Thus *"tribulation* worketh *patience*; and patience, *experience*; and experience, *hope."*

THE LOVE OF GOD
SHED ABROAD IN OUR HEARTS

"And hope maketh not ashamed; because the love of God is shed abroad in our hearts by the Holy Ghost, which is given unto us" (Ver. 5).

Does the reader long for the love of God to flood his heart and soul? Then let us retrace our steps once more. "The love of God...shed abroad in our hearts" is the result of the *hope* that comes from the *experience* produced by *patiently* enduring *tribulation*.

This "hope" that still looks to God in faith for glorious things to come *"maketh not ashamed."* It does not leave us embarrassed or frustrated,

"For the Scripture saith, Whosoever believeth on Him shall not be ashamed" (Rom. 10:11).

Indeed this "hope" brings us into ever-closer fellowship with God and an ever-deeper appreciation of Himself. "Hope maketh not ashamed, *because the love of God is shed abroad in our hearts by the Holy Ghost which is given unto us."*

What believer with even a limited degree of Christian experience will deny that spiritual tests have brought him closer to God and have helped him to appreciate more fully His wonderful love?

Thus *"we rejoice in tribulations also, knowing that tribulation worketh patience; and patience, experience; and experience, hope. And hope maketh not ashamed, because the love of God is shed abroad in our hearts by the Holy Ghost which is given unto us."*

Does the world offer anything to compare with this?

> Loved with everlasting love;
> > Led by grace that love to know;
> > Spirit of my God above,
> > Thou hast taught me it is so.
> > Oh, this full and perfect peace!
> > Oh, this transport all divine!
> > In a love that cannot cease,
> > I am His, and He is mine.
>
> Heaven above is softer blue,
> > Earth around is sweeter green;
> > Something lives in every hue,
> > Christless eyes have never seen.
> > Birds with gladder songs o'erflow;
> > Flow'rs with deeper beauty shine,
> > Since I know, as now I know,
> > I am His, and He is mine.
>
> His forever, only His;
> > Who the Lord and me shall part?
> > Ah, with what a rest of bliss,
> > Christ can fill the loving heart!
> > Heav'n and earth may fade and flee,
> > Firstborn light in gloom decline;
> > But while God and I shall be,
> > I am His, and He is mine.
>
> > —G. Wade Robinson

Chapter V — Romans 5:6-21

CHRIST'S DEATH FOR US DISPENSATIONALLY CONSIDERED

THE ANSWER TO MAN'S HELPLESSNESS, HIS SINFULNESS AND HIS WILLFULNESS

"For when we were yet without strength, in due time Christ died for the ungodly.

"For scarcely for a righteous man will one die; yet peradventure for a good man some would even dare to die.

"But God commendeth His love toward us, in that while we were yet sinners, Christ died for us.

"Much more, then, being now justified by His blood, we shall be saved from wrath through Him.

"For if when we were enemies we were reconciled to God by the death of His Son, much more, being reconciled, we shall be saved by His life.

"And not only so, but we also joy in God through our Lord Jesus Christ, by whom we have now received the atonement."

—Rom. 5:6-11

THE PERSONAL ASPECT

Three times in the above passage we read that Christ died for us, and the lesson is progressive.

Ver. 6: "When we were yet *without strength*...Christ died for the ungodly."

Ver. 8: "While we were yet *sinners*, Christ died for us."

Ver. 10: "When we were *enemies* we were reconciled to God by the death of His Son."

Thus, in our *helplessness*, in our *sinfulness*, yes, in our *willfulness*, Christ died for us.

1. *"When we were yet without strength"* (Ver. 6).

Rom. 5:6 views the unbeliever as one *without God,* and as such, utterly helpless. He *cannot* lift himself from his fallen state. He *cannot* subdue his evil passions. He *cannot* overcome the results of his sin. Without God he is "without strength."

But for such, thank God, Christ died. "When we were yet *without strength,* in due time Christ died for the ungodly." In infinite grace, He took the place of utter helplessness—death—with and for us, that He might bring us through with Him to resurrection life and power.

Many people are loath to admit their moral and spiritual helplessness, but the hymn writer was more candid when he said, *"My best resolves I only break."*

Even physically we are so helpless that *every night* we must change our clothing and lie down on a bed, an item of furniture specially constructed for the purpose, and give ourselves over to unconsciousness, our very lives protected only by the hand of God. For perhaps eight hours out of every twenty-four we must thus give ourselves over to God's care. Then, finally, comes death, when we must in utter helplessness give up life itself. The list of antediluvians in Gen. 5 records ages of more than 900 years, but in every case the closing words are, *"and he died."* [1]

But apart from all this, heaven is God's abode, and it is for *Him* to tell us *if* and *how* we may be admitted. He graciously does this in Rom. 5:6, where He says, *"When we were yet without strength, in due time Christ died for the ungodly."* Only as we accept this in faith may we *"rejoice in hope of the glory of God"* (4:25; 5:1,2).

But the passage says that "when we were yet without strength, in due time *Christ died for the ungodly,"* and if men object to being called helpless they surely do not generally appreciate being called *"ungodly."* To such we say, churchgoing, philanthropy, love for your family, financial integrity and all these good things do not make you *godly.* If I should

---

1. With the exception of Enoch, who *"was translated that he should not see death"* (Gen. 5:24; Heb. 11:5).

introduce you to a friend as "a godly person," would you not be embarrassed? Yet you are offended if I call you *un*godly.

But Rom. 5:6 contains wonderful news for the person who will acknowledge his ungodly state: *"Christ died for the ungodly,"* not for *some* of the ungodly, or for an elect few, but *"for the ungodly."* From this it follows that any unsaved, ungodly reader of these lines may believe God's Word and say, *"Christ died for ME."*

2. *"While we were yet sinners"* (Ver. 8).

Sinfulness is more serious than helplessness. A just judge must *condemn* sin and exact a full penalty for it. *"But God commendeth His love toward us, in that, while we were yet sinners, Christ died for us."* Thus God *did* exact the just penalty for sin as, in infinite love, He paid the debt *Himself!*

The preceding context renders this passage the more precious:

"For scarcely for a righteous man will one die; yet peradventure for a good man some would even dare to die" (Ver. 7).

Sternly honest men are generally resented by the less-righteous populace, yet for "a *good* man," a kind, generous, upright man, "*some—might—even* dare to die."

"But God commendeth His love toward us, in that, while we were yet sinners, Christ died for us" (Ver. 8).

What love! Though our sins may rise as a mountain before us, we need not despair, for every Christian believer can bear witness to the words of Paul, the *chief* of sinners (I Tim. 1:15), that *"while we were yet sinners Christ died for us."* He died for us *in our sin.*

To the reader who denies that he is a sinner, we say, Surely *you* are the *only one* of that opinion! Or, do you consider sin too lightly? Do you suppose that only drunkards, harlots and criminals are sinners, but not the self-righteous? Then consider this: God gave His only Son, His dearly beloved Son, to suffering, shame and death, to purchase eternal life and heaven for you, and you reject His gift—*and* the love that has provided it at such infinite cost.

Do you protest that you have *not* rejected this gift, that you just have not done *anything* about it? Nonsense! If I proffered you a costly gift which you desperately needed and you "just did nothing about it," would you not have rejected that gift—and offended me? Then, the *love* that offers you life through Christ, the *Person* of the Giver, and the *infinite cost* of the gift, all bear witness that while you "do nothing about it," you reject God's great gift and grievously insult Him.

But if you receive the gift in faith, the following verse will prove the more precious to you:

"Much more then, being now justified by His blood, we shall be saved from wrath [2] through Him" (Ver. 9).

What calm assurance should be ours as we consider that Christ died for us *as sinners*. Thus, having been "justified by His blood," we shall surely be saved from wrath through Him who paid the price of our redemption.

3. *"When we were enemies"* (Ver. 10).

Think of it! God has good news for us even in our *willfulness*, our *enmity* against Him! *"When we were enemies,"* says Paul, *"we were reconciled to God by the death of His Son."*

Here we can almost hear some reader object: "Of all things, don't charge me with being an *enemy* of God. I'm a religious person, I go to church regularly, I even *give* to the church." Ah, but God does not say that the unsaved are not *religious*. Perhaps 999 out of 1,000 are religious. The point is that by your ungodly, sinful life, and certainly by rejecting God's gift of salvation, you have made yourself an enemy of God. You may not be an enemy against the "God" *you* have conjured up in your own mind, but you are certainly an enemy against *God*, the God of the Bible.

But despite all this God still sends His ambassadors out to offer reconciliation to all His enemies everywhere—*"by the*

---

2. Consider this in connection with I Thes. 5:9-11 and the coming "day of wrath."

death of His Son." Think of it! We who believe are reconciled to God, *not* by some effort or payment offered by us to placate God, but *"by the death of HIS Son."* He bore the enmity as His own creatures mocked Him, spat in His face and nailed Him to a tree. This is grace indeed! And this is not all, for the whole passage reads:

"For if, when we were enemies, we were reconciled to God by the death of His Son, *much more*, being reconciled, we shall be saved by His life.

"And not only so, but we also joy in God through our Lord Jesus Christ, by whom we have now received the atonement [Lit., *reconciliation*[3]" (Vers. 10,11).

The argument of this passage is that if, as His enemies, we were reconciled to God by the death of His Son, *much more* "being reconciled," we may be assured that our living Savior will keep us safe. And not only are believers *safe* in Christ, but all the while we "*joy* in God through our Lord Jesus Christ, by whom we have now received," not only help in our *helplessness*, or the forgiveness of our *sins*, but "the *reconciliation*," by which we are brought nigh to God and *experience* His love toward us.

THE HISTORICAL PERSPECTIVE

"Wherefore, as by one man sin entered into the world, and death by sin; and so death passed upon all men, for that all have sinned:

"(For until the law sin was in the world: but sin is not imputed when there is no law.

"Nevertheless death reigned from Adam to Moses, even over them that had not sinned after the similitude of Adam's transgression, who is the figure of Him that was to come.

"But not as the offence, so also is the free gift. For if through the offence of one many be dead, much more the grace of God, and the gift by grace, which is by one Man, Jesus Christ, hath abounded unto many.

---

3. We do not understand why the KJV translators here departed from their own *Received Text*, which reads *katallagee*. This word and its verb are everywhere else rendered *"reconciliation"* and *"reconcile."* Also, *reconciliation*, not atonement, is the subject of *this passage*. Both times in Verse 10 the verb is rendered "reconciled."

"And not as it was by one that sinned, so is the gift: for the judgment was by one to condemnation, but the free gift is of many offences unto justification.

"For if by one man's offence death reigned by one; much more they which receive abundance of grace and of the gift of righteousness shall reign in life by one, Jesus Christ.)

"Therefore as by the offence of one judgment came upon all men to condemnation; even so by the righteousness of one the free gift came upon all men unto justification of life.

"For as by one man's disobedience many were made sinners, so by the obedience of one shall many be made righteous.

"Moreover the law entered that the offence might abound. But where sin abounded, grace did much more abound;

"That as sin hath reigned unto death, even so might grace reign through righteousness unto eternal life by Jesus Christ our Lord."

—Rom. 5:12-21

It should be carefully noted that in Rom. 5:6,8 and 10, the Apostle uses the past tense: "*When we were* yet without strength....*while we were* yet sinners....*when we were* enemies." Why is this? Certainly Christ died for *us* long before any of us were even born. The answer is that he speaks historically, dispensationally. This should be evident from the fact that he says in Ver. 6 that "*in due time* Christ died for the ungodly." This agrees with Gal. 4:4: "*When the fulness of the time was come, God sent forth His Son....*" But it becomes the more evident as we proceed to the remainder of the chapter: Vers. 12-21. In these verses the Apostle shows that in using the pronoun "we" in Vers. 6,8 and 10, he refers to the human race historically.

The Apostle had a broad outlook and a keen sense of his place—and our place—in history,[4] and the harmony, the design of this whole latter part of Romans 5 in its relation to Vers. 6-11 is beautiful to behold. The three leading characters of the passage are *Adam, Moses and Christ*.

By *Adam* we have the *entrance* of sin (Ver. 12).

---

4. For an in-depth discussion of this subject, see the author's booklet, *The Knowledge of the Mystery*.

By *Moses*, the *knowledge* of sin (Ver. 20).

By *Christ*, the *forgiveness* of sins (Vers. 20,21).

A comparison of Vers. 12-21 with Vers. 6-10 may be outlined as follows:

From Adam to Moses ("when we were yet without strength") we have *the reign of death* through Adam (Vers. 6,14).

From Moses to Christ ("while we were yet sinners") we have *the reign of sin* through the Law (Vers. 8,20,21).

From Christ to the Present ("when we were enemies") we have *the reign of grace*, through Christ (Vers. 10,20,21).

Before proceeding further with Vers. 12-21 it should be carefully noted that the above references are (1) to Adam, not at his creation, but after the fall, (2) to Moses, not at his birth, but later at Sinai, where he delivered the Law, and (3) to Christ, not at His birth or earthly ministry, but at His exaltation in heaven as the taster of death "for every man" (Heb. 2:9). This is how Paul consistently proclaimed Him. The Law was still in force until Paul was raised up to proclaim *"the preaching of the cross,"* nor was any revelation given as to the abolition of the Law covenant until Paul's *"But now"* of Rom. 3:21 (Cf. Acts 2:46; 3:1; 22:12,13).

FROM ADAM TO MOSES
THE REIGN OF DEATH THROUGH ADAM

"Wherefore as by one man sin entered into the world, and death by sin; and so death passed upon all men, for that all have sinned:

"(For until the law sin was in the world, but sin is not imputed when there is no law.

"Nevertheless death reigned from Adam to Moses, even over them that had not sinned after the similitude of Adam's transgression, who is the figure of Him that was to come" (Vers. 12-14).

We have here to do with God's dealings with men during the period *"from Adam to Moses," "until the law," "when there was no [Mosaic] law."* During this period of history it was demonstrated that "death passed upon all men," not because the Law of Moses had condemned them to death, but simply because they were the offspring of fallen Adam, and depraved *by nature*. Entirely apart from the Law, *"sin, when it is finished, bringeth forth death"* (Jas. 1:15). Thus *"death reigned from Adam to Moses, even over them that had NOT sinned after the similitude of Adam's transgression."*

It should be observed that while sin entered into the world "by one man," Adam, death "passed upon all men for that [because] *all* have sinned," i.e., *in Adam*. We cannot say, *"It was no fault of mine,"* for we were in Adam, we *were* Adam when he sinned. We cannot dissociate ourselves from Adam any more than the branch can separate itself from the tree, or the tree from its root.

The period from Adam to Moses illustrates historically the helplessness referred to in Ver. 6. During these 2500 years there was no written Law to condemn sinners to death (Ver. 13). Nevertheless they died, for entirely apart from the Law sin in its very nature corrupts and destroys.

In the first genealogy of the Bible, referred to above, there are antediluvians who lived up to 969 years of age [5] but, with one notable exception, they all died, setting the pattern for a historical demonstration of the fact that with Adam's sin *"death passed upon all men."* Thus *"death reigned from Adam to Moses."*

Yet many of those who lived before Moses were saved and accepted by God. Examples are Abel, Enoch, Noah and Abraham. How could they be saved? Paul answers as, again speaking historically, he says, *"When we were yet without strength, in due time, Christ died for the ungodly"* (Ver. 6). This was not yet revealed to them, nor is there any indication that they looked forward to the death of a coming Christ for salvation. Rather we are told that they believed God's word *to them*. But *we now know* that the *basis* of their acceptance with God was the redemptive work of Christ, for

---

5. See the author's *Methuselah and Paul*.

Paul, in Rom. 3:25, declares "His [Christ's] righteousness for the remission of sins *that are past.*"

In Ver. 13 the Apostle goes on to explain that sin, while active from Adam to Moses, *"is not imputed when there is no law,"* i.e., there can be no *"transgression"* where there is no law to transgress (4:15). *"Nevertheless death reigned from Adam to Moses,"* as we have seen, and it reigned *"even over them that had not sinned after the similitude of Adam's transgression,"* i.e., over those who had not violated a specific command as Adam had.

Adam's headship over the race as its progenitor was typical of "Him that was to come" (Ver. 14), but here the likeness ends, as is seen from the repeated use of the phrase "*not* as," in the following verses.

"But *not* as the offence, so also is the free gift . . . . And *not* as it was by one that sinned, so is the gift . . ." (Vers. 15,16).

"The grace of God, and the gift by grace" is "much more" than a recovery from the effects of Adam's offence, "much more" than a reinstatement to the position Adam held before the fall. And this grace, through Christ, *"hath abounded unto many."*

" . . . for the judgment was by one to condemnation, but the free gift is of many offences unto justification" (Ver. 16).

One sin brought condemnation to all, but grace and the "free gift" bring justification not only from one sin, but from "many offences" (Ver. 16) *and* to many people (Ver. 15).

"For if by one man's offence death reigned by one: much more they which receive abundance of grace and of the gift of righteousness, shall reign in life by one, Jesus Christ.)" (Ver. 17).

This is the end of a long parenthesis begun at Ver. 13, but it is filled with precious truth. As *"death reigned"* because of one man's sin, "much more" those who receive the "abundance of grace and of the gift of righteousness, *shall reign* . . . ." Observe carefully: not those who toil and strive and sacrifice "shall reign," but those who *receive* the *"abundance of grace"* and receive *"the gift of righteousness"*—these "*shall* reign in life by one, Jesus Christ" (Ver. 17). Does not the very phrase, *"the gift of righteousness,"* indicate that righteousness cannot be achieved or earned by the children of Adam?

Ver. 18 by no means teaches universal reconciliation, as some hold. "As by the offence of one judgment came upon all men to condemnation; even so by the righteousness [6] of one the free gift came upon all men" *who receive the gift*, as is evident from the preceding verse, and consistent with the verse that follows:

"For as by one man's disobedience many were made sinners, so by the obedience of one shall many be made righteous" (Ver. 19).

This passage, then, leads us from the "first Adam," by whom sin and death entered and spread like a cancer over the whole human race, to the "last Adam," by whom believers receive *"abundance of grace and of the gift of righteousness."*

FROM MOSES TO CHRIST

THE REIGN OF SIN THROUGH THE LAW

"Moreover the law entered that the offence might abound..." (Ver. 20).

The dispensation of Law covered the period of time from the giving of the Law by Moses to the revelation of grace by the *glorified* Lord *to and through Paul*.

We have already seen that the covenant of the Law was *not* done away immediately at the crucifixion of Christ, for the Pentecostal believers still remained under the Law, careful *not* to start a sect separate from Judaism (Acts 2:46; 3:1; 22:12,13).[7] True, the Law was "abolished"[8] *by* the cross, but it was not until our Lord in heaven commissioned Paul that "the righteousness of God without the Law [was]

---

6. Here "the righteous act." The idea is that of *accomplished* righteousness, i.e., in the death of the cross.

7. See the author's *How and When?*

8. Not as the Word of God, but as a covenant (See Ex. 19:5).

manifested" (Rom. 3:21), and the dispensation of grace ushered in.

We have also seen that the Law was *"added because of transgressions"* (Gal. 3:19), *"that sin, by the commandment might become exceeding sinful"* (Rom. 7:13) and *"that the offence might abound"* (Rom. 5:20 above).

This purpose was indeed fulfilled, for now the *written Law* pronounced men sinners and condemned them to death. Paul, in I Cor. 15:56, declares pointedly that "the *sting* of death is *sin*," and that "the *strength* of sin is the *Law*."

Is it objected that the Law was not given to the human race, but only to Israel? True, but Israel was God's representative nation. Any who wished to approach God had to come through Israel since the Gentiles had long ago been "given up," and Israel was the only nation on earth God recognized. Thus we read in Rom. 3:19:

"Now we know that what things soever the law saith, it saith to them who are under the law; that every mouth may be stopped and all the world may become guilty before God."

During the dispensation of the Law the *guilt* of man was being demonstrated as "sin...*reigned*" (5:21). There was no way of escape for, *"kept under the law,"* they were *"shut up* unto the faith which should *afterwards* be revealed" (Gal. 3:23).

But how then were Moses, Aaron, David, Daniel and other Old Testament believers saved? Paul gives the answer in Rom. 5:8 where, speaking historically, he says:

"While we were yet sinners, Christ died for us."

They did not yet know this, for it was not "revealed," "testified," "manifested" until the "due time" *through Paul* (Gal. 3:23; I Tim. 2:6,7; Tit. 1:3). *They* found peace of heart only as they believed what God said *to them*. But we now know the secret as it is revealed in this very chapter of Romans. It was only on the basis of the all-sufficient redemption wrought by Christ that any man was ever saved.

THE PRESENT DISPENSATION
THE REIGN OF GRACE THROUGH CHRIST

"....But where sin abounded, grace did much more abound;

"That as sin hath reigned unto death, even so might grace reign, through righteousness, unto eternal life, by [9] Jesus Christ our Lord (Vers. 20,21).

The above passage corresponds with Ver. 10: "When we were *enemies* we were reconciled to God by the death of His Son."

Sin had surely risen to its height during Paul's early years. Christ had been crucified and even after His resurrection His enemies had stood by that awful deed. Israel had joined the Gentiles in declaring war on God and His anointed Son (Psa. 2:1-3) and Saul of Tarsus was the leader of the revolt. It was no longer merely a matter of sin; it was now *rebellion*.

Saul's bitter hatred of Christ knew no bounds.

Luke says: "As for Saul, *he made havoc of the Church*,[10] entering into every house, and haling[11] men and women, committed them to prison" (Acts 8:3).

The saints at Damascus said: "Is not this he that *destroyed* them which called on this name in Jerusalem...?" (Acts 9:21).

To the Galatian believers the Apostle himself wrote: "...*beyond measure I persecuted the Church of God and wasted it* [*laid it waste*]" (Gal. 1:13).

"But where sin abounded, grace did much more abound...."

As Saul, *"being exceedingly mad"* against the disciples, *"persecuted them even unto strange cities"* (Acts 26:11), God stepped in to intervene. While on his way to Damascus, *"yet breathing out threatenings and slaughter against the disciples*

---

9. "Through" and "by" here are both the Greek *dia*.

10. The *Messianic* Church, of course.

11. Dragging.

of the Lord" (9:1), he was overtaken and *saved* by the very One whom he had so bitterly persecuted.[12]

Surely God had responded to the abounding sin of man with His overabounding grace! Little wonder the Apostle says of this:

"And the grace of our Lord was exceeding abundant....

"This is a faithful saying, and worthy of all acceptation, that Christ Jesus came into the world to save sinners, *of whom I am chief"* (I Tim. 1:14,15).

But it is even more deeply significant that the Apostle *continues* to say:

"Howbeit FOR THIS CAUSE I OBTAINED MERCY, THAT IN ME FIRST JESUS CHRIST MIGHT SHOW FORTH ALL LONGSUFFERING, FOR A PATTERN TO THEM WHICH SHOULD HEREAFTER BELIEVE ON HIM TO LIFE EVERLASTING" (Ver. 16).

Thus Saul, who until lately had been the leader of the persecution against Christ, the personification of the *enmity* that existed between God and man, now became not only the herald, but *the living demonstration* of the overabounding grace of God, burning out his life to proclaim to others *"the gospel of the grace of God"* (Acts 20:24).

But again we must ask: On what basis could God justly save one who was the avowed and bitter enemy of Christ, with even the blood of the Lord's disciples on his hands? The answer is again: On the basis of the death of Christ for us. In our *helplessness*, in our *sinfulness*, yes, in our *wilfulness*, *"Christ died for us."*

Thus we read in Col. 1:21,22:

"And you, that were sometime alienated and *enemies* in your mind by wicked works, yet now hath He *reconciled,*

"In the body of His flesh *through death,* to present you holy and unblameable and unreprovable in His sight."

---

12. Master stroke! By saving Saul, the Lord not only robbed the opposition of its leader, but put him on the other side, as it were, making him the champion of the Christ he had formerly opposed!

It is *wonderful* that "when we were yet *without strength, in due time Christ died for the ungodly.*"

It is *more wonderful* that "while we were yet *sinners* Christ died for us."

It is *most wonderful* that "when we were *enemies*, we were reconciled to God by the death of His Son."

Amazing truth: "By the death of *His Son*"! It would have been gracious indeed had He said, "Give me the instigators behind this outrage against My Son! Give Me Judas, Caiaphas, the chief priests and, not least, Saul of Tarsus. I will punish *them* and be reconciled to the rest." This would have been more than mankind had any reason to expect. But, wonder of wonders, He has reconciled us to Himself by the death of *His* Son, His beloved, sinless Son! That death, so unjust and cruel, has become the just payment for our sins and the basis upon which God can now show the fulness of His love for sinners. Indeed, His gracious and loving question now is, "Will *you* be reconciled to Me?" (See II Cor. 5:20).

Thus we are now living under *the reign of grace*. As "DEATH REIGNED from Adam to Moses" (Rom. 5:14); as SIN REIGNED *"unto death"* after "the Law entered" (Vers. 20,21), so now grace abounds, THAT GRACE MIGHT REIGN *"through righteousness unto eternal life by Jesus Christ our Lord"* (Vers. 20,21).

THE UNPARDONABLE SIN

Surely Rom. 5:20,21 is the antidote for the deep anxiety that has haunted so many because of the popular teaching on the unpardonable sin.

Those who know "the gospel of the grace of God" will not strike fear into the hearts of their hearers by the threat of an *unpardonable* sin, for

"...we have redemption through His blood, THE FORGIVENESS OF SINS ACCORDING TO THE RICHES OF HIS GRACE" (Eph. 1:7).

"...WHERE SIN ABOUNDED, *GRACE DID MUCH MORE A-BOUND*, THAT...GRACE MIGHT *REIGN*..." (Rom. 5:20,21).

Surely there is no room for an *unpardonable* sin here. It has been rightly said that sinners who die in unbelief in this dispensation of grace will go to the lake of fire with all their sins *unpardoned*, but not because one of them was *unpardonable*.

The unpardonable sin must be considered in the light of dispensational truth. All through Old Testament times Israel had resisted the Father. The Father, in turn, had sent the Son, who had taught and labored among them, only to be rejected too. Now the Son was to send the Spirit, and this generation in Israel would have her last chance to be saved. Hence the Lord's warning:

"Wherefore I say unto you, All manner of sin and blasphemy shall be forgiven unto men: but the blasphemy against the Holy Ghost shall not be forgiven unto men . . . neither in this world [age], neither in the world [age] to come" (Matt. 12:31,32).

Our Lord spoke these words on the same principle which the writer's father had in mind when he said to his young son: "Now this is the *second* time I've spoken to you. *If I have to speak again—!!!*" Indeed, we have the actual account of Israel's commission of the unpardonable sin in early Acts [13] (e.g., Acts 7:51).

Thus to us, as to Paul, has been committed "the gospel of the *GRACE* of God," and "the ministry of *RECONCILIATION*," in which we proclaim God's offer of *grace* to His *enemies*, pleading with them to be reconciled to Him (II Cor. 5:20,21) while there is still time (II Cor. 6:1,2).

> Jesus, the name that charms our fears,
>   That bids our sorrows cease;
> 'Tis music in the sinner's ears;
>   'Tis life, and health, and peace.
>
> He breaks the power of cancelled sin,
>   He sets the prisoner free.
> His blood can make the foulest clean;
>   His blood availed for me.
>
> —Charles Wesley

---

13. See the author's *Acts, Dispensationally Considered*, Vol. I, Pp. 236-240, where the subject is discussed at length.

Chapter VI — Romans 6:1-23
SHALL WE CONTINUE IN SIN?

CRUCIFIED, BURIED AND RAISED WITH CHRIST

"What shall we say then? Shall we continue in sin that grace may abound?

"God forbid. How shall we that are dead to sin live any longer therein?

"Know ye not that so many of us as were baptized into Jesus Christ were baptized into His death?

"Therefore we are buried with Him by baptism into death: that like as Christ was raised up from the dead by the glory of the Father, even so we also should walk in newness of life.

"For if we have been planted together in the likeness of His death, we shall be also in the likeness of His resurrection.

"Knowing this, that our old man is crucified with Him, that the body of sin might be destroyed, that henceforth we should not serve sin.

"For he that is dead is freed from sin.

"Now if we be dead with Christ, we believe that we shall also live with Him:

"Knowing that Christ being raised from the dead dieth no more; death hath no more dominion over him.

"For in that He died, He died unto sin once; but in that He liveth, He liveth unto God.

"Likewise reckon ye also yourselves to be dead indeed unto sin, but alive unto God through Jesus Christ our Lord."

—Rom. 6:1-11

A PIVOTAL PASSAGE

The above is a pivotal passage of the *Epistle to the Romans*, the hinge between doctrine and practice.

The opening verses recall 3:8, where the Apostle brands

as *slanderers* those who charge *him* with teaching, *"Let us do evil that good may come."* Here, however, he deals with this teaching doctrinally and sweeps the ground from under it.

"God forbid!"[1] he cries: *"How shall we that are dead to sin, live any longer therein?"* (Ver. 2).

It is true—and he affirms it—that "our unrighteousness" enhances "the righteousness of God" (3:5) and that His "truth" shines the more brightly against the background of "my lie"—*"unto His glory"* (3:7). It is also true that God's *grace* is magnified by man's sin, especially since *"where sin abounded, grace did much more abound"* (5:20).

It is natural, therefore, and right, that as we behold God's grace to sinners, and particularly to the chief of sinners, we should exclaim, "How merciful and loving is our God!"

But does it follow from this that we should continue in sin so that His grace may continue to abound, or may abound still more?

The very thought is repulsive to the Apostle, but the teaching must be answered lest grace be turned into a license for wrong-doing. This the Apostle does by posing a question of his own:

"How shall we that are dead to sin, live any longer therein?" (6:2).

CRUCIFIED WITH CHRIST

True, the most saintly Christian has not yet died to sin *experientially*. Like Paul, he finds sin very much alive in him. But *God* has *pronounced* us dead to sin *in Christ*; He views the "old man" as having been *"crucified with Him"* (Ver. 6), and this is what is *most* important—and presents the greater reason why we should *not* continue in sin. Thus the Apostle continues:

"Know ye not,[2] that so many of us as were baptized into Jesus Christ were baptized into His death?" (Ver. 3).

---

1. The phrase has the sense of *"Far be it!"* or *"Perish the thought!"*

2. This is the first of Paul's "know ye nots." The others are: Rom. 6:16; 7:1; I Cor. 3:16; 5:6; 6:2,3,9,15,16,19; 9:13,24; II Cor. 13:5.

His tone of reproof implies that his readers *should* have known this basic fact of salvation, yet even today many, yes, *most* believers fail to grasp it. Thus his words *"Know ye not?"*, after 1900 years, bear a stern rebuke to those who will not listen.

Determined to make this passage (Vers. 3,4) teach baptism by water, many declare that the word "into" in Ver. 3 should have been translated "unto." [3]

Whatever being baptized "unto" Christ might mean is not clear, but it is clear, as we compare Scripture with Scripture, that the Greek *eis* here is correctly rendered "into." We may get the sense of the Apostle's language by comparing it with I Cor. 12:13, where we read that "by [4] one Spirit are we all baptized *into* one body." Could *eis* here possibly be rendered "unto"? In Gal. 3:27 the sense is equally clear, and again with respect to baptism. There the Apostle declares:

"For as many of you as have been baptized *into* Christ have put on Christ."

Could he have stated any more clearly that believers are now *in Christ* because they have been "baptized *into* Christ," and so have *"put on Christ"*?

But *how* are we baptized into Christ? *By faith*, as a comparison with the preceding verse indicates:

"For ye are all the children of God BY FAITH IN CHRIST JESUS,

"FOR [not *and*] as many of you as have been baptized into Christ have put on Christ."

If Rom. 6:3 teaches water baptism it clearly teaches *salvation* by water baptism as, indeed, many claim that it does, but according to Gal. 3:26,27, we are "baptized into Christ" *"by faith in Christ Jesus."*

---

3. Years ago the author's Baptist pastor used this argument, adding that the Greek *eis* is translated "unto" 203 times in the *Authorized Version*. What he neglected to say was that it is translated "into" 563 times!

4. "By" is correct, for the Greek *en* here is in the instrumental case. The sense of the passage bears this out. It is a mistake to assume that *en* necessarily means "in." See Matt. 5:34, where *en* is also correctly rendered "by."

It should be carefully noted that we are baptized into Jesus Christ as, by faith, we are baptized *into His death* (Ver. 3). Calvary is ever the meeting place between Christ and the sinner.

We must come to Calvary, as it were, acknowledging in faith: "This is not *His* death He is dying. Death has no claim on Him. He is dying *my* death."

"The soul that *sinneth*, it shall die" (Ezek. 18:20).

"By one man sin entered into the world, and death *by sin*" (Rom. 5:12).

"The wages of *sin* is death" (Rom. 6:23).

"And *sin*, when it is finished, bringeth forth death" (Jas. 1:15).

Our Lord never sinned; He had no death to die. Why, then, did He hang there in agony and disgrace, shedding His life's blood for sins He had never committed? There is only one answer, beloved reader: He died *your* death and *mine*.

You object that this is symbolic and representative, but not *real*? Then let us go over it again: Was His *death* not real? The scourging, the spitting, the crown of thorns, the crucifixion to a tree—*not real?* And was His death not really *our* death, the payment for *our* sins? Surely they were not the payment for *His* sins; He had committed none. His death then, as our Representative, is not to be classed with the "mysteries" of the Roman Church; there is nothing mystical about it. It is rather very real, though indeed part of the great "mystery," or *secret*, first revealed to Paul. And the moment we place our trust in Him *as such*, as the One who died *our* death, in that moment we are made one with Him, "baptized into His death," and so into Himself. This too is most real. As He was baptized into our death *by grace* (cf. Luke 12:50), so we are baptized into His death *by faith* (Gal. 3:26,27). Or, to put it in another way: As He, by grace, became one with us in our death, so we, by faith, become one with Him in His death—*"crucified with Him"* (Ver. 6; cf. Gal. 2:20).

No one was ever baptized into Christ or made one with

Him who did not first recognize that Christ came to Calvary to represent *him* and pay the penalty for *his* sins.

Human nature does insist upon intruding into God's peerless plan of salvation, and this is how water came to be injected into Rom. 6:3,4. The passage does not mention the word *water*, but millions of people assume it is there.

One thing is certain: Make Rom. 6:3,4 teach *water* baptism and you have stripped it of all its meaning and power and beauty. One of the greatest heresies in the history of the Church has been the disparagement of our divine baptism into Christ by changing it into a religious rite. But read as it is, the passage expresses one of the most sublime truths of Scripture, the truth of our union, our *being made one* with Christ.

What an answer God has given to the question: *"Shall we continue in sin that grace may abound?"*

How can those who are "dead to sin" consistently continue living in sin? See the blessed truth of Rom. 6:1-3, and the rest of the chapter will fall beautifully into place.

BURIED AND RAISED WITH CHRIST

"Therefore we are buried with Him by baptism into death, that like as Christ was raised up from the dead by the glory [5] of the Father, even so we also should walk in newness of life.

"For if we have been planted together in the likeness of His death, we shall be also in the likeness of His resurrection" (Rom. 6:4,5).

It is of paramount importance to observe that the Apostle *continues* here to answer the question, *"Shall we continue in sin that grace may abound?"* In Ver. 4 he goes on to show that as we have been crucified *with Christ*, so we have also been buried and raised *with Him* to walk in newness of life.

Some who agree that Ver. 3 refers to the supernatural baptism by which believers are made one with Christ, nevertheless hold that Ver. 4 refers to *water* baptism. They argue that since we have been crucified with Christ, *"there-*

---

5. I.e., the glorious power (John 11:40).

fore" we should be "buried with Him by [water] baptism...."
But there are many insurmountable objections to this view.

1. *Never, anywhere* does the Bible refer to the *burial* of believers *in water*.[6] Search the Scriptures and see.

2. We do not bury the bodies of our departed loved ones in water, nor did they do this in Bible times. Men were buried in the earth or in tombs in the rocks, but *not* in water.

3. W. G. T. Shedd significantly states that "...the Greek word *sunthapto*[7] is applicable only to burial in earth. No one would render it by 'immerse.' ...when a person unacquainted with the original reads in the English version of a 'burial in baptism,' or 'by baptism,' a burial in water is the only idea that enters his mind; an idea which the Greek positively *excludes*....Had *sunthapto* been translated literally, by 'entombed,' instead of 'buried,' this text would never have been quoted, as it so frequently has been, to prove that Christian baptism is immersion."[8]

4. In Acts 8:38 we read that Philip and the Ethiopian eunuch "went down *both* into the water, *both* Philip and the eunuch; and he baptized him." If this passage proves that the eunuch was *immersed*, as many think it does, does it not also prove that Philip *immersed himself* at the same time? The passage states: "They went down *both* into the water, *both* Philip and the eunuch." Can "into the water," here, be made to mean "under the water"? Yet our immersionist friends use this passage to prove their "water burial" theory.

5. Rom. 6:4 does not state that believers are buried *like* Christ; it states that they are buried *with* Him. The prefix *sun* clearly makes it a "co-burial." By faith they are united to Christ in *His* death, burial and resurrection (Rom. 6:6; Col. 2:10-12).

---

6. It must not be assumed that the word *baptism* in Scripture always refers to *water* baptism. Some other Bible baptisms are: in, or with, the Holy Spirit (Matt. 3:11), in fire (Matt. 3:11), in death (Luke 12:50), "in the cloud and in the sea" (I Cor. 10:2), into Christ (Rom. 6:3; Gal. 3:27; Col. 2:12), and into the Body of Christ (I Cor. 12:13).

7. We believe he meant *thapto*. *Sunthapto* means "buried *together with*," as in Rom. 6:4.

8. Shedd, *Dogmatic Theology*, Vol. II, P. 586.

6. If the believer is "crucified with Christ" and "raised to walk in newness of life" the moment he places his faith in Christ, when is he "buried with Christ"? Is it possible for a clergyman to "bury" one *"with Christ"* who has already been "raised *with Christ*"? Would it not be strange and illogical if *after* having given us resurrection life in Christ, God should now ask us to be *buried* by a clergyman!

7. When one is "raised" from *water* baptism has the "old man" actually been buried? And is it actually the "new man" who is raised "to walk in newness of life"? Do not *both* the old and new natures come out of the waters of baptism exactly as they went in?

8. If Rom. 6:4 refers to water baptism, does it not unquestionably teach water baptism *for salvation*?[9]

Thus it is clear that in Rom. 6:4 the Apostle continues to pursue his argument of Ver. 3. As the believer is "crucified *with Christ*," *"baptized into His death,"* so he is buried and raised *"with Him,"* by the same supernatural baptism—by which, indeed, he is also glorified *together with Him* (Eph. 2:5,6).

Col. 2:10-12 sets forth this same truth of our death, burial and resurrection *with* and *in* Christ. There, under the heading, *"Ye are Complete in Him"* (Ver. 10), the Apostle goes on to elucidate:

Ver. 11: *"In whom* also ye are *circumcised*..." (Death to the flesh).

Ver. 12: *"Buried with Him* in baptism...."

Ver. 12: "wherein *also* ye are *risen with Him* through the faith of *the operation of God*...."

Thus the "newness of life" referred to in Rom. 6:4 is a *sharing* of Christ's resurrection life. This, we believe, is the explanation of the Apostle's desire, expressed in Phil. 3:10, 11, to *"know...the power of His resurrection"* and so *"attain*

---

9. The author's booklet, *Just Asking*, deals with the "water burial" theory at greater length.

unto the resurrection of the dead" (Cf. Rom. 8:11; Eph. 1:19,20).

In Rom. 6:5, therefore, the Apostle speaks *logically* rather than chronologically. His subject is not our future resurrection, but the present *resurrection life* which is ours *in Christ*.

Human nature is so determined to have some part in this whole transaction that some even read water baptism into this verse, arguing that in water baptism we have a "likeness" of our burial and resurrection with Christ. But a careful reading will show that the word "likeness" is used in the sense of "sameness." The verse clearly states that we were "planted *together*," i.e., planted together *with Christ*, having died the *same* death—*His* death—and therefore also sharing in the *same* resurrection—*His* resurrection.

BURY THAT CORPSE!

"Knowing this, that our old man is crucified with Him, that the body of sin might be destroyed, that henceforth we should not serve sin.

"For he that is dead is freed from sin.

"Now if we be dead with Christ, we believe that we shall also live with Him.

"Knowing that Christ being raised from the dead dieth no more; death hath no more dominion over Him.

"For in that He died, He died unto sin once; but in that He liveth, He liveth unto God.

"Likewise reckon ye also yourselves to be dead indeed unto sin, but alive unto God through Jesus Christ our Lord" (Rom. 6:6-11).

Paul's way is always: *doctrine* first, then the *application*. We find this even *within* sections of his epistles. Here it is:

"...our old man [10] is crucified with Him, *that the body of sin might be destroyed*, that henceforth we should not serve sin" (Ver. 6).

In the larger context it is the same. The "old man" *has been* crucified and buried with Christ; now accept this by

---

10. I.e., the old Adamic nature, the old self.

faith and bury that "dead body"—*experientially*. We have this idea again in Col. 3:9,10 and Eph. 4:22,24. The former passage states, "ye *have put off* the old man...and *have put on* the new man,..." while the latter exhorts, "...*put off*... the old man...and...*put on* the new man...." The former refers to a positional *fact*, the latter to *the practical application* of that fact.

Why, then, was the "old man" crucified with Christ? The answer is, "that the body of sin[11] might be *destroyed*" (Ver. 6), i.e., that the "corpse" might be *buried*.

Some sincere Christians are forever striving to *improve* the old nature. Their minds continually dwell upon it. They inject psychological medicines, they try to give it will power, they dress it up, they strive and pray for *improvement*, when God says that the "old man" *has been put to death in Christ* and should now be *"reckoned...dead indeed"* (Ver. 11), and *buried* (Ver. 6), with the "new man" *"alive unto God"*! How sad that so many devout Christians should be forever bemoaning their sinful *state*, while ignoring the glorious *standing* God has so graciously *given* us *in Christ!*

The path to deliverance from sin, then, is not *works*; it is *faith*. *God says* that we cease "serving sin" as we take Him at His Word, *"reckoning"* the "old man" to be *"dead indeed."*

It is true that experientially *"the flesh lusteth against the Spirit, and the Spirit against the flesh,"* because *"these are contrary the one to the other"* (Gal. 5:17), but the secret to victory in this battle lies not in fighting, but in an appreciation of the *fact* that the battle has already been won for us through Christ, that He died our death so that we may now "bury" the old self, as it were, and forget him and focus all our attention on Christ and our new life in Him.

The struggle with the old nature is futile. Wrestle with a chimney sweep and you only become soiled. We need not, and should not, be occupied with the "old man," but should rather take God at His Word as to the *death* of the "old man,"

---

11. Another appellation for the old nature, since the old nature operates through the body.

rejoicing that "henceforth" we need no longer "serve [be slaves to] sin" (Ver. 6), since "he that is dead is freed from sin" (Ver. 7; cf. Phil. 3:13,14).

In Ver. 8 the Apostle again speaks *logically* rather than chronologically. His subject is not the future resurrection of the dead, but our new life in Christ. Becoming one with Christ in His death, we become one *with Him*, and thus one with Him in His resurrection also.

Our Lord will never die again; death is not His master (Ver. 9). *"For in that He died, He died unto sin once:* [12] *but in that He liveth, He liveth unto God,"* never to die again (Ver. 10; Rev. 1:18).

Before leaving this passage it should be noted here also that we are not only to reckon ourselves "dead indeed unto sin," but also *"alive unto God, through Jesus Christ our Lord"* (Ver. 11). As we have been "baptized into His death," we have also been raised with Him *"to walk in newness of life"* (Ver. 4). God help us to be occupied with Christ and our new life in Him!

Thus the redemptive work of Christ in the sinner's behalf stands between the believer and *his sins* (I Cor. 15:3; Eph. 1:7), between the believer and *his sin* (II Cor. 5:21), and between the believer and *his sinning* (Rom. 6:1-14).

ALIVE FROM THE DEAD

"Let not sin therefore reign in your mortal body, that ye should obey it in the lusts thereof.

"Neither yield ye your members as instruments of unrighteousness unto sin; but yield yourselves unto God, as those that are alive from the dead, and your members as instruments of righteousness unto God.

"For sin shall not have dominion over you; for ye are not under the law, but under grace."

—Rom. 6:12-14

---

12. Here the word "once" is intensified. The Greek for "once" is *hapax*, but here the prefix *ep* has been added: *ephapax*, meaning "once and once only," or "once for all." How powerfully this answers the Roman Catholic doctrine of the "perpetual" offering up of "the flesh and blood of Christ" in *the Sacrifice of the Mass!* (See also Heb. 9:25-28; 10:10-14). This subject is dealt with at length in the author's booklet, *Rome's Greatest Blunder.*

Whereas the keywords to the earlier part of Romans 6 are *"believe"* and *"reckon"* (Vers. 8,11), the keywords to the latter part are *"Let not...neither yield"* (Vers. 12,13). The earlier part of the chapter is chiefly concerned with the *heart*, "for with the heart man believeth" (10:10), but the latter is chiefly concerned with the *will*, for we have come now from the *secret* of godly living to the *practical application* of that important secret.

Note the words, *"Let not"* and *"mortal body"* in Ver. 12. While we are indeed still *"waiting for...the redemption of our body"* (8:23), we may rejoice that the old self has been *"crucified with Christ."* We have no obligation to him, nor need we yield to his desires. In other words, the Apostle is saying in effect: "You have accepted by faith *what God says* about your sins and your old nature, therefore *refuse* to yield your members 'as instruments of unrighteousness unto sin.'"

But how is this accomplished? The answer is, by "accentuating the positive": "...but *yield* [13] *yourselves unto God*, as those that are alive from the dead, and your members as instruments of righteousness unto God" (Ver. 13).

This is objective living indeed, and the only practical solution to the problem of sin in our members. It meets the negative with a positive. It harmonizes with what the Apostle says in Gal. 5:16:

"This I say then, Walk in the Spirit, and ye shall not fulfill the lust of the flesh."

Many suppose that walking in the Spirit is a mystical sort of thing. They would overcome sin by trying to *feel* spiritual! But Paul's meaning is rather, *"Be occupied with the things of the Spirit,"* i.e., study the Word, spend time in prayer, rejoice in your heavenly position and blessings, witness for Christ, etc. As these things hold your interest sin will be crowded out. When as a boy, the author complained that he was made to work too hard, his mother would

---

13. The same word is rendered "present" in Rom. 12:1, but we feel that here, at least, the *Authorized Version* has more accurately represented the sense.

answer: "Oh, that's good. *It will keep you out of mischief!*" She was right and we, her children, will never cease to thank God that our parents gave us good, constructive things to do *"to keep us out of mischief!"*

"For sin shall not have dominion over you: for ye are not under the law, but under grace" (Ver. 14).

Our "members," our hands, feet, eyes, tongues, have all been defiled by sin, but the defilement need not go on unchecked. We are not under sin's domain; it no longer "reigns" as it once did (Rom. 5:20,21). The Apostle says in Gal. 2:19:

"For I through the law am *dead to the law*, that I might live unto God."

The old self has already died *for* sin and *to* sin *in Christ*, thus sin has no further claim upon us. And—amazing grace!—God will gladly use these poor, defiled members as "instruments of righteousness," as we yield ourselves to Him (Ver. 13).

The Law says: "You are a sinner and must die," but *grace* says that *"Christ died for our sins"* (I Cor. 15:3). He died our death, and we have come through with Him to resurrection life and a standing in grace. The Law is the great Accuser, always demanding the death penalty—and the Law is always *right*, for "the *sting* of death is *sin*, and the *strength* of sin is the *law*" (I Cor. 15:56).

"But thanks be to God, who giveth us the victory through our Lord Jesus Christ" (I Cor. 15:57).

"That as sin hath reigned unto death, even so might *grace reign* through righteousness unto eternal life by Jesus Christ our Lord" (Rom. 5:21).

"*Let not* sin therefore reign in your mortal body....Neither yield ye your members...unto sin....FOR SIN SHALL NOT HAVE DOMINION OVER YOU: FOR YE ARE NOT UNDER THE LAW, BUT UNDER GRACE" (Rom. 6:12-14).

What an answer to the question: "Shall we continue in sin that grace may abound?"!

WHOSE SLAVE AM I?

Before considering Vers. 15-23 in detail we should observe the *two* lines of truth which run throughout the chapter with regard to the believer's deliverance from sin.

First, *judicially, positionally*, the believer *has been delivered* from bondage to sin:

6:7: "...*he that is dead is freed from sin.*"

6:18: "*Being then made free from sin....*"

6:22: "...*being made free from sin....*"

6:14: "*For sin shall not have dominion over you, for ye are not under the law but under grace.*"

6:17: "*But God be thanked, that ye were the servants of sin, but ye have obeyed from the heart that form of doctrine which was delivered you.*"

6:20: "...*ye were the servants of sin....*"

From these passages it is evident that *in God's sight, positionally*, the believer *has been delivered* from the bondage of sin.

However, this same chapter also establishes the fact that *experientially* the believer may *submit himself* to the slavery of sin:

6:12: "*Let not sin therefore reign in your mortal body....*"

6:13: "*Neither yield ye your members...unto sin....*"

6:16: "...*to whom ye yield yourselves servants to obey, his servants ye are to whom ye obey....*"

6:19: "*I speak after the manner of men because of the infirmity of your flesh....*"

To the "carnal" Corinthian believers Paul listed "fornicators...adulterers...thieves...drunkards" and the like, as those who would be shut out from "the kingdom of God" (I Cor. 6:9,10), and he could have said, *"and such are some of you,"* for some of these failing Christians had indulged in the grossest immorality. But he did not say this. He said rather, "And such *were* some of you," and added:

"...but ye are washed, but ye are sanctified, but ye are justified in the name of the Lord Jesus Christ, and by the Spirit of our God" (Ver. 11).

Thus the Scriptures, and especially the Pauline epistles, make a sharp distinction between the believer's *standing* and his *state*, between his *position* and his *condition*.

Unless *both* these lines of truth are borne in mind it will be impossible to understand Chapters 6-8 of Romans. Let us, then, consider Rom. 6:15-23 in detail.

"What then? shall we sin because we are not under the law, but under grace? God forbid.

"Know ye not, that to whom ye yield yourselves servants to obey, his servants ye are to whom ye obey; whether of sin unto death, or of obedience unto righteousness?

"But God be thanked, that ye were the servants of sin, but ye have obeyed from the heart that form of doctrine which was delivered you.

"Being then made free from sin, ye became the servants of righteousness.

"I speak after the manner of men because of the infirmity of your flesh: for as ye have yielded your members servants to uncleanness and to iniquity unto iniquity, even so now yield your members servants to righteousness unto holiness.

"For when ye were the servants of sin, ye were free from righteousness.

"What fruit had ye then in those things whereof ye are now ashamed? for the end of those things is death.

"But now, being made free from sin and become servants to God, ye have your fruit unto holiness, and the end everlasting life.

"For the wages of sin is death; but the gift of God is eternal life through Jesus Christ our Lord."

How fallen human nature seeks excuses to sin! In Ver. 1 it was, *"Shall we continue in sin that grace may abound?"* Here it is, *"Shall we sin because we are not under the law, but under grace?"* Paul answers both with a reproachful *"Know ye not?"* [14] Here he says:

> "Know ye not, that to whom ye yield yourselves servants [15] to obey, his servants ye are to whom ye obey; whether of sin unto death, or of obedience unto righteousness?" (Ver. 16).

Slavery has by no means been abolished in America or anywhere else. Millions are in bondage to the desires of the flesh. At this writing America is witnessing one of the greatest demonstrations of such slavery. Alcoholism, cigarette smoking, dope addiction, sex perversion and other forms of health-destroying habits have enslaved millions. Once smoking was considered merely a mildly "bad habit," in which even some Christians indulged. But now it has been conclusively proved and widely published that cigarette smoking is related to various forms of cancer and to other types of physical illness. All cigarette packages *must by law* carry a conspicuous advertisement stating: "Warning: The Surgeon General Has Determined That Cigarette Smoking is Dangerous to Your Health." But has the sale of cigarettes decreased? Are the big tobacco companies going out of business? Far from it! Their sales continue to soar. Why? Simply because that little weed has men, women and young people *enslaved*. Even young Christians are finding out that one doesn't just "give up smoking." Mark Twain frankly acknowledged this in his quip: "I'm sure I could quit smoking; in fact, I've done so a thousand times."

Thank God, supernatural power is available to the believer to find deliverance from such bondage. The chains fall away as we yield ourselves to God as *His* bondmen. But mark well, it is *the one or the other*. "His servants ye are to whom ye obey; *whether of sin unto death, or of obedience unto righteousness*" (Ver. 16).

"Death," in Paul's epistles, does not always refer to

---

14. Not that so many of the Roman believers necessarily sought license to sin, but rather that the old sin nature, even the *religious* sin nature, is so apt to arrive at the above conclusions. How many religious people have objected to Paul's great message of grace, saying, "If you tell people they are not under the Law but under grace, it gives them a license to sin."

15. This is the familiar Greek word *doulos*, "bondman," or "slave," though it is frequently used of *subjection* apart from *forced* bondage.

eternal death, or "the second death." Sometimes the word is used in a comparative sense with regard to the Christian's experience. If the believer yields his life to God, he will blossom and bloom; if not, he will wither and die—as far as his Christian experience is concerned. Hence such passages from Paul *to believers* as the following:

Rom. 8:6: "For to be carnally minded is death, but to be spiritually minded is life and peace."

Gal. 6:8: "For he that soweth to his flesh shall of the flesh reap corruption, but he that soweth to the Spirit shall of the Spirit reap life everlasting."

It should be noted that these Roman Christians, once slaves to sin, had now "obeyed from the heart that *form* of doctrine" which he had delivered to them. "Being then made free from sin," they had become "the servants [bondmen] of righteousness" (Vers. 17,18).

So it should be carefully noted that they were "made free from sin" (positionally, "in Christ") by obeying *"from the heart"* the *"doctrine"* which Paul proclaimed.

The word "form," here, is also used in II Tim. 1:13, where the Apostle says:

"Hold fast the *form* of sound words which thou hast heard of me . . . ."

This places great emphasis upon the importance of Paul's God-given message to us, and it points up the fact that through him God has brought to light important new revelations. This is especially so, as we have seen, with respect to the death and resurrection of Christ.

Paul's "preaching of the cross" is a great advance upon what Peter said with regard to the cross at Pentecost. There Peter *blamed* his hearers for the death of Christ and bade them: *"Repent, and be baptized every one...in the name of Jesus Christ for the remission of sins..."* (Acts 2:38).

But Paul's "preaching of the cross" was the proclamation of its *all-sufficiency*, not only to save from sin, but to make the believer *one with Christ*, so taking him through to resurrection life and a position in the heavenlies at the right hand of God.

In the same way Paul's preaching of the resurrection of Christ was a great advance upon Peter's preaching of the resurrection at Pentecost. At Pentecost Peter *warned* his hearers that the One whom they had crucified was alive again (Acts 2:32,36,37), whereas Paul associates the resurrection with our justification (Rom. 4:25) and declares that believers have been raised *with Christ* and made to share His resurrection life (Eph. 2:5,6; Rom. 6:4).

Thus, with regard to the resurrection of our Lord, the Apostle earnestly exhorts Timothy, in II Tim. 2:7-9:

"Consider what I say; and the Lord give thee understanding in all things.

"Remember that Jesus Christ, of the seed of David, was raised from the dead according to my gospel;

"Wherein I suffer trouble as an evil-doer, even unto bonds; but the Word of God is not bound."

How blessed the "new slavery" to righteousness is, the Apostle now points out. Explaining *why* he has used the metaphors of *slave* and *master*, he says in Rom. 6:19:

"I speak after the manner of men *because of the infirmity of your flesh*: for as ye have yielded your members servants [slaves] to uncleanness and to iniquity unto iniquity, even so now yield your members servants [slaves] to righteousness unto holiness."

He well knew that in the believer bondage to sin originates in *the weakness of the flesh*, which is totally depraved (Ver. 19; cf. 8:3). Ah, but we are delivered experientially from the mastery of sin as we yield our members to "righteousness, unto holiness."[16]

Paul well knew the blessedness of this divine bondage. He endured many discouragements in the work of the Lord, and might have given up a thousand times, but *he could not*. "The love of Christ, he said, *"constraineth us"* (II Cor. 5:14).

---

16. "Holiness" is *not* sinlessness; it is *to be set apart as sacred to God*. Thus bondage to God and righteousness brings us close to Him in a very blessed relationship—*and this is what delivers us from the tyranny of the flesh.*

Not his love *to* Christ, but the love *of* Christ to him and to all, bore him along like an ocean tide,[17] so that he could not cease pleading with men to be reconciled to God who, in infinite love, had *"made Him [Christ] to be sin for us...that we might be made the righteousness of God in Him"* (II Cor. 5:20,21).

This is what it means to be "*under* grace," to have "grace *reign*" "in our mortal bodies." It is the bondage of love and gratitude, the slavery of a thankful, adoring heart.

"For when ye were the servants [slaves] of sin," says the Apostle, "ye were free from righteousness." You boasted that you did not *have to* submit to God's claims. You said, "I do *what I please*," not realizing that sin had you enslaved. Moreover, the Apostle asks:

"What fruit had ye then in those things whereof ye are now ashamed? for the end of those things is death" (Ver. 21).

Ah, this is an important question, which every unbeliever should ask himself. What is the *fruit* of my service to sin? It is "shame" now, says the Apostle, and at the end, *death*. "The motions of sins[18]...did work in our members *to bring forth fruit unto death*" (7:5).

"But now, being made free from sin, and become servants to God, ye have your fruit unto holiness, and the end everlasting life" (6:22).

How beautiful! The fruit of our service to God is, for the present, *"holiness."* By doing God's will we are brought *closer to Him*; we come to know Him more intimately and to experience His love more fully. *"...and the end, EVERLASTING LIFE,"* all by His matchless grace! and this contrast could not be expressed more pointedly than it is in the next verse, the closing verse of this section:

"For the wages of sin is death; but the gift of God is eternal life, through Jesus Christ our Lord" (Ver. 23).

Does this not speak volumes with respect to the contrast between slavery to sin and slavery to God? "The *wages of*

---

17. This is the sense of the word rendered "constraineth" here.
18. Even if they are the sins of *self-righteousness* and *self-satisfaction*, which God despises most of all.

sin"—and they are high indeed—"*death*," but "the *gift* of God"—ah, sin's wages cannot compare with this!—"*eternal life,* [19] through Jesus Christ our Lord."

And so the Apostle concludes his answer to the questions: *"Shall we continue in sin that grace may abound?"* and *"Shall we sin because we are not under the law, but under grace?"* (Vers. 1,15). In this final argument he enquires as to *the "fruit"* and *the result*, "the end," of such a course. The question, *"Why can't we do this or that?"* may make the commission of sin seem like the enjoyment of liberty, but before long such questions produce lamentations like, *"I can't help it; I can't stop it."* Sin, indulged in, is like the chain which a Roman tyrant forced a blacksmith to make—*for himself*. "Make it longer," demanded the emperor each time the blacksmith appeared before him. "Add more links. It must be longer still, much longer," until finally he had the poor wretch tied and nearly smothered in the chains of his own forging and thus cast into the fire.

Thank God, we who have placed our trust in Christ are no longer under the reign of sin. We *need* not yield to its demands. We have been crucified with Christ and raised to walk in newness of life, to serve another Master—*"and the end, everlasting life!"*

> Jesus, in Thy transporting Name
>   What glories meet our eyes!
> Thou art the angels' sweetest theme,
>   The wonder of the skies.
>
> Oh, may our willing hearts confess
>   Thy sweet, Thy gentle sway;
> Glad captives of Thy matchless grace,
>   Thy loving rule obey.
>
>   —Author unknown

---

19. *His* life.

Chapter VII — Romans 7:1—8:4

ANOTHER HUSBAND
CORRESPONDENT DEATH

"Know ye not, brethren, (for I speak to them that know the law), how that the law hath dominion over a man as long as he liveth?

"For the woman which hath an husband is bound by the law to her husband so long as he liveth; but if the husband be dead, she is loosed from the law of her husband.

"So then if, while her husband liveth, she be married to another man, she shall be called an adulteress: but if her husband be dead, she is free from that law, so that she is no adulteress, though she be married to another man.

"Wherefore, my brethren, ye also are become dead to the law by the body of Christ; that ye should be married to another, even to Him who is raised from the dead, that we should bring forth fruit unto God.

"For when we were in the flesh, the motions of sins, which were by the law, did work in our members to bring forth fruit unto death.

"But now we are delivered from the law, that being dead wherein we were held; that we should serve in newness of spirit, and not in the oldness of the letter."

—Rom. 7:1-6

Whereas in Chapter 6 the basic theme was deliverance from *sin* as a *master*, in Chapter 7 and the first four verses of Chapter 8 the basic theme is deliverance from the *Law* as a *husband*. The first six verses of Chapter 7 set the pace by the use of three significant phrases: *"bound by the law"* (Ver. 2), *"dead to the law"* (Ver. 4), and *"delivered from the law"* (Ver. 6). Indeed, the word "law" is found 23 times in this chapter.

Here we must be careful to note, however, that throughout Chap. 7 the word "law" is sometimes used in the abstract, of law *as such*, while at other times it refers particularly to the Law of Moses. Also, the last verses of Chap. 7 and the

first few of Chap. 8 refer to no less than five *specific* laws:
1. *"the law of God"* (7:22).   2. *"the law of my mind"* (7:23).
3. *"the law of sin...in my members"* (7:23).   4. *"the law of sin and death"* (8:2).   5. *"the law of the Spirit...life in Christ"* (8:2).

Some have concluded, erroneously, that because Paul here addresses *"them that know the law,"* this letter must have been written primarily to Jews. Such have overlooked the address on the envelope: *"To the Romans."* We have already demonstrated that the church at Rome was made up overwhelmingly of Gentiles in the flesh (Rom. 1:13,14; 11:13; 15:15,16).

If, however, the Apostle did refer here to the Law of Moses, it would be answer enough that *Christian* Gentiles in the Church at Rome would be familiar with this because the Old Testament would comprise the bulk of the Scriptures they possessed and read.

We do not believe, however, that the Law of Moses is referred to in Rom. 7:1,2, for, as to Ver. 2, Roman women surely would not be subject to Hebrew Law. Rather the Apostle refers here to law in the abstract, to law *as such*. The Romans had a deep interest in law. They were the great law-makers of the ages. Their famous Senate established a system of law, many of the components of which are found on our statute books today. Indeed, British and American law are founded basically on Hebrew and Roman law.

Those who know the law understand that death dissolves all bonds. It terminates all financial obligations and temporal responsibilities—*and* it strips the deceased of all his earthly riches, authority and rights. Thus the Apostle speaks more explicitly in Ver. 2:

"For the woman which hath an husband is bound by the law [i.e., legally bound] to her husband so long as he liveth; but if the husband be dead, she is loosed from the law of her husband."

Some have taken this last phrase to refer to the *authority* of her husband, but we feel it refers to the law concerning her marriage to her husband. In either case her obligations as his wife are dissolved.

WHO IS THE HUSBAND?

More important to the interpretation of this verse is the question, *"Who is the husband?"* Some take him to be the old nature, i.e., we are bound to the old nature until it has died—in Christ. Others, including this author, believe that the husband here is the Law of God.[1] The unbeliever is not *legally* bound to the old nature, nor was there any contractual agreement involved. But there was a contractual agreement between Israel and the Law, as representative of God's will.

It is true, of course, that the Law was a marital covenant between God and Israel (Ex. 19:4,5; Jer. 3:1,20; 31:32), in which God was to love and care for Israel and Israel was to love and obey God. But in another sense God presided over a marriage between Israel and the Law, in which the Law was given authority over Israel, and Israel promised to obey.

Thus the "woman" in Rom. 7:2 is legally bound to her husband until he dies, and "if, while her husband liveth, she be married to another man, she shall be called an adulteress" (Ver. 3), neither her relationship to her former husband, nor that to the present husband being truly sacred. How often in Scripture Israel is called an adulteress for departing from the Law and going after strange gods.

It has been argued that since the Romans to whom Paul wrote never were under the Law, this passage could not apply to them, but this is not wholly so. True, the Law was given *to Israel* but it nevertheless *affected* the Gentiles as well. Gentiles who wished to be accepted of God had to become Israelites religiously, submitting to the Law and the rite of circumcision (Isa. 56:6,7). Under the dispensation of the Law, the world's *only* way of approach to God was *through Israel*, and if that dispensation had continued this would still have been the case. Thus the Apostle rightly

---

1. In either case the relationship is used as an *illustration*.

states that death dissolves the believer's bondage to the Law, without reference to Israel or the Gentiles.

Furthermore, we have already seen that those in deepest paganism *"show the work of the law written in their hearts"* (Rom. 2:15; cf. 1:32).

Attention should be called to the fact that in 7:1 the word "man" (Gr., *anthropos*) has the sense of a *person*, man or woman.[2] In Ver. 2, however, it is not the "woman," the weaker vessel, that dies, but the *husband* (Gr., *aner*). Did the Law, then, *die*? Yes, not as the Word of God, indeed, but as a covenant, or contract. Had Israel obeyed the Law, they would have become God's special people in the fullest sense, and forever. As we know, however, they never did or could keep their agreement. Thus God, in due time having demonstrated their need of *salvation* from sin, graciously gave Christ to pay the penalty for the broken Law and thereby *cancelled it*.

That the Covenant of the Law did die is clear from Paul's epistles:

Eph. 2:15: "HAVING ABOLISHED IN HIS FLESH THE ENMITY, EVEN THE LAW OF COMMANDMENTS contained in ordinances; for to make in Himself of twain [Jew and Gentile] one new man, so making peace."

Col. 2:14: "BLOTTING OUT THE HANDWRITING OF ORDINANCES THAT WAS AGAINST US, WHICH WAS CONTRARY TO US, and took it out of the way, NAILING IT TO HIS CROSS."

II Cor. 3:11: "For if THAT WHICH IS DONE AWAY was glorious, much more that which remaineth is glorious."

All this agrees with Ver. 6 of our text:

"But now we are delivered from the law, THAT BEING DEAD WHEREIN WE WERE HELD..." (Cf. Ver. 2).

Furthermore, in the Old Testament we find the death of the Law clearly typified. Recall how, in the face of Israel's flagrant disobedience, God said to Moses: *"Let them make Me a sanctuary that I may dwell among them"* (Ex. 25:8). Would not this be a breach of the covenant He had just made with

---

2. Because the woman is *"of the man"* (Gen. 2:21-23; I Cor. 11:8). Hence we speak of the human race as *"man*kind."

them, and which they had ratified? They had not "obeyed" His voice "indeed." Already they were about to desecrate the very first commandment. But did you notice the first article of furniture God commanded Moses to make for the tabernacle? The words are: "And they shall make *an ark*..." (Ex. 25:10). But what is an ark? A ship? A basket? Not *this* ark, for the very same word here rendered "ark" (organically, *coffer*), is translated "coffin" in the last verse of Genesis. This harmonizes with the use to which this ark was put, for in Ex. 25 the commandment is given:

"And thou shalt put into the ark [coffin] the testimony which I shall give thee.

"And thou shalt make a mercy seat of pure gold...."

"And thou shalt put the mercy seat above, upon the ark, and in the ark shalt thou put the testimony that I shall give thee.

"AND THERE WILL I MEET WITH THEE, AND I WILL COMMUNE WITH THEE FROM ABOVE THE MERCY SEAT..." (Ex. 25:16,17, 21,22).

Beautiful type! The Law had hardly been given when God said: "Put it in a coffin and cover the coffin with a *mercy seat*" (to be sprinkled with atoning blood, Lev. 16:14,15), "and *there*, from the mercy seat, I will meet with you."

It should be most carefully observed that the Old Testament Scriptures do not hint that these instructions were even typical, much less *what* they might have typified. It is only *now*, as we look back at these instructions in the light of Paul's epistles, that *we* recognize them as typical, and exclaim: "God had this in mind all the while! This was indeed His *eternal* purpose, though kept secret until revealed through the Apostle Paul!"

One further point should be brought out before proceeding further with this passage. We know that *historically* there was at first "no law," i.e., no Mosaic Law. Then, after 2500 years, "the law entered" to convict men of sin, "but where sin abounded, grace [after 1500 more years] did much more abound, that...*grace might reign.*" Just so it is in the life of the individual believer. When lost, he went on his way unconvicted of his sins. At some point in his life, however, "the law entered" and he was brought under conviction for his disobedience to God, fearing the consequences of his conduct. But, finally looking to Christ, who *"died for our sins,"* the dispensation of grace began *in his life!* The Law and its condemning power had been abolished *for him* (Gal. 3:13) and *grace reigned!*

DOUBLE DEATH

"Wherefore, my brethren, ye also are become dead to the law by the body of Christ; that ye should be married to another, even to Him who is raised from the dead, that we should bring forth fruit unto God.

"For when we were in the flesh, the motions of sins, which were by the law, did work in our members to bring forth fruit unto death.

"But now we are delivered from the law, that being dead wherein we were held; that we should serve in newness of spirit, and not in the oldness of the letter" (Rom. 7:4-6).

Why this sudden change from the thought of the *husband* having died to that of the *wife* having died—to the husband? Is it not to show that the husband (the Law in this case) having died, the wife has also died *to him*. And we believers have indeed died to the Law, having been *crucified with Christ* when He, in His death, nailed the Law to His cross. And our having been crucified with Him does indeed leave us free to be "married to another," even to *"Him who is raised from the dead"* (Ver. 4).

The believer's *body* did not die to the Law, but *Christ's* body did (Ver. 4); we have become "dead to the law *by the body of Christ.*" He shed His life's blood that we might be free from the Law's dominion and be *His* forever (See Gal. 2:19,20). Moreover, the fruit that issued from the former union could only be "unto death," for as we shall see more fully later on, *"the motions*[3] *of sins, which were by the law, did work in our members to bring forth fruit unto death"* (Ver. 5). But the fruit that issues from our union with the resurrected Christ brings forth fresh new life.

All the foregoing, we believe, confirms the *Authorized*

---

3. Emotions, passions.

rendering of Ver. 6: "But now we are delivered from the law, *that being dead wherein we were held*," rather than the R.V. rendering,[4] *"having died to that wherein we were holden."*

And now, says the Apostle, it is ours to serve our beloved Savior and Lord *"in newness of spirit, and not in the oldness of the letter"* (Ver. 6). As in Heb. 10:19,20 he contrasts the old, dead way of approach to God (altars, sacrifices, etc.) with the "new and living way," so in II Cor. 3:6 and here in Rom. 7 he draws a contrast between serving God "in newness of spirit," and "in the oldness of the letter."[5]

> Free from the Law, O happy condition!
> Jesus hath bled and there is remission.
> Cursed by the Law and bruised by the fall,
> Grace hath redeemed us, once for all.
>
> Philip P. Bliss

Indeed, our relationship to the Law has been *doubly* dissolved; it has died to us and we have died to it. And now we can serve this blessed One "who loved us and gave Himself for us" (Gal. 2:20; Eph. 5:25), not in the old, dry, dead, "religious" way, because the Law says we *must*, but in fresh, joyous "newness of spirit," our words and works expressing our gratitude and love.

THE LAW AND SIN

"What shall we say then? Is the law sin? God forbid. Nay, I had not known sin, but by the law; for I had not known lust, except the law had said, Thou shalt not covet.

"But sin, taking occasion by the commandment, wrought in me all manner of concupiscence. For without the law sin was dead.

"For I was alive without the law once; but when the commandment came, sin revived, and I died.

"And the commandment, which was ordained to life, I found to be unto death.

"For sin, taking occasion by the commandment, deceived me, and by it slew me.

---

4. Followed by most modern versions.

5. I.e., the Law (II Cor. 3:6-15).

*"Wherefore the law is holy and the commandment holy, and just, and good.

"Was then that which is good made death unto me? God forbid. But sin, that it might appear sin, working death in me by that which is good; that sin by the commandment might become exceeding sinful.

"For we know that the law is spiritual: but I am carnal, sold under sin."*

—Rom. 7:7-14

Anyone who would intelligently proclaim grace must understand the bearing which the Law has upon the unbeliever, for God consistently proclaims grace against the background of the Law.

We have already taken note of three important phrases in Romans 7 regarding the believer and the law in a general way: Ver. 2: "*bound by* the law," Ver. 4: "*dead to* the law," Ver. 6: "*delivered from* the law." This is the history of everyone who has come to trust in Christ, and this was so even of Gentile believers who lived in Paul's day. True, Gentiles in Old Testament times were never directly under the Law, but *to become God's people* they would have had to accept the covenant of the Law. They *could not be* God's people without accepting the conditions of the Covenant, which were: *obedience or death*. As we know, however, this covenant was abolished by the death of Christ. So we, Gentile believers, once sought to please God by obeying His revealed will. We were *bound* by the Law. But then we heard and believed God's good news about Christ dying our death and by faith were "crucified with Christ." Thus we are *dead* to the Law and *delivered* from the Law.

If freed from the Law, then, can we not live in sin? Yes, we *can*, but *"shall we?"* (6:2,15). Did we not come to Christ in the first place to be *delivered from* sin? And did He not die our death so that the "old man" might truly be "a thing of the past"?

But do we not *need* the Law to help us to live aright? No, for God would not have us do His will because we must, or to gain His favor. He, like any normal parent, would have us do His will because we *love* Him and respond in gratitude to

His love for us. Such an attitude needs no law to threaten it. Does a loving mother need a law to make her care for her children? Does a grateful employee need a law to make him serve his employer faithfully?

But now arises the question of Rom. 7:7: *"Is the law sin?" "God forbid* [such a thought]!" the Apostle cries.

"Nay, I had not known sin, but by the law: for I had not known lust [6] except the law had said, Thou shalt not covet.

"But sin, taking occasion by the commandment, wrought in me all manner of concupiscence [covetousness]. For without the law sin was dead" (Vers. 7,8).

Here an illustration may help. A patch of waste, barren soil receives fresh rain and the warming rays of the sun, but brings forth only weeds. Is there something evil about the rain and the sun? No, the fault lies with the soil, which contains only the germs of noxious weeds. So, there is nothing wrong with the Law. The fault lies rather with the sinful human heart which reacts adversely to the holy Law of God.

"I had not known coveting," says the Apostle, "except the law had said, Thou shalt *not* covet." And my sinful heart, rebelling against the commandment, replied in effect, "Why can't I have what I want and do what I please?" and *"wrought in me all manner of covetousness."*

"Without the law sin was dead," he continues. As a fallen son of Adam it did not trouble him. And the Law being dead (in him) *he* was alive, revelling in the "freedom" of doing what he pleased. "But when the commandment came," he says, "sin revived and I died," i.e., the Law made him conscious that sin was alive in him and that *he* was dead, powerless to deliver himself from it. Thus, he says, *"the commandment, which was ordained to life,*[7] I found to be unto death" (Ver. 10).

---

6. "Lust" and "covet," in Ver. 7, and "concupiscence," in Ver. 8, are all the same word, meaning *"strong desire."*

7. In the sense of Lev. 18:5 and our Lord's words in Luke 10:28: *"This do and thou shalt live."*

It should be observed how through this whole passage the blame for man's condition and condemnation is placed, not on God's law, but on man's sin.

Ver. 8: "...*sin*, taking occasion by the commandment, wrought in me all manner of concupiscence."

Ver. 9: "...when the commandment came, *sin* revived, and I died."

Ver. 11: "...*sin*...deceived me...."

Ver. 13: "...*sin*, working death in me...."

In Vers. 12-14 the Apostle draws the valid conclusion that there is nothing wrong with the Law or the Commandment.[8] These are holy, and just, and good, and spiritual, though not adapted to purify the heart of fallen man. The Law in the very holiness of its nature, excites in man increased pride and rebellion and sin, but the fault does not lie with the Law, nor with its precepts, but with the corrupt nature of man.

"Was then that which is good made death unto me?" Would something *good* produce death? No. The law only shows sin up to be what it is—*utterly sinful* (Ver. 13). Thus it is not the Law that must be held accountable for my death, "but *sin*...working death in me by that [the Law] which is good."

"For we know that the law is spiritual, but I am carnal, sold under sin" (Ver. 14).

This is his concluding response to the question of Ver. 7, *"Is the law sin?"* but it is also an introduction to the latter part of the chapter (Vers. 15-25). This portion of the Romans Epistle has been the subject of no small degree of controversy, and deserves the most thoughtful consideration.

PAUL'S STRUGGLE WITH THE OLD SELF

"For that which I do I allow not: for what I would, that do I not, but what I hate, that do I.

"If then I do that which I would not, I consent unto the law that it is good.

---

8. That which is enjoined.

"Now then it is no more I that do it, but sin that dwelleth in me.

"For I know that in me (that is, in my flesh) dwelleth no good thing: for to will is present with me, but how to perform that which is good I find not.

"For the good that I would I do not: but the evil which I would not, that I do.

"Now if I do that I would not, it is no more I that do it, but sin that dwelleth in me.

"I find then a law, that, when I would do good, evil is present with me.

"For I delight in the law of God after the inward man:

"But I see another law in my members, warring against the law of my mind, and bringing me into captivity to the law of sin which is in my members.

"O wretched man that I am! who shall deliver me from the body of this death?

"I thank God through Jesus Christ our Lord. So then with the mind I myself serve the law of God; but with the flesh the law of sin.

"There is therefore now no condemnation to them which are in Christ Jesus, who walk not after the flesh, but after the Spirit.

"For the law of the Spirit of life in Christ Jesus hath made me free from the law of sin and death.

"For what the law could not do, in that it was weak through the flesh, God sending His own Son in the likeness of sinful flesh, and for sin, condemned sin in the flesh:

"That the righteousness of the law might be fulfilled in us, who walk not after the flesh, but after the Spirit."

—Rom. 7:15—8:4

The above passage sets forth an aspect of the Christian life that we should all understand. If we do not understand it discouragement must inevitably result, but rightly understood, this passage can contribute much toward a steady, balanced Christian experience.

OUT OF ROMANS 7 INTO ROMANS 8?

Some able men of God have held that in Romans 7 we have Paul's experience under the Law and in Romans 8 his experience under grace, the former fraught with discouragement and the latter with victory and blessing. Hence the advice: "Get out of Romans 7 and into Romans 8."

We reject this view for two important reasons:

1. Paul penned these two chapters *at the same writing*, not even a chapter division appearing in the original. The same man who wrote Rom. 8:1,2 prefaced this declaration with the words of 7:22-25. Evidently he rejoiced in the truth of Rom. 8:1,2 *while* experiencing Rom. 7:22-25.

2. Sincere and godly believers acknowledge that their experience has conformed closely to that described by Paul in Rom. 7:14-25. Here we must ask those who hold that Rom. 7 concerns Paul's experiences while still under the Law: Does not the old nature in *you* constantly strive to gain control? Do *you* have no problem at all with the "old man"? Have you *consistently* overcome the flesh in *your* experience as a Christian? Do *you* not honestly have to confess with Paul that "to will is present with me, but how to perform that which is good I find not"? Have *you* found out how to *consistently* perform the good and overcome the evil?

Romans 7 should deeply concern us for this chapter describes the spiritual experience of no less a saint than the Apostle Paul, and that of every sincere believer in the Lord Jesus Christ.

FIVE IMPORTANT LAWS

To correctly understand Rom. 7:15—8:4 we must recognize five important laws referred to.

Basically a law is a *fixed rule*. This definition holds true of the laws of nature, of civil and moral laws, and also of the holy Law of God. In the above passage the Apostle, by divine inspiration, discusses several laws which every child of God should thoroughly understand. Some believe they see as many as seven laws enumerated in this part of Paul's great *Romans* epistle. We will deal here with five that are clearly visible.

THE MORAL LAW OF GOD
(Romans 7:22)

By the moral Law of God we mean the Law that God gave through Moses, centered in the Ten Commandments (Ex. 32:15,16; John 1:17). This law represented a covenant which God made specifically with Israel (Ex. 19:5,6). The penalty for breaking this covenant was death (II Cor. 3:7).

But while the Law was given particularly to Israel, we have seen that it nevertheless *concerns* the Gentiles as well. In Rom. 2:14,15 Paul declares that *"the Gentiles, which have not the law"* nevertheless *"show the work of the law written in their hearts, their conscience also bearing witness, and their thoughts the meanwhile accusing or else excusing one another."*

Thus, while the Gentiles were already condemned by the moral law, written in their hearts by God, God now gave this law *written on tables of stone* to His chosen nation, as a basis for a covenant which He would use to show them that they too were sinners. Almost immediately the people of Israel began breaking the Law so that they, like the Gentiles, were brought in guilty before God. [9] This is specifically stated in Rom. 3:19:

"Now we know that what things soever the law saith, it saith to them who are under the law; that every mouth may be stopped, and all the world may become guilty before God."

This is also taught in Romans 5, where we read that *"by one man sin entered into the world"* (Ver. 12), and that later *"the law entered that the offence might abound"* (Ver. 20). Thus, while the *covenant* of the Law was made with Israel alone, it at the same time emphasizes *man's* sin.

THE LAW OF INDWELLING SIN
(Romans 7:23)

Another law clearly enunciated in Romans 7 is that of indwelling sin, found at work even in the life of the most consecrated saint of God.

---

9. Space forbids us to deal here with the function of the *ceremonial* law.

This constant, aggressive assertion of the Adamic nature within us the Apostle calls *"the law of sin which is in my members."* Freely acknowledging the operation of this law within himself, he says:

"The law [of God] is spiritual; but I am carnal, sold under sin.... For I know that in me (that is in my flesh) dwelleth no good thing, for to will is present with me, but how to perform that which is good I find not. For the good that I would I do not; but the evil which I would not, that I do...I find then a law, that when I would do good, evil is present with me. For I delight in the law of God after the inward man, but I see another law in my members, warring against the law of my mind, and bringing me into captivity to the law of sin which is in my members" (7:14,18,19,21,22,23).

Does this mean that Paul was not the true man of God that the Scriptures present to us? No, for he does not discuss here his general manner of life, but his problem—the problem we all encounter—*with sin.*

The Apostle's forthright confession should have a humbling effect upon us all for it comes from the heart of a man who was doubtless far more godly than we.

But a recognition of the law of indwelling sin should also prove encouraging to the believer. It is as if God would say to us: "Write it down; fix it clearly in your mind: In you, that is to say, in your old self, is *no good thing*: it is totally corrupt. But it has been crucified with Christ." Thus the path to victory lies not in a subjective examination of the old nature, much less in attempts to improve the old nature, but in an objective occupation with *Christ*, in whose blessed Person we now stand before God, justified from every sin.

This does not mean that we should not often confess our sins to God, asking His parental forgiveness, but it does mean that we should not continually dwell upon our sins and the depravity of the old nature.

Every true believer longs to be free from sin, and some wonder why God does not remove the old nature with its depraved tendencies. Ah, but if He did this now, if we did not experience the inner strife between the Spirit and the flesh, so "contrary the one to the other" (Gal. 5:17), in a word, if we were not ever tempted by sin, how could we possibly reach the lost about us? Would there not be a great gulf fixed between them in their sinfulness and us in our perfection?

THE LAW OF THE RENEWED MIND
(Romans 7:22,23)

Does the above argument from Scripture indicate that believers may settle down in sin, not taking it too seriously when they stumble and fall? No indeed, for there is another law which forbids this. This law the Apostle calls *"the law of my mind."* The law of indwelling sin, he says, wars against "the law of my mind." What, then, is this *"law of my mind"*?

The observant student of the Scriptures will note that Paul's epistles have much to say about the believer's renewal of mind, brought about by the Holy Spirit's work as He applies His Word to the heart. It begins at conversion, when one who hitherto viewed the Bible in the light of other things now begins to view other things in the light of the Bible.

That it is not the body, or the old nature, but the *mind* that is thus renewed is clear from Col. 3:10:

"[Ye] have put on the new man, which is RENEWED IN KNOWLEDGE AFTER THE IMAGE OF HIM THAT CREATED HIM."

In the passage we are considering the Apostle makes it clear that he himself has received this "renewing of the mind," declaring that he does not condone, indeed "hates" the wrong he does (7:15), that he longs to do right and does *not* wish to do wrong (Vers. 18,19), that he "*delights* in the law of God" (Ver. 22), and with his mind serves the law of God (Ver. 25).

This renewing of the mind in the believer he calls a *law*. It is now *"the law of my mind,"* he says, to *earnestly desire* to do God's will. This law operates in every believer. Anyone who does not abhor sin and desire to please God had better question his salvation, for true believers come to Christ not to be free *to* sin, but to be delivered *from* sin. Their minds, once alienated from God by sin, have now been renewed as they have been reconciled to God (Col. 1:20,21).

But the renewing of the mind is not consummated at conversion. More and more we should see sin and righteousness, truth and error, in their true light. Thus the Apostle says with regard to the evil about us:

"...be not conformed to this world, but BE YE TRANSFORMED BY THE RENEWING OF YOUR MIND..." (Rom. 12:2).

And concerning the evil *in* us, the Old Adamic nature, he exhorts:

"...put off...the old man, which is corrupt according to the deceitful lusts, and BE RENEWED IN THE SPIRIT OF YOUR MIND" (Eph. 4:22,23).

THE LAW OF SIN AND DEATH
(Romans 8:2)

But, whether the mind is renewed or not, there is another very basic law to consider, a law which we see in operation all about us: *"the law of sin and death."*

This too is an inexorable, unchangeable *law*. One of the basic lessons of Scripture is that *sin brings death*, and this is also one of the basic facts of life.

Ezek. 18:4: "...the soul that sinneth, it shall die."

Rom. 5:12: "...by one man sin entered into the world, and death by sin, and so death passed upon all men, for that all have sinned."

Rom. 6:23: "...For the wages of sin is death...."

Jas. 1:15: "...sin, when it is finished, bringeth forth death."

To face up to the full effects of this law, however, it must be noted that not only physical death is included in "the law of sin and death," but also the death (*not* the annihilation) of the whole man in the lake of fire (Rev. 20:11-15). [10]

The "law of sin and death" is terrible indeed to contemplate, and some believers in Christ, who truly long to please God, are naturally alarmed at the thought of appear-

---

10. See the Author's *Man, His Nature and Destiny* (Pp. 26-36; 169,170).

ing before the Lord at the Great White Throne to answer for their many sins.

Such fears, thank God, are needless, for not only is it clear from the record in Rev. 20 that only the lost will appear at this final judgment, but an understanding of still another unchangeable, irrevocable law mentioned in Romans 8 will quickly allay any such fears.

THE LAW OF THE SPIRIT
LIFE IN CHRIST
(Romans 8:2)

"There is therefore now no condemnation to them which are in Christ Jesus," says Rom. 8:1. This simply because they are *"in* Christ Jesus," *"accepted in the Beloved"* (Eph. 1:6) and pronounced *"complete in Him"* (Col. 2:10). This is a judicial matter. With our sins imputed to Christ and His righteousness imputed to us, we are fully justified before the bar of a just and holy God (See Rom. 3:21—4:8).

But more than judicial considerations are involved in the believer's deliverance from "the law of sin and death." *"The law of the Spirit,"* says the Apostle, *"hath made me free from the law of sin and death"* (Rom. 8:2). What, then, is *"the law of the Spirit"*?

We are aware that in Rom. 8:2 the complete phrase appears to be: *"the law of the Spirit of life in Christ Jesus,"* but this phraseology is puzzling to say the least. Through many years we have asked many friends what *"the law of the Spirit of life in Christ Jesus"* might be. We have never received a satisfying answer to this question.

Since there is virtually no punctuation in the Greek, however, the matter is easily cleared up by placing a colon or a dash between the words "Spirit" and "of" in the English reading. Nor, we believe, would this violate what the translators meant to express. Or, a legitimate ellipsis could be supplied thus: *"The law of the Spirit, [that] of life in Christ Jesus."* This is evidently the correct rendering, for *"life in Christ"* is indeed *"the law of the Spirit."*

Not only are believers *justified* before God; they also receive *life in Christ* upon believing; life imparted by the Holy Spirit.

John 3:36: "He that believeth on the Son hath everlasting life; and he that believeth not the Son shall not see life...."

I John 5:11,12: "And this is the record, that God hath given to us eternal life, and THIS LIFE IS IN HIS SON.

"HE THAT HATH THE SON HATH LIFE; AND HE THAT HATH NOT THE SON OF GOD HATH NOT LIFE."

"The law of the Spirit," then, is *"life in Christ Jesus."* The moment one places his faith in Christ, that same moment the Spirit imparts *life, eternal life, the life of Christ Himself*. This is an immutable *law*. True faith in Christ *always* produces this result.

Now with all this in mind let us consider the real argument of Rom. 8:2 and its bearing on "the law of sin and death."

"For the law of the Spirit, [that] of life in Christ Jesus, hath made me free from the law of sin and death."

Does this mean that one divine law violates another, or conflicts with it? No, but one *supersedes* the other. The story is told of a Christian cobbler in England, working in his shop as an atheist entered. Soon the atheist began ridiculing the miraculous element in the Scriptures, declaring that the laws of nature rendered the miraculous impossible.

Using the cobbler's knife as an illustration, he said, "For example, if you let that knife go, the law of gravitation would cause it to fall to the ground, and nothing could stop it." Hereupon the cobbler, with a flip of the wrist, tossed the knife upward so that it stuck in the ceiling! Was the law of gravitation suspended during this time; had it been violated in any way? No, its downward pull was in operation all the while the knife was flying upward and as it stuck in the ceiling, but a stronger law superseded it: the law of the cobbler's deliberate action.

It is indeed a *law* that sin results in death, and seeing we have sinned we *must* die. Ah, but the believer *has died—in Christ!* (Rom. 6:6; Gal. 2:20). And since our Lord overcame death and came forth in resurrection life, so do we, *in Him*.

Much more could be said about "the law of the Spirit," by which we have "life in Christ Jesus," indeed, much more could be said about all these laws, but the above will at least prepare us to better understand Romans 7:15-25, one of the most difficult portions of the *Romans* epistle.

Thank God, He operates by laws, laws that are an essential part of His very nature, so that we can rely on Him fully and stand unshaken as the storm of life rages about us.

WHO'S WHO?

What student of the Word can read Romans 7:15-25 without being reminded of Galatians 2:20? *"I am crucified with Christ—nevertheless I live—yet not I . . . ."*

Indeed, in Rom. 7:15-25, *more* than in Gal. 2:20 or any part of Paul's epistles, the question keeps arising: Of whom does the Apostle speak here, of the "old man," the "new man," or the *whole* man? Here we must ask God for special insight to grasp the *sense* of His Word. In some cases, however, the meaning is quite clear.

In Ver. 18 the words "in me" obviously refer to the "old man," for he immediately explains, "that is, in *my flesh*." But in Ver. 15 the words "I allow not" and "I hate" clearly refer to the "new man."

In Ver. 17 the "*sin* that dwelleth in me" must, of course, be associated with the "*old* man," but the *"me"* in which the sin dwells is the *whole* man, or the man as a whole, while the word "I" in "it is no more *I* that do it" clearly refers to the "*new* man."

In Ver. 21 the phrase "evil is *present with* me" might at first seem to mean that evil is *at hand* to tempt, but the preceding verse (Ver. 20), followed by the words "I find then a law," indicates that in Ver. 21 he speaks of sin *in* him. Why then does he use the term *"present with"*? The explanation is found in the identity of the person referred to. Here the

"I" that "would do good" is obviously the "new man," and the "old man," who does the evil, is *"present with"* him, both the old and the new residing in the *whole* man.

These are but examples of the problem and its basic solution. The child of God who sincerely desires to please Him and recognizes the fact that the old nature and the new dwell side-by-side within will not find it too difficult to understand "Who's Who" in this passage.

The phrase *"it is no more I that do it,"* found twice in this passage (Vers. 17,20), might seem to the careless reader to indicate that Paul is shedding the blame for the sins he commits. This is by no means the case. It is rather a note of rejoicing that the new man in him has *no connection* with sin. It *does not* and *cannot* sin, for it is Christ in him. The new man is the resurrected man, living the resurrection life of Christ. Also, the Apostle does what he urges *us* to do in Rom. 6:11; he reckons himself to be *"dead indeed"* unto sin, for while the old nature is still active in us experientially, and will be until "the redemption of the body," [11] it has died *so far as God is concerned*, for He sees us now in the person of His crucified, buried, risen Son. Thus the same man who cried, *"O wretched man that I am! Who shall deliver me...?"* could also exclaim, *"I thank God, through Jesus Christ our Lord"* and *"There is therefore now no [more] condemnation"!*

FURTHER LESSONS
FROM ROMANS 7:14-25

1. This passage teaches unequivocally that the believer has two natures; that the Adamic nature is *not* eradicated at his conversion to Christ or at any time before his going to be with Christ. It teaches further that the old nature *cannot* be *improved*, for it is totally bad.

We have seen that the way to victory over the flesh is not by wrestling, but by faith, by "reckoning" ourselves to be "dead indeed" unto sin, accepting God's Word that the old

---

11. This is why Gal. 5:5 declares that *"we, through the Spirit, WAIT for the HOPE of righteousness* [i.e., perfect, personal righteousness] *by faith."*

man was crucified with Christ. But it does not follow from this that the old nature is dead experientially, otherwise why the exhortations to *consider* him dead? *Judicially* he has indeed been put to death in Christ, and it is now for us to appropriate this truth in our daily experience.

2. The Apostle's words in Ver. 18: *"How to perform that which is good I find not"* are a humbling confession from the heart of no less a saint of God than Paul, yet it expresses a simple fact of any believer's experience, for who has yet learned how to consistently "perform that which is good"?

We have a similar truth set forth in Gal. 5:17:

"For the flesh lusteth against the Spirit, and the Spirit against the flesh, and these are contrary the one to the other, *so that ye cannot do the things that ye would.*"

It goes without saying that the Apostle does not mean to condone sin here on the ground that we *cannot* do otherwise. His meaning is rather that whereas we yearn to be forever rid of temptation and sin, the flesh within us keeps badgering us so that we cannot settle down to living a sinless life. Thus the Christian life must be a step-by-step experience, daily appropriating by faith the help that God, in grace, provides.

3. This passage further shows us that the believer cannot boast that he, by nature, is any better than others. The truth of the matter is described in the words of a young Christian sailor who was accused of thinking that he was better than others. "Oh no," said the sailor, "you've got that all wrong. We don't think we're any better—but we're *better off!*"

4. The fact that this passage was penned as an honest confession by Paul himself should prove encouraging to believers who long, as he did, to live godly lives. Does the old nature continually try to dominate your experience? Then, in that respect at least, you are like Paul! But you must be like him in the rest too. Acknowledging recurrent failures, the Apostle nevertheless protests that this is *not* because he approves of sin or condones it in any way. Hear him: "I long to do good, I *delight* in the law of God, I *hate* sin, I do not

'allow' it, but how to perform that which is good I find not. O wretched man that I am!"

Thus Paul did not take sin lightly, for if anything is clear from this passage it is the fact that he *delighted* in that which was right and *hated* that which was wrong, seeking earnestly to overcome it.

5. This passage also teaches us that Paul did not exalt himself, for here he confesses humiliating facts about his personal life which might well cause some to despise him. Elsewhere he calls himself the chief of sinners (I Tim. 1:15) and "less than the least of all saints" (Eph. 3:8). He did, however, defend his God-given *position* and *message*. A consideration of the whole of Eph. 3:8 will explain why:

"Unto me, who am less than the least of all saints, *is this grace given*, THAT I SHOULD PREACH AMONG THE GENTILES THE UNSEARCHABLE RICHES OF CHRIST."

He was both the herald and the living example of *what had been accomplished at Calvary*. If his position as God's appointed ambassador of grace could be undermined, so could the message he was sent to proclaim. But the above verse is proof enough that he did not exalt himself in thus defending his position.

NO CONDEMNATION
TO THOSE WHO ARE IN CHRIST JESUS

"There is therefore now no condemnation to them which are in Christ Jesus, who walk not after the flesh, but after the Spirit.

"For the law of the Spirit of life in Christ Jesus hath made me free from the law of sin and death.

"For what the law could not do, in that it was weak through the flesh, God sending His own Son in the likeness of sinful flesh, and for sin, condemned sin in the flesh;

"That the righteousness of the law might be fulfilled in us, who walk not after the flesh, but after the Spirit."

—Rom. 8:1-4

We come now to one of the most amazing and wonderful

chapters of the *Epistle to the Romans* and, like so many other passages in the epistle, it opens with the word *"therefore."*

"Therefore," as we know, is a key word in the study of logic, where it is used so consistently that the sign ∴ has been designated to represent it.

It is not strange, then, that we find this word used, in one form or another, no less than 70 times in the Romans Epistle, for Romans is a logical, as well as a theological, treatise.

As we have already begun to point out, the word "therefore" stands out prominently in Paul's discussion of *the logic of the plan of salvation*,[12] in which he presents a series of logical propositions.

The *first* of these propositions is found in Rom. 2:1 where, having proved that *all* men are sinners, including even the most self-righteous, he declares:

"Therefore thou art inexcusable...."

Then, demonstrating the fact that the Law cannot justify, but can only condemn the sinner, he offers his *second* logical proposition in Rom. 3:20:

"Therefore by the deeds of the law there shall no flesh be justified in His [God's] sight...."

Following this declaration with the good news that *"now the righteousness of God without the law is manifested.... through the redemption that is in Christ Jesus,"* he takes a *third* logical step in the proposition of Rom. 3:28:

"Therefore we conclude that a man is justified by faith, without the deeds of the law."

Then an in-depth discussion of the imputation of the believer's sins to Christ and of Christ's righteousness to the believer leads the Apostle to his *fourth* logical proposition in Rom. 5:1:

"Therefore being justified by faith, we have peace with God through our Lord Jesus Christ."

---

12. See the author's booklet, *The Logic of the Plan of Salvation*.

This, in turn, leads him into a discussion of the believer's deliverance from the bondage of sin (Chapter 6) and of the Law (Chapter 7), to his *fifth* logical proposition in Rom. 8:1:

"There is *therefore* now no condemnation to them which are in Christ Jesus...."

This proposition is his introduction to a precious chapter, in which the utter inefficacy of the Law is set over against the glorious efficacy of the Holy Spirit's working in and through the believer, a chapter which opens with *"no condemnation"* and closes with *"no separation."*

ROMANS 8:1
AND THE AUTHORIZED VERSION

"There is therefore now no condemnation to them which are in Christ Jesus, who walk not after the flesh, but after the Spirit" (Rom. 8:1).

Much discussion has revolved around the question of the authenticity of the latter part of Rom. 8:1 as found in the *Authorized*, or *King James Version* of the Bible—and this by men who equally believe in the divine inspiration of the Holy Scriptures. The question is: Do the words "who walk not," etc., belong in Ver. 1 as in the AV, or only in Ver. 4, where they also occur? [13]

Many believe that at Ver. 1 this clause is a "gloss" [14] added by a copyist who may have feared that careless living might result from the unqualified statement of Rom. 8:1*a*.

Certainly the words *"who walk not after the flesh, but after the Spirit"* cannot be a *qualifying* clause, for our security as believers does not depend upon our walk but upon our God-given position *in Christ*; not upon our success in Christian living, but upon *"this grace wherein we stand"* (Rom. 5:2). God has not made *another* covenant like the Covenant of the Law, saying in effect, "*If* you 'walk not after the flesh but after the Spirit' *then* you will not suffer condemnation." The believer in Christ is freed from condemnation *simply*

---
13. For an in-depth discussion of this subject, see Appendix No. 1.
14. A word of explanation or correction inserted between the lines or in the margin of a manuscript.

because he is "in Christ Jesus," not because he succeeds in walking after the Spirit or in overcoming the lusts of the flesh (See Rom. 6 and 7).

No such problem exists where Ver. 4 is concerned, for here the phrase "who walk not," etc., *fits perfectly*. God, in grace, did for us what the Law could not do, *so that "the righteousness of the Law might be fulfilled in us, who walk not after the flesh, but after the Spirit."*

But if, on the other hand, the latter part of Rom. 8:1 is to be considered *in any sense* a statement of *fact*, surely it belongs in parentheses so that the force of Rom. 8:1*a* along with 8:2-4 may not be destroyed, but fully appreciated. Consider how powerful this passage is if we read 8:2-4 immediately following 8:1*a*, omitting the parenthesis and including the words "who walk not," etc., only at Ver. 4.

"There is therefore now no condemnation to them which are in Christ Jesus.

"For the law of the Spirit [i.e.,] of life in Christ Jesus hath made me free from the law of sin and death.

"For what the law could not do, in that it was weak through the flesh, God sending His own Son in the likeness of sinful flesh, and for sin, condemned sin in the flesh:

"That the righteousness of the law might be fulfilled in us, who walk not after the flesh but after the Spirit."

Thus the believer is free from the condemnation of sin simply because he is *"in Christ Jesus"* (Ver. 1). He has been *"made accepted in the Beloved"* (Eph. 1:6) and has been pronounced *"complete in Him"* (Col. 2:9,10). Blessed standing! Even before our Lord revealed all the facts involved to the Apostle Paul, He said to those who sought to kill Him:

"Verily, verily I say unto you, He that heareth My word and believeth on Him that sent Me, *hath everlasting life, and shall not come into condemnation, but is* [has] *passed from death unto life"* (John 5:24).

The believer has been freed from condemnation and death because "the law of the Spirit," that of "life in Christ," has made him free, *not* from the law of sin in his members (7:23), but from *"the law of sin and death"* (8:2). We have already discussed this latter law (Pp. 173,174).

The impotence of the Mosaic Law to save, as set forth in Ver. 3, is often stressed in Paul's epistles and, indeed, was strongly emphasized in his *first recorded sermon*, delivered in the synagogue in Antioch of Pisidia. The climax of his message, and that upon which all the rest converged, is found in Acts 13:38,39:

"Be it known unto you therefore, men and brethren, that through this man is preached unto you the forgiveness of sins;

"And by Him all that believe are justified from all things, FROM WHICH YE COULD NOT BE JUSTIFIED BY THE LAW OF MOSES."

The impotency of the Law is further emphasized in Heb. 7:18,19, where the Apostle declares:

"For there is verily a disannulling of the commandment going before FOR THE WEAKNESS AND UNPROFITABLENESS THEREOF.

"FOR THE LAW MADE NOTHING PERFECT...."

But while "the law made nothing perfect...*the bringing in of a better hope did*" (Ver. 19). *"For what the law could not do, in that it was weak through the flesh, God, sending His own Son in the likeness of sinful flesh"* accomplished! (Rom. 8:3). *How* did He accomplish it? Read on:

"...sending His own Son in the likeness of sinful flesh, and for sin, [He] condemned sin in the flesh" (Ver. 3).

We know that originally God created man in His own image and after His likeness (Gen. 1:26). After the fall, however, Adam "begat a son in *his own* likeness" (Gen. 5:3). And thus *"by one man sin entered into the world, and death by sin"* (Rom. 5:12).

Twenty-five hundred years later *"the law entered that the offence might abound"* (5:20). Mark well, "that the *offence* might abound." The Law could not justify—it could only condemn sinful man, thus God in grace sent "His own Son, *in the likeness of sinful flesh*" specifically *"for sin,"* to *"condemn sin in the flesh"*—*His* flesh (Rom. 8:3).

It should be carefully noted that our Lord did not appear

"in the likeness of sinful flesh" in the sense that He too was tainted by sin. The thought is rather that He did *not* appear in the likeness of unfallen Adam, with all of Adam's glory and physical well-being. Rather He appeared in the likeness of *fallen* Adam and his progeny, weakened as it had been by sin.

It should also be observed that God sent His own Son in the likeness of fallen man that sin might be *"condemned ...[Gr., katekrinen] in the flesh"* (Ver. 3).

Thus we read in Eph. 2 that our Lord "abolished *in His flesh*...the law of commandments" and that we who were "far off" have been "made nigh *by the blood of Christ"* (Vers. 13,15).

Similarly, Col. 1:21,22 declares that we who were once "alienated and enemies" have now been reconciled *"in the body of His flesh, through death."* Peter, after his acquaintance with Paul, also added his testimony, declaring that our Lord,

"...His own self bare our sins *in His own body on the tree*..." (I Pet. 2:24).

After having seen this, and *only* after having seen it, are we in a position to serve God acceptably, not in response to any *"Thou shalt"* or *"Thou shalt not,"* but from sheer *gratitude* and *love*, the natural response to *grace!* Our blessed Lord justifies believing sinners,

"That the righteousness of the law might be fulfilled in us, *who walk not after the flesh, but after the Spirit"* (Rom. 8:4).

> Jesus, Thy blood and righteousness
> My beauty are, my glorious dress.
> Midst flaming worlds, in these arrayed,
> With joy shall I lift up my head.
>
> Bold shall I stand in that great day,
> For who aught to my charge shall lay?
> Fully absolved from these I am:
> From sin and fear, from guilt and shame.
>
> —John Wesley

Chapter VIII — Romans 8:5-39
LIFE IN THE SPIRIT
THE CHRISTIAN WALK

"For they that are after the flesh do mind the things of the flesh; but they that are after the Spirit the things of the Spirit.

"For to be carnally minded is death; but to be spiritually minded is life and peace.

"Because the carnal mind is enmity against God: for it is not subject to the law of God, neither indeed can be.

"So then, they that are in the flesh cannot please God.

"But ye are not in the flesh, but in the Spirit, if so be that the Spirit of God dwell in you. Now if any man have not the Spirit of Christ, he is none of His.

"And if Christ be in you, the body is dead because of sin; but the Spirit is life because of righteousness.

"But if the Spirit of Him that raised up Jesus from the dead dwell in you, He that raised up Christ from the dead shall also quicken your mortal bodies by His Spirit that dwelleth in you.

"Therefore, brethren, we are debtors, not to the flesh, to live after the flesh.

"For if ye live after the flesh, ye shall die: but if ye through the Spirit do mortify the deeds of the body, ye shall live."
—Rom. 8:5-13

Before proceeding with Rom. 8:5 it should be observed that the Greek word *sarx*, generally rendered "flesh" in the AV, has a wide range of meaning. Sometimes it refers to the *body* or the *substance* of the body, as in Rom. 1:3; 2:28; and 4:1. In many other cases, however, and especially often in Paul's epistles, it refers to the Adamic nature in man, human nature. In the believer it is the "old man" or the old *self*. This is the meaning of the word "flesh" as we find it in Rom. 8:5-13, the passage we are now to consider.

As we have seen, the believer now has the Spirit of God within him, but he also still has the "flesh," the old Adamic nature. Thus he may be saved by the grace of God, yet "walk" according to the flesh, as indeed many do, even though Christ died for us that we might walk according to the Spirit.

The difference lies in that which occupies the mind. Those who are after the flesh, says the Apostle, "mind," or set their minds upon, "the things of the flesh" (Ver. 5), or the things that the flesh enjoys: worldly pleasure, sensual satisfaction, earthly gain, even intellectual or religious attainment. But those who walk according to the Spirit set their minds on "the things of the Spirit": pleasing God, serving Christ, spending time with the Word and in prayer, rejoicing in their "all spiritual blessings in heavenly places in Christ," etc. Thus the Apostle says in Col. 3:1,2:

"If ye then be risen with Christ, *seek those things which are above, where Christ sitteth on the right hand of God.*

"*Set your affection on things above, not on things on the earth.*"

In Rom. 8:6,7 the word "carnal" is this same word *sarx*, generally rendered "flesh"; thus to be "carnally minded" is to have the mind set upon the things of the flesh. *This* spells death, says the Apostle, *"but to be spiritually minded is life and peace."*

But has not the believer been delivered from death? Yes, as the penalty for sin, but as we have seen, believers may still die as far as their Christian experience is concerned (See Rom. 8:12,13; Gal. 6:8; Eph. 5:14). The words "die" and "death" here must be taken in the light of the context. If we walk after the Spirit we will thrive and blossom and bloom, experientially, but if we walk after the flesh we will wither and die. Has the reader never seen a dead Christian? Paul saw many of them, saved but fruitless; hence his admonition *to believers*: *"Awake thou that sleepest and arise from the dead . . ."* (Eph. 5:14). For the unbeliever there is no alternative, but the believer in Christ will do well to remember the Apostle's wise counsel:

"...to be carnally minded is death; but to be spiritually minded is life and peace" (Rom. 8:6).

The Apostle sounds these words of admonition because the flesh, the old self, though counted dead in Christ—and this is of basic importance—is still very active in our *experience*, and his activity always tends toward death. Thus *"he that soweth to his flesh shall of the flesh reap corruption"* (Gal. 6:8), and *"to be carnally minded is death"* (Rom. 8:6). Let us then heed the exhortation, always occupied with the glorious alternative fact that *"to be spiritually minded is life and peace."*

Verse 7 declares that the "old man" is a *rebel* against God. "The carnal mind [the mind of the flesh] is *enmity against God*; for it is *not subject* to the law of God, neither indeed *can* be." He is his own god and wants his own way.

Thus the Apostle says of those who are "*in* the flesh," i.e., who are still unregenerate and without the new nature,

"So then they that are in the flesh cannot please God" (Ver. 8).

The unregenerate man may be cultured, intellectual, generous, kind, even religious, but he *cannot* please God. With all his virtues he is still *at enmity* with God for, rejecting God's estimate of his condition and refusing God's saving grace through Christ, he goes on in his self-righteousness, and this God will not abide. There is one thing, above all, that God will not accept from the sinner, and that is "back talk." Those who would experience the joy of sins forgiven and of acceptance with God must stop saying things in their own defense. Rather they must plead guilty and throw themselves upon the mercy of the court. It is not sin that keeps men out of heaven, but a wrong attitude. Christ died to pay the penalty for our sins and will accept the vilest who come to Him in faith, but self-righteousness He abhors.

That Verse 8 refers to the unsaved is clear from the contrast that follows:

"But ye are not in the flesh but in the Spirit, if so be that the Spirit of God dwell in you. Now if any man have not the Spirit of Christ, he is none of His" (Ver. 9).

Some hold that "the Spirit of Christ" here does not refer to the Holy Spirit, but to an attitude. This cannot be, for while believers indeed should show "the spirit of Christ," or a Christian spirit, in their relationship with others, it cannot be said of those who lack this that they are "none of His." Furthermore, the next verse goes on to say, *"And if Christ be in you,"* not merely a Christian spirit, a proper attitude, but *Christ*, who, like the Father, dwells within us through the Spirit (Cf. Eph. 2:22).

But what does the Apostle mean by declaring:

"And if Christ be in you, *the body is dead because of sin;* but the Spirit is life because of righteousess" (Ver. 10).

How is the body [1] "dead" because of sin? Evidently the answer is that *God* counts it dead—and this is profoundly important. It matters little what we might think, or how we might look at things, but it *does* matter profoundly that *God* sees the believer's old self as having died in Christ, "because of sin." And it matters too that *"the Spirit is life because of righteousness,"* i.e., that the Holy Spirit within us is our life because our sins have been righteously dealt with and Christ's righteousness imputed to us.

Note the difference between the adjective, "dead," and the noun, "life," in Verse 10. The Holy Spirit within us is not merely alive (as opposed to "dead"); He is our *life!* Recall Verse 2, where we are told that "the law of the Spirit" is "life in Christ." When we receive Christ as our Savior we are justified—*and more*, for the Spirit imparts *life*.

Verse 11, which follows, is important as a conclusion to the preceding verses. Generally it has been considered a *prediction* of our future resurrection, but this is incorrect. Read carefully, and note that it is *not* our *dead* bodies, but our *"mortal"* bodies that the Holy Spirit quickens to help us overcome sin.

The whole subject here is the Christian walk and the Spirit's aid in this. Thus the Apostle concludes:

---

1. The vehicle through which the old nature operates.

"But if the Spirit of Him that raised up Jesus from the dead dwell in you, He that raised up Christ from the dead shall also quicken your mortal bodies by His Spirit that dwelleth in you" (Ver. 11).

The thought is that if the Spirit of God, who raised Christ from the *dead*, dwells in you, He that raised up Christ from the *dead* will surely "quicken," or give life to, your *mortal*[2] bodies, i.e., to help you to overcome the desires of the flesh.

That this is the meaning is evident from the verse that follows:

"Therefore, brethren, we are debtors, not to the flesh, to live after the flesh" (Ver. 12).

How many Christians live in an "I can't help it" frame of mind! They recline, as it were, on a couch, with two favorite mottoes on the wall above: *"The Spirit is Willing, But the Flesh is Weak"* and *"He Knoweth Our Frame; He Remembereth That We Are Dust."* But this "after all I'm only human" attitude is an affront to God, who in grace has given us needed aid, to be appropriated by faith: the Holy Spirit within to strengthen these mortal bodies against sin, even when, in our weakness, we are most vulnerable.

Therefore *we are debtors*, not to sin, but to *God* who has so graciously provided help for us in our weakness. With this help at hand at all times, it is *wrong*, now, to excuse ourselves with the words, "I can't help it."

We shall see more of this when we consider Verse 26: *"the Spirit helpeth our infirmities."* Meantime let us vow that by God's grace we will *appropriate* the help of the Holy Spirit, through whom God raised Christ from the dead seeking, like Paul, to experience *"the power of His resurrection"* (Phil. 3:10).

"For if ye live after the flesh, ye shall die;[3] but if ye through the Spirit do mortify the deeds of the body, ye shall live" (Ver. 13).

May God convict us of our *responsibility*—"we are *debtors*" —to be thriving, flourishing believers, *"strengthened...by*

---

2. Liable, or subject to death.

3. In the sense discussed above with regard to Verse 6.

His Spirit in the inner man" (Eph. 3:16), and bearing much of "*the fruit of the Spirit*" (Gal. 5:22) for His glory.

SONSHIP

"For as many as are led by the Spirit of God, they are the sons of God.

"For ye have not received the spirit of bondage again to fear; but ye have received the Spirit of adoption, whereby we cry Abba, Father.

"The Spirit itself beareth witness with our spirit, that we are the children of God:

"And if children, then heirs; heirs of God and joint-heirs with Christ; if so be that we suffer with Him, that we may be also glorified together."

—Rom. 8:14-17

Does Verse 14 above mean that those who do not consistently yield themselves to the leading of the Holy Spirit are not the sons of God? No. He is speaking of being *led* rather than being *forced*, drawing a contrast between those under the Law and those under grace. It will be well here to examine the dispensational setting.

Under the Law God's people were not invited to seek the leading of the Holy Spirit in their walk. Their fellowship with God depended rather upon their *obedience* to the *Law*. "*Thou shalt*" and "*Thou shalt not*" were the characteristic phrases of God's Word through Moses.

By contrast, during the coming millennial reign of Christ, God's people will be *controlled* by the Spirit. Hear the Word of God on the subject:

"For I will take you from among the heathen [nations] and gather you out of all countries, and will bring you into your own land.

"Then will I sprinkle clean water upon you, and ye shall be clean: from all your filthiness, and from all your idols, will I cleanse you."

"And I will put My Spirit within you, and CAUSE you to walk in my statutes, AND YE SHALL KEEP MY JUDGMENTS AND DO THEM" (Ezek. 36:24,25,27).

God gave His people a foretaste of this at Pentecost while Christ's return and the establishment of His kingdom were being offered (Acts 2:29-31; 3:19-26). There, we read, *"they were all filled with the Holy Spirit"* (Acts 2:4) in fulfillment of our Lord's promise: *"Ye shall be baptized with the Holy Spirit not many days hence"* (Acts 1:5). Thus we search in vain for a single sin or blunder in the conduct of the believers at Pentecost and for some time thereafter.

But this soon changed as the King and the kingdom were rejected and "this present evil age" set in. The Galatian believers were not all filled with the Spirit; they "bit and devoured one another." And surely the Corinthian believers were not all filled with the Spirit, for Paul had to send them at least one letter of stern rebuke. Nor were the Colossians all filled with the Spirit, for they had to be warned against dangerous heresies that had crept in among them.

Today the filling with the Spirit is a *goal* (Eph. 5:18) to be attained by grace through faith, as we allow ourselves to be *"led by the Spirit of God"* (Rom. 8:14).

"For the flesh lusteth against the Spirit, and the Spirit against the flesh; and these are contrary the one to the other, so that ye cannot do the things that ye would.

"But if ye be led of the Spirit, ye are not under the law" (Gal. 5:17,18).

To put it simply:

1. In the *past*, fellowship with God depended upon *obedience* to the *Law*.

2. In the *present* dispensation, *grace* and *faith* are elevated to their highest place. *Grace provides* the needed help of the Holy Spirit, and this help is *appropriated by faith*. We are neither simply *commanded* to obey God, nor does the Holy Spirit arbitrarily take *control* and *"cause"* us to obey. Rather God's people enjoy fellowship with Him as they yield themselves to the *leading* of the Spirit.

3. In the *future*, when our Lord reigns on earth, the Holy Spirit will *control* the people of God and *"cause"* them to obey His will (Ezek. 36:24-27).

A POSITION AS FULLGROWN SONS

"For ye have not received the spirit of bondage again, to fear; but ye have received the Spirit of adoption, whereby we cry, Abba [which being translated is] Father" (Ver. 15).

There has been much misunderstanding about the meaning of the word "adoption" in this verse. In defining this word *three* of the Bible Dictionaries in the Author's library *mis*interprets its meaning. One typical definition reads:

> "Adoption is an act by which a person *takes a stranger into his family*, acknowledges him as his child, and constitutes him heir of his estate....In the New Testament, adoption denotes the act of God's grace by which, on being justified through faith, we are received into the family of God, and made heirs of the inheritance of heaven."

That this is the sense of our English word *adoption* no one will deny, but it is certainly *not* the meaning of the word here rendered "adoption." Perhaps no passage of Scripture will throw more light on the meaning of the Greek word here than Gal. 4:1-7 where, in one of his great historical statements, the Apostle says:

"Now I say, that the heir, as long as he is a child, differeth nothing from a servant, though he be lord of all;

"But is under tutors and governors until the time appointed of the father.

"EVEN SO we, when we were children, were in bondage under the elements of the world:

"But when the fulness of the time was come, God sent forth His Son, made of a woman, made under the law,

"To redeem them that were under the law, that we might receive the adoption of sons.

"And because ye are sons, God hath sent forth the Spirit of His Son into your hearts, crying, Abba, Father.

"Wherefore thou art no more a servant, but a son; and if a son then an heir of God, through Christ."

According to this passage, "adoption" is the "placing as a son"—a fullgrown son. This is the definition of the Greek word *huiothesia*, as given by Young, Robinson and others, while Thayer, referring to the adoption for which believers still wait, calls it "the consummate condition of the sons of God, which will render it evident that they are the sons of God."

The adoption of children, as we speak of it in English today, refers to the taking in of other people's children. This is *not* the meaning of the Greek *huiothesia*, for according to Gal. 4:1-7 this "placing as sons" affected those *already* children. This is not to imply, of course, that a stranger could not also be taken in and given a place as a full-grown son, but the point is that "adoption" here does not refer to mere acceptance into the family, but to *a declaration of full sonship*, with all its rights and privileges—and responsibilities.

In the life of the Hebrew boy there came a time, "appointed of the father," when "adoption" proceedings took place and the boy was *declared* to be the son and heir of the father.

Before that time he had been a son, indeed, but "under tutors and governors." He had been told what he must and must not, what he might and might not, do. In this he differed nothing from a servant.

But finally the "time appointed" arrives! He is growing up now. It is assumed that he will no longer need overseers to keep him in check. There has come to be a natural understanding and co-operation between father and son. And so the "adoption" proceedings take place: a *declaration*, public and official, that the lad now enters into all the rights and privileges of full sonship.

Such is the meaning of the word *adoption* as used in the writings of Paul.[4] How all this opens up the meaning of Rom. 8:15: "For ye have not received *the spirit of bondage again, to fear; but ye have received the Spirit of adoption*,

---

4. The author's booklet on *Sonship* goes into this subject more comprehensively, dealing also with the "adoption" of Israel and the "adoption" of Christ.

whereby we cry Abba [or] Father." True, we Gentile believers were once strangers and aliens, graciously taken into the family of God, but a careful examination of the above and related passages on "adoption" will clearly reveal that more than present-day adoption is meant.

The believer in this "dispensation of the grace of God" is not only saved from the penalty of sin, but is accepted as *the Father's fullgrown son in Christ, God's beloved Son.* He is given a position *in Christ* in the heavenlies at God's right hand, with free access to all the riches of the Father.

This is what so thrilled the heart of Paul as he exclaimed:

"Blessed be the God and Father of our Lord Jesus Christ, who hath blessed us with all spiritual blessings in heavenly places in Christ:

"According as He hath chosen us in Him before the foundation of the world, that we should be holy and without blame before Him in love:

"Having predestinated us unto the adoption of children [Gr., *huiothesian*] [5] by Jesus Christ unto Himself, according to the good pleasure of His will.

"To the praise of the glory of His grace, wherein He hath made us accepted in the Beloved" (Eph. 1:3-6).

But all the above does not militate against the idea that we are God's *born* children. Indeed, the opposite is the case, for the Apostle specifically states that *as fullgrown sons* we come into a deeper appreciation of the fact that we *are* God's children *by birth:*

"For...ye have received...*the Spirit of adoption*," he says, *"whereby we cry Abba, Father,"* and adds:

"The Spirit itself beareth witness with our spirit, that we are the children [6] of God:

"And if children [born ones], then heirs; heirs of God and joint-heirs

---

5. Here the AV translators departed from their own text. *Textus Receptus* reads "huiothesian," the placing as *sons,* i.e., grown sons, while the Greek for "children" is *nepioi.*

6. Here the word is *tekna,* "born ones." There is no English word for this, but the Scots have a word for it: *"bairn."* A mother might speak of the child she bore as her *"bairn."*

with Christ; if so be that we suffer with Him, that we may be also glorified together" (Rom. 8:16,17).

As *"joint-heirs with Christ"* we share in all of Christ's riches; not part belonging to each, but *all to both*. All He has is ours (I Cor. 3:21-23; II Cor. 4:15). *In Him* and *with Him* we are "blessed with all spiritual blessings in heavenly places" (Eph. 1:3). Some have erroneously equated this "joint-tenancy" with "tenancy in common," but in any case it is a "tenancy by *coparceny*," in which the coparceners, whatever their number, constitute but one heir. Thus we may also be assured that *"if so be that we suffer with Him,"* we shall also be *"glorified together."* With this thought the Apostle introduces the subject of our present sufferings and the glory to come (Rom. 8:18-27).

> What a prospect, child of glory,
>   Does the future hold in store!
> By the wildest flights of fancy
>   Thou couldst never ask for more.
> Heir of God, joint-heir forever,
>   With His own beloved Son!
> God could not to you have promised
>   More of bliss than He has done.
>
>   —Author unknown

We must always remember that this position of sonship and all that goes with it is ours by grace alone, *in Christ*. We could never have attained to the place where God could simply *trust us* to do what is right and wise and good. It was rather when we came to a realization of our utter *unworthiness* and placed our trust in Christ, God's perfect Son, that God accepted us, and *sees us now in His beloved Son, the Lord Jesus Christ*. And this is our position from the very moment that we place our trust in Christ, for Eph. 2:5,6 clearly states that,

"Even when we were dead in sins, [God] hath quickened us together with Christ (by grace ye are saved),

"And hath raised us up together, and made us sit together in heavenly places in Christ Jesus."

Thus, immediately, without any period of probation, He

places us not under the Law but, *as* and *in* His Son, under *grace*. Blessed thought!

But will not this produce careless living? *NO!* Such love will accomplish what the Law never could. It is natural that those whose hearts have been won by grace will now *long* to serve God acceptably, that their hearts will call upon Him as "Father," for love begets love (I John 4:10,19). Any other response is *un*natural and inconsistent.

"For sin shall not have dominion over you, FOR ye are not under the law, but under grace" (Rom. 6:14).

"For ye have not received the spirit of bondage again to fear; but ye have received the Spirit of adoption [sonship], whereby we cry, Abba, Father" (Rom. 8:15).

The Law from without, with its prohibitions, commands and threatenings, could only produce fear, but the Spirit resides within to produce that revolutionary change that causes us, as grown sons, to look to God and call Him *"Father"* with an intimacy that the Law forbade. No threat hangs over God's people today. Rather, we rejoice in *"this grace wherein we stand"* (Rom. 5:2). As to carnal Christians, they do well to carefully consider all these reasons why the Apostle bids us walk worthy of our calling (Eph. 4:1).

PRESENT SUFFERING AND THE GLORY TO COME

"For I reckon that the sufferings of this present time are not worthy to be compared with the glory which shall be revealed in us.

"For the earnest expectation of the creature waiteth for the manifestation of the sons of God.

"For the creature was made subject to vanity, not willingly, but by reason of Him who hath subjected the same in hope.

"Because the creature itself also shall be delivered from the bondage of corruption into the glorious liberty of the children of God.

"For we know that the whole creation groaneth and travaileth in pain together until now.

"And not only they, but ourselves also, which have the firstfruits of the

Spirit, even we ourselves groan within ourselves, waiting for the adoption, to wit, the redemption of our body.

"For we are saved by hope: but hope that is seen is not hope, for what a man seeth, why doth he yet hope for?

"But if we hope for that we see not, then do we with patience wait for it."
—Rom. 8:18-25

Many of God's dear children suffer much for Christ in addition to normal human suffering, yet none so much as did the Apostle Paul. By the time he had written this letter to the Romans he had already suffered the untold hardships recorded in II Cor. 11:23-28: unremitting labor, imprisonments, scourgings, beatings, close calls with death, stonings, shipwrecks, long hours clinging to debris out at sea, all kinds of perils, weariness, pain, hunger, cold, nakedness—this and much more, *in addition* to "the care of all the churches" that constantly weighed upon his heart and mind.

Yet it is this toiling, suffering, persecuted Apostle of Christ who says, both by divine inspiration and from an intimate knowledge of the God he represents:

"...I RECKON that the sufferings of this present time are NOT WORTHY TO BE COMPARED with the glory which shall be revealed in us" (Rom. 8:18).

In II Cor. 4:17 he refers to these sufferings as "light afflictions" which will continue "but for a moment," and compares them with the "far more exceeding and eternal weight of glory" to come. Thus the present sufferings are an *investment* in glory to come; a very profitable investment, the "light," "momentary" sufferings gaining for us *"a far more exceeding and eternal weight of glory."*

What an encouragement this should be to suffering Christians everywhere, and especially to those who are suffering for Christ. And mark well, this glory to come will not merely be revealed *to* us; it will be revealed "*in* us." *We* shall be glorified!

Nor are we alone in our sufferings. Indeed a suffering creation awaits with "earnest expectation" our "manifestation" as "the sons of God," for the creation too "was made subject to vanity," or *futility*, "not willingly, but by reason of Him who hath subjected the same"[7] (Ver. 20).

Thank God, as the curse upon man also brought a curse upon the creation about him,[8] this curse will be removed when believers are manifested as the sons of God:

"Because the creature itself also shall be delivered from the bondage of corruption into the glorious liberty of the children of God" (Ver. 21).

What a deliverance! *"From the bondage of corruption into the glorious liberty of the children of God"!*

When our Lord was on earth the masses did not recognize Him. Some said: "Why is He so important? Isn't He the carpenter's son? And His mother and brothers and sisters, aren't they all here with us?" He was the Son of God, but they did not recognize this. And if this was so with Him, how much more is it so with us. We pass among the throngs and rub elbows with them every day, but no one says, "There goes a child of God!" But when our Lord is *manifested*, *"then shall we also be manifested with Him in glory"* (Col. 3:4). And our manifestation with Christ at the Rapture will be but a foretaste of our manifestation together as the sons of God when He is crowned as King of kings and Lord of lords. Then the change in creation will be revolutionary! This is *really* what creation has been waiting for.

Now most of the sounds which emanate from this poor, bleeding world are in the minor key. The wind sighs, the ocean moans, cattle low and bleat, wild beasts roar and howl and scream, the owl hoots, the dove mourns; only a few birds sing, but this not in the sense that man can sing. Each knows only one simple refrain of not more than a bar or two, nor do they *really* sing for *joy*.

But what a difference there will be at the manifestation of the sons of God! What a difference when creation is "deliv-

---

7. Ver. 20 is obviously a parenthesis up to the words "in hope," which complete the sentence of Ver. 19: "The creation waiteth for the manifestation of the sons of God...in hope."

8. "Cursed is the ground for thy sake" (Gen. 3:17).

ered from the bondage of corruption into the glorious liberty of the children of God"! Many Old Testament Scriptures describe this change and some of them picture creation itself as joyful! For example:

"Make a joyful noise unto the Lord all the earth....let the floods clap their hands; let the hills be joyful together before the Lord; for He cometh to judge the earth" (Psa. 98:4-9).

"The wilderness and the solitary place shall be glad for them; and the desert shall rejoice, and blossom as the rose.

"It shall blossom abundantly, and rejoice even with joy and singing..." (Isa. 35:1,2).

"Sing, O heavens; and be joyful, O earth; and break forth into singing O mountains; for the Lord hath comforted His people" (Isa. 49:13).

"For ye shall go out with joy, and be led forth with peace: the mountains and the hills shall break forth before you into singing, and all the trees of the field shall clap their hands" (Isa. 55:12).

But there is an important dispensational lesson for us to learn with regard to the sufferings of humanity and of creation. Rom. 8:22,23 states:

"For we know that the whole creation groaneth and travaileth in pain together until now.

"And not only they, but ourselves also, which have the firstfruits of the Spirit, even we ourselves groan within ourselves, waiting for the adoption, to wit, the redemption of our body."

"The whole creation"—"even we"—"until now." These are important phrases to consider. "The nations" and "the people" of Israel (Psa. 2:1) have long sought to bring in "times of refreshing" *without Christ*, but all in vain. Statesmen have failed to abolish war and bloodshed. Magistrates have failed to eradicate vice and crime. The medical profession has failed to eliminate sickness and death. The scientists have failed to subdue the violent forces of nature. Educators have failed to dispel ignorance and superstition—even religion is a Babel of confusion. Indeed there has not been any *real* improvement along these lines. The whole creation groans and travails in pain together *"until now."*

The great promised change has not yet come.

What greater proof could we have that the kingdom of Christ has *not* been established on earth? When our Lord came preaching "the gospel of the kingdom" He healed thousands of sick people, and when Peter, after Pentecost, *offered* Messiah's return and the establishment of His kingdom, thousands more were healed in His name. These healings were "signs" of Messiah's royal rights (Isa. 35:5,6; Acts 2:22; John 20:30,31; Mark 16:17,18).

But then the King and His kingdom were finally and officially rejected and all those who had been healed ultimately died. And this condition has continued without interruption *"until now."* This explains why present-day "healings" must so often be questioned and why they *never* last, the healers themselves finally succumbing to death.

The late J. C. O'Hair was right when he said that despite all the healers, all the physicians, all the medicines and drugs—and all the prayers of God's people, the death rate still remains "one apiece." We all groan and travail in pain *"together, until now,"* and there will be no change until the "glorious manifestation of the sons of God." Lest any reader might presume that the above does not apply to believers, let us refer again to read Ver. 23:

"And not only they, but ourselves also, which have the firstfruits of the Spirit, even we ourselves groan within ourselves, waiting for the adoption, to wit, the redemption of our body."

This is not the place for an in-depth examination of the so-called "healing question," but suffice it to say that much disillusionment would be avoided if *the Pauline epistles* were recognized as containing God's Word *for today* as to sickness and healing, for today's healers are leaving behind them a long sad trail of disappointment and shaken faith. How many who teach "faith healing," for example, recognize those cases in which the Apostle Paul in his later ministry could not, certainly did not, heal beloved brethren who were sick? And how many of them can say with Paul:

"...Most gladly therefore will I rather glory in my infirmities, THAT THE POWER OF CHRIST MAY REST UPON ME.

"Therefore, *I take pleasure in infirmities*, in reproaches, in necessities, in persecutions, in distresses for Christ's sake; FOR WHEN I AM WEAK, THEN AM I STRONG" (II Cor. 12:9,10).

What could be clearer than the words of Rom. 8:23,24, that *we*, who "have the firstfruits of the Spirit, *even we* ourselves groan within ourselves, WAITING for the adoption, to wit, the redemption of our body. For we are saved by *hope*," i.e., we are saved from despair over our infirmities by the blessed "hope" of "the redemption of our body," and therefore we *"with patience wait for it"* (Ver. 25).

Thank God, we wait for something far better than the mere *healing* of our sick bodies, however. We wait for *glorified* bodies:

"For our conversation is in heaven, from whence also we look for the Savior, the Lord Jesus Christ;

"Who shall change our vile body, that it may be fashioned like unto His glorious body, according to the working whereby He is able even to subdue all things unto Himself" (Phil. 3:20,21).

Before leaving this section, let us note three things for which, basically, the instructed believer waits:

1. We *wait* for God's Son from heaven (I Thes. 1:9), to take us out of this world to be with Him (I Thes. 4:16-18; Tit. 2:13).

2. We "*wait* for the redemption of the body" (I Cor. 15:51-53; Phil. 3:20,21).

3. We "through the Spirit *wait* for the hope of righteousness [9] by faith" (Gal. 5:5).

Thus *"we rejoice in hope of the glory of God"* (Rom. 5:2), joyfully anticipating the fulfillment of God's gracious promises to those who trust Him in "this present evil age."

THE SPIRIT'S HELP

"Likewise the Spirit also helpeth our infirmities; for we know not what we should pray for as we ought: but the Spirit itself maketh intercession for us with groanings which cannot be uttered.

---

9. I.e., perfect, personal righteousness not yet attained in this life.

> "And He that searcheth the hearts knoweth what is the mind of the Spirit, because He maketh intercession for the saints according to the will of God.
>
> "And we know that all things work together for good to them that love God, to them who are the called according to His purpose."
>
> —Rom. 8:26-28

It should be noted here that while there is *"one Mediator between God and men"* (I Tim. 2:5) the believer has *two* divine *Intercessors*: one in heaven and one on earth; the Lord Jesus Christ at the Father's right hand, and the Holy Spirit within. The Lord Jesus intercedes where our *salvation* is concerned:

> "Who is he that condemneth? It is Christ that died, yea rather, that is risen again, who is even at the right hand of God, who also *maketh intercession for us*" (Rom. 8:34).

> "Wherefore He is able also to *save them to the uttermost* that come unto God by Him, *seeing He ever liveth to make intercession for them*" (Heb. 7:25).

The Holy Spirit, however, intercedes for us with respect to Christian *experience*. This is the teaching of Rom. 8:26. As "the Spirit itself [Himself] beareth witness with our spirit, that we are the children of God" (Ver. 16), so *"likewise* [He] also helpeth our infirmities; for we know not what we should pray for as we ought: but the Spirit itself [Himself] maketh intercession for us with groanings which cannot be uttered [I.e., inexpressible by us]" (Ver. 26).

Those who hold that believers should receive all they ask for in faith should consider this passage, for here the Apostle clearly states that *"we know not what we should pray for as we ought."* Indeed, this is why the Spirit makes intercession for us. How well it is for us in "this present evil age" that we do *not* receive all we ask for, even in faith! What problems we would create for ourselves if we did receive all we asked even in believing prayer!

Our Lord's "whatsoever" promises in Matt. 21:22, *et al*, were made with the establishment of His kingdom in view, when all will be filled with the Spirit and will know what to pray for, but in this age of darkness (Eph. 6:12) we often find ourselves saying, "I don't even know how to pray or what I should ask for." Hence God has given us His Spirit who, dwelling within, *"maketh intercession for us with groanings which cannot be uttered"* (Ver. 26).

We have indicated that the "likewise" of Ver. 26 refers back to Ver. 16; that as the Spirit bears witness with our spirit that we are the children of God, so "likewise" He *prays for us* with groanings that cannot be uttered. Some, however, feel that the "likewise" refers to the Spirit's groanings, taking us back to Vers. 22,23. As the "whole creation *groaneth*," and "even we...*groan* within ourselves," so "likewise the Spirit also," helping our infirmities, "maketh intercession for us with *groanings* which cannot be uttered."

In any case, His intercession *"for us"* with *"groanings which cannot be uttered"* indicates how infinite is His love for us.

Best of all, "He that searcheth the hearts" [I.e., God, I Sam. 16:7] "knoweth what is the mind of the Spirit, because *He* [the Spirit] *maketh intercession for the saints according to the will of God"* (Ver. 27). That is, God, who searches the heart, knows what in our prayers is merely the expression of our own finite, fallible mind, and what is the mind of the Spirit, who always prays for us *"according to the will of God."*

How important to rightly divide the Word of truth at this point! We are to pray now *not* like the importunate widow (Luke 18:2-7), nor according to Matt. 21:22 or Matt. 18:19, expecting whatever we ask in faith, but from acknowledged ignorance, weakness and need, always in subjection to the will of our wise and loving heavenly Father.

There is an additional reason for praying in this way during "this present evil age," for the Apostle continues:

"And we know that all things work together for good to them that love God, to them who are the called according to His purpose" (Ver. 28).

There are two things in Romans 8 that "we know":

(1) *"We know that the whole creation groaneth and travaileth in pain together until now"* (Ver. 22). The great prophesied change has not yet taken place. At Pentecost there seemed to be bright hope that the favored nation would repent and that Messiah would return to bring peace, prosperity and blessing, but *"His citizens hated Him, and sent a message after Him, saying, We will not have this man to reign over us"* (Luke 19:14; cf. Acts 7:51-59). Thus "the whole creation" continues to groan and travail in pain together *"until now,"* with no prospect of a change until our Lord comes in power and glory to *take* the throne that is rightfully His. But (2) in the meantime, *"we know that all things work together [10] for good to them that love God;[11] to them who are the called according to His purpose"* (Ver. 28).

We should also compare two passages in this chapter which refer to what *"we know not"* and to what *"we know."* "*We know not* what we should pray for as we ought" but, thank God, "*we know* that all things work together for good, to them that love God; to them who are the called according to His purpose" (Vers. 26,28).

What a strong ally we have in the Holy Spirit, who intercedes for us with groanings that cannot be uttered! What an ally in the Lord Jesus Christ, who also intercedes for us at the Father's right hand! And what a loving, faithful heavenly Father, who works all things out for our good!

But does this intercession indicate that the Father would not be willing of Himself to keep us secure, or to work all things out for our good? By no means, the language is couched so that finite man can understand for, actually, the very presence of our crucified, risen Lord at the Father's right hand is an effective plea in our behalf:

> Five bleeding wounds He bears,
> Received at Calvary;

---

10. Not luckily, but by design. God *causes* them to work together for our good.

11. Not to them that love God *enough* (See I John 4:10). Rather he is here contrasting those who love God with those who are unbelievers and do not.

> They pour effectual prayers;
>   They strongly plead for me.
> "Forgive him, oh, forgive," they cry,
>   "Nor let that ransomed sinner die."
>
> —Charles Wesley

So with the intercession of the Spirit in our behalf. This rather demonstrates the fact that God Himself—the Spirit a member of the Trinity—is deeply and personally interested in our weakness, and concerned that we pray aright, with requests that He can grant for our good.

This explains Phil. 4:6,7, where we find the highest form of prayer during the present dispensation:

"Be careful [anxious] for nothing, but in everything, by prayer and supplication, with thanksgiving, LET YOUR REQUESTS BE MADE KNOWN UNTO GOD, AND...."

"And" what? *"And whatsoever ye shall ask in prayer, believing, ye shall receive"*?

NO! This would be *tragic* today. Thus the passage reads:

"...let your requests be made known unto God,

"AND THE PEACE OF GOD, WHICH PASSETH ALL UNDERSTANDING, SHALL KEEP [Lit., GARRISON] YOUR HEARTS AND MINDS THROUGH CHRIST JESUS."

Here is ample proof that God is not deaf to the cries of His people in this evil age. He urges them to pour out all their hearts to Him. There is nothing about which He does not wish to hear. He says, "Tell Me *everything* and be anxious about *nothing*, for I'll work it all out for your good."

The late Pastor Edward Drew once told of a young man who had an important position with a large firm with an outpost high up in the frigid zone. One day he was called into the main office and told that he must take a journey far into the North by plane, train, ship and even dog-sled to their northern outpost. "When?" he asked. "Well, we want you to start tomorrow," was the answer. "But gentlemen," he remonstrated, "I am not ready. I haven't the slightest idea what might be necessary for such a journey." "We know you don't," replied the officer in charge, "but *we* do. We have everything planned and have provided every detail to the very end of your journey." Thus God has graciously provided for us—to the very end of our journey here.

"Whatsoever ye shall ask in prayer, believing, ye shall receive"? We have something much better than that now! In the darkness of this "evil age," we are instructed to take all our burdens to the Lord "with thanksgiving," being anxious for nothing since He has promised to work all out for our good. What more could we ask for! Little wonder the Apostle breaks out in the doxology of Eph. 3:20,21:

"Now unto Him that is able to do EXCEEDING ABUNDANTLY ABOVE ALL THAT WE ASK OR THINK, according to the power that worketh in us,

"Unto Him be glory in the Church, by Christ Jesus, throughout all ages, world without end. Amen."

THE CALLED ACCORDING TO HIS PURPOSE

"For whom He did foreknow, He also did predestinate to be conformed to the image of His Son, that He might be the firstborn among many brethren.

"Moreover whom He did predestinate, them He also called: and whom He called, them He also justified; and whom He justified, them He also glorified."

—Rom. 8:29,30

The above passage is a good introduction to the great truths of Romans 9. Anyone who reads Rom. 8:29,30 thoughtfully must be struck with the importance of *not* reading more into the Scriptures than they say or clearly imply.

This passage will help to explain what is meant by the phrase, *"the called according to His purpose,"* in Ver. 28.

First, Ver. 28 does *not* say that God's people are "called according to His purpose *to call them*," nor do we believe that this is the sense. Rather we believe that His purpose here refers to *"the eternal purpose which He purposed in Christ*

Jesus our Lord," the great subject of Paul's epistles (See Eph. 1:3-11; 3:1-11). This purpose, of course, *includes* individual believers.

Thus, covering the whole span from foreknowledge to glory, the Apostle says:

"For whom He did foreknow, He also did predestinate to be conformed to the image of His Son, that He might be the firstborn among many brethren" (Ver. 29).

But what is the "foreknowledge" referred to here? This is important, for *"whom He did foreknow,* He also did predestinate to be conformed to the image of His Son."

Does His foreknowledge here refer to the mere fact that He knew beforehand *who would be saved*? Hardly, for then God could predestinate only on the basis of what He knew—merely knew—men would do. Thus man's actions would govern God's!

It is true that God foreknew *all things* and therefore could elect reasonably rather than arbitrarily or capriciously (I Pet. 1:2), but this has no bearing *here,* for Rom. 8:29 does not state that God knew something—or all things—*about* us; it says He foreknew *us*: "For *whom* He did foreknow, He also did predestinate . . . ."

To understand this statement we must bear in mind that in Scripture, as in modern English, to *know* a person, or group of persons, is to recognize, to have regard for, or interest in, or a close acquaintance with. The following Scripture passages will bear this out:

"You only have I known of all the families of the earth . . ." (Amos 3:2 regarding Israel).

"And then will I profess unto them, *I never knew you*: depart from Me ye that work iniquity" (Matt. 7:23).

". . .ye have known God, or rather *are known of God* . . ." (Gal. 4:9).

Thus to foreknow a person is *to know him beforehand,* i.e., to recognize or regard him beforehand.

The argument so often heard, that "God foreknew everybody," denies the above facts and, indeed, the very passage we are considering, for "whom He did foreknow, He also did predestinate to be conformed to the image of His Son" and surely *all men* will not be conformed to the image of God's Son.

Predestination is to be distinguished from foreknowledge here, in that God's foreknowledge has special reference to the *person* foreknown, while predestination has reference rather to *that to which* the person foreknown is predestinated.

Before leaving Verse 29, we should note the fact that God will conform believers to the image of His Son *"that He might be the firstborn among many brethren."* In one sense our Lord is "the *only* begotten Son" of God (I John 4:9), but in another—and due to His redemptive work at Calvary—He is *"the firstborn among many brethren"* (See 8:16,17, where the word "children" is *tekna*—"born ones").

Being careful again not to read into a passage what it does not say, we should note that Vers. 29,30 present the *method* by which God leads His people, step by step, from foreknowledge to glory. "For whom He did *foreknow*, He also did *predestinate* ....Moreover whom He did predestinate, them He also *called*; and whom He called, [12] them He also *justified*; and whom He justified, them He also *glorified*."

Mark well that Vers. 29 and 30 are both in the past tense, for as far as God is concerned He sees us already glorified in Christ. The *Epistle to the Ephesians* has much to say about this, as in 2:4-6:

"But God, who is rich in mercy, for His great love wherewith He loved us,

"Even when we were dead in sins, hath quickened us together with Christ (by grace ye are saved),

"And hath raised us up together, and made us sit together in heavenly places in Christ Jesus."

---

12. This does not state, or imply, that He justified *all* those whom He called (Matt. 22:14). We will deal further with this word when we reach Chapter 9. At this point let us note that this passage deals only with believers, indicating the *method* by which God brings them to glory.

This is how God sees us in grace, and we may *now occupy* this God-given position by faith and appropriate the *"all spiritual blessings"* that go with it, until that blessed day when our Lord comes for us *Himself* and takes us physically, in glorified bodies, to be with Him (I Cor. 15:51-54; I Thes. 4:16-18).

There is a tendency among believers to minimize the reality of our position in Christ. Actually it should greatly encourage fainting, doubting Christians that *God* sees them *already in heaven*, and beckons them to rise experientially by faith above this sin-cursed world and *"seek those things which are above, where Christ sitteth on the right hand of God"* (Col. 3:1).

WHO CAN BE AGAINST US?

"What shall we then say to these things? If God be for us, who can be against us?

"He that spared not His own Son, but delivered Him up for us all, how shall He not with Him also freely give us all things?

"Who shall lay anything to the charge of God's elect? It is God that justifieth.

"Who is He that condemneth? It is Christ that died, yea rather, that is risen again, who is even at the right hand of God, who also maketh intercession for us."

—Rom. 8:31-34

We come now to the grand climax of the doctrinal part of Romans.

"If God be for us, who can be against us?"!

This makes us think of the small boy who had been constantly badgered by neighborhood bullies. It seemed that every day he came home with a bloody nose, a black eye, or scratched elbows or knees, until one day he walked confidently through their midst—hand in hand with his father. This time his tormentors drew back, saying, "We'd better leave him alone; his father is with him."

Ah, but Rom. 8:31 is more *grand* than this! It is the more powerful because it is put in the form of a challenge. It breathes defiance and confidence, taking us back to a line from one of John Newton's great hymns: *"Thou may'st smile at all thy foes."*

How wonderful to have *God* for us! He manifested this attitude toward us in the greatest gift ever given to mankind, *the Lord Jesus Christ*, His beloved Son, delivering Him to shame and death that even the vilest sinner may be redeemed and justified before the bar of justice. And the giving of this infinite gift proves that there is *no good thing* that He would withhold from us: *it is "the gift that includes all others."* [13]

To *begin* to appreciate the bestowal of this infinite gift, we must consider (1) *the love that prompted it* (John 3:16), (2) *its priceless value* (II Cor. 9:15), (3) *our deep need of it* (Rom. 6:23), and (4) *how gratuitous the offer* (Rom. 4:5; 10:13).

In this brief passage of the Word of God seven short phrases stand out, any one of which would provide material for many hours of Bible study. They are:

1. *"spared not"*   4. *"for us all"*
2. *"own Son"*   5. *"with Him"*
3. *"delivered up"*   6. *"freely give"*
    7. *"all things"*

Two of these demand our special attention in this volume: *"spared not"* and *"delivered up."*

In His love and compassion for doomed sinners, God *"spared not* His own Son, but *delivered Him up* for us all."

The words "spared not" have a rough, stern sound. Despite our Lord's divine and essential majesty, despite His infinite and perfect holiness, despite the humiliation He had already endured *for sinners*, despite the agonized prayer, *"Father if it be possible, let this cup pass from Me,"* despite the "exceeding sorrow," the bloody sweat, the "strong crying and tears," despite the infinite disgrace and agony involved—despite all this the Father spared Him not, but delivered Him up to bear a load that would have sunk a world to hell.

We can understand how even a merciful God "spared not

---

13. See the author's booklet under this title.

the angels that sinned" (II Pet. 2:4) in those days of antediluvian wickedness. We can understand how He "spared not the old world" (Ver. 5) with its vile revelry and godlessness. We can understand how He "spared not" Israel, "the natural branches" of His olive tree (Rom. 11:21) when they stood by the awful deed committed at Calvary. But the infinite purpose and grace that impelled Him *not* to spare His own sinless, spotless Son but to deliver *Him* up for us all, that *we* might be spared—this is utterly beyond our comprehension. "Rooted and grounded in love," we should ever keep measuring "the breadth, and length, and depth, and height" of this, God's great purpose in Christ (Eph. 3:17,18).

The words "delivered up," in our text, have the idea of giving up, or giving over to another, or to another's power— *as a last necessity*. Could a million worlds have paid for man's sin, God would gladly have robbed the heavens of them, or spoken a million more into space, but material transactions cannot right moral wrongs, much less can they impart spiritual life. The price of man's redemption could be nothing less than the suffering and death of Christ, God's beloved Son.

As we ponder all this we *begin* to see the power of the Apostle's argument as to the infinite character of God's love for us.

"He that spared not His own Son, but delivered Him up for us all, HOW SHALL HE NOT WITH HIM ALSO FREELY GIVE US ALL THINGS?" (Rom. 8:32).

Thus God has *"saved us, and called us with an holy calling, not according to our works, but according to His own purpose and [His own] grace, which was given us in Christ Jesus before the world began"* (II Tim. 1:9).

It is because those who love God are "the called according to His purpose" that He works all out for their good. It is on this basis alone that we can say with confidence: *"If God be for us, who can be against us?"* What if some have gone to one-sided and unscriptural extremes in this matter? This should not harden our hearts to what God has said about it. Rather than questioning these truths and minimizing "the glory of His grace," let us stand amazed and grateful that He has saved *us*.

But if Vers. 31,32 are the text, Vers. 33,34 are the sermon—with a four-fold assurance for wavering believers of our eternal security in Christ. Consider the four headings carefully:

1. *"Who Shall Lay Anything to the Charge of God's Elect?"* The answer: *"It is God That Justifieth"* (Ver. 33), and this is what *really* matters.

2. *"Who is He That Condemneth?"* Again the answer: *"It is Christ That Died"* (Ver. 34). He paid the penalty for our sins that we might *not* be condemned. But more:

3. *"Yea, Rather, That is Risen Again"* (Ver. 34). We have seen at Rom. 4:25 that as our Lord died to pay the debt of our sins, He arose again to prove that the debt was fully paid. Who, then, can condemn us?

4. *"Who is Even at the Right Hand of God, Who Also Maketh Intercession For Us"* (Ver. 34). How can we be condemned while God's precious Son, our Savior, appears in His presence *in our behalf?* (Cf. Heb. 7:25; 9:24).[14]

What blessed assurance for the fainting believer! True, Satan accuses, the Law condemns, and our hearts acknowledge that daily we sin in thought, in word and in deed. But our glorious Lord defeated Satan at the Cross, making a show of him openly (Col. 2:15), and as to the Law, He took that out of the way, "nailing it to His Cross" (Col. 2:14). As to the sins our hearts must continually acknowledge, has not God justified us, did not Christ die to pay our debt and rise to prove it paid—and does He not intercede for us at this very moment? Let us then put aside our doubts and fears, rejoicing that "if God be for us" we are eternally secure.

Does this promote lax conduct in the believer? Indeed

---

14. It will be observed that in the *Authorized Version* the words *"It is,"* in Vers. 33 and 34, appear in italics, having been supplied by the translators. If omitted, the answer to each challenge becomes a question, thus: *"Who shall lay anything to the charge of God's elect? God that justifieth? Who is he that condemneth? Christ that died?"* etc. Indeed, Ver. 35 continues in this way. Either way, however, the sense is not changed.

not. In fact God's infinite grace to us offers the greatest possible incentive to holy living, an incentive that the Law could not possibly provide. Let us not tell God what *we think* will promote more godly or more careless conduct among His people! *He says* that it is *His grace* that "teaches," or disciplines us to live "soberly, righteously and godly in this present world" (Tit. 2:11,12).

But the Apostle is not yet through emphasizing the believer's security in Christ. In closing this important section of his *Epistle to the Romans* he takes us from the courtroom to the Father's House, as it were, where we learn the final lesson as to this precious truth.

WHO SHALL SEPARATE US?

"Who shall separate us from the love of Christ? shall tribulation, or distress, or persecution, or famine, or nakedness, or peril, or sword?

"As it is written, For Thy sake we are killed all the day long: we are accounted as sheep for the slaughter.

"Nay, in all these things we are more than conquerors through Him that loved us.

"For I am persuaded that neither death, nor life, nor angels, nor principalities, nor powers, nor things present, nor things to come,

"Nor height, nor depth, nor any other creature, shall be able to separate us from the love of God, which is in Christ Jesus our Lord."

—Rom. 8:35-39

"Who shall separate us from the love of Christ?" Could the believer possibly have greater assurance of his eternal security than this? The writer has known several individuals in his experience who thought the doctrine of the believer's eternal security in Christ to be a dangerous heresy. They countered every Scripture on the subject with another to refute it. But in each of these cases it was this great truth, *"Who shall separate us from the love of Christ,"* that finally persuaded them.

It is significant that the Apostle Paul never tells us about his love for Christ, but he is always telling us about Christ's love for him and for others! The Law commands: *"Thou shalt love the Lord thy God,"* but grace puts it the other way, telling us how deeply *God* loves *us*—and this begets love in return. "We love Him *because He first loved us*" (I John 4:19). The Apostle experienced discouragements that would have caused him to give up the work of the Lord a thousand times, but *he could not*. Why? He says, *"the love of Christ constraineth us"* (II Cor. 5:14); it bore him along like a strong tide. No doubt he had this very thing in mind when he continued writing in Romans 8.

"For Thy sake we are killed all the day long...accounted as sheep for the slaughter" (Ver. 36).

And therefore defeated? Far from it! Listen:

"Nay, in all these things we are more than conquerors through Him that loved us" (Ver. 37).

Not only do we win the battle; we are "more than conquerors," for these adversities serve to draw us into still closer fellowship with Him, thus enriching our Christian experience.

Thus this great chapter opens with *"no condemnation"* and closes with *"no separation,"* and the Apostle, gathering all the forces of creation together, whether they be time, space, or matter, declares that *none* of them can separate us from "the love of God, which is [manifested] in Christ Jesus" (Vers. 38,39). Whether it be death or life, heavenly principalities, things present or to come, height or depth or any created thing, none of them, nor all together, can threaten our security or separate us from the love of God, which He has manifested to us in Christ Jesus.

> The work which His goodness began,
>   The arm of His strength will complete;
> His promise is "Yea and Amen"
>   And never was forfeited yet.
>
> Things future and things that are now—
>   Not all things below, nor above,
> Can make Him His purpose forego,
>   Or sever my soul from His love.
>
>   —Augustus M. Toplady

Chapter IX — Romans 9:1-33

THE OPENING OF THE DISPENSATIONAL SECTION OF ROMANS

PAUL'S SORROW OVER HIS UNBELIEVING KINSMEN

"I say the truth in Christ; I lie not, my conscience also bearing me witness in the Holy Ghost.

"That I have great heaviness and continual sorrow in my heart.

"For I could wish that myself were accursed from Christ for my brethren, my kinsmen according to the flesh."
—Rom. 9:1-3

Why this sudden change in subject? The Apostle has taken eight chapters to lead us step by logical step to the great truths of 8:33-39. One would think he would now be ready for the application of these truths to our practical lives, as found in Chapters 12 to the end. How appropriate this would seem to be at this point!

Instead, there is a sudden interruption, while for three chapters Paul deals with the fall of Israel and her present position before God.

There is scarcely a mention of this in the first eight chapters. There he proclaims grace and complete justification through faith in Christ alone to Jew and Gentile alike, placing them on a common level. Had he forgotten the promises of God that Israel should be His *"peculiar,"* His *"special"* people? Once he had been a zealot for His nation. Had he now become a traitor, indifferent to their fate? He *must* now reconcile the world-wide offer of grace and justification by faith alone with the special blessings promised to Israel. This he does in the dispensational parenthesis of Chapters 9—11.

Indifferent? A casual reading of Chapters 1—8 might make it appear so, but he swears before God that this is not so. If the opening verses of Chapter 1 express his love for the Gentiles, the opening verses of Chapter 9 express, with deep feeling, his love for his unbelieving kinsmen. *"Great heaviness and continual sorrow"* filled his heart for them. Indeed, he affirms with an oath that he could wish himself accursed from Christ in their stead.

This is not less than the love that Moses himself showed toward the sinful nation in his impassioned prayer of Ex. 32:31,32:

"...Oh, this people have sinned a great sin, and have made them gods of gold.

"Yet now, if Thou wilt forgive their sin—; and if not, blot me, I pray Thee, out of Thy book which thou hast written."

Luke, in *The Acts of the Apostles*, confirms Paul's burden for Israel, for there, while laboring faithfully among the Gentiles to whom he had been sent, we find the Apostle's heart continually turning back to Jerusalem and his kinsmen there.

Note the words "could" and "wish" in Rom. 9:3, however, for sincerely as he might *"wish"* that he *"could"* take their place, he could not so soon forget his own Spirit-inspired words of 8:35: *"Who shall separate us from the love of Christ?"*

ISRAEL'S PLACE OF PRIVILEGE

"Who are Israelites; to whom pertaineth the adoption, and the glory, and the covenants, and the giving of the law, and the service of God, and the promises;

"Whose are the fathers, and of whom as concerning the flesh Christ came, who is over all, God blessed for ever. Amen."

—Rom. 9:4,5

The Apostle begins, then, by acknowledging that Israel does have a special place in the program of God—just as he bids us Gentile believers to "remember" that *we*, in time past, *"were without Christ, being aliens from the commonwealth of Israel, and strangers from the covenants of promise, having no hope and without God in the world"* (Eph. 2:11,12). To Israel, exclusively, pertained:

"the adoption and the glory," for the time *will* come when "all Israel shall be saved" and will be glorified, as they are publicly declared to be the sons of God (Hos. 1:10).

"and the covenants," the "covenants of promise" having been made with Israel alone, not with the Gentiles (Eph. 2:12).

"and the giving of the law, and the service of God," God's Word and worship also having been committed exclusively to Israel (Ex. 25:8-16,21,22).

"and the promises," all those exciting predictions of Israel's coming glory under Christ, her King (Isa. 35; 60:1-3; 61:3-6).

"whose are the fathers," Abraham, Isaac and Jacob, for whose sakes God would ever love them (Rom. 11:28).

"and of whom, as concerning the flesh, Christ came, who is over all, God blessed forever. Amen." This last is by far Israel's greatest honor, though she does not now recognize it.

THE BASIC THEME OF CHAPTERS 9—11

Before going further into the actual text of Chapter 9, we quote here a very penetrating passage by J. Sidlow Baxter:

"The apostle has now completed his main argument (i-viii), showing how the Gospel saves the individual human sinner. Glorious though this Gospel is, however, he simply cannot leave off there and affect blindness to the acute problem which it raises in relation to the nation Israel. If Gentiles are now accepted, justified, given sonship and promise, on equal footing with the Jews, what about Israel's special covenant relationship with God? Does not this new 'Gospel' imply that God has now 'cast away His people which He foreknew' (xi. 2)?

"If the new 'Gospel' *does* mean that, are not God's dealings with Israel the most hypocritical enigma and irony of history? Were not the covenant people the repository of most wonderful Messianic promises? Were not the godly among them right in anticipating Messiah's coming as that which would end the sufferings of their people, when the scattered tribes should be regathered as one purified Israel, and the nation, so long ruled by the Gentiles, should at last be exalted *over* them? Yet now that Messiah had come, instead of consummation for Israel there was the most reactionary of all paradoxes—those to whom the covenant promises were given were apparently shut out, and all the long-looked-for benefits were going to Gentile outsiders!

"Well, that is the background problem of Romans ix-xi, and it is vital to realise it in considering any of the foreground statements separately. But besides this, if we are going to interpret truly *any* of these Pauline statements on the Divine sovereignty, we must keep to the *point* and the *scope* of the passage. As to the former, Paul's purpose is to show that (*a*) the present by-passing of Israel nationally is not inconsistent with the Divine promises (see ix. 6-13); (*b*) because Israel's present sin and blindness nationally is overruled in blessing to both Jews and Gentiles as individuals (see xi. 23 - xi. 25); (*c*) and because 'all Israel *shall* yet be saved' at a postponed climax, inasmuch as 'the gifts and calling of God are irreversible' (see xi. 26-36).

"As to the *scope* of the passage, it will by now have become obvious that it is all about God's dealings with men and nations historically and dispensationally, and is *not* about individual salvation and destiny beyond the grave. Now *that* is the absolutely *vital* fact to remember in reading the problem-verses of these chapters, especially the paragraph ix. 14-22.

"John Calvin is wrong when he reads into these verses election either to salvation or to damnation in the eternal sense. That is not their scope. They belong only to a Divine economy of *history*. Paul opens the paragraph by asking: 'Is there then unrighteousness with God?'—and the rest of the paragraph is meant to show that the answer is 'No'; but if these verses referred to *eternal* life and death, there *would* be unrighteousness with God;

and that which is implanted deepest in our moral nature by God Himself would protest that even God has no honourable right to create human beings whose destiny is a predetermined damnation.

"No, this passage does not comprehend the *eternal* aspects of human destiny: Paul has already dealt with those in chapters i-viii. It is concerned (let us emphasize again) with *the historical and dispensational*. Once that is seen, there is no need to 'soften down' its terms or 'explain away' one syllable of it. Even the awesome words to Pharaoh (verse 17) can be faced in their full force—'Even for this same purpose have I raised thee up, that I might show My power in thee, and that My name might be declared throughout all the earth.' The words 'raised thee up' do not mean that God had raised him up from *birth* for this purpose: they refer to his elevation to the highest throne on earth. Nay, as they occur in Exodus ix. 16, they scarce mean even *that*, but only that God had kept Pharaoh from dying in the preceding plague, so as to be made the more fully an object lesson to all men.

"Moreover, when Paul (still alluding to Pharaoh) says, 'And whom He [God] will, He *hardeneth*' (verse 18), we need not try to soften the word. God did not override Pharaoh's own will. The hardening was a reciprocal process. Eighteen times we are told that Pharaoh's heart was 'hardened' in refusal. In about half of these the hardening is attributed to Pharaoh himself; in the others, to God. But the whole contest between God and Pharaoh must be interpreted by what God said to Moses before ever the contest started: 'The king of Egypt *will not* . . .' (Exod. iii. 19). The will was already set. The heart was already hard. God *overruled* Pharaoh's will, but did not *override* it. The hardening process developed inasmuch as the plagues forced Pharaoh to an issue which *crystallised* his sin.

"Thus Pharaoh was made an object-lesson to all the earth (Rom. ix. 17). But Pharaoh's *eternal* destiny is not the thing in question; and moreover in thus making an example of this 'vessel of wrath' who was 'fit for [such] destruction' (verse 22), God was working out a vast purpose which was not only righteous, but overrulingly *gracious* towards many millions of 'vessels of mercy which He had afore prepared unto glory,' as we learn in verse 23!

"It is always important to distinguish between Divine foreknowledge and Divine predestination. God foreknows everything that every man will do; but He does not *predetermine* everything that every man does. Nay, that would make God the author of sin!

"God foreknew that Esau would despise his birthright; that Pharaoh would be wicked; that Moses would sin in anger at Meribah; that the Israelites would rebel at Kadesh-Barnea; that Judas would betray our Lord; that the Jews would crucify their Messiah: but not one of these things did God *predetermine*. To say that He did would involve Him in the libellous contradiction of predetermining men to commit what He Himself declared to be *sin*. God did *not* predetermine these sinful acts of men; but He *did* foreknow them, and anticipate them, and overrule them to the fulfilling of His further purposes.

"We mention this because it involves Esau, Pharaoh, and Moses, all of whom Paul cites in Romans ix. Let us say two things emphatically of Pharaoh in particular: (1) God did not create him to be a wicked man; (2) God did not create him to be a damned soul. And, with mental relief, let us further say that God could never create *any* man either to be wicked or to be eternally damned. 'Is there unrighteousness with God? God forbid!' In Romans ix we simply must *not* read an after-death significance into what is solely historical. Moses, because of his sin at Meribah, was denied entrance into the promised land; but would we argue that this punishment extended in any way to the salvation of his soul beyond the grave? Thousands upon thousands of Israelites died in the wilderness because of that grievous sin at Kadesh-Barnea; but were they all lost souls beyond the grave? Look up some of the generous offerings and acts of devotion mentioned earlier in connection with some of them!" (*Explore the Book*, by J. Sidlow Baxter, Vol. VI, Pp. 87-90, Marshall, Morgan and Scott, Ltd.)

A THEOLOGICAL BATTLEGROUND

"Not as though the Word of God hath taken none effect. For they are not all Israel which are of Israel:

"Neither because they are the seed of Abraham, are they all children, but, In Isaac shall thy seed be called.

"That is, They which are the children of the flesh, these are not the children of God: but the children of promise are counted for the seed.

"For this is the word of promise, At this time will I come, and Sarah shall have a son.

"And not only this; but when Rebecca also had conceived by one, even by our father Isaac;

"(For the children being not yet born, neither having done any good or evil, that the purpose of God according to election might stand, not of works, but of Him that calleth,)

"It was said unto her, The elder shall serve the younger.

"As it is written, Jacob have I loved, but Esau have I hated."

—Rom. 9:6-13

Chapter 9, beginning with this passage, has long been a theological battleground. Actually there has been much needless acrimony over this chapter, largely because some have read into it what it does not say, even using Ver. 13 to teach that God loves only the elect and hates all the non-elect.

Surely the above passage has nothing to do with predestination to heaven or hell. It does not say, nor imply, that God gave eternal life to Jacob but consigned Esau to eternal damnation, much less that God loved Jacob and hated Esau *before they were born*. Nor yet does "the purpose of God according to election," in Ver. 11, have to do with eternal salvation and reprobation, but rather with His purpose to make the descendants of Jacob, rather than those of Esau, His special people.

The words "as it is written," in Ver. 13, should lead true Bereans to go back to the Old Testament record and take note that God did not say that He loved Jacob or hated Esau *personally*, any more than Gen. 25:23 says that Esau should serve Jacob personally—which he never did.

Both Verses 12 and 13 refer to Jacob and Esau only as representative of the races they fathered. As to Ver. 12, we have the very words of God to Rebekah *in their context* in Gen. 25:23:

"And the Lord said unto her, TWO NATIONS are in thy womb, and TWO MANNER OF PEOPLE shall be separated from thy bowels; THE ONE PEOPLE shall be stronger than THE OTHER PEOPLE; and the elder shall serve the younger."

As to the quotation in Ver. 13, these words were spoken long after Jacob and Esau had died and their progeny had become great races of people. Whereas the quotation in Ver. 12 is taken from a passage in Genesis, the *first* book of the "Old Testament," that in Ver. 13 is taken from a passage in Malachi, the *last*. This passage (Mal. 1:1-4) is also very revealing as to whom God is discussing, Jacob and Esau personally, or the races that sprang from them:

"The burden of the word of the Lord TO ISRAEL by Malachi.

"I HAVE LOVED YOU, saith the Lord. Yet ye say, Wherein hast Thou loved us? WAS NOT ESAU JACOB'S BROTHER? saith the Lord, YET I LOVED JACOB,

"AND I HATED ESAU, AND LAID HIS MOUNTAINS AND HIS HERITAGE WASTE FOR THE DRAGONS OF THE WILDERNESS.

"Whereas Edom [Esau] saith, We are impoverished, but we will return and build the desolate places; thus saith the Lord of hosts, They shall build, but I will throw down; and they shall call them, The border of wickedness, and, The people against whom the Lord hath indignation forever." (Cf. also Ezek. 35:9,15).

Thus it was *representatively* and *comparatively* and *dispensationally* that God "loved Jacob" and "hated[1] Esau." To Israel, represented by Jacob, He gave a fruitful land, the written Law, the tabernacle and temple worship and much more that was denied to the offspring of Esau. Esau's

---

1. A glance at Luke 14:26; John 12:25, *et al*, should convince the discerning student that the word "hate" (Gr., *miseo*), used here in Rom. 9:13, does not always contain the idea of enmity but sometimes, as in this case, involves a strong preference for one over another.

descendants have, ever since their father's day, been known as children of the desert, and are today the nomadic tribes of Araby, characterized by their father's independent, lawless spirit.

Surely it would not be strange if God had said in Malachi that He had hated Esau personally, even in the accepted sense for, unlike Jacob, with all his faults, he obviously had no interest in the things of God. Esau was "a cunning hunter" (Gen. 25:27), who did not wish to stay at home with those who were "heirs together of the same promises." A sinewy son of the desert with its boundless horizons and lawless freedom, he loved to roam the wilderness and go where and when he chose, though often he did return to Isaac who, unhappily, *"loved Esau because he did eat of his venison"* (Gen. 25:28).

But more took place in Esau's lifetime to mold the character of those who should spring from his loins. Heb. 12:16 calls him a *"profane person...who for one morsel of meat sold his birthright,"* and the Genesis record states that he "*despised* his birthright," not only in his hunger, but after he had been well fed (Gen. 25:34).

When one considers all that is involved in the birthright in a Hebrew family, it is evident that Esau had not sold *his* birthright on the spot. No one sells his birthright on the spot. "Profane" man that he was, he had despised it in his heart long before he sold it for a morsel of food.

It would not be strange, we say, that God should hate Esau. What *is* strange is that He should love Jacob, who had serious flaws in his own character. The great difference between them was, however, that whereas Esau despised his birthright and the blessings that went with it, Jacob deeply desired these. The manner in which he obtained them was unquestionably ignoble, but God looked past all this at Jacob's sincere longing for *His blessings and Himself,* making him the progenitor of the favored nation and its Messiah. This is doubtless one reason why Psa. 146:5 says, *"Happy is he that hath the God of Jacob for his help...."*

THEY ARE NOT ALL ISRAEL
WHICH ARE OF ISRAEL

As Paul's heart bled because his nation was not saved from sin (Rom. 9:1-3; 10:1-3) so the nation itself chafed under the bondage of Rome and some argued that if Jesus was the Messiah God's Word had failed, for rather than having delivered them from Roman bondage it seemed that God had abandoned them.

This, says the Apostle, was not so, for *"they are not all Israel which are of Israel,"* as their own national history and their own prophetic Scriptures proved.

The promise to Abraham had not been, "In *all* thy seed shall all the nations of the earth be blessed," but *"In thy seed shall all the nations of the earth be blessed"* (Gen. 22:18), and this distinction had already been demonstrated in a positive manner. Abraham had one son by Hagar, his bondslave, and later another by Sarah, his legitimate wife, who bore him a son when he was 100 years of age and she 90 (Gen. 17:17; 21:1-5). Abraham had pleaded with God that Ishmael might be accepted (Gen. 17:18) but God's answer was: *"In Isaac shall thy seed be called"* (Gen. 17:19; 21:12). Ishmael was the product of unbelief. Abraham and Sarah had sought to help God fulfill His promise, as it were, before it was "too late." But God fulfilled His promise even when it seemed all hope was gone, and commanded Abraham:

"Cast out the bondwoman and her son: for the son of the bondwoman shall not be heir with the son of the freewoman" (Gal. 4:30).

Thus Ishmael and all his offspring were excluded from the promised seed (Rom. 9:7-9). But lest it should be argued that the offspring of Ishmael were not Abraham's *legitimate* seed anyway, the Apostle goes on to point out that Isaac in turn had two sons by the *same* wife, one of whom, along with all his progeny, was also excluded from the promised seed (Rom. 9:10-13).

Thus, as we have already stated, "the purpose of God

according to election," in Ver. 11, has nothing whatever to do with the election of individuals to salvation or damnation, but with His sovereign right to choose Israel rather than the offspring of Esau to further His purposes. But even the opening words of this verse do not teach *arbitrary* election; they only teach that election is *"not of works, but of Him that calleth."*

No doubt the general doctrine of election is indirectly involved here, but why balk at this? *"Shall not the Judge of all the earth do right?"* *Must* we assume that He is callous, or arbitrary, much less capricious in His elective acts? Robert Shank rightly says of Rom. 9:11:

"Paul asserts only the inherent freedom of God, as a sovereign Creator, to act without becoming accountable to His creatures. But this must not be construed to mean that God is not governed by moral principles inherent in His own holy character and that He is at liberty to be arbitrary or capricious. God is governed in His actions, not by His creatures, but by the moral integrity of His own Person" *(Life in the Spirit*, by Robert Shank, P. 343, Westcott Publishers).

The basic argument of Rom. 9:6-13 is, of course, that *"they are not all Israel, which are of Israel,"* for as we shall see, not even all the physical offspring of *Jacob* who lived in Paul's day were "the children of promise." Some of them were willful unbelievers.

IS THERE UNRIGHTEOUSNESS WITH GOD?

"What shall we say then? Is there unrighteousness with God? God forbid.

"For He saith to Moses, I will have mercy on whom I will have mercy, and I will have compassion on whom I will have compassion.

"So then it is not of him that willeth, nor of him that runneth, but of God that showeth mercy.

"For the Scripture saith unto Pharaoh, Even for this same purpose have I raised thee up, that I might show My power in thee, and that My name might be declared throughout all the earth.

> "Therefore hath He mercy on whom He will have mercy, and whom He will He hardeneth."
>
> —Rom. 9:14-18

While recognizing the fact that God is still speaking historically here of His right to deal with men as *He* sees fit, it must be acknowledged that more than this is indirectly involved.

There are two sides to grace, and Romans deals with them both. One side is represented in Rom. 10:12,13:

> "For there is no difference between the Jew and the Greek: for *the same Lord over all is rich unto all that call upon Him.*
>
> "For WHOSOEVER SHALL CALL UPON THE NAME OF THE LORD SHALL BE SAVED."

This is grace indeed; salvation full and free, offered to all who will simply *"call upon the name of the Lord."*

But there is another side to grace—a side against which many people rebel. It is the side that proclaims salvation as wholly of God, entirely apart from man's will or his works.

Having shown that God is not answerable to man for His elective acts, the Apostle asks and answers a question that this fact has raised in many a mind: *"Is there unrighteousness with God?"* Such a conclusion the Apostle utterly repudiates, showing that it was in perfect righteousness—and mercy—that God said to Moses:

> "...I will have mercy on whom I will have mercy, and I will have compassion on whom I will have compassion" (Ver. 15).

This is Paul's second reference to the incident in which Moses so fervently interceded for his wayward people. They had broken the very first of the Ten Commandments and had worshipped a golden calf. Surely God would have been wholly righteous had He destroyed them all. But was it therefore *un*righteous of Him to have mercy on those whom He chose to spare? especially with Calvary in view? As we know, He spared the whole nation at this time, so that ever after Israel owed all her blessings to the God of *mercy* and *compassion*.

Note that the negative does not yet enter in here. He speaks only of God's sovereign right to show *mercy* and *compassion*—according to His will—toward those condemned by sin, showing that "it is not of him that willeth, nor of him that runneth," i.e., not of man's will, nor of his works, *"but of God that showeth mercy"* (Ver. 16).

But now, having vindicated God's sovereignty in showing mercy, the Apostle proceeds further to vindicate His sovereignty in exercising judgment and wrath.

"For the Scripture saith unto Pharaoh, Even for this same purpose have I raised thee up, that I might show My power in thee, and that My name might be declared throughout all the earth.

"Therefore hath He mercy on whom He will have mercy, *and whom He will He hardeneth*" (Vers. 17,18).

Before exclaiming: "That *is* unrighteous!" let us examine the passage and the record in Exodus thoughtfully.

Is it possible that God *arbitrarily* chooses individuals, one here, another there, to harden and destroy? Does not His *foreknowledge* enter into His dealings with men; are there no *moral principles* involved? Is God a despot, a tyrant, who creates some men simply to destroy them? And shall we assume that because there are passages on election in which no conditioning factor is mentioned, that therefore none exists?

The phrase *"raised thee up"* surely does not indicate that God had *created* Pharaoh to make an example of him, for there were doubtless many other Egyptians as obstinate as Pharaoh and they were all drowned together in the Red Sea. His meaning was doubtless that He had raised Pharaoh up to his position as *the highest ruler in the world* so that His contest with him might have historical consequence. And this it did. As a result the Israelites, rescued from their oppressors, could sing:

"The people shall hear, and be afraid....The dukes of Edom shall be amazed; the mighty men of Moab, trembling shall take hold upon them; all the inhabitants of Canaan shall melt away" (Ex. 15:14,15).

Forty years later Rahab of Jericho said to the spies from Israel:

> "I know that the Lord hath given you the land, and that your terror is fallen upon us, and that all the inhabitants of the land faint because of you.
>
> "For we have heard how the Lord dried up the water of the Red Sea for you, when ye came out of Egypt....
>
> "And as soon as we had heard these things, our hearts did melt, neither did there remain any more courage in any man because of you: for the Lord your God, He is God in heaven and in earth beneath" (Josh. 2:9-11).

Still later the Gibeonites said to Joshua:

> "From a very far country thy servants are come because of the name of the Lord thy God; for we have heard the fame of Him, and all that He did in Egypt" (Josh. 9:9).

Indeed, to this day, wherever throughout the world the record in Exodus is read, God's purpose in raising up Pharaoh is realized, i.e., *"to show My power in thee, and that My name might be declared throughout all the earth."*

But what about the declaration that *"whom He will He hardeneth"*? F. L. Godet rightly says of this: "There would be something revolting to the conscience in supposing that God could Himself have impelled Pharaoh inwardly to evil" (*Commentary on the Epistle to the Romans*, by F. L. Godet, Zondervan Publishing Co.). This is true, for *"God cannot be tempted with evil, neither tempteth He any man"* (James 1:13).

But do not the Scriptures *say* that God hardened Pharaoh's heart? Did not God tell Moses *in advance* that He would do so (Ex. 4:21)?

Yes, but do not conclude from this that "poor, dear Pharaoh" had a tender, trusting heart, which was then hardened by God, for this would implicate God in double dealing. Those who reason thus have God sending Moses and Aaron to Pharaoh to say, *"Let My people go"*; then whispering in Pharaoh's ear, as it were: *"Don't you do it!"* Indeed, this would involve God in *both* dishonesty and injustice, for, according to this theory, God sent Moses and Aaron to say to Pharaoh, "Let My people go"; then influenced Pharaoh *not* to let them go, and *then* judged him for not letting them go!

The truth is that God hardened Pharaoh's heart only *indirectly* and *instrumentally*. He knew beforehand the haughty pride of the one who would say, *"Who is the Lord, that I should obey His voice to let Israel go? I know not the Lord, neither will I let Israel go"* (Ex. 5:2), and God was about to *show* Pharaoh who the God of Israel was!

Thus while Pharaoh hardened his heart against God's demand, it was God who made the demand, bringing about the circumstances in which He knew Pharaoh's self-will would be asserted. And so, by judgment and respite, by wrath and compassion, Pharaoh's hard heart was further hardened.

The hearts of many criminals have been similarly hardened when appealed to by the alternate exercise of judgment and mercy. Shall we then charge those who have employed these measures with directly hardening the criminals' hearts?

Much has been said and written about "irresistible grace." Perhaps "resistible grace" should be given equal time!

All this has its application to us who live in the dispensation of the grace of God. We have seen that the Lord is *"rich unto all that call upon Him"* and that *"whosoever shall call upon the name of the Lord shall be saved"* (Rom. 10:12,13). This is wonderful grace: salvation, purchased for us by the blood of Christ and bestowed as a free gift upon all who will receive it in faith.

But Romans 9 deals with the other side of grace, which teaches us that it is *He* who in providence and love works conviction in the heart and saves the believing sinner. *And*, as He convicts and saves some, He inevitably hardens others, not directly, but indirectly, as we have seen in the case of Pharaoh.

The Universalists, claiming that God created Pharaoh to harden him, use Rom. 9:17 in a way that can only *incriminate* God; *He* uses it to *vindicate* Himself, to show that there is *not* unrighteousness with Him. Suppose He had *not* sent judgments upon Pharaoh in increasing severity. Suppose He had *not* shown mercy after each but the last of these judgments. Pharaoh would never have been so wholly without excuse.

The words, *"whom He will He hardeneth,"* in Rom. 9:18, surely teach one important lesson: It is folly to trifle with God or to enter into contest with Him, for while you will become harder of heart and more willful in the process, *He will assuredly prevail* and you will be utterly defeated. This happened even with the favored nation, Israel—and it is for this reason that the Apostle discusses this subject here.

THE POTTER AND THE CLAY

"Thou wilt say then unto me, Why doth He yet find fault? For who hath resisted His will?

"Nay but, O man, who art thou that repliest against God? Shall the thing formed say to him that formed it, Why hast thou made me thus?

"Hath not the potter power over the clay, of the same lump to make one vessel unto honor, and another unto dishonor?

"What if God, willing to show His wrath, and to make His power known, endured with much longsuffering the vessels of wrath fitted to destruction:

"And that He might make known the riches of His glory on the vessels of mercy, which He had afore prepared unto glory,

"Even us, whom He hath called, not of the Jews only, but also of the Gentiles?"

—Rom. 9:19-24

The objection of 9:14 answered, the Apostle now anticipates and answers another: *"Why doth He yet find fault? For who hath resisted His will?"* This is by no means a hypothetical question, for God *does* find fault with unbelievers. He *condemns* them, and says: "*You* would not receive the love of the truth. *This* is why I gave you up to a lie" (See II Thes. 2:10-12).

Surely Pharaoh could have no legitimate criticism of God simply because he failed to successfully resist His will. We have seen that God did *not* inwardly impel Pharaoh to defy Him. That which essentially caused him to harden his heart did not proceed from God but from his own sinful nature. Thus God *could*, and did, find fault with Pharaoh. *He*, not God, was to blame for his overthrow.

Paul's *"Nay but,"* in Ver. 20, however, indicates that there is a more basic question which must take precedence over the one just asked. He states it in the form of a challenge:

> "Nay but, O man, who art thou that repliest against God? Shall the thing formed [2] say to him that formed it, Why hast thou made me thus?"

To "reply against" means to *talk back*. The Apostle says in effect, "Who are you to talk back to God?" The words, *"Oh man,"* in this context emphasize man's profound inferiority to God. "Oh man—poor, condemned, wretched, sinful, dying man! Who are you to talk back to God?" The condemned criminal is in no position to enter into debate with "the Judge of all the earth."

Unregenerate man supposes that if God shows mercy to one He is under obligation to show mercy to all, which He is not, though indeed He *does* offer salvation to all who will receive it in faith. Who can find fault with that? [3]

One of the first lessons we need to learn as sinners is that God owes no man *anything*. He has fully as much right to make of us what He pleases as the potter has a right to make what *he* pleases out of that lump of clay. Certainly none of us has any right to "stay His hand, or say unto Him, What doest Thou?" (Dan. 4:35). But we ask again, shall we assume from this that He is callous or capricious in His elective acts?

Surely the potter has complete power over the clay, but God exercises this power in accordance with the highest

---

2. Note: "formed," not "created." The Universalist claim that Judas was "born for such a role as this" is illegitimate and an affront to God.

3. For a further discussion of Election see Appendix No. II.

moral principles—His own. In Israel's case He used it to display His mercy; in Pharaoh's to display His wrath upon sin, making of the one a "vessel unto honor," and of the other a "vessel unto dishonor."

Thus, rather than debating the issue, we are wiser to place ourselves in the hands of the Master Potter, beseeching Him to make of us vessels unto honor. Indeed, this is especially appropriate where the believer in Christ is concerned, for the Potter is not yet finished with us. Thus the Apostle declares in II Tim. 2:20,21 that if we purge ourselves from spiritual uncleanness He will make of us *"[vessels] unto honor, sanctified, and meet for the Master's use...."*

As to Ver. 22, how clearly the words *"willing"* and *"endured with much longsuffering"* indicate that God does not induce the sinner to sin. Also, it should be carefully observed that the terms *"fitted to destruction,"* in Ver. 22, and *"afore prepared unto glory,"* in Ver. 23, are by no means synonymous. The word "fitted," used with regard to Pharaoh, is in the Middle Voice, and means *self-fitted*, while "afore prepared" means *made ready beforehand*. In this case God "endured with much longsuffering" the brazen obstinacy of Pharaoh that He might "make known the riches of His glory on the vessels of mercy" whom Pharaoh had been oppressing. Who could find fault with that?

Indeed, He still "endures with much longsuffering" the rebellion of an unbelieving world, that He might "make known the riches of His glory on the vessels of mercy,"

"Even us, whom He hath called, not of the Jews only, but also of the Gentiles" (Ver. 24).

"The Lord is not slack concerning His promise, [4] as some men count slackness, but is LONGSUFFERING to usward, NOT WILLING THAT ANY SHOULD PERISH, but that all should come to repentance" (II Pet. 3:9).

Thus the longsuffering that delays our Lord's return to judge and reign spells for mankind one great, wonderful

---

4. To return to earth to judge and reign (II Pet. 3:3,4).

word: "SALVATION"—*"even as our beloved brother Paul... hath written unto you"* (II Pet. 3:15).

THE FUTURE JEWISH REMNANT

"As He saith also in Osee [Hosea], I will call them My people which were not My people; and her beloved which was not beloved.

"And it shall come to pass, that in the place where it was said unto them, Ye are not My people, there shall they be called the children of the living God.

"Esaias also crieth concerning Israel, Though the number of the children of Israel be as the sand of the sea, a remnant [5] shall be saved:

"For He will finish the work, and cut it short in righteousness; because a short work will the Lord make upon the earth.

"And as Esaias said before, Except the Lord of Sabaoth had left us a seed, we had been as Sodoma, and been made like unto Gomorrha."

—Rom. 9:25-29

The Apostle, having shown from Israel's own history that "they are not all Israel which are of Israel," now proceeds to further establish this fact from their prophetic Scriptures. Indeed, he now cites Hosea and Isaiah to prove that only by God's grace will even a "remnant" be saved when, at last, He begins to fulfill His kingdom promises to Israel.

Many commentators apply Verses 25,26 to Gentiles being saved today, but an examination of the Old Testament passages reveals that they refer rather to redeemed Israel as Jehovah's *reconciled wife*. He had given her "a bill of divorcement" (Isa. 50:1) and had called her "Lo-ammi," *"Not My People"* (Hos. 1:9,10) because of her spiritual adultery, but He never ceased loving her or abandoned His promise and purpose to make her His own indeed. This will take place after God has "finished the work and cut it short in righteousness" (Ver. 28), i.e., after He has judged Israel and the nations in the great tribulation.

This all concerns Israel *as a nation*, of course, but of whom will the redeemed nation be comprised? From all that we have considered above, it will surely not include all of the

---

5. I.e., only a remnant.

physical descendants of Abraham, nor even all those of his descendants living at that time. At its beginning it will rather include only a "remnant," a comparatively small number of the whole nation, as indicated in the quotation from Isaiah in Verses 27,28. This is not inconsistent with the history of the favored nation, for Isaiah said of Judah and Jerusalem even in his own day:

"Except the Lord of Sabaoth [hosts] had left us a seed, we had been as Sodoma, and been made like unto Gomorrha" (Ver. 29: cf. Isa. 1:9).

Thus the "seed" through whom all nations will be blessed will be the believing remnant of the future—along with Abraham and all his believing seed, who will have been resurrected to participate in the kingdom blessing (See Luke 13:28,29). [6]

Even in the history of the present dispensation, God has always worked through believing remnants. When Modernism rose to deny the fundamentals of the faith, just after the turn of the century, it was the faithful remnant, the minority, who cared enough to get out of apostate denominations and stand boldly for the truth. But because they were in the minority, does it follow that they lost the battle? By no means, for the majority lost God's presence and blessing in their midst, and the largest churches were often the most devoid of spiritual life, while the faithful minority enjoyed the power and blessing of the Holy Spirit and were used of God to send thousands of missionaries forth to evangelize the heathen—and the civilized heathen here at home.

It will be the same with the New Evangelicalism and its compromises with the world and apostate religion. All their "big time" operators, all their highly organized campaigns, all their popularity notwithstanding, they will lose—have already largely lost—God's power and blessing, while the remnant, the faithful minority, will win the spiritual victories.

---

6. In dealing here with God's promise regarding Abraham's multiplied seed (Gen. 22:17,18), we by no means deny the truth of Gal. 3:16. See the author's *A Simple Solution To a Difficult Problem*, where this subject is discussed at length.

GOD'S PRESENT WORK AMONG THE GENTILES

"What shall we say then? That the Gentiles, which followed not after righteousness, have attained to righteousness, even the righteousness which is of faith.

"But Israel, which followed after the law of righteousness, hath not attained to the law of righteousness.

"Wherefore? Because they sought it not by faith, but as it were by the works of the law. For they stumbled at that stumblingstone;

"As it is written, Behold I lay in Sion a stumblingstone and rock of offence: and whosoever believeth on Him shall not be ashamed."

—Rom. 9:30-33

God has shown in the case of His own beloved Israel that He is not a respecter of persons. He *will* maintain justice. Israelites were not counted for the promised seed *just* because they were the physical descendants of Abraham. When the favored nation rejected Christ, she was temporarily set aside while God sent salvation to the Gentiles to provoke Israel to jealousy (See 11:11).

The Gentiles had not "followed after righteousness," but now God offered it to them through Christ, whose righteousness is *imputed* to believers, and many of them received it in faith (Ver. 30).

But Israel, seeking to obtain the righteousness of the law, did not obtain it. Why? Because they sought it by works rather than by faith (Vers. 31,32). Mark well, the Apostle does not say that they had failed to obtain righteousness because *God* had not elected them to salvation, but because *they* had sought to gain it by works rather than by faith. This is important, appearing as it does, at the close of such a chapter as Romans 9.

"They stumbled at that stumblingstone," says the Apostle (Ver. 32). They persisted in a futile effort to *earn* God's favor instead of receiving it by faith in Christ who, in love and grace, had paid the full penalty for their sins. This has since been a constant embarrassment to them, a stone over

which they have continually stumbled (See Acts 4:11,12; I Cor. 1:23).

> Not what these hands have done
>   Can save my guilty soul:
> Not what this toiling flesh hath wrought
>   Can make my spirit whole.
>
> Not what I feel or do
>   Can give me peace with God:
> Not all my prayers, or sighs, or tears
>   Can ease this awful load.
>
> Thy love to me, O God,
>   Not mine, O Lord, to Thee,
> Can rid me of this dark unrest
>   And set my spirit free.
>
> Thy work alone, Lord Jesus,
>   Can ease this weight of sin;
> Thy blood alone, O Lamb of God,
>   Can give me peace within.
>
> I praise the God of grace,
>   I trust His love and might;
> He calls me His, I call Him mine;
>   My God, my joy, my light!
>
>   —Horatius Bonar

Chapter X—Romans 10:1-21
ISRAEL'S FAILURE UNDER THE LAW
HER UNBELIEF
AND RESISTANCE TO GRACE

"Brethren, my heart's desire and prayer to God for Israel is that they might be saved.

"For I bear them record that they have a zeal of God, but not according to knowledge.

"For they, being ignorant of God's righteousness, and going about to establish their own righteousness, have not submitted themselves unto the righteousness of God.

"For Christ is the end of the law for righteousness to every one that believeth."

—Rom. 10:1-4

Is Paul's "heart's desire and prayer" here for the salvation of the *nation* Israel, or for that of the individuals comprising the nation? In a sense the question is academic, for the salvation of the nation would include all the individuals in it, while the salvation of the individuals would in fact *be* the salvation of the nation.

In the light of the prophetic Scriptures, however, the question is more than academic, for the salvation of Israel *as a nation* is consistently associated with the return of Christ to earth to reign (See 11:26).

There are some indeed who teach that Paul proclaimed, even *offered*, the kingdom to Israel right up until Acts 28. This is an error. Paul did exactly what we would—or should —do when preaching to Jews: he confirmed Peter's message, proving that "Jesus is the Christ," as the *basis* for preaching justification by faith without the Law (Acts 13:38,39). There is no Scripture to indicate that Paul ever proclaimed, much less offered, the kingdom to Israel as Peter had done at Pentecost (Acts 2:29-36; 3:19-26), nor *could* he have done so, for God had sent him *away from* Jerusalem, the seat of government, with the words *"they will not receive thy testimony concerning Me"* (Acts 22:18-21).

In Paul's earliest epistle he already states that in Judaea, where the national capital was situated and the rulers assembled, Israel had "filled up their sins" and that "wrath [had] come upon them to the uttermost" (I Thes. 2:16).

Evidently all hope of national salvation was gone for the present, for the Apostle states that the majority of the nation had been *"blinded"* (11:7), that God had judicially "given them *the spirit of slumber*" (11:8), that they had *"fallen"* (11:11,12), had been *"cast away"* (11:15), had been *"broken off"* (11:19,20), were *"not spared"* (11:21) and had been *"concluded...in unbelief"* (11:32).

Indeed, the Apostle goes even farther, declaring that the nation will not be saved until *"there shall come out of Sion the Deliverer, and shall turn away ungodliness from Jacob"* (11:26).

All this proves conclusively that Paul could not have been praying at this time for the salvation of *national* Israel. Rather it is now his "heart's desire and prayer to God" that he might be used to *"save some of them"* (11:14).

ZEALOUSLY RELIGIOUS
—BUT LOST

"For I bear them record, that they have a zeal of God..." (Ver. 2).

Sad condition! Zealous in the things of God, but *not saved!* Paul knew something about this, and sympathized. Some time later, addressing a multitude at his last visit to Jerusalem, he said:

"I am...a Jew...brought up in this city at the feet of Gamaliel, and taught according to the perfect manner of the law of the fathers, and was ZEALOUS TOWARD GOD, as ye all are this day" (Acts 22:3).

And to the Galatians he wrote:

"[I] profited in the Jews' religion above many my equals in mine own nation, being MORE EXCEEDINGLY ZEALOUS of the traditions of my fathers" (Gal. 1:14).

But in his intense *zeal for God*, Paul had *persecuted* the *Church of God*. Hear his own testimony:

"...beyond measure I persecuted the Church of God [1] and wasted it [i.e., laid it waste]" (Gal. 1:13).

Luke adds his testimony in confirmation:

"As for Saul, he made havock of the church..." (Acts 8:3).

His condition then, as theirs now, sprang from two oft-related problems: *ignorance* and *obstinacy*.

They were ignorant of God's righteousness and refused to submit themselves to it (Ver. 3). Oh, they knew all the details of the Law, but they had not grasped the true *purpose* of the Law—nor, seemingly, did they wish to grasp it. A sad picture this. The Jew, with God's Book in his hand, wilfully blind to what that Book says about *him* as guilty before God.

Still "going about to establish their own righteousness," says the Apostle, *they "have not submitted themselves* unto the righteousness of God." Like the Pharisees and lawyers of our Lord's day, they *"rejected the counsel of God against themselves"* (Luke 7:30). Israel's "going about" and "not submitting" illustrates the "willing" and "running" of 9:16.

How like multitudes of religious, but unsaved, people today! Not realizing that divine righteousness demands perfection, and thus not realizing that they need a *Savior*, they continue *"going about to establish their own righteousness."* In their obstinacy they insist: "*I* can do it; *I* can make it," refusing to *"submit themselves unto the righteousness of God."*

But neither the nation Israel, nor individuals in Israel, nor sinners today can be saved while rejecting "the counsel of God against themselves." Not until one acknowledges his desperate plight, under the condemnation of sin, and turns in faith to Christ who died for our sins, can he ever be saved.

---

1. I.e., the Church of God of that day, not to be confused with "the Body of Christ," the Church of the present dispensation.

The people of Israel impatiently waited to be saved—from their troubles, but not from their *sins*. But they will never be saved from their troubles until they are *first* saved from their sins. The Scriptures make this unmistakably clear.

The angel who announced our Lord's birth to Joseph, said:

"...thou shalt call His name Jesus: for He shall SAVE HIS PEOPLE FROM THEIR SINS" (Matt. 1:21). [2]

When Peter offered the kingdom to Israel at Pentecost, he said:

"Unto you first God, having raised up His Son Jesus, sent Him to bless you in TURNING AWAY EVERY ONE OF YOU FROM HIS INIQUITIES" (Acts 3:26).

Thus Paul declares that when Israel is finally "saved":

"There shall come out of Sion the Deliverer, and shall TURN AWAY UNGODLINESS FROM JACOB" (Rom. 11:26).

CHRIST THE END OF THE LAW FOR RIGHTEOUSNESS

Does Verse 4 mean that Christ is the *fulfillment* of the Law, or the *termination* of the Law "to every one that believeth"? Actually *both* are true.

Christ is "the end of the Law" in the sense that He was the *Goal* to which the Law led:

"Wherefore the law was our schoolmaster to *bring us unto Christ*, that we might be justified by faith" (Gal. 3:24).

But in this very context the Apostle goes on to say,

"But after that faith is come, *we are no longer under a schoolmaster*" (Ver. 25).

Thus Christ is also the *termination* of the Law for righteousness to those who believe:

"Having *abolished* in His flesh the enmity, even the law of commandments, contained in ordinances; for to make in Himself of twain one new man, so making peace" (Eph. 2:15).

---

2. This passage is sometimes used as a general gospel verse. Actually it refers to the salvation of "His people," i.e., His covenant people, Israel.

> *"Blotting out the handwriting of ordinances that was against us, which was contrary to us, and took it out of the way, nailing it to His cross"* (Col. 2:14).

Efforts to keep the Law will never establish one's righteousness; rather they will establish his *un*righteousness. God's righteousness, required by the Law, was manifested in Christ alone, *in whom* our sins were judged at Calvary, *by whom* their penalty was fully paid, and *through whom* we may now be justified by faith. This is why Paul declares that it is his desire:

> "[To] be found in Him, *not* having mine own righteousness, which is of the law, but that which is through the faith of Christ, [3] the righteousness which is of God by faith" (Phil. 3:9).

THE RIGHTEOUSNESS OF THE LAW
VS.
THE RIGHTEOUSNESS OF FAITH

> "For Moses describeth the righteousness which is of the law, That the man which doeth those things shall live by them.
>
> "But the righteousness which is of faith speaketh on this wise, Say not in thine heart, Who shall ascend into heaven? (that is, to bring Christ down from above),
>
> "Or, Who shall descend into the deep? (that is, to bring up Christ again from the dead.)
>
> "But what saith it? The word is nigh thee, even in thy mouth, and in thy heart: that is, the word of faith, which we preach."
>
> —Rom. 10:5-8

Here the Apostle invokes the name of Moses, doubtless because of the great reverence in which he was held by the Jews. Quoting from Lev. 18:5, he says that Moses has described for us the righteousness of the Law, i.e., the righteousness to be obtained by keeping the Law. And *how* is this "righteousness of the law" obtained? By *doing* it, says Moses, not by just talking about it. "The man which *doeth* those things shall live by them" (Rom. 10:5). Actually Lev. 18:5 reads, "which IF a man do, he shall live in them."

---

3. See the author's booklet, *The Faith of Christ*.

This is indeed a "big IF"! Thus in Gal. 3:10 the Apostle, again quoting from Moses (Deut. 27:26), says:

> "For as many as are of the works of the law are under the curse, for it is written, Cursed is every one that CONTINUETH not in ALL things which are written in the book of the law to DO them."

In Vers. 6-8 of our text the Apostle does not quote, but refers to another declaration by Moses, describing "the righteousness of *faith*." The passage, Deut. 30:11-14, reads:

> "For the commandment which I command thee this day, it is not hidden from thee, neither is it far off.
>
> "It is not in heaven, that thou shouldst say, Who shall go up for us to heaven, and bring it unto us, that we may hear it, and do it?
>
> "Neither is it beyond the sea, that thou shouldst say, Who shall go over the sea for us, and bring it unto us, that we may hear it and do it?
>
> "But the word is very nigh unto thee, in thy mouth and in thy heart, that thou mayest do it."

What Moses is saying is, in effect: "This law is 'not hidden from you'; it is simple and plain. You don't have to send to heaven to bring it down to your level, or send your philosophers across the sea to other lands to get *their* learned opinions about it. God has brought it down to *you* and as you receive it as *His word* you are saved." Is it not significant that immediately following these words in Deut. 30:11-14, Moses says, "*He* is thy life."

Many Israelites were trying earnestly to keep the Law, every jot, every tittle—*in order to save their souls*. Their first concern was not God, but self. They were lost because, having made the Law their means of obtaining righteousness, they had utterly failed to keep it.

But there were others, like David, who simply believed the Law to be *the Word of God to them* and sought to keep it *on that basis*. This was "the obedience of faith," and such delighted to do the Law, in spite of many failures, and loved to meditate on it day and night (Psa. 1:2). Moreover, these were by far the best "Law keepers." Thus even the Law became to these "the word of faith," and Paul says, "This is what *we* preach" in proclaiming Christ.[4] The word of God to us: *"To him that worketh not, but believeth...his faith is counted for righteousness"* (Rom. 4:5), is as authoritative today as was the word of God to Abel to bring a blood sacrifice, or the word of God through Moses to keep the Law. When God says: "Bring a blood sacrifice as an atonement for your soul," what will *faith* do? It will bring a blood sacrifice. When God says, "Repent and be baptized for the remission of sins," what will *faith* do? It will repent and be baptized (See Mark 1:4; Acts 2:38). When God says, "To him that worketh NOT, *but believeth* on Him that justifieth the ungodly, his faith is counted for righteousness," what will *faith* do? Faith will rejoice and say, *"What grace!"* This is what Paul emphasizes in Rom. 10:6-8. No one need go to heaven to bring Christ down to us, or descend into the deep to bring Him up from the dead, as though He were not already a risen, living Savior. Ah, no. All that we need to know about Him is right here in our Bibles; in our mouth as we read it, and in our heart as we believe it.

BY WORKS AFTER ALL?

"That if thou shalt confess with thy mouth the Lord Jesus, and shalt believe in thine heart that God hath raised Him from the dead, thou shalt be saved.

"For with the heart man believeth unto righteousness; and with the mouth confession is made unto salvation.

"For the Scripture saith, Whosoever believeth on Him shall not be ashamed.

"For there is no difference between the Jew and the Greek: for the same Lord over all is rich unto all that call upon Him.

"For whosoever shall call upon the name of the Lord shall be saved."
—Rom. 10:9-13

---

4. The opening chapter of the author's book, *Things That Differ*, shows how all the Old Testament saints were saved *by faith*, though this was demonstrated by their approaching God in the way which *He* had prescribed. Here suffice it to say that the list in Hebrews 11, of those who "obtained a good report" from God contains many variables, but *one* constant. Abel brought the right sacrifice, Enoch walked with God, Noah built an ark, etc., but they "all obtained a good report" only because these works demonstrated their *faith* in God's word to them. Thus the constant, *"by faith,"* pervades the whole chapter.

In these sublime words the Apostle Paul sets forth God's simple plan of salvation in this "dispensation of the grace of God." This, he says, is *"the word of faith, which we preach."* How grateful we should be that *both* Jews and Gentiles are included in this program while God's blessings to Israel *as a nation* are being held in abeyance!

The alarming extent to which the Church has departed from Paul's "gospel of the grace of God," however, is evidenced by the fact that today even many Fundamentalists, who claim to preach "the word of faith," have introduced into the very words of Paul in Vers. 9-11 the element of meritorious works.

How often babes in Christ are urged to get to their feet in public testimony on the basis of these words! They are reminded that, in addition to believing, "if thou shalt *confess with thy mouth*...thou shalt be saved" (Rom. 10:9).

Frequently Christian workers, not rightly dividing the Word of truth, support this argument by an appeal to the words of our Lord in Matt. 10:32,33:

"Whosoever therefore shall confess Me before men, him will I confess also before My Father which is in heaven.

"But whosoever shall deny Me before men, him will I also deny before My Father which is in heaven."

And thus the element of meritorious works is injected into "the word of faith, which we preach." Newborn babes in Christ are given to feel that a heart faith is not enough to make them secure; that not until they have risen in public testimony is their salvation fully confirmed.

While few of our leading Fundamentalists would stand by any explicit statement to that effect, we dare say that most of them in their comments on these verses give the impression that this is so.

But what, then, does the Apostle mean by these words? Does he not plainly say, *"If thou shalt confess...thou shalt be saved"*? Yes, but here again, as with so many other passages of Scripture, a traditional meaning has been superimposed upon the actual words of God.

What does the English word "confess" mean? Simply to "acknowledge," to "admit." And this is exactly what the original Greek word means too, nor does Rom. 10:9,10 say anything about confessing *before men*.

The trouble is that the idea of confession has been changed to *profession*—even *public* profession—and multitudes have followed the tradition of the fathers instead of examining the Word to see what it actually *says*. Thus "the word of faith" has been perverted.

But, it may be argued, does not the Apostle clearly say, "If thou shalt confess *with thy mouth*...thou shalt be saved"? Indeed he does, and he adds, "and shalt believe *in thine heart*."

Let us consider this thoughtfully. Is it with the physical organ which pumps blood into our veins that we believe in Christ as our Savior? No! All admit that this is merely a figure of speech; that somehow the heart is associated with believing. Yet some would insist that it is with the physical mouth that we must confess in order to be saved. Can mutes then not be saved? And what does the Apostle mean in Acts 28:27, where he quotes Isaiah's words: "And their *eyes* have they *closed*"?

Must we not see that the heart and mouth in Romans 10 are both used symbolically? While believing is naturally associated with the heart, confessing is naturally associated with the mouth.

If indeed the Apostle meant that with the physical mouth public "profession" must be made for salvation, then salvation is *not* by faith alone after all, but by faith plus works. If, not only before men, but before God as well, a question mark is placed after the name of the believer who has not testified before men, then most assuredly, salvation is *not* "the word of faith, which we preach."

The Apostle says that we must *confess* and *believe* to be saved. This is different, and here quite naturally the heart and mouth become symbolically significant.

As if anticipating the misinterpretation of his words, the Spirit-inspired Apostle continues:

"For the Scripture saith, Whosoever BELIEVETH on Him shall not be ashamed" (Ver. 11).

"For whosoever shall CALL upon the name of the Lord shall be saved" (Ver. 13).

This is "the word of faith, which we preach."

It is when the sinner comes to the end of himself and *confesses, acknowledges* that Jesus is Lord, and *believes* in Him as the risen, living Savior, that he is saved. Any work of righteousness he might add for salvation would be useless, for salvation is *"by grace...through faith...not of works"* (Eph. 2:8,9). And so:

"With the heart man BELIEVETH"[5] (Ver. 10).

"With the mouth CONFESSION is made" (Ver. 10).

"For whosoever BELIEVETH on Him shall not be ashamed" (Ver. 11).

"For...whosoever shall CALL upon the name of the Lord shall be saved" (Ver. 13).

Years ago a Christian woman kept urging her unsaved husband to attend large Saturday night evangelistic services. He went, week after week, to please her. It seemed to her, after a time, however, that he was under deep conviction, so as they walked home together she asked him, "Dear, why didn't you go forward tonight?" He replied, "I guess I'm just a coward. I didn't have the courage to get up out of my seat and go forward. Maybe next week." But is salvation, then, by courage or by faith? by some human effort, or by trusting in the finished work of Christ? Yet this man and his wife had associated being saved with going forward in a gospel meeting, and there are multitudes like them.

We do not for a moment mean to minimize the importance of Christian testimony. Only, we would not frighten God's dear children into witnessing for Him. We would not cast doubt upon their salvation just because they have not had

---

5. Intellectual issues interest the *head*; moral issues the *heart*.

the courage to bear public testimony, nor give them to feel that salvation is incomplete without human works. Some of the finest people—and the best Christians—are very retiring, and find it difficult to ever express themselves publicly. Above all, we would not adulterate the message of grace, or alter the written Word of God.

Read *as it is* Romans 10:9-13 does not in any way qualify "the gospel of the grace of God." Read *as it is* it presents God's simple, wonderful plan of salvation for poor, lost sinners in "this present evil age."

TWO TWOSOMES

Rom. 10:12,13 involves two important twosomes that should be considered before we proceed to the closing section of the chapter. They are:

1. "There is no difference."
2. "Whosoever shall call upon the name of the Lord shall be saved."

THERE IS NO DIFFERENCE

This statement is found twice in Paul's *Epistle to the Romans*: once in connection with *sin* and once in connection with *grace*. In Rom. 3:22,23 the Apostle shows *why* justification must of necessity be "by [God's] grace, through the redemption that is in Christ Jesus," while in Rom. 10:12,13 he shows *how* it is freely bestowed upon all who "call upon the name of the Lord."

THERE IS NO DIFFERENCE
FOR ALL HAVE SINNED
AND COME SHORT OF THE GLORY OF GOD
(Rom. 3:22,23)

During the early years of the *Berean Searchlight* the author had a Jewish friend named Sam, from whom he frequently bought paper for the printing of the magazine. At one time, as we were "discussing" prices, Sam said, "If you get me down any lower I'll go bankrupt," to which I responded, "If I ever beat a son of Abraham in business, I'll surely be a shrewd businessman!" and then, "Sam, are you and I blood relatives?" His eye twinkled as he said, "No, I'm a son of Abraham." "That's right," I responded, "but tell me, are you by chance a son of Adam?" He knew the Hebrew Scriptures well enough to see the point, and said, "You got me that time!"

Sam and I *were* blood relatives, having both descended from fallen Adam, and thus were *both sinners*, for *"by one man sin entered into the world, and death by sin; and so death passed upon all men, for that all have sinned"* (Rom. 5:12).

Thus there never was any essential difference between Jew and Gentile, *"for all have sinned and come short of the glory of God."* But it is interesting to see how God *demonstrated* this historically, dispensationally; how He *made* a difference to show that there *is* no difference, how He made an *artificial* difference to show that there is no *essential* difference.

Certainly God made a difference when He chose Abraham from all this pagan world and said:

"And I will make of thee a great nation, and I will bless thee, and make thy name great; and thou shalt be a blessing" (Gen. 12:2).

"And in thy seed shall all the nations of the earth be blessed..." (Gen. 22:18).

And certainly there was still a great difference between Israel and the rest of the world, when God said:

"Ye have seen what I did unto the Egyptians, and how I bare you on eagles' wings, and brought you unto Myself.

"Now therefore, if ye will obey My voice indeed, and keep My covenant, then ye shall be a peculiar treasure unto Me above all people, for all the earth is Mine:

"And ye shall be unto Me a kingdom of priests, and an holy nation" (Ex. 19:4-6).

The goal of prophecy was Christ as King over Israel, and Israel as head of the nations (Jer. 23:5,6) and the very first verse of the "New Testament" introduces Christ as *"the son of David, the son of Abraham"* (Matt. 1:1), the patriarchs to whom the kingdom and the land of Canaan, respectively, had been promised.

Thus it is not strange that Paul declares:

"Now I say that Jesus Christ was a minister of the Circumcision [the Jew], for the truth of God, TO CONFIRM THE PROMISES MADE UNTO THE FATHERS:

"And that the Gentiles might glorify God for His mercy..." (Rom. 15:8,9).

There we have the prophetic program: Christ confirming —and one day fulfilling—God's promises to Israel, and the Gentiles glorifying Him for His mercy. Be it noted, however, that the Gentile nations will not glorify God for His mercy to them until the promises to Israel have been fulfilled, for it is through *redeemed* Israel that the nations will ultimately be blessed.

Thus when our Lord ministered on earth there was still a difference between Israel and the Gentiles. When a Gentile woman came to Him for help, He responded by saying, *"I am not sent but unto the lost sheep of the house of Israel"* (Matt. 15:24).

Pitying the woman, He helped her, but not until He had driven home to both her and His disciples the fact that she had no claim whatsoever on Him. Thus too, when He first sent His twelve apostles forth He said:

"Go not into the way of the Gentiles, and into any city of the Samaritans enter ye not:

"But go rather to the lost sheep of the house of Israel" (Matt. 10:5,6).

As we know, however, the King and His glorious kingdom were rejected as Israel refused her own Messiah and condemned Him to death. However, in infinite mercy He prayed for them from the cross, imploring the Father to forgive them (Luke 23:34).

Thus it is that even after our Lord's ascension to heaven there was still a great difference, positionally, between Israel and the Gentiles. This is evident from the fact that in his great Pentecostal message Peter addressed only his

Jewish kinsmen (Acts 2:14,22,36), declaring to them that God had raised Christ from the dead to sit on David's throne (Vers. 29-31), and later saying to them:

"Ye are the children of the prophets, and of the covenant which God made with our fathers, saying unto Abraham, And in thy seed shall all the kindreds of the earth be blessed.

"Unto you first God, having raised up His Son Jesus, sent Him to bless you in turning away every one of you from his iniquities" (Acts 3:25,26).

It is most important to notice that up to this point Peter never said that there was "no difference" between Jew and Gentile. We do not find this until the raising up of Paul. But as Stephen was stoned and a message was sent after the ascended Christ, saying, *"We will not have this man to reign over us"* (See Luke 19:14), the nation Israel had surely proved herself no different from the Gentiles as far as sin is concerned. It had now been demonstrated historically that *"there is no difference, for all have sinned and come short of the glory of God"* (Rom. 3:22,23), and Paul uses this last to prove that justification must, in the nature of the case, be by the free grace of God and through the redemption that is in Christ Jesus (Rom. 3:22-24; cf. Gal. 3:22).

THERE IS NO DIFFERENCE
FOR THE SAME LORD OVER ALL
IS RICH UNTO ALL THAT CALL UPON HIM
(Romans 10:12)

Gentiles could be saved in Old Testament times, but only by approaching God *through Israel*, recognizing Israel's temple as God's appointed place of worship, and submitting to circumcision and the Law. This is clearly stated in Isa. 56:6,7:

"Also the sons of the stranger, that join themselves to the Lord, to serve Him, and to love the name of the Lord, to be His servants, every one that keepeth the sabbath from polluting it, and taketh hold of my covenant [circumcision];

"Even them will I bring to My holy mountain, and make them joyful in My house of prayer: their burnt-offerings and their sacrifices shall be accepted upon Mine altar; for Mine house shall be called an house of prayer for all people."

But now that Israel had joined the Gentiles in their rebellion against Christ and had been given up by God along with the Gentiles, God had graciously saved Saul, the leader of the rebellion, and had sent him forth as *Paul the Apostle*, with a message of *"grace and peace"* to all men everywhere. Thus we have the second use of the phrase *"there is no difference"* in Rom. 10:12. As the Apostle declares in Rom. 3:22,23 that *"there is no difference, for all have sinned,"* so now in Rom. 10:12,13 he proclaims the glad message:

"For THERE IS NO DIFFERENCE BETWEEN THE JEW AND THE GREEK; FOR THE SAME LORD OVER ALL IS RICH UNTO ALL THAT CALL UPON HIM.

"FOR WHOSOEVER SHALL CALL UPON THE NAME OF THE LORD SHALL BE SAVED."

WHOSOEVER SHALL CALL

Rom. 10:12,13 in turn introduces us to another important twosome, for the declaration, *"Whosoever shall call upon the name of the Lord shall be saved,"* a quotation from Joel 2:32, is found twice in the "New Testament": in Acts 2:21 and here. A comparison of these two quotations is most revealing.

Once it is quoted by *Peter* and once by *Paul*; once at the *beginning* of the Acts period and once at the *end*; once while God was still pleading with Israel to accept her King and once after a judicial blindness had settled upon the nation; once while Israel was God's covenant people and once after God had begun to break down the middle wall of partition between Jew and Gentile, and Paul, as God's appointed apostle of grace, had been sent to declare that before God *"there is no difference between the Jew and the Greek."*

We must first consider the quotation of this passage by Peter if we would appreciate the wonder of its use some years later by Paul.

THE QUOTATION BY PETER

It should be observed first of all that Peter quotes the verse right along with its foregoing context. This point is very important to the understanding of Peter's address in Acts 2.

The passage in Joel is about Pentecost and the Tribulation, and the prediction concerning Pentecost as quoted by Peter is followed immediately by that concerning the Tribulation:

"And I will show wonders in heaven above, and signs in the earth beneath; *blood, and fire, and vapor of smoke:*

"*The sun shall be turned into darkness, and the moon into blood,* before that great and notable day of the Lord come:

"And it shall come to pass, that whosoever shall call on the name of the Lord shall be saved" (Acts 2:19-21).

Has this as yet come to pass?

Do we see these signs today?

Is the Day of the Lord now being ushered in?

Every thoughtful Bible student will answer *"No"* to all three of these questions. Yet we must remember well that it is in connection with these terrors which were—and are—to usher in "the day of the Lord," that the prophet says: *"And it shall come to pass, that whosoever shall call on the name of the Lord shall be saved."*

Most certainly *this prophecy has not yet been fulfilled.* These are not "the times of the signs" and surely this is not "the day of the Lord," but the day of man. This is why war and bloodshed go on practically without interruption and our ablest statesmen meet in vain to discuss plans for peace and safety.

But God had a *secret* purpose which Peter did not yet know. The signs of the Tribulation were not *immediately* to follow those of Pentecost. Indeed, the signs of Pentecost were to vanish away again and God was to offer His enemies everywhere *reconciliation* by grace, through the blood of the cross which, in the eternal purpose, had *"slain the enmity"* between God and man and had made it possible for Him to be *"just, and [at the same time] the justifier of him which believeth in Jesus"* (Rom. 3:26).

Here is where Paul's quotation of Joel 2:32 comes in.

THE QUOTATION BY PAUL

Paul, it will be noticed, quotes the statement from Joel entirely out of its context. This might be considered an illegitimate use of Scripture, except that he wrote by divine inspiration and that it was God Himself who was now to use this same statement in an infinitely more wonderful setting:

"FOR THERE IS NO DIFFERENCE BETWEEN THE JEW AND THE GREEK; FOR THE SAME LORD OVER ALL IS RICH UNTO ALL THAT CALL UPON HIM.

"FOR WHOSOEVER SHALL CALL UPON THE NAME OF THE LORD SHALL BE SAVED" (Rom. 10:12,13).

Now, let us ask again: Has *this* come to pass? and every saint cries, "Yes! Hallelujah! Are not *we* some of the 'whosoever'?"

As significant as it is that Peter quotes this statement directly in its prophetic context, it is even more significant that Paul now quotes it in this new setting.

The signs which began at Pentecost finally vanished away again and the horrors predicted did not—have not even yet—come to pass. God is not now saving whosoever calls in the sense predicted by Joel and proclaimed by Peter.

The wonderful fact is, however, that God has now sent out a "whosoever" offer of eternal salvation *by His interruption of the program predicted by Joel and the ushering in of the present dispensation of grace.*

How blessed is our lot! How much more we, both Jewish and Gentile believers, have than Peter ever dreamed of on the day of Pentecost! To think that in "this present evil age," salvation is offered to all as a free gift from God, and that the vilest sinner may be *"justified freely by His grace, through the redemption that is in Christ Jesus,"* entirely apart from religion or works! And to think that believers, as ambassadors for Christ, have the high honor to deliver this message to the lost![6]

GOD'S PATIENCE WITH ISRAEL

"How then shall they call on Him in whom they have not believed? and how shall they believe in Him of whom they have not heard? and how shall they hear without a preacher?

"And how shall they preach except they be sent? as it is written, How beautiful are the feet of them that preach the gospel of peace, and bring glad tidings of good things!

"But they have not all obeyed the gospel. For Esaias saith, Lord, who hath believed our report?

"So then faith cometh by hearing, and hearing by the Word of God.

"But I say, Have they not heard? Yes verily, their sound went into all the earth, and their words unto the ends of the world.

"But I say, Did not Israel know? First Moses saith, I will provoke you to jealousy by them that are no people, and by a foolish nation I will anger you.

"But Esaias is very bold, and saith, I was found of them that sought Me not; I was made manifest unto them that asked not after Me.

"But to Israel He saith, All day long have I stretched forth My hands unto a disobedient and gainsaying people."

—Rom. 10:14-21

The above is another significant passage *concerning Israel*. In fact Chapters 9, 10 and 11 all revolve around the nation Israel. Israel has a most important place in God's program and some day—who knows how soon—she will be the center of this world's glory.

But it is a fact of life that Israel is not now exalted above the nations. Rather she is struggling just to maintain a foothold in the land once promised to her. Why is this? The answer is found in Romans 9-11, and especially in the above passage.

---

6. The above paragraphs on Rom. 10:13 may also be found, with slight variations, in the author's four-volume set, *Acts, Dispensationally Considered*, at Acts 2:21.

Verses 14 and 15 are generally taken out of context and used as an appeal for foreign missionary service. No doubt the passage can be legitimately *adapted* to make such an *application*, but the context clearly shows that the Apostle is using this argument to prove that Israel herself, not God, is to blame for her present condition.

He contends that "the gospel of peace and...glad tidings of good things" had been proclaimed to them by God-ordained preachers, thus *they* were responsible for not having called upon the name of the Lord to be saved (Vers. 13-15).

"But they have not all *obeyed* the gospel, For Esaias saith, Lord, who hath believed our report?" (Ver. 16).

Indeed, the last phrase of the foregoing verse indicates, as does Chapter 9, that only a small minority had believed, while the nation, as such, had turned a deaf ear to the good news.

Summing up Vers. 14,15, the Apostle says:

"So then, *faith* cometh by *hearing*, and hearing by *the Word of God*" (Ver. 17).

Many people quote this passage without really thinking it through, or connecting it with the preceding context, especially Verses 14,15. The point is that one can believe only what he hears (or reads), and he can hear only *what has been said*. So faith in God comes only by *hearing God*, and we can hear (or read) only *what He has said*.

Thus the Apostle now concludes his argument as to Israel's unbelief and obstinacy in a passage we all do well to heed, Verses 18-21.

Note carefully that each of these verses begins with the word "But." They are *answers to objections* which might be raised in defence of Israel's unbelief.

"But I say, Have they not heard? Yes verily, their sound went into all the earth, and their words unto the ends of the world" (Ver. 18).

Citing Psa. 19:1-4 here, the Apostle argues that since the

knowledge of God has gone to the ends of the earth, is it possible that *Israel*, His chosen people, could not have heard the gospel? They would be the *first* to hear any message from God.

> "But I say, Did not Israel know? First Moses saith, I will provoke you to jealousy by them that are no people, and by a foolish nation I will anger you" (Ver. 19).

Conceding that Israel has *heard* the good news, did she *"know"*?, i.e., did she *understand* it? In answering this question, the Apostle cites Deut. 32:21 and applies it to Israel's present situation. Israel understood very clearly, for God had provoked them to jealousy by "a foolish *nation*," by those who were considered "no people."

It is a mistake to teach, as many do, that the Apostle refers here to the sending of the gospel to the *Gentiles* to provoke Israel to jealousy, as in Rom. 11:11, for *before* sending the gospel to the Gentiles, God had provoked Israel to jealousy by the little flock of His Jewish followers.

In Matt. 21:43 we have our Lord's words to the rulers of Israel:

> "Therefore say I unto you, The kingdom of God shall be taken from you, and given to a nation bringing forth the fruits thereof."

This too is often interpreted to refer to salvation being sent to the Gentiles. But our Lord did not refer to salvation. He declared that *the kingdom* would be *taken from* the rulers in Israel. And He did not say that this kingdom would be given to the Gentiles, but to "*a nation* bringing forth the fruits thereof." The Gentiles were not "a nation," much less a nation bringing forth the fruits of the kingdom. Indeed, the "nation" to which He referred is clearly mentioned in Luke 12:32, where He says to the little flock of His followers:

> "Fear not, little flock; for it is your Father's good pleasure *to give you the kingdom*."

In this connection it must not be forgotten that our Lord had already appointed the twelve apostles as the chief rulers in this kingdom, next to Himself (Matt. 19:28).

Similarly here, in Rom. 10:19, the Apostle refers not to the Gentiles, but to *a nation*, considered "a foolish nation," "no people" by the recognized rulers. How the members of the Sanhedrin must have stormed as the "little flock" preached Christ and the resurrection right in their midst and led thousands to faith in Him!

Pursuing his argument further, the Apostle says:

"But Esaias is very bold, and saith, I was found of them that sought Me not; I was made manifest unto them that asked not after Me" (Ver. 20).

That this *cannot* refer to the sending of salvation to the Gentiles is evident from two important facts. First, this verse *and* Ver. 21 are taken from Isa. 65:1,2, a passage which clearly refers to Israel, not the Gentiles. Second, the Apostle does not say, "Esaias is *very gracious*" or *"very kind,"* as if the passage referred to the sending of the gospel to the Gentiles. He says, *"Esaias is very BOLD,"* and the words which follow show that He refers to the presentation of Christ during the Pentecostal era to those who did not wish to have anything to do with Him, i.e., to the rulers of Israel. This is especially clear from the latter part of Isa. 65:1: *"I said, Behold Me, Behold Me, unto a nation that was not called by My name."*

Thus it is evident that the word "But" in Ver. 21 does not indicate a change in subject from the Gentiles to Israel. Rather it is the Apostle's fourth answer to any possible objection. Beginning for the fourth time with the word "But," he argues that God says to Israel (in Isa. 65:2):

"All day long I have stretched forth My hands unto a disobedient and gainsaying people" (Ver. 21).

Had not Israel heard (Ver. 18)? Or had she perhaps not understood (Ver. 19)? Impossible! Indeed Isaiah uses language that is *"very bold,"* in which God says to rebellious Israel, "You did not want Me, but here I am, Behold Me! Behold Me!" But finally God had to give the nation up, at least for the present, with the words:

"All day long I have stretched forth My hands unto a disobedient and gainsaying people" (Ver. 21).

How significant that this passage argues at length, not for God's sovereign *right* to set Israel aside, but rather as a vindication of His having done so because *they* would not heed His strongest entreaties to acknowledge Jesus Christ as their Savior and Lord. And this constitutes an appeal to unbelievers today.

> Is this the kind return
>   And these the thanks we owe?
> Thus to abuse eternal love
>   Whence all our blessings flow?
>
> To what a stubborn frame
>   Has sin reduced our mind!
> What strange, rebellious wretches we,
>   And God as strangely kind!
>
> Turn, turn us, mighty God,
>   And mould our souls afresh.
> Break, sovereign grace, these hearts of stone,
>   And give us hearts of flesh.
>
> —Isaac Watts

Chapter XI — Romans 11:1-36
ISRAEL AND THE GENTILES IN THE PROGRAM OF GOD

ISRAEL'S PRESENT CONDITION NOT COMPLETELY ABANDONED

"I say then, Hath God cast away His people? God forbid. For I also am an Israelite, of the seed of Abraham, of the tribe of Benjamin.

"God hath not cast away His people which He foreknew. Wot ye not what the Scripture saith of Elias? how he maketh intercession to God against Israel, saying,

"Lord, they have killed Thy prophets, and digged down Thine altars; and I am left alone, and they seek my life.

"But what saith the answer of God unto him? I have reserved to Myself seven thousand men, who have not bowed the knee to the image of Baal.

"Even so then at this present time also there is a remnant according to the election of grace.

"And if by grace, then is it no more of works; otherwise grace is no more grace. But if it be of works, then is it no more grace; otherwise work is no more work."

—Rom. 11:1-6

AN INTRODUCTORY WORD

Since the *fulfillment* of the promises concerning Israel apparently ceased after the ascension and Pentecost, many theologians have come to the conclusion that God could not have meant exactly what He said when He promised that Christ would sit on the throne of David in Jerusalem, as King of Israel.

They believe that God is completely and forever through with Israel and that all the promises made to them should be understood in a "spiritual" sense. Confusing the earthly Jerusalem with "the Jerusalem which is above," they hold that Christ is *now* sitting on the throne of David, that heaven is Canaan, the Church "spiritual" Israel, etc., a far cry from merely recognizing symbolic language!

We object to this whole system of interpretation. It is as illegitimate as if a man should promise to give his son a gold watch on his birthday but, grieved with his son before the birthday arrives, he "keeps his promise" *by giving a grandfather clock to another person altogether!*

There is, in fact, nothing spiritual about this interpretation of the Scriptures. It is *carnal and sinful*, not spiritual, to seek to explain away Scriptural difficulties by arbitrarily altering the plain Word of God. We hold that a pleasing name, "spiritualization," has been given to a system of Bible interpretation which is nothing less than vicious.

Years ago, in one of the *Richmond Hill Discussions*[1] we presented Zech. 8:23, where we read that ten men out of all nations will take hold of the skirt of a Jew, pleading to be with him.

Our opponent "explained" this passage by altering it. He maintained that this prophecy is being fulfilled now. The Bible was written by the Jew, he said, also our Lord was a Jew, and the Gentiles are now coming to Christ and the Bible for blessing.

We responded that the 13th verse says of these same people:

"...AS YE WERE A CURSE AMONG THE HEATHEN...SO WILL I SAVE YOU AND YE SHALL BE A BLESSING."

Were Christ and the Bible ever a *curse* to the Gentiles? Did God have to *save* either Christ or the Bible to make them a blessing!

As we come to the "New Testament" Scriptures we find the obvious, natural interpretation placed upon these "Old

---

[1]. A series of ten debates on dispensationalism, held in Richmond Hill, N.Y., in which the author participated.

Testament" prophecies. When our Lord's birth approached, the angel announced:

> "...the Lord God shall give unto Him the throne of His Father David; and He shall reign over the house of Jacob forever, and of His kingdom there shall be no end" (Luke 1:32,33).

A dozen, perhaps scores of "New Testament" Scriptures could be cited in this connection. But the spiritualizers alter these too, insisting that Christ is *now* reigning over "the house of David," i.e., the Church, His "covenant people" today, and that the "Body of Christ" is the same as the "kingdom of Christ," over which He shall reign forever.

Many spiritualizers contend that our Lord's disciples were unspiritual when they asked, after His resurrection:

> "Lord, wilt Thou at this time restore again the kingdom to Israel?" (Acts 1:6).

It can hardly be denied that these disciples expected nothing less than a restoration of the theocracy in greater glory, with Christ as King. But was this a sign of ignorance or lack of spiritual perception? We believe not. Indeed, we read with regard to our Lord's contact with His disciples just after His resurrection:

> "Then opened He their understanding, that they might understand the Scriptures" (Luke 24:45).

And then, with their eyes *opened to understand the Scriptures*, our Lord spent *"forty days"* with them, *"speaking of the things pertaining to the kingdom of God"* (Acts 1:3). How then could they have been so carnal or ignorant in asking the question of Acts 1:6? Actually it is the so-called "spiritualizers" who are carnal in altering the plain Word of God and are ignorant of the great truths that render such a course completely unnecessary. If one sees and acknowledges the Mystery revealed through Paul, there is no need to alter any prophecy to make it harmonize with the present dispensation.

The "spiritualization" of the prophetic Word is a serious error for three important reasons:

1. It leaves us at the mercy of theologians. If the Scriptures do not mean what they obviously, naturally seem to mean, just what else do they mean, and who has the authority to decide? Then perhaps salvation, after all, is *not* by grace. Perhaps it *is* by works. Perhaps these Scriptures too really mean something else—and who has the authority to interpret them for us?

If the "spiritualization" of the Scriptures is valid, then we are indeed left at the mercy of theologians, and future theologians may wrest from us what today's theologians have agreed to allow us. Nor will it do any good to turn to the Scriptures to see what *God* says, for God does not always mean what He says, and only trained theologians can correctly interpret His Word for us! This is the position of the Church of Rome, which arrogates to herself *final authority* in spiritual matters, but this leads to a vicious cycle indeed, for where would Rome get her authority *from?!*

2. It affects the veracity of God. It is a thrust at His very honor. If the obvious, natural meaning of the "Old Testament" promises is not to be depended upon, how can we depend upon *any* promise of God? Then, when He says that *"Christ died for our sins,"* He may also mean something else. This is unthinkable of God.

It is only *just* that the promis*ee* should have a fair understanding of the promise for, promised something, he will have a right to *claim* exactly what he has been promised. A little child, confused over an ambiguous explanation of a Scripture passage, is supposed to have asked: "If God didn't mean what He said, why didn't He say what He meant?"

3. It is the mother of apostasy. When Luke 1:32,33 is "spiritualized" the Modernist, or Liberal, agrees wholeheartedly. He agrees that the throne of David and the house of Israel in this passage must be viewed in a "spiritual" sense—*and so must the next few verses!* Thus Christ was not *really* born of a virgin. This is merely a picture, drawn to impress us with the purity of His person!

And the Modernist denies the resurrection in the same way. Concerning Acts 2:30-32 it is argued that since Christ apparently will not *really* occupy the throne of David, *neither was He really raised from the dead!* The Scriptures which say so must be "spiritually" interpreted!

And here comes a "Jehovah's Witness," claiming to be one of the 144,000. Ask him which tribe he is from and he will explain that not physical, but "spiritual" Israelites are referred to in the prophecy of the 144,000. Yet we are distinctly told that there are to be *12,000 from each tribe, and the tribes are named!*

Rome employs the same reasoning. She is seeking to establish the kingdom of Christ on earth—*herself being that kingdom!*

Those who have resorted to the "spiritualization" of the prophetic Scriptures because they cannot otherwise account for the seeming cessation in their fulfillment in this present age, will find the solution to their problem in the recognition of the "Mystery." We repeat: Recognize the Mystery and there will be no need to alter prophecy.

In Romans 11 the Apostle Paul, to whom the Mystery was revealed, utterly annihilates the teaching that God is through with Israel and has transferred all her blessings to the Church, the Body of Christ.

THE BELIEVING REMNANT

The great truths of Romans 11 are vital to a clear understanding of God's program for this age and that which is to come.

Chapters 9 and 10 explain why God finally gave Israel up (temporarily) and ceased dealing with her as a nation. This, as we have seen, has caused some to conclude that God is through with Israel and has raised up the Church, the Body of Christ, in her stead. Paul answers this error in Chapter 11, and shows that her "casting away" is neither total nor permanent.

The latter part of Ver. 1, along with Ver. 2-5 and Ver. 15, clearly indicate the sense of Ver. 1. *"Hath God cast away*

His people?" i.e., completely and permanently? And the answer is, *"God forbid!"*

Ver. 15 indicates that God *has* cast away the nation Israel, but Paul's argument that God has reserved to Himself a remnant (Vers. 2-5) shows that in Ver. 1 he means that God has not cast *all* Israel away.

In proof of this he declares, *"I also am an Israelite,"* i.e., God has not cast *me* away! Surely no one was better qualified than Paul to advance this argument, for he was not only a pure-blooded son of Abraham, but he belonged to the small, but noble, tribe of Benjamin.

The fact that he did not say "you yourselves are Israelites," or "There are many believing Israelites among you" (seemingly the best proof of all that God had not totally cast Israel away), is another proof that the church at Rome was made up overwhelmingly of Gentile believers and not of Jewish converts won to Messiah by some who had returned to Rome after Pentecost.[2] This is further confirmed by his words in Ver. 13, where he says, *"I speak to you Gentiles...."*

There is a temptation to interpret the words "His people which He foreknew" to refer only to the remnant; *they* had not been cast away. However, the ensuing context clearly indicates that the Apostle still refers to the whole nation, whom God had indeed foreknown, and that because of His plans for *the nation* He had not cast them *all* away. Many "Old Testament" Scriptures confirm this viewpoint, as e.g.:

I Sam. 12:22: "For the Lord will not forsake His people for His great name's sake: because it hath pleased the Lord to make you His people."

Jer. 31:37: "Thus saith the Lord; If heaven above can be measured, and the foundations of the earth searched out beneath, I will also cast off all the seed of Israel for all that they have done, saith the Lord."

These and other "Old Testament" passages prove that God had purposed never to cast Israel away entirely or permanently. Yet other passages, like II Kings 23:27, indicate

---

2. See *Introduction*.

that He was even then about to temporarily cast *the nation* aside *as such*:

> "And the Lord said, I will remove Judah also out of My sight, as I have removed Israel, and will cast off this city Jerusalem, which I have chosen, and the house of which I said, My name shall be there."

Does not this remind us of our Lord's sad words in Matt. 23:37-39:

> "O Jerusalem, Jerusalem, thou that killest the prophets, and stonest them which are sent unto thee; how often would I have gathered thy children together, even as a hen gathereth her chickens under her wings, and ye would not!
>
> "Behold, your house is left unto you desolate.
>
> "For I say unto you, Ye shall not see Me henceforth till ye shall say, Blessed is He that cometh in the name of the Lord."

All this confirms Paul's argument in Rom. 11:1-5.

The words "cast away" in Vers. 1,2 (Gr., *apotheo*) mean to thrust from oneself, to cast off by way of rejection, and we should let them have their full force rather than toning them down with such terms as "set aside." The same term in Ver. 15 is a slightly different Greek word (*apobole*), but is such a close synonym that it is likewise futile to use it to soften the facts of God's dealings with Israel at this time.

The point of the passage is that God has not cast away *all* Israelites. At one time Elijah thought He had done so! The worship of Baal had practically become Israel's state religion. Under Ahab and Jezebel the multitudes bowed down before this pagan god. Elijah had valiantly challenged this vile, idolatrous religion, and had "triumphed gloriously," but almost immediately he had to flee for his life from the wicked Jezebel, and when God found him, utterly dejected, he said, as it were, "Lord, where have *You* been? I have been very jealous for You, but what encouragement have You given me?"

> "...they have killed *Thy* prophets, and digged down *Thine* altars; and *I* am left alone, *and they seek my life*" (Ver. 3; cf. I Ki. 19:10,14).

God's answer to His distraught prophet is both heart-warming and majestic:

"I have reserved to Myself seven thousand men, who have not bowed the knee to the image of Baal" (Ver. 4).

So many men courageous enough to refuse to yield to Baal worship? And under such pressure?! Yes, *by the grace of God!* It is sad that in the New Evangelicalism of our day permissiveness is so prevalent. Few, if any, of the Neo-evangelicals have sought and found the grace to say *"No!"* to the pressures of a backsliding Christian leadership. Rather they themselves have brought the Church to such a low ebb, spiritually.

Mark well, however: God did not say, "Luckily about 7000 are standing true." How could they stand true except by His grace? Rather He said, *"I have reserved to Myself seven thousand men."* Thus the record of Scripture cites not merely the heroism of this believing remnant, but God's purpose in reserving them to Himself. All the glory must go to Him, without whom the remnant would have been as cowardly and wicked as the rest.

In Paul's day, many Jews who had trusted Christ as their Savior and were standing true to Him had to suffer greatly at the hand of their kinsmen. This they were able to do only by the grace of God, just as they had been saved by the grace of God. Yet we must not confuse *"grace to help"* (Heb. 4:16) with saving grace. Thus the Apostle continues:

"Even so then at this present time also there is a remnant according to the election of grace.

"And if by grace, then is it no more of works; otherwise grace is no more grace. But if it be of works, then is it no more grace; otherwise work is no more work" (Vers. 5,6).

Grace is not grace if mingled with works. The two principles are mutually exclusive (Rom. 4:4,5). Thus in salvation there is no "your part" to perform; it is the *gift* of God's love, to be received in simple faith (Rom. 6:23; Eph. 2:8,9).

Is some reader determined to be saved by his own efforts? Then that reader will have to suffer all that Christ went through to pay the penalty for his sins—and that will take all eternity in "the lake of fire."[3]

Paul was part of the remnant according to the election of grace. He richly deserved to be cast away with his rebellious kinsmen, but was saved by the grace of God (I Tim. 1:13-16). This should mean much to us Gentiles in the flesh, for we certainly did not deserve to be numbered among the people of God.

UNBELIEVING ISRAEL JUDICIALLY BLINDED

"What then? Israel hath not obtained that which he seeketh for; but the election hath obtained it, and the rest were blinded.

"(According as it is written, God hath given them the spirit of slumber, eyes that they should not see, and ears that they should not hear;) unto this day.

"And David saith, Let their table be made a snare, and a trap, and a stumblingblock, and a recompense unto them:

"Let their eyes be darkened, that they may not see, and bow down their back alway."

—Rom. 11:7-10

"What then?" Or, "What does all this add up to?" The answer is: *"Israel hath not obtained that which he seeketh for, but the election hath obtained it, and the rest were blinded"* (Ver. 7).

What was it that Israel sought for but did not obtain? *Righteousness.* They did not obtain it because *"going about to establish their own righteousness,"* they refused to *"submit themselves unto the righteousness of God"* (Rom. 10:3). They *"followed after the law of righteousness,"* but failed to obtain righteousness. *"Wherefore? Because they sought it not by faith, but as it were by the works, of the law, for THEY STUMBLED AT THAT STUMBLINGSTONE"* (Rom. 9: 31,32). They were not willing to accept God's righteous-

---
3. See the author's discussion of this subject in *Man, His Nature and Destiny*, Pp. 133-137.

ness, imputed *by grace*, and, as we have just seen, if it be by grace it is *not* by works, and if by works, it is *not* by grace (Ver. 6).

It should be observed that Verse 7 does not say that "the rest were *blind*," but that they "were *blinded*."[4] Had they been blind, there might have been some excuse for their attitude, but they had not been blind. They *knew* that they had failed, day after day, year after year, to keep God's Law, but unwilling to "give up" and cry to God for mercy, they continued "going about to establish their own righteousness." Thus God finally gave them up and allowed a judicial blindness to settle down upon them. To understand the meaning of the word "blinded" (Gr., *poroo*), in Ver. 7, the closing words of Ver. 7 should be read along with Ver. 8:

"... and the rest were blinded *(According as it is written, God hath given them the spirit of slumber, eyes that they should not see, and ears that they should not hear)....*"

Here we have two more of Paul's metaphors. In Rom. 10:8-10 it was the mouth and the heart; here it is the eyes and the ears. And significantly, where "slumber" takes over, not only the eyes but also the ears are affected. When one falls asleep he becomes blind, and also deaf to the things about him. Thus God gave Israel up to her self-blindness, giving her "the spirit of slumber...unto this day" (Ver. 8).

In Vers. 9,10 the Apostle quotes from David, in Psa. 69, to place even greater emphasis on the folly of self-righteousness, showing how God, in judgment, had turned Israel's blessings into curses because of this attitude.

In David's day, most people simply sat on the ground to dine, usually in a circle, with the food placed before and about them. Due to the heat of the Palestinian climate they often ate out of doors, on blankets and rugs. This was an opportune time for an enemy to surprise them, seated on the

---

4. We cannot accept the definition of the Greek *poroo* and *porosis* as "harden" and "hardness," except in the sense of a stupefying or dulling of the *senses*. Uniformly this word is associated with a lack of spiritual perception, and this is naturally associated with *blindness*. Moreover, in the very next verse, Ver. 8, the Apostle himself defines it as *"the spirit of slumber."*

ground and surrounded by dishes, food, etc. In such a case their "table" became a "trap" and a "stumblingblock," for under such circumstances it would be difficult to arise quickly to their feet. They would be apt to stumble over the dishes, the food, the servants and other obstacles.

Applied to Israel in Paul's day, and to religious but unsaved people in ours, it might be said, "Let their special privileges become a trap to them. Let their possession of God's Word and their form of worship become to them, not a blessing, but a curse; a 'recompense' for their self-righteous attitude." The Apostle continues:

"Let their eyes be darkened, that they may not see, and bow down their back alway" (Ver. 10).

How graphic! They would not acknowledge their sinful condition; they insisted on gaining salvation by their own efforts. Therefore, saith God, "Let their eyes be darkened," so that they may not recognize their condition, and "bow down their back alway" with a load they cannot possibly bear, i.e., they were judicially blinded and must bear the futility of their self-righteousness.

ISRAEL'S FALL AND RECOVERY

"I say then, Have they stumbled that they should fall? God forbid: but rather through their fall salvation is come unto the Gentiles for to provoke them to jealousy.

"Now if the fall of them be the riches of the world, and the diminishing of them the riches of the Gentiles; how much more their fulness!

"For I speak to you Gentiles, inasmuch as I am the apostle of the Gentiles, I magnify mine office:

"If by any means I may provoke to emulation them which are my flesh, and might save some of them.

"For if the casting away of them be the reconciling of the world, what shall the receiving of them be, but life from the dead?

"For if the firstfruits be holy, the lump is also holy; and if the root be holy, so are the branches."

—Rom. 11:11-16

It should be carefully observed that the above passage

does *not* deal mainly with *the blessing of the Gentiles* through the fall of Israel, important as this fact is. Rather it deals basically with the fact that God still has Israel on His heart and in His plans; that she will recover from her present fallen condition and rise to great glory. See the thrust of his contention as he pursues his argument that God has not cast the favored nation away forever:

1. "Have they stumbled that they should fall[5] [i.e., beyond recovery]?" (Ver. 11).

   a. "God forbid; but rather through their fall salvation is come unto the Gentiles for *to provoke them* [Israel] *to jealousy*" (Ver. 11).

   b. "Now if the fall of them be the riches of the world...how much more their fulness!" (Ver. 12).

2. "For I speak to you Gentiles, inasmuch as I am the apostle of the Gentiles; *I magnify mine office*" (Ver. 13).

   a. "If by any means I may provoke to emulation them which are my flesh, and might save some of them" (Ver. 14).

   b. "For if the casting away of them be the reconciling of the world, what shall the receiving of them be, but life from the dead?" (Ver. 15).

And to this he adds: "For if the *firstfruit* be holy, the *lump* is also holy; and if the *root* be holy, so are the *branches*" (Ver. 16). We take the "firstfruit" here to be those who at Pentecost foreshadowed the salvation of the nation, "the lump." Likewise with the "root" and the "branches," though, in the light of the following context the "root" in this case may go back all the way to Abraham.

A brief but important digression is necessary here. While it is true that one reason why Paul magnified his office as the Apostle of the Gentiles was to provoke his kinsmen to jealousy (that they might envy what he had), it remains a fact that it was by divine inspiration that he wrote:

---

5. The Greek for "fall" here is not the same as that which occurs twice in the next two sentences. Here the word is *ptaio*, to fall beyond recovery. It is in the aorist, and denotes a *precipitous* fall. But in the next two occurrences it is *paraptoma*, to *fall aside*, or *fall away*, as a soldier might fall from the ranks. Both words, however, are used in a moral or spiritual sense. Indeed, both are sometimes rendered "offense" in KJV.

"For I speak to you Gentiles, inasmuch as I am the apostle of the Gentiles: I magnify mine office" (Ver. 13).

It is of profound importance to bear this firmly in mind. We live in a day when the unique character of Paul's apostleship is minimized, if not denied. He is considered to be merely "one of the apostles." Some even think that the eleven made a mistake in choosing Matthias to fill Judas' place—that in God's mind *Paul* was the twelfth apostle.

We have demonstrated, however, in many *Searchlight* articles, plus our books, *Things That Differ*, *Moses and Paul*, *Our Great Commission*, and *Acts, Dispensationally Considered*, that Paul's apostleship was wholly separate and distinct from that of the twelve and that, indeed, he would not have qualified for a position among them.

Those who ignore or deny the distinctiveness of Paul's apostleship and ministry, or fail to give it its due emphasis, minimize what *God* has magnified. Certainly to undermine Paul's position as the God-appointed apostle of grace is to undermine the very "dispensation of the grace of God" itself, for Paul was the living demonstration of the grace he proclaimed. Hence his battles in defense of his apostleship. Be it noted, however, that while he indeed magnified his office, he never exalted himself.

Now, back to Israel's fall and recovery.

THE DIMINISHING OF THEM

The present "diminishing" of Israel, mentioned in Ver. 12, doubtless has reference to both her national and spiritual loss. Presently Israel is not the "head" among the great nations of the world (Deut. 28:13); rather she is the "tail" (28:44). And rather than imparting spiritual light to the nations, she herself is blinded, as we have seen.

We believe, however, that the "diminishing" of Israel refers also to their *numerical* diminution. This, according to Ex. 34, Lev. 26, Deut. 28, and other Old Testament passages, was to be one of the important evidences of God's displeasure with Israel if they forsook Him. These passages go into great detail to warn Israel that God, who had promised to multiply them and enlarge their borders would, if they departed from Him, cut them off, for the time being, by pestilence, famine and sword until they were "few in number" and their borders had been tragically reduced.

How conspicuously this has been fulfilled in the experience of the favored nation since she joined the Gentiles in rebellion against God and His Christ (Psa. 2:1-3; cf. Acts 4:25-27)!

The *total world population* of Jews, or Israelites, today is about 14,353,790.[6] Does this sound like a great number? Then compare it with the population of other religious groups:

```
Christians[7] .............................954,766,700
Muslims ...............................538,213,900
Hindus ................................524,273,500
Buddhists..............................249,877,300
Confucianists ..........................186,104,300
Israelites .............................. 14,353,790
```

Thus Israel is diminutive, numerically, when compared with the other leading religions of the world. There are more than *66 times as many* "Christians" in the world as Israelites, more than *37 times as many* Muslims, and even more than *13 times as many* Confucianists. Yet it was the people of Israel that God promised to multiply "as the stars of heaven and as the sand which is upon the seashore."

Or, consider national comparisons:[8] the approximate populations of:

```
China .................................864,000,000
India ..................................625,000,000
USSR .................................258,000,000
Japan .................................113,000,000
```

---

6. All totals in the following section are taken from the *Hammond Almanac* of 1980.

7. Nominal, of course. Those who profess the name of Christ.

8. We have purposely omitted the United States of America because its population is made up of so many different nationalities.

Germany	61,000,000
Italy	56,000,000
France	53,000,000
Egypt	38,000,000
Israel	3,700,000

From the above it may readily be seen that even the populations of nations like Japan, Germany, Italy and France are many times that of Israel. Even Egypt has more than ten times her population, and compared with China and India she is tiny indeed.

As we have said, God promised to multiply the seed of *Israel* "as the stars of heaven and as the sand which is upon the seashore."[9] Indeed, 3500 years ago, after Israel had been in slavery for 400 years (Acts 7:6), and many had succumbed to their hardships or had been put to death (e.g., Ex. 1:22), even then, during their 430 years in Egypt, their numbers had grown from 70 souls to an estimated two to three million[10] (See Ex. 12:40,41; Deut. 10:22). Yet *now*, after *three and a half millenniums* they still number less than 15,000,000 souls, other nations and religions vastly outstripping them.

Blame this on Hitler and all the persecutors of Israel down through the centuries—and they richly deserve to be blamed—but it still remains a fact that *God* permitted it, and again and again Israel's own Scriptures give us the reason. In addition to the many promises of Israel's multiplication we have in the chapters referred to above three passages which should be cited here with regard to Israel's prosperity vs. her "diminishing":

Ex. 34:24: "For I will cast out the nations before thee, and enlarge thy borders; neither shall any man desire thy land."

The multiplying and enlarging of Israel was to be her portion as she believed and obeyed God. Through unbelief

---

9. We have already noted that this multiplied seed, first promised to Abraham, was to come through Isaac and then Jacob.

10. This is estimated from the fact that shortly after their deliverance from Egypt the total number of *men* "from twenty years old and upward," who were "able to go forth to war" was 603,550 (Num. 1:45,46).

and disobedience, however, the following was to become—and has become—her lot:

> Deut. 28:62: "And ye shall be left few in number, whereas ye were as the stars of heaven for multitude; because thou wouldest not obey the voice of the Lord thy God."

> Lev. 26:17: "And I will set My face against you, and ye shall be slain before your enemies, they that hate you shall reign over you, and ye shall flee when none pursueth you."

How often through the past centuries these last two passages have been fulfilled! Even today, *a small minority* of Israelites has but a *tenuous* hold on a *small part* of the land once promised to her. If only those of the once-favored people could see that this is a fulfillment of God's warnings, so often reiterated in their own Scriptures—and if only they would take to heart the words of the Apostle Paul, the Hebrew of the Hebrews who loved them so deeply, and receive salvation by grace through faith in Christ!

Speaking of small numbers, the "remnant according to the election of grace" is indeed, as in Isaiah's day, "a very small remnant" (Isa. 1:9), so small that in the thousands of speaking engagements in "Gentile" churches which this author has filled through the years, few indeed have been the believing Jews who have met with us. So small has been their number that where even two or three have been present, the pastor of the church has been wont to lean over during the preliminaries and whisper, "We have some Jewish believers in this church."

Do we cite all these statistics and facts to belittle Israel? *By no means!* for the author has for many years had a special love in his heart for the Jews, and looks forward with eager anticipation to the day when God again raises her to great glory, and His original promises to her shall be fulfilled; when "the nations shall come to [her] light, and kings to the brightness of [her] rising" (Isa. 60:3).

Little wonder the Apostle Paul calls the present situation "this *mystery* among the Gentiles" (Col. 1:27), for it is certainly not the fulfillment of *prophecy* concerning them!

(See Rom. 11:25; cf. 15:8,9). Old Testament prophecy says nothing about the salvation of the Gentiles through Israel's fall. This is the gift of God's grace, and we Gentiles in the flesh should be humbly grateful every time we meet with Gentile believers to worship Israel's God and her Messiah, now the Head of "the Church which is His Body."

We do not have available space here to discuss the great volume of Old Testament prophecy which deals with Israel's restoration, but this is the thrust of Paul's great argument in Rom. 9-11, and especially in Chapter 11. God has *not* cast Israel away, either completely or permanently, but only "in part" and "until" (Rom. 11:25), i.e., her judicial blinding is only *partial* and *temporary*. She *will* be restored to glory greater by far than any she has experienced in the past. And this will affect the nations too, for "if the *fall* of them" is now "the riches of the world," think of the riches that will flow to the Gentiles through Israel's salvation and rise! Old Testament prophecy abounds with descriptions of this wonderful time of blessing under Messiah's reign.[11] Consider some of Paul's statements in Rom. 11 alone:

Ver. 2: "God hath not cast away His people [i.e., permanently or completely] which He foreknew."

Ver. 5: "...there is a remnant according to the election of grace."

Ver. 7: "Israel hath not obtained that which he seeketh for; *but the election hath obtained it....*"

Ver. 12: "Now if the fall of them be the riches of the world, and the diminishing of them the riches of the Gentiles; *how much more their fulness!*"

Ver. 15: "For if the casting away of them be the reconciling of the world, *what shall the receiving of them be, but life from the dead!*"

Ver. 26: "*And so all Israel shall be saved;* as it is written, There shall come out of Sion the Deliverer, and shall turn away ungodliness from Jacob."

We have often wondered what our "spiritualizing" brethren can possibly do with such passages as Rom. 11:7,12 and

---

11. The author has written on this subject at some length in his *Things That Differ*, Pp. 49-53.

15—and have never read one clear answer to the Apostle's declarations in these verses.

Surely the "election" in Ver. 7 must refer to the election *from Israel*.

As to Ver. 12, how can "their fulness" refer to anything but the "fulness" of the *same nation* that had *fallen* and been *diminished*?

And must not the second "them" in Ver. 15 refer to the same nation as the first "them"? Granted, the second "them" is not found in the Greek—it is not needed there—but it is certainly included in the English as a legitimate ellipsis. Unquestionably this verse teaches that while Israel's "casting away" brought about "the reconciling of the world," [12] the "receiving of them" will be "life from the dead." How can the second "them" be legitimately "spiritualized" to refer to another company altogether?

THE BLESSING OF THE GENTILES TODAY

While the Apostle's chief purpose in Chapter 11 is to prove that God is *not* "through with Israel," as the "spiritualizers" teach, it is enlightening to consider what he says here regarding the blessing of the Gentiles during this present "dispensation of the grace of God." Let us consider this in the light of its background.

According to all covenant and prophecy, the Gentiles were —and are—to be blessed through the *rise* of Israel. Note only the two following passages of Scripture:

" . . . in blessing I will bless thee, and in multiplying I will multiply thy

---

[12]. Note, "the reconciling of the *world*," not merely the reconciling of the Gentiles (Cf. Rom. 11:32). In II Cor. 5:19 we read that (at Calvary) "*God was in Christ, reconciling the world unto Himself*," but historically He could not reconcile them to Himself until Israel, as well as the Gentiles, had been "cast away" (Rom. 11:12), for *reconciliation* postulates alienation. Hence, it was *by* the cross that God thus reconciled the world to Himself, but historically, *when* Israel was "cast away." This reconciliation, of course, is *God's part* in the reconciliation of God and men to each other, for He still sends us out to His enemies, with the ministry of reconciliation, beseeching them in His name, *"Be ye reconciled."*

seed as the stars of the heaven, and as the sand which is upon the seashore; and thy seed shall possess the gate of his enemies;

"AND IN THY SEED SHALL ALL THE NATIONS OF THE EARTH BE BLESSED..." (Gen. 22:17,18).

"Arise and shine; for thy light is come, and the glory of the Lord is risen upon thee.

"For, behold the darkness shall cover the earth, and gross darkness the people, BUT THE LORD SHALL ARISE UPON THEE, AND HIS GLORY SHALL BE SEEN UPON THEE.

"AND THE GENTILES SHALL COME TO THY LIGHT, AND KINGS TO THE BRIGHTNESS OF THY RISING" (Isa. 60:1-3).

This will take place at a future time, but surely it is not happening today. Today the situation is different indeed.

Whereas Israel, according to prophecy, is to be given *supremacy* over the nations (Isa. 60:10-12; 61:6), this is clearly not so today. Israel, as a nation, has been cast out of God's favor, as the Gentiles had been many centuries before, but both Jews and Gentiles as individuals are now offered reconciliation by grace through the shed blood of Christ (II Cor. 5:14-21; cf. Rom. 11:32,33).

According to covenant and prophecy, the Gentiles are to be blessed through Israel's *instrumentality* (Gen. 22:17,18; Zech. 8:13), but today they are being blessed through Israel's *obstinacy* (Acts 13:44-46; Rom. 11:28-32).

According to prophecy the Gentiles are to be blessed through Israel's *rise* (Isa. 60:1-3; Zech. 8:22,23). But today the Gentiles are being blessed through her *fall*: *"through their fall salvation is come unto the Gentiles"* (Rom. 11:11; cf. Vers. 12,15).

Thus the salvation of Gentiles—and Jews—today is not based on any *covenant* but only on God's *grace*; not on the fulfillment of any *prophecy*, but upon His eternal purpose, *"the mystery...kept secret since the world began,"* but made known in due time through the Apostle Paul (Rom. 11:25; Eph. 3:1-4).

THE OLIVE TREE
THE ROOT AND THE BRANCHES

"And if some of the branches be broken off, and thou, being a wild olive tree, wert grafted in among them, and with them partakest of the root and fatness of the olive tree;

"Boast not against the branches. But if thou boast, thou bearest not the root, but the root thee.

"Thou wilt say then, The branches were broken off, that I might be grafted in.

"Well; because of unbelief they were broken off, and thou standest by faith. Be not highminded, but fear:

"For if God spared not the natural branches, take heed lest He also spare not thee.

"Behold therefore the goodness and severity of God: on them which fell, severity; but toward thee, goodness, if thou continue in His goodness: otherwise thou also shalt be cut off.

"And they also, if they abide not still in unbelief, shall be grafted in: for God is able to graft them in again.

"For if thou wert cut out of the olive tree which is wild by nature, and wert grafted contrary to nature into a good olive tree: how much more shall these, which be the natural branches, be grafted into their own olive tree?"

—Rom. 11:17-24

In employing the familiar figure of the olive tree, the Apostle Paul further presses home his argument that God has not cast Israel away either totally or finally—and he cautions believing Gentiles not to be highminded because God has, for a season, replaced unbelieving Israel with them.

In determining exactly whom the olive tree, its root, its natural branches and its grafted-in branches represent, it will help us to remember that in Romans 9—11 the Apostle deals with *dispensational position*, not with the doctrine of justification by faith.

It is almost universally agreed that the original olive tree represents Israel. As to the branches that were broken off, it is also generally agreed that these represent unbelieving

Israel, the majority who had been "cast away," the remaining branches representing the believing remnant. This harmonizes with what we considered in the earlier part of the chapter:

"Even so then at this present time also *there is a remnant according to the election of grace*" (Ver. 5).

"What then? Israel hath not obtained that which he seeketh for: but *the election hath obtained it, and the rest were blinded*" (Ver. 7).

But who are the branches from "the *wild* olive tree" that, "contrary to nature," were grafted into "the good olive tree"? Surely they are not the Gentile nations for (1) they are said to be believers. (2) The nations will not be "broken off," but *blessed* when unbelieving Israel is saved and grafted in again, and (3) the Gentile nations today are certainly not living from "the root and fatness of the olive tree."

Could the grafted-in branches, then, represent the Church, the Body of Christ, as some teach? Again, no, for (1) the Body *contains* the believing remnant who are *left in* the olive tree. (2) The Jewish believers *in the Church*, the Body of Christ, did not come from the "wild olive tree," and (3) it is *Gentile believers*, not the Church as such, who are warned lest they be "broken off" so that those Jews who "abide not still in unbelief" might be grafted in again.

In considering the figure of the olive tree, we would remind our readers that while indeed the Church today is a "joint body" of Jewish and Gentile believers, with one as welcome as the other, it is a simple fact that the Jewish believers constitute a *very small* minority of the whole, as we have seen. Practically speaking, therefore, Paul calls God's work today "this mystery among *the Gentiles*" (Col. 1:27), and refers to the completion of the Body as "the fulness of *the Gentiles*" (Rom. 11:25). This is not strange when we consider the small minority of Gentile proselytes among the Jews when Israel was God's people.

We agree with Dr. Arthur C. Custance that the olive tree is associated, symbolically, with Israel's *spiritual history*.[13]

---

13. *The Doorway Papers*, Vol. VI, Pp. 66-69. Zondervan Publishing House.

"The root" doubtless represents Abraham, and "the fatness," the blessings that came to him through faith. Since the nation that sprang from him, however, did not continue in faith, the vast majority of the branches were "broken off." Meantime Gentile believers, "branches" from a "wild olive tree," were grafted in among the believing branches that had been left in the good olive tree.

This agrees beautifully with what the Apostle himself says about believing Gentiles in the Body of Christ:

"And he [Abraham] received the sign of circumcision, a seal of the righteousness of the faith which he had yet being uncircumcised; that he might be the father of all them that believe, though they be not circumcised; that righteousness might be imputed unto them also" (Rom. 4:11).

"And if ye be Christ's, then are ye Abraham's seed, and heirs according to the promise" (Gal. 3:29).

Gentiles, Abraham's seed?! Of course, if they are *in Christ*. Was He not Abraham's seed?

Once more we must remind our readers, however, that the Apostle, in using this symbol of the olive tree, with its "broken off" and "grafted in" branches, is dealing basically with *dispensational position*, not with the doctrine of justification by faith, else it would surely teach that believers may be lost again, repudiating the very doctrine which he proclaims with such emphasis in Chapter 8: the eternal security of the believer in Christ. But the metaphor of the olive tree in Romans 11 harmonizes perfectly with the doctrinal chapters of Romans *when we see the dispensational aspect of Chapter 11*.

If the Apostle were dealing with doctrinal issues here, the branches that were broken off would certainly *not* be grafted in again, for the actual branches that were broken off, having resisted the Holy Spirit at Pentecost, were not to be forgiven either in that age *or in "the age to come."* They had committed an unpardonable sin (Matt. 12:31,32; cf. Acts 7:51). Thus the *individuals* who were "broken off" will not be "grafted in again." They lived and died without Christ.

But Paul is not referring to individual salvation here, thus he says that if "they," i.e., the *nation*, "abide not still in unbelief," *they will* be grafted in again (Rom. 11:23). Likewise the Gentile believers who were grafted in "stand," i.e., *in that position*, only "by faith," and if they continue not "in His goodness" they too will be "cut off" (Ver. 22). Indeed, the passage clearly teaches that the "grafted in" branches *will* be broken off again, and the "broken off" branches grafted in to "their own olive tree."

Thus, viewed dispensationally, this passage by no means militates against the doctrine of eternal security.

This opens up an aspect of the Rapture of the Church that is too little considered. This "blessed hope" gladdens, and should gladden, the heart of every instructed and sincere believer. However there are *two* aspects of the Rapture that should have a sobering effect upon us.

First, it is clearly at the Rapture that the Gentile branches [14] will be broken off so that Israel might be grafted in again. I.e., when the Gentile branches cease to "continue in His goodness" and fail to fulfil their God-ordained function, they will be "broken off" and taken out of this world. Believers who profess to love the Lord Jesus should carefully consider the fact that our rapture to heaven will mark the end of our opportunity to reach our fellowmen with the gospel of the grace of God.

Second, it will be "at that day" that all the members of the Body, dead and alive, will be caught up for a meeting with the Lord in the air, to "receive rewards" or "suffer loss" for their conduct and their service for Christ (I Cor. 3:9-15; II Cor. 5:10; cf. I Thes. 4:17; I Cor. 4:5; II Tim. 4:8). These are solemn facts to consider as God, in His grace, leaves us here to work and witness for the Lord Jesus Christ.

---

14. Jewish believers in the Body will, of course, also be taken up at the Rapture for, as we have said above: "The Body *contains* the believing remnant who are *left in* the olive tree." As we have seen, however, the Body is composed overwhelmingly of Gentiles in the flesh and is therefore viewed *practically* as a Gentile Church (Acts 28:28; Col. 1:27; Rom. 11:25).

BE NOT HIGHMINDED

It was when Israel vainly considered herself merely the *object* rather than the *agent* of God's blessing that the branches were broken off, and the Apostle warns us of similar consequences if *we* become conceited.

"Boast not against the branches," he says, and when you are tempted to boast, remember *"thou bearest not the root, but the root thee"* (Rom. 11:18). This warning is sorely needed at a time when even those who call themselves Christians are often prone to anti-semitic attitudes. Thus he continues:

"...because of unbelief they were broken off, and thou standest by faith. Be not highminded, but fear.

"For if God spared not the natural branches, take heed lest He also spare not thee.

"Behold therefore the goodness and severity of God: on them which fell, severity; but toward thee, goodness, if thou continue in His goodness: otherwise thou also shalt be cut off" (Vers. 20-22).

In the next section of the chapter the Apostle again exhorts Gentile believers lest they be wise in their own conceits (Ver. 25).

How humble, then, and grateful we should be for the blessings He has so graciously bestowed upon us who had no claim upon Him!

PROPHECY AND THE MYSTERY

"For I would not, brethren, that ye should be ignorant of this mystery, lest ye should be wise in your own conceits; that blindness in part is happened to Israel, until the fulness of the Gentiles be come in.

"And so all Israel shall be saved: as it is written, There shall come out of Sion the Deliverer, and shall turn away ungodliness from Jacob:

"For this is My covenant unto them, when I shall take away their sins."

—Rom. 11:25-27

To understand God's plan for the ages, and for the age in which we live, we must recognize the fact that the basic division in the Word of God is *not* that between the so-called

"Old" and "New" Testaments. It is rather that between *prophecy* and "the *mystery*"; between that which "God hath *spoken* by the mouth of all His holy prophets since the world began" (Acts 3:21), and that which was *"kept secret* since the world began" until revealed through the Apostle Paul (Rom. 16:25).

The prophets of "Old Testament" times had much to say about the blessing of the Gentiles through the *rise* of Israel (Isa. 60:1-3), but nothing whatever about the blessing of the Gentiles through the *fall* of Israel as we learn of it here in Romans 11. This latter was a secret (Gr. *musterion*) first made known to and through Paul. Thus what God is doing today is not in fulfillment of "Old Testament" predictions, but of His secret, eternal purpose in Christ; it is not based on covenants, but on God's *grace* alone.

Our Lord, when on earth, said to the Samaritan woman:

"Ye worship ye know not what: We know what we worship, for SALVATION IS OF THE JEWS" (John 4:22).

But after Paul had testified to the Jews from Jerusalem to Rome, almost in vain, he said:

"Be it known therefore unto you, that THE SALVATION OF GOD IS SENT UNTO THE GENTILES and that they will hear it" (Acts 28:28).

This latter, the salvation of the Gentiles through Israel's *rejection* of Christ, had never been prophesied; it was a secret, *"hid in God"* (Eph. 3:9), *"hid from ages and from generations"* (Col. 1:26), *"in other ages not made known"* (Eph. 3:5), *"kept secret since the world began"* (Rom. 16:25), until God made it known through Paul.

We could scarcely wish for a better example of this distinction between prophecy and the mystery than that which is found here in Rom. 11:25-27.

As to God's dealings with men *today*, the Apostle says:

"I would not, brethren, that ye should be ignorant of *this mystery*, lest ye should be wise in your own conceits; *that blindness in part is* [has] *happened to Israel, until the fulness of the Gentiles be come in"* (Ver. 25).

Mark well: we Gentile believers should understand "this mystery" lest we become conceited, for *we* had never been *promised anything* (Eph. 2:11,12). We have been saved by *grace*, and *partial* [15] blindness has overtaken Israel only *until* the full complement of the Gentiles has been brought in. And then....

"...all Israel shall be saved, AS IT IS WRITTEN, There shall come out of Sion the Deliverer, and shall turn away ungodliness from Jacob:

"For THIS IS MY COVENANT UNTO THEM, when I shall take away their sins" (Rom. 11:26,27).

Here we return from the *mystery*, with its riches of *unpromised grace*, to *prophecy* and God's *covenant* with Israel.

"For the gifts and calling of God are without repentance" (Ver. 29).

It will be *the return of Christ to earth*, not the efforts of the Church or of the world's statesmen, that will finally bring in the millennial reign with its peace and prosperity. Of those who expect these blessings to be brought in by human effort, the late J. C. O'Hair once said: "If our rulers, or scientists, or religious leaders think that *they* are going to bring in the kingdom, they are going to have to back it in, for certainly they are not headed that way!" The God-instructed believer knows that the Deliverer will come from *Sion*, not from Washington, Moscow, Paris or Rome.

It should be carefully noted, however, that "all Israel" will be saved when the Deliverer comes to *"turn away ungodliness from Jacob."* Israel has always wanted to be saved—from tyranny, from persecution, from trouble—but has shown no great longing to be saved from sin. Yet she will never be saved from her afflictions *until she is saved from her sins*. Many Scripture passages confirm this fact; among them the following:

---

15. It has been debated whether the words "in part" (Ver. 25) mean that only *part of the nation* were blinded, or that the unbelieving nation was only *partially blinded*. We believe that a careful examination of Romans 11, and especially of Verses 5 and 7, provide the answer. Not all, but only "part," though admittedly the greater part, were blinded.

"...thou shalt call His name JESUS: for He shall save His people FROM THEIR SINS" (Matt. 1:21).

"Unto you first God, having raised up His Son Jesus, sent Him to bless you, in turning away every one of you FROM HIS INIQUITIES" (Acts 3:26).

"...There shall come out of Sion the Deliverer, and shall turn away UNGODLINESS from Jacob" (Rom. 11:26).

All this should speak to us Gentiles, as well as to the Jews, for we are all too prone to become "wise in [our] own conceits." If we Gentile believers accept God's grace in true humility we will rejoice at the prospect of Israel's future redemption. What a day that will be for them—*and* for the Gentile nations!

"...if the fall of them be the riches of the world, and the diminishing of them the riches of the Gentiles, HOW MUCH MORE THEIR FULNESS!" (Rom. 11:12).

Before passing on from this section of Romans 11 it should be acknowledged that we Bible-believing Christians are quite aware that worldly men laugh at us for believing that Christ will return to this earth. We can brook their sneers, however. Indeed *we* might laugh at *them*, as they trust in leaders who solemnly write peace pacts only to tear them up again, as they have done for millenniums. Do *they* think that God will allow this earth *forever* to be a scene of sickness and misery and death, of greed and hate and intrigue, of war and bloodshed and devastation?

THE SCRIPTURAL MOTIVE FOR JEWISH MISSIONARY WORK

"As concerning the gospel, they are enemies for your sakes: but as touching the election, they are beloved for the fathers' sakes.

"For the gifts and calling of God are without repentance.

"For as ye in times past have not believed God, yet have now obtained mercy through their unbelief;

"Even so have these also now not believed, that through your mercy they also may obtain mercy.

"For God hath concluded them all in unbelief, that He might have mercy upon all.

"O the depth of the riches both of the wisdom and knowledge of God! how unsearchable are His judgments, and His ways past finding out!

"For who hath known the mind of the Lord? or who hath been His counselor?

"Or who hath first given to Him, and it shall be recompensed unto him again?

"For of Him, and through Him, and to Him, are all things: to whom be glory forever. Amen."

—Rom. 11:28-36

In dealing with Romans 1:16 we saw that the words *"to the Jew first,"* in that passage, do *not* mean that the Jew today has a priority on the gospel, or that this is the Scriptural motive for missionary work among the Jews. Rather the Scriptural motive for Jewish missionary work is found in the passage quoted above.

Here we learn that *"they are enemies,"* i.e., they have been alienated from God, *"for your sakes,"* though still *"beloved for the fathers' sakes"* [16] (Ver. 28).

Thus follows the great argument for missionary work among the Jews:

"For as ye [Gentiles] *in times past have not believed God, yet have now obtained mercy through their unbelief,*

"*Even so have these also now not believed, that through your mercy, they also may obtain mercy*" (Vers. 30,31).

In this present dispensation, while God is bringing millions of Gentiles to Himself, His grace to us should produce in us a great love for Israel.

What a holy incentive for the Gentile believer to bring the gospel to the Jew! What light and power it will add to his message! Blessed is the missionary to Israel who is intelligently motivated by the above truth!

---

16. Not "for the Father's sake," but "for the fathers' sakes." They are still beloved because of the promises made to their fathers: Abraham, Isaac and Jacob. *"For the gifts and calling of God are without repentance"* (Ver. 29).

Tell the Jew that he has a prior claim on God and he will agree with you, but will reject Christ. But show him from the Scriptures *why* Israel is in her present condition, why it appears as though God has abandoned her for some nineteen hundred years, why she is *not* now first among the nations; then show him that it was for his own benefit that God gave the nation up for a season—

Show him that the Gentiles were "given up" long before the Jews, and that God has now concluded all in unbelief only that He might have mercy upon all and offer *individuals* everywhere, Jews and Gentiles alike, *reconciliation* by grace, through faith in Christ who died for us—show him that it is the divine purpose to "reconcile *both* [Jews and Gentiles] unto God in *one body* by the cross, having slain the enmity thereby" (Eph. 2:16), and with this Scriptural approach you are more apt to get results.

We must not forget, however, that at least six times in Romans 11 the Apostle cautions us Gentile believers lest *we* begin to think that we are merely the objects, rather than the agents, of God's blessing.

"For God hath concluded them all in unbelief, *that He might have mercy upon all*" (Ver. 32).

At the tower of Babel God concluded the *Gentiles* in unbelief and gave them up, scattering them over the face of the earth (Gen. 11:9; cf. Rom. 1:24,26,28). Later He concluded *Israel* in unbelief (Acts 22:18) and gave the nation up, scattering them over the face of the earth, where we find them today (Acts 28:25-27). And what have we now? a world of individual lost sinners to whom God offers salvation by grace, through the death of His Son for our sins at Calvary. Little wonder the exclamation of Ver. 33 follows:

"O THE DEPTH OF THE RICHES BOTH OF THE WISDOM AND KNOWLEDGE OF GOD! HOW UNSEARCHABLE ARE HIS JUDGMENTS, AND HIS WAYS PAST FINDING OUT!"

Who could have thought of this amazing plan to show sinners their need of Christ? Indeed, who could have thought of such a plan as God devised for our salvation? It has been said that God asked the angels, from Michael and Gabriel on down: "What can I do to save these sinners and still maintain My righteousness? And then what can I do to show them their *need* of salvation?" Not an angel, it is said, had a plan to offer. Only God could devise such a plan, for *"God is love."* Only He could think of coming into the world *Himself* as one of us, to represent us and pay our debt for us. Even His judgments upon the nations and upon His own nation are "unsearchable," for He "concluded them all in unbelief, *that He might have mercy upon all,"* casting them out—*into the arms of grace!*

Indeed, the Apostle goes on to express the above sentiment as he asks, "Who can fathom the mind of God or be His counselor?" (Ver. 34), or "who can claim that he received from God that which he had first given to Him?" (Ver. 35). God will never be man's debtor. He is the supreme Giver, the supreme Benefactor. Even if we accept *His free gift* of eternal life and *then* give our lives in unremitting service for Him, He will still outdo us by rewarding us richly at "the judgment seat of Christ" (I Cor. 3:14). The rewards which believers will receive for faithful service and testimony are all over and above "the gift of God" which is "eternal life, through Jesus Christ our Lord."

"For of Him, and through Him, and to Him, are all things" (Ver. 36). This includes creation, its history and culmination, but here it applies particularly to our salvation, which was planned *by* Him, wrought *through* Him and will one day redound to *His* eternal glory! Thus the Apostle closes this important part of his epistle with the words: *"to whom be glory forever. Amen."*

> When all Thy mercies, O my God,
>   My rising soul surveys,
> Transported with the view, I'm lost
>   In wonder, love and praise!
>
> —Joseph Addison

Chapter XII — Romans 12:1-21

THE OPENING OF THE PRACTICAL SECTION OF ROMANS

YOUR REASONABLE SERVICE

"I beseech you therefore, brethren, by the mercies of God, that ye present your bodies a living sacrifice, holy, acceptable unto God, which is your reasonable service.

"And be not conformed to this world, but be ye transformed by the renewing of your mind, that ye may prove what is that good, and acceptable, and perfect will of God."

—Rom. 12:1,2

It is typical of Paul to follow doctrine with exhortation, to *apply* his teachings in a practical way. This is the more appropriate, however, where his *Epistle to the Romans* is concerned, for the practical appeal of the closing chapters brings to a conclusion the series of logical arguments that comprise the epistle. These arguments are presented progressively in the following steps: "*Therefore* thou art inexcusable" (2:1), "*Therefore* by the deeds of the law there shall no flesh be justified in His [God's] sight" (3:20), "*Therefore* we conclude that a man is justified by faith, without the deeds of the law" (3:28), "*Therefore*, being justified by faith, we have peace with God through our Lord Jesus Christ" (5:1), "There is *therefore* now no condemnation to them which are in Christ Jesus" (8:1), and "I beseech you *therefore* ... that ye present your bodies a living sacrifice, holy, acceptable unto God" (12:1).

The opening appeal of this final section of the Romans epistle is like the text of a sermon. Every phrase, every word is significant.

Who is the *"I"* whom the Spirit inspired to voice this appeal? It is none other than the Apostle Paul, who had placed himself at the divine disposal as a bondman, a slave of

Christ, with no will but his Lord's; who had willingly "suffered the loss of all things" for Christ, counting them but rubbish (Phil. 3:8). Sent to us through such an instrumentality, this appeal surely constitutes nothing less than the Word of God to us, His children.

"*I beseech.*" Not "I *command*," or "I *direct*," but "I *beg*, I *beseech.*" The epistles of Paul do contain commands and directives, but where the consecration of lives to Christ is concerned, the God-inspired Apostle writes as he did to Philemon, *"Though I might...enjoin thee...yet for love's sake I rather beseech thee..."* (Phile. 8,9). What an amazing word is this from God who, in matchless grace, rescued us from our condemned state and made us His own! He had the full and perfect right to place us, like Israel of old, under the iron hand of the Law but, having saved us by grace, He continues ever to deal with us in grace.

"I beseech *you.*" Who are the "you" but *"Gentiles in the flesh,"* only lately *"without Christ...having no hope and without God in the world,"* indeed *"alienated and enemies... by wicked works"* (Eph. 2:11,12; Col. 1:21). Surely our reconciliation to Him through Christ was a gift of grace, grace enough to keep us praising Him for all eternity. Yet He *continues* to deal with us in grace more abundant than that ever shown to any race or class of people.

"By the mercies of God." What a basis for his appeal! Perhaps we should read the first eleven chapters of Romans all over again to appreciate the force of the entreaty—along with all the rest of his writings! *"Justified from all things," "baptized into Christ," "seated in the heavenlies," "blessed with all spiritual blessings"*; these and a thousand other benefits are offered as the basis for his appeal: *"I beseech you therefore, brethren, by the mercies of God...."*

"That ye present your bodies." Does He not wish our souls and spirits too? Of course He does (I Thes. 5:23), but the word *"present"* takes care of that, for if we indeed *present* our bodies to Him He has the whole man! It is true that a man

may own a slave who may serve him with the greatest inner reluctance. He may be inwardly rebellious. But surely this will not be the case when we willingly *present* our bodies to God, for in so doing we have already yielded the inner man to His will.

"A living sacrifice." This, of course, stands in contrast to the slain sacrifices required of Israel. God would have us *live* a life of sacrifice for Him day by day. He would have us sacrifice *ourselves*. Paul could justly make this appeal for he knew what it was to toil tirelessly for Christ. He had suffered "weariness and painfulness...hunger and thirst... cold and nakedness" for His Lord, but discouraged though he must often have become, he *could not* stop. He said: *"The love of Christ constraineth us"*[1] (II Cor. 5:14). How disappointing, then, to see so many believers today who cannot seem to get started in a life of sacrifice for the One who gave His all—Himself—for them.

"Holy, acceptable unto God." The word rendered "holy" means "set apart as sacred." God would have us present ourselves to Him as those whom He has set apart for Himself, His own sacred possession. I.e., He would have us present ourselves to Him because *He loves us*, and *we* love *Him*. Such sacrifice alone is "acceptable" to Him, just as a husband desires nothing less from his wife than a life lived for him *because she loves him*.

"Which is your reasonable service." The word "service," here, occurs also in Rom. 9:4, where we are told that to Israel belonged "the service of God." The word actually refers to "divine service" (Heb. 9:1), or worship. And the word "reasonable" is that from which our word *logic* is derived. Think it through. Does not all logic and reason tell us that a life of worshipful sacrifice is due to the One who, in compassion and love, bore for us the shame and suffering that was *our* due?

---

1. I.e., "bears us along like an ocean tide."

"And be not conformed to this world." [2] In Gal. 1:4 we read that our Lord *"gave Himself for our sins, that He might deliver us from this present evil world."* Yet we are ever prone to adapt ourselves to our environment. Hence the Apostle's exhortation: "and be *not* conformed."

Many Christians suppose that they can better win the lost to Christ if they adapt themselves to their worldly environment and go along with their unsaved friends to show them that they are no different. But God says, *"Be different. Be not conformed."* Indeed, it is only as men see that we *are* different that they can be impressed with our testimony. Thus the Apostle continues:

"But be ye transformed, by the renewing of your mind." II Cor. 3:18 expresses it beautifully. It is as we are occupied with Christ that we are *"transformed* [3] *into the same image from glory to glory."* Thus this transformation takes place *"by the renewing of your mind."*

"...seeing ye have put off the old man with his deeds;

"And have put on the new man, which is renewed in knowledge after the image of Him that created him" (Col. 3:9,10).

"That ye may prove what is that good, and acceptable, and perfect will of God." Be sure to take in the sweep of Paul's words here. He says in effect: "If you will present yourself to God as a living sacrifice, holy and acceptable *to Him*, you will *prove for yourself* that His will is good, and acceptable, and *perfect"—for you!* Looking back you will be able to say, "I could have wished for nothing better. I would have wanted it no other way." So graciously has God planned for our happiness, both temporal and eternal!

---

2. We cannot accept the argument that the Greek *aion* should *always* be rendered "age." We believe that generally the word has to do with *environment* rather than *time*. We use the word "world" thus in the hymn, "When I rise to worlds unknown." Surely in Heb. 11:3 it *cannot* refer to time. The words *"so that"* forbid this. See also Eph. 3:9; Heb. 1:2,3, where the word appears in connection with the creation.

3. The same Greek word, *metamorphoo*, from which our *metamorphosis* is derived.

THE ONE BODY
AND THE FUNCTIONS OF ITS MEMBERS

"For I say, through the grace given unto me, to every man that is among you, not to think of himself more highly than he ought to think; but to think soberly, according as God hath dealt to every man the measure of faith.

"For as we have many members in one body, and all members have not the same office:

"So we, being many, are one body in Christ, and every one members one of another.

"Having then gifts differing according to the grace that is given to us, whether prophecy, let us prophesy according to the proportion of faith;

"Or ministry, let us wait on our ministering: or he that teacheth on teaching;

"Or he that exhorteth on exhortation: he that giveth, let him do it with simplicity; he that ruleth, with diligence; he that showeth mercy, with cheerfulness."

—Rom. 12:3-8

Many commentators hold that Vers. 6-8 refer to the ministries of the elected or appointed officers of the church, but could there be an *office* of "mercy shower" (Ver. 8)? The more this writer has pondered over this whole passage, the more he is convinced that it has to do with the various "offices," or functions, of a *living body*, the Body of Christ (Ver. 4).

After exhorting us to be *"transformed by the renewing of [our] mind,"* the Apostle raises his finger, as it were, to make a very important statement to *"every man"* among us about this renewed mind and its relation to Christian service and fellowship. Appealing to his Apostolic authority, he says:

"For I say, through the grace given unto me, to every man that is among you, not to think of himself more highly than he ought to think;[4] but to think soberly, according as God hath dealt to every man the measure of faith" (Ver. 3).

---

4. Some, noticing that the words "of himself," in this verse, are printed in italics in KJV, have come to the conclusion that these words were incorrectly, or at least unnecessarily, supplied by the translators. They hold that the

In many Christian assemblies there are one or more individuals who have this problem. They overrate themselves, and this indeed does affect their general thinking. They are apt to think of themselves as quite intellectual, and this is bound to have an adverse effect upon the oneness of the assembly and upon their own ministry for Christ. Thus Paul earnestly exhorts "every man[5] that is among you" *not* to overrate himself but to "think soberly, according as God hath dealt to every man the measure of faith" (Ver. 3).

The word "soberly" is very appropriate here, for generally in Scripture it stands over against *intoxication*, and even believers are sometimes prone to think *intemperately*, rather than realistically about their natural abilities. "Think soberly," says the Apostle, according to the measure of the faith which God, in His providence, has given you to use your gifts for Him. Paul himself was the greatest example of such temperate thinking (See I Cor. 2:1,4,5).

Rom. 12:4,5 clearly indicates that the Apostle says all this with the unity of the Body in view. As Ver. 3 begins with the word "For," so does Ver. 4. He is still pursuing the same thought.

There are many members in the human body, he says, yet all do not have the same office. Indeed, there is practically *no* equality in the body. Yet all the members work *with* and *for* each other since all are mutually dependent upon one another. When one is injured, or in danger, the others

---

passage has to do with *thinking* too highly, rather than with *thinking of one's self* too highly. I.e., they feel that the Apostle here warns against a spirit of *intellectualism* rather than against personal conceit. We ourselves once held this view and felt that there is support for this interpretation in Paul's words in I Cor. 4:6 where, omitting the supplied words "of men," the passage reads: *"that ye might learn in us not to think above that which is written."* But can this be what Paul is saying here when the Scriptures were at that time still incomplete and Paul himself was proclaiming blessed truths which had not yet been written in the Scriptures, and was endorsing the gift of prophecy, as in I Cor. 14:1: "*...desire spiritual gifts, but rather that ye may prophesy*"? Thus we believe that the *King James Version* translators were correct in rendering Rom. 12:3, *"not to think of himself."*

5. Such exhortations as these generally include the women too. He addresses the men (1) because they are in authority in the assembly and (2) because "the woman is *of* the man" (I Cor. 11:8). Thus even our term "*man*kind" refers to all humanity, male and female.

immediately come to its aid. *"So we, being many,"* he says, *"are one body in Christ, and every one members one of another"* (Ver. 5). *"Having then gifts differing according to the grace that is given to us,"* let each of us use *his* gift to the utmost advantage for the edification of the Body and the glory of God. This is the sense of Vers. 6-8.

Now that the Scriptures are complete, the gift of prophecy has passed away according to I Cor. 13:8. But prophecy was *then* in order, indeed it is placed *first* here, as it is in I Cor. 14:1. Thus the Apostle exhorts those who have this gift to use it *"according to the proportion of faith,"* i.e., to proclaim *what the Spirit has revealed to him,* not permitting human pride to alter the Spirit's revelation in any way.

"Ministry" (Ver. 7) is simply service, aid. Is the reader's gift that of service, perhaps lowly service, to others or to the church? Then, says Paul, "Give yourself to it." Some joyously engage in loving service in the assembly for a time, but soon begin to feel that their position is inferior to that of others, to whom God has given other positions. This is a sad mistake, for God honors the most menial task done *for Him.* Indeed, it appears that He often honors these more than the more glamorous exploits.

Likewise he who has been given the gift of *teaching* should give himself to teaching, and he who has the gift of *exhortation*—also an important endowment—to exhortation (Vers. 7,8).

But is *"giving"* a "gift" (Ver. 8)? Yes, it is a gift which *all believers* should "covet earnestly." Giving should never be done ostentatiously, however, or with pretense. Rather it should be done *"with simplicity."* Some have rendered the words *en haploteti* "with liberality," perhaps because giving done "with simplicity" is so apt to be generous giving. There is one thing this writer has consistently observed during more than fifty years in the work of the Lord: those who contribute most faithfully and sacrificially generally do so with sublime simplicity, while others are so accustomed to spending upon themselves or to hoarding their God-given riches that they never acquire the gift of giving. This is a great pity in the light of II Cor. 8:9.

"He that *ruleth*" (Ver. 8). The Greek *ho proistamenos* means *to stand in front, to lead* (not the same as *episkopos*, bishop or overseer). This, says the Apostle, should be done "with diligence," i.e., with "earnest care." This is important since so much leading in Christian assemblies is done in a careless, haphazard fashion, so that the service lacks what it should supply in edification. This is not to deny that *ho proistamenos* applies to more than the leading of public services.

Finally, "he that *showeth mercy*" should do so "with *cheerfulness*" (Ver. 8). Showing *mercy* with a sanctimonious spirit robs it of the very quality of *mercy*. Let mercy, then, be tendered with a cheerful attitude, whether shown to the guilty or to the needy.

THE CHRISTIAN'S RESPONSIBILITY WITH REGARD TO HIMSELF AND OTHERS

"Let love be without dissimulation. Abhor that which is evil; cleave to that which is good.

"Be kindly affectioned one to another with brotherly love; in honor preferring one another;

"Not slothful in business; fervent in spirit; serving the Lord;

"Rejoicing in hope; patient in tribulation; continuing instant in prayer;

"Distributing to the necessity of saints; given to hospitality.

"Bless them which persecute you: bless, and curse not.

"Rejoice with them that do rejoice, and weep with them that weep.

"Be of the same mind one toward another. Mind not high things, but condescend to men of low estate. Be not wise in your own conceits.

"Recompense to no man evil for evil. Provide things honest in the sight of all men.

"If it be possible, as much as lieth in you, live peaceably with all men.

"Dearly beloved, avenge not yourselves, but rather give place unto wrath: for it is written, Vengeance is Mine; I will repay, saith the Lord.

"Therefore if thine enemy hunger, feed him; if he thirst, give him drink; for in so doing thou shalt heap coals of fire on his head.

"Be not overcome of evil, but overcome evil with good."

—Rom. 12:9-21

This part of the *Epistle to the Romans* is as truly about grace as are Chapters 5 and 8. Here we have grace in its *outworking*, God's grace *shining through* the believer. The careless reader may see here only a list of exhortations, but to the earnest, diligent student of Scripture it is a blessed passage indeed. As Verses 3-8 deal with Christian *service*, the remainder of the chapter deals with Christian *conduct*.

The first thing that strikes us as we examine these verses is that the characteristics here commended are diametrically opposite to those the world considers important. Love, humility, patience, hope, prayer, longsuffering—these are not exactly what the world recommends for success! With the world it is rather self-confidence, aggressiveness, insistence upon one's rights, etc. But somehow the unregenerate man cannot see that this is precisely the reason why the world is in its present deplorable condition, with greed, strife, hate, rebellion and violence threatening to undo us. Let us then consider thoughtfully and prayerfully what God would have us, His dear children, be and do.

"Dissimulation" in Ver. 9 is, of course, *hypocrisy*. In the world about us there is much veneer, much sheer hypocrisy, in human relations. Mrs. Smith tells Mrs. Jones how *very happy* she is to see her again and how *very lovely* she looks today, and walks away grumbling to herself about the one woman she cannot bear! And many men do the same in other ways. "Don't let this be so among you," says the Apostle: *"Let love be without dissimulation."* And Peter agrees in those beautiful words of I Pet. 1:22: *"Love one another with a pure heart fervently."*

When Mrs. Howard Taylor first went to China as a missionary many years ago, she was disappointed to find that it seemed much harder to love the Chinese near at hand than it had been to love them from a distance. Realizing that this was a severe handicap to her ministry among them, she prayed in desperation: "Lord, I don't really love these Chinese people and I am sure they sense that I don't really love them. Please help me to love them heartily; otherwise I might as well go back to England." This was the beginning of Mrs. Taylor's great missionary exploits in China.

The words *"abhor"* and *"cleave,"* in Ver. 9, are also most significant. Notice how *thoroughly opposite* they are. Don't even touch the one; consider it abhorrent, but cling tightly to the other so as not to let it go! The same idea is found in II Tim. 2:22: *"Flee* also youthful lusts, but *follow* righteousness...." *Flee* from the one as for your life, but *pursue* the other as you would a quarry in the hunt.

The exhortation to *"abhor that which is evil"* and *"cling to that which is good"* should be prayerfully considered by Christians who too readily conform to this world, constantly flirting with those things that dishonor God, to see how close they can come to them.

In Ver. 10 the Apostle goes from *agape* love (Ver. 9) to *"brotherly love."* In the Greek it is *philadelphia*, which differs from *agape* in several subtle respects. Perhaps the word "brotherly" will best help us to grasp the meaning of the term here. The love of brother to brother is not exactly the same as that of husband to wife (cf. Eph. 5:25, where it is *agape*) but it is strong nevertheless, and believers should be thus "kindly affectioned" toward each other, gladly preferring the other where honor is concerned. In Phil. 2:3 we have the same basic exhortation:

"Let nothing be done through strife or vainglory, but in lowliness of mind let each esteem other better than themselves."

Indeed, we have an outstanding example of this quality in the attitude and conduct of two noted Christian gentlemen: Apollos, and Paul himself.

Apollos, an "eloquent" man, and "mighty in the Scriptures," had evidently been greatly used of God to bring blessing to the Corinthian believers. Soon, however, there arose divisions among the Corinthians as to whom they should follow: Paul, Apollos, Cephas or Christ (I Cor. 1:12). To correct this situation Paul wrote to the Corinthians rebuking them for their sectarian attitude and assuring them that there was no rivalry between him and Apollos, the two mainly concerned, at the same time reminding them that believers are now one body in Christ, the blessed truth which he had taught them at the first.

While there was indeed no rivalry between him and Apollos, the fact remained however, that Apollos had unwittingly "stolen the hearts" of the believers there, as it were, placing Paul in the shade. Yet with all this we read in I Cor. 16:12 that Paul "greatly desired" Apollos to return to Corinth to minister the Word there. What selflessness! And Apollos showed the same humble spirit, for the passage goes on to say that *"his will was not at all to come at this time."* Evidently he was determined not to take advantage of his popularity at Corinth. This was "brotherly love" indeed, and grace in action!

Ver. 11 actually has nothing to do with business matters as we think of business. Rather it refers to whatever needs to be done. In that which God has given us to do we should not be slothful in zeal, but *"fervent in spirit, serving the Lord."* What good will intellectual acumen, or eloquence or any other human faculty do to bring needed blessing to the hearts of those with whom we come into contact, if these God-given abilities are not coupled with a warm, zealous, fervent spirit, by one who is sincerely "serving the Lord"?

How beautifully the three parts of Ver. 12 go together! "*Rejoicing* in hope; *patient* in tribulation; continuing *instant* in prayer." The world knows nothing of *rejoicing* in hope! They merely keep hoping for the best, not knowing of the *"hope we have as an anchor of the soul, both sure and steadfast"* (Heb. 6:19). They hope—if they ever think about it—that God will finally deal kindly with them, but are ignorant of the hope of the Bible, that eager anticipation of things surely to come to pass.

Should we be called upon to endure *"tribulation,"* we

should do so with *"patience,"* indeed, tribulation is used, in the providence of God, to teach us patience. Thus,

"...we glory in tribulations also; knowing that tribulation worketh patience;

"And patience, experience; and experience, hope:

"And hope maketh not ashamed, because the love of God is shed abroad in our hearts by the Holy Ghost which is given unto us" (Rom. 5:3-5).

And all the while we are to *continue* "instant in prayer." Never in Paul's epistles are we instructed to pray for long periods of time. Rather the Apostle bids us to be "*instant* in prayer." Is there a problem? Pray about it, *instantly*, now! Does a servant of God come to mind? Pray for him—now, while you are thinking of him. Do you need light on the Word? or guidance for your life? or special grace for a difficult situation? Pray—*now*.

Ver. 13 has to do with generosity of heart. Note, he does not promote reckless extravagance. He speaks of "distributing to the *necessity* of saints," i.e., to saints in need. Note too that the emphasis is on the *saints*. Otherwise we could all speedily go bankrupt! On the five occasions when Paul urges generosity it is always generosity *to the saints*. He himself took up great "collections" from the Gentile churches to provide for the needs of "the poor saints which [were] at Jerusalem" (Rom. 15:26). He does not mean that we should be unmindful of the sufferings of humanity, but simply that our first responsibility is toward our brethren in Christ. Gal. 6:10 states it well:

"As we have therefore opportunity, let us do good unto all men, especially unto them who are of the household of faith."

This is the answer to the social gospel of the neo-evangelicals and liberals. Many of these think that the Church's first order of business is to relieve the world's physical and material needs. Thus millions are being given financial aid whether or not they are willing to work (cf. II Thes. 3:10) and regardless of how they spend the funds they receive. Meanwhile less and less of the Church's finances are used to bring our God-given message of grace to the teeming millions, rich and poor, who are without Christ and without hope. Our material aid, then, should go *first* to relieve *"the necessity of saints,"* so that together we may be the better able to meet *the still greater need*, the *spiritual* need, of the multitudes about us who are lost.

After the author's father had spent nearly 50 years in city missionary work, he asked us: "Which branch of our ministry do you feel has been most productive spiritually: the institutional meetings, the Bible conferences, the mothers' sewing classes (where we provided the materials and helped them to make clothing for their families), the free clothes dispensary, the free food distribution—which?" It did not take much thought or discussion to arrive at the answer to this question. The Bible conferences, with men of God like Mr. Newell, Dr. Gaebelein, Dr. Ironside, and later Pastor J. C. O'Hair, *teaching the Word*; these had been *by far* the most productive spiritually—in revolutionizing lives and turning souls "from darkness to light," from judgment to justification, from eternal perdition to eternal life and the conscious joy of sins forgiven.

The words *"given to hospitality"* continue in this vein. The believer should be "given to" hospitality, quick to take some friend or stranger into the warmth and fellowship of his household, especially another believer. We do not ignore the fact that this is becoming more difficult in our day, when soaring inflation practically forces some wives to take on secular employment just so that the family may be adequately provided for. Doubtless God understands this as He understands the difficulties associated with obedience to other Scriptural exhortations. Nevertheless it is a pity that in these hectic days old-fashioned hospitality has become almost non-existent and we have lost much by bidding it, or having to bid it, farewell. Every believer, surely, should have a hospitable spirit, seeking opportunities to receive others into the home for Christian fellowship. Bishops, or overseers in the church especially, says the Apostle, should be "lovers of hospitality" (Tit. 1:8).

Probably referring to possible persecution from those without, but still dealing with our own attitude of heart as believers, the Apostle goes on to say:

"Bless them which persecute you: bless, and curse not" (Ver. 14).

In I Pet. 2:23 we read of our Lord, that,

"...when He was reviled, He reviled not again; when He suffered, He threatened not..."

And Paul says the same of himself in I Cor. 4:12:

"...being reviled we bless; being persecuted we suffer it."

This self-abnegation is a virtue that the world, doubtless, scorns above all, but which God honors and blesses.

Verse 15 is a beautiful passage on Christian *sympathy*. Talk about psychology! Here you have sanctified psychology! How many of us, even among pastors and Christian workers, need to learn that one does not comfort a burdened heart by merely being jolly, nor does one bring blessing to a glad heart by being "a wet blanket"! Sympathy is a sharing, an understanding, of another's feelings and this is exactly what this verse is about. "*Rejoice* with them that do rejoice," says the Spirit-inspired Apostle, "and *weep* with them that weep." This is the gracious outworking of what we find in I Cor. 12:26 concerning the Body of Christ:

"And whether one member suffer, all the members *suffer with it;* or [if] one member be honored, all the members *rejoice with it.*"

And Ver. 16 (of Rom. 12) naturally follows:

"Be of the same mind *one toward another*," i.e., let love and trust and sympathy and interest be mutual.

"Look not every man on his own things, but every man also on the things of others" (Phil. 2:4).

This is most important, for we are all prone to be self-centered, taking little interest, if any, in the things that concern others. And the Apostle goes on to press this home in the light of his original exhortation in Ver. 3: "*Mind not high things, but condescend to men of low estate. Be not wise in your own conceits."* Even apart from Christianity this is wise counsel. Prov. 26:12 says:

> "Seest thou a man wise in his own conceit; there is more hope of a fool than of him."

How very much the Apostle has to say in his epistles about high-mindedness! How often he warns against conceit! And how, here, he rebukes our pretense in looking down on men of low estate!

"Recompense to no man evil for evil" (Ver. 17). Note the *"no man."* We should not even recompense evil for evil to the ungodly. Paul emphasizes this in I Thes. 5:15:

> "See that none render evil for evil unto any man; but ever follow that which is good, both among yourselves, and to all men."

"Provide things honest in the sight of all men" (Ver. 17). Paul himself was a good example of this. Not only was his integrity impeccable, but there were occasions when, for the sake of his ministry, he made sure that others had reason to *know* this to be so, especially where financial matters were concerned.

As we know from Rom. 15:25,26, Paul was even now about to go to Judaea with an offering "for the poor saints...at Jerusalem." *Poor saints—at Jerusalem?* Yes, and this confirmed the validity of *Paul's* apostleship and message. When the Pentecostal program was in force we read of these same saints: *"Neither was there any among them that lacked"* (Acts 4:34), but now this program was fast passing from the scene and, having sold their houses and lands for the common good (Acts 4:34,35) the Judaean saints now found themselves in great distress. Thus Paul, fulfilling his agreement with the leaders of the church at Jerusalem (Gal. 2:10), had initiated a massive effort to raise funds for these needy saints. The Gentile churches of Macedonia and Achaia (Rom. 15:26), along with those of Galatia (I Cor. 16:1) and others, were all taking part in this great love-offering.

This undertaking placed upon Paul a great responsibility, thus, for the sake of his testimony, he arranged to *make certain* that no one could ever question his financial integrity in this matter. When he wrote to the church at Corinth about this he had already "given order to the churches of Galatia" (I Cor. 16:1) as to the procedure.

They were to be taking up offerings, preparing for Paul's arrival (with delegates from other cities). *Then*, he said, *"whomsoever ye shall approve by your letters, them will I send to bring your liberality unto Jerusalem"* (I Cor. 16:3). Mark well, the Corinthian church was to submit *written approval* of the delegates *they* selected to go to Jerusalem with their offering. And then he adds, most modestly: *"And if it be meet that I go also, they shall go with me"* (Ver. 4). Of course, they *could* go separately!

Surely Paul would be the one to oversee the transportation of the great offering from all the Gentile churches to the Judaean saints. Was not he the promoter of this whole undertaking? Ah, but it must not be forgotten that only recently some there had even questioned his apostleship. Thus he did not take even the above for granted but, in a delicately-worded suggestion, in which he still rightly maintains his role as leader, he says, "If it be meet [appropriate] that I go also, *they* shall go with *me*."

In II Cor. 8:20,21 he again refers to the care which he exercised in seeing to it that this great offering reached Jerusalem without any possibility of blame ever being attached to him or the others who delivered it:

"Avoiding this, that no man should blame us in this abundance which is administered by us:

"Providing for honest things, not only in the sight of the Lord, but also in the sight of men."

A great lesson, this, in fiscal responsibility, and a wholesome example of the importance of his own words here in Rom. 12:17: *"Provide things honest in the sight of all men."*

The Apostle concedes, of course, that even the most sincere conduct and motives may be misunderstood, or even deliberately misinterpreted, thus he continues:

"If it be possible, as much as lieth in you, live peaceably with all men" (Rom. 12:18).

When it is impossible to live peaceably with others, he implies, at least be sure that the difficulty does not lie with you. And then, with a touching expression of his love for them, to soften hurt feelings over wrongs done them by others, he brings his exhortation to a conclusion:

"Dearly beloved, avenge not yourselves, but rather give place unto wrath: for it is written, Vengeance is Mine; I will repay, saith the Lord.

"Therefore, if thine enemy hunger, feed him; if he thirst, give him drink: for in so doing thou shalt heap coals of fire on his head.

"Be not overcome of evil, but overcome evil with good" (Vers. 19-21).

It is natural, with most of us, to *resist* wrath and to resist the *person* who would do us wrong. But this would come perilously close to displaying the very attitude our adversary displays—and that would be wrong. Rather let us back away from our adversary's wrath; give him room. *"Give place unto wrath, for it is written, Vengeance is Mine, I will repay, saith the Lord."* It would be a mistake to take our problems out of His hands just because we are angry.

In Ver. 25 the Apostle quotes from Prov. 25:21,22 which, however, adds the words *"and the Lord shall reward thee"!* In feeding your enemy when he is hungry and giving him drink when thirsty, you will heap "coals of fire on his head," a metaphor for the remorse caused by repentance.

> So artists melt the sullen ore of lead,
>   By heaping coals of fire upon its head.
> In the kind warmth the metal learns to glow,
>   And, pure from dross, the silver runs below. [6]

How appropriate are the Apostle's words: *"Be not overcome of evil, but overcome evil with good"* (Ver. 21). If we resist and challenge those who would persecute us we will only be overcome of evil. But if we make friends of our enemies we will have overcome evil with good.

The story is told of an ancient general who said to his defeated enemy, "I will destroy you," and then prepared for

---

6. Author unknown.

him a lavish feast. As they dined together, his "enemy" said, "I understood you to say you were going to *destroy* me." "True," replied the general. "Have I not destroyed my enemy and made him my friend!"

Indeed, this is how God "destroyed" *His* chief enemy on earth, Saul of Tarsus. He *saved* him, thus robbing the opposition of its leader and making of Saul the great Apostle Paul, the herald and the living example of His grace to sinners.

> Aloud we sing the wondrous grace
>   Christ to His murderers bare;
> Which made the tort'ring cross its throne,
>   And hung its trophies there.
>
> Jesus, this wondrous love we sing!
>   And whilst we sing, admire!
> Breathe in our souls, and kindle there
>   The same celestial fire.
>
> Swayed by Thy dear example, we
>   For enemies will pray
> With love their hatred—and their curse
>   With blessings—will repay.
>
>   —Author unknown

Chapter XIII — Romans 13:1-14

THE CHRISTIAN
AND HIS GOVERNMENT,
HIS NEIGHBOR AND HIS LORD

SUBJECTION TO THE POWERS THAT BE

"Let every soul be subject unto the higher powers. For there is no power but of God: the powers that be are ordained of God.

"Whosoever therefore resisteth the power, resisteth the ordinance of God: and they that resist shall receive to themselves damnation.

"For rulers are not a terror to good works, but to the evil. Wilt thou then not be afraid of the power? do that which is good, and thou shalt have praise of the same:

"For he is the minister of God to thee for good. But if thou do that which is evil, be afraid; for he beareth not the sword in vain: for he is the minister of God, a revenger to execute wrath upon him that doeth evil.

"Wherefore ye must needs be subject, not only for wrath, but also for conscience' sake.

"For for this cause pay ye tribute also: for they are God's ministers, attending continually upon this very thing.

"Render therefore to all their dues: tribute to whom tribute is due; custom to whom custom; fear to whom fear; honor to whom honor."

—Rom. 13:1-7

Our studies in Romans have now taken us to the subject of the Christian and his government.

It is amazing that so many Christians are not aware of the truth of Ver. 1 above. They do not know that *"the powers that be are ordained of God,"* so that ultimately *"there is no power but of God."*

It is true that we are living under "the dispensation of the grace of God" (Eph. 3:1-4), but we are also living under the dispensation of Human Government. This dispensation, instituted in Noah's day (Gen. 9:5,6), has never been brought to a close. *God ordained human government*, holding man responsible for the life of his brother. The decree: "Whoso sheddeth man's blood, *by man* shall his blood be shed" (Gen. 9:6), makes *man* responsible even to execute capital punishment and this, of course, includes all lesser penalties.

More than this: the particular "powers that be" are God-ordained. Generally God gives nations exactly the kind of rulers they deserve. *Some* of these are wicked and immoral, "the basest of men," yet they are "ordained of God" (Dan. 4:17) and responsible to Him. To the pagan and arrogant Nebuchadnezzar, Daniel said:

"...the God of heaven hath given thee a kingdom, power, and strength, and glory" (Dan. 2:37).

And to this king, in his pride, a voice later came from heaven condemning him to insanity until he should learn the lesson that,

"...the Most High ruleth in the kingdom of men, and giveth it to whomsoever He will" (Dan. 4:32).

Our Lord said to Pilate:

"...Thou couldst have no power at all against Me, except it were given thee from above..." (John 19:11).

Indeed, *six times* in this one brief passage in Romans (13:1-7) the Apostle declares that the governments over us are ordained *by God*.

Thus earthly rulers may be arbitrary or oppressive or corrupt, but God says: *"Be subject,"* just as He directs the wife to be subject to her husband, the child to his parents, the servant to his master. Abuse of authority in any of these cases does not change the established order of God, for without such order all would be chaos. This is not the popular philosophy of the day, but it is the path to harmony and to man's greatest happiness. The affirmation that we are responsible to obey only "reasonable" laws leaves the question of subjection open to each man's interpretation. This philosophy has driven many a nation to anarchy.

Peter confirms Paul in this matter and, indeed, both proclaim God's Word to us:

> "Submit yourselves to every ordinance of man for the Lord's sake: whether it be to the king, as supreme;
>
> "Or unto governors, as unto them that are sent by him, for the punishment of evildoers, and for the praise of them that do well" (I Pet. 2:13,14).

But the Apostle Paul states this principle negatively as well as positively:

> "Whosoever therefore resisteth the power, resisteth the ordinance of God: and they that resist shall receive to themselves damnation [condemnation]" (Ver. 2).

Surely this world is headed straight toward the coming "Great Tribulation," for in ever greater measure *"the mystery of iniquity* [or *lawlessness*] *doth already work"* (II Thes. 2:7), and lawlessness seems to be taking over. But, as we say, this will end not in the liberty men claim to seek, but in the anarchy and horror of the "Great Tribulation."

In Verses 3,4 the apostle makes an important statement that is true of law enforcement in general, whether under a dictatorship or a democracy. Rulers, he says, are not a terror to good works, but to evil. They seldom bother the law-abiding citizen, but the law-breaker must always be looking over his shoulder. Thus, he continues, if you do not wish to be afraid, do what is good, but if you do what is evil *"be* afraid," for he does not carry "the sword" in vain. Indeed, "he is *the minister of God*," all unwittingly, "a revenger to execute wrath upon him that doeth evil" (Ver. 4).

Do not forget, dear reader, that under God you can sleep restfully at night because of the police force that God has ordained. Even in this day of political and social upheaval, as evidently in Paul's day, these basic observations are true.

As an obedient Christian you are not, certainly need not be afraid of the policeman, but *someone* is, and that someone would rob or harm you if it were not for the God-ordained police force.

But he presses the argument farther in Vers. 5-7, pointing out that we should be subject to government, not only for fear of wrath but "for conscience' sake" (Ver. 5), i.e., out of obedience to *God*. As we have seen above, Peter says: "Submit yourselves to every ordinance of man *for the Lord's sake*" (I Pet. 2:13). We should submit ourselves to "the powers that be" not merely out of fear, or even to be good citizens, but to be *good Christians*. Indeed, this is why, under God's providence, "ye pay tribute also," for your rulers, from the top down, "attend continually upon this very thing," i.e., *your* safety.

"Therefore," says the Apostle, *"render...to all their dues; tribute to whom tribute is due...,"* etc. (Ver. 7).

Those who, in our day, complain of corrupt government and assume the prerogative to decide whether or not they should pay taxes should reflect that Paul lived under the wicked Nero and his corrupt administration and *he* bids us to pay our taxes (Vers. 6,7), and our Lord, also living under pagan Rome, taught His disciples to pay their taxes (Matt. 22:16-21; 17:24-27). This is *God's Word* on the matter.

God is not a God of confusion, allowing every one to do what is right in his own eyes; He is a God of order, and under the present conditions, considering man's fallen state, it is best that the masses "be subject unto the higher powers," and this responsibility devolves especially upon God's own people.

SHOULD CHRISTIANS GO TO WAR?

With all the above as a background perhaps we are now in a better position to consider the question which so many sincere children of God have asked: *Should Christians go to war?*

Believers in Christ, doubtless, find war more repugnant than do others, yet we, above all men, know that we are to bow in obedience to the Word of God, so that for us the vital question is: *Does the Bible teach that Christians should go to war when called upon by their governments to do so?*

Fortunately God has not left us without light on this subject, for as Paul, by divine inspiration, instructs us as to the relationships that should exist between husband and wife, parents and children, masters and servants so, as we have already begun to see, he instructs us about the proper relationship between the Christian and his government.

In Paul's day men did not apply or volunteer for a position on the police force or in the armed services. They were *all drafted*, and it is against this background that the Apostle says: *"Be subject unto the higher powers,"* for they are *"ordained of God"* (Rom. 13:1). And recall, he declares of the individual officer that this "minister of God to thee...*beareth not the sword in vain"* (Ver. 4). The sword, of course, was the instrument of capital punishment, which God has authorized "the powers that be" to inflict.

But someone asks: Is war compatible with "the dispensation of grace"? In answer we remind our readers that this is also the dispensation of Human Government as we have seen above, and that it is Paul, the Apostle of grace who, by divine inspiration, declares that God has ordained "the powers that be" and that we are to "be subject" to them.

But does not the Word of God say, "Thou shalt not kill"? Yes, but the word "kill" in Ex. 20:13 has the sense of *murder*. This is obvious from the fact that God Himself, in the same Law, directed the people of Israel to *slay* the *murderer* (Num. 35:16,17,18,19,21,30,31),[1] in compliance with His command inaugurating the dispensation of Human Government: "Whoso sheddeth man's blood, *by man* shall his blood be shed" (Gen. 9:6). This is not murder, as some argue; it is the execution of God's command. If our rulers faithfully carried out this command our land would not be filled with violence and murder as it now is.

Surely most of those who refuse to carry arms today would

---

[1]. The word rendered "kill" in Ex. 20:13 is the root of the word rendered "murderer" eight times in Num. 35 above.

be quick to call for the police if they were being robbed! And is it not highly probable that most of those who refuse to go to war do so primarily, not because they do not want to kill another—none of us would *want* to do this—but because they are deathly afraid that *they* might be wounded or killed? Thus it is not, in such cases, conviction, but fear, that makes pacifists of them.

Some, of course, have argued that some specific war has been unwarranted or even immoral. But do *we* really *know* this to be so? The average person, even the average politician, knows little indeed about all the *facts* involved in any war. Obviously our highest rulers and military leaders know *most* about them. Thus the responsibility for *any* war which they may declare rests upon *their* shoulders, not upon ours, for God has commanded us to obey *them*. We have already discussed the impropriety of every man deciding for himself which laws he shall obey.

Did not Paul know, when he wrote Romans 13, that the kingdoms of this world are sustained by armies; that the Babylonian Empire had been conquered by the sword of Persia, and Persia by the sword of Greece, and Greece by the sword of Rome, and that Rome would one day be overthrown by another's sword?[2] Yet it is he—yes, it is *God* through him—who says: *"Be subject."*

But perhaps the most searching objection is: How can a God of love sanction war? To this we reply that God's love *is* indeed *infinite*, but so is His *justice*. Strange, is it not, that men do want God to be infinite in mercy and love, but not in justice or in His wrath upon sin. But God is infinite in *all* His attributes because *He* is infinite. It was in perfect and infinite justice, therefore, that He condemned *all men* to death as the penalty for sin. Thus those who hold that it is unjust of God to command a young man to go to war and, perhaps, be killed by a bullet, should ask themselves whether it would not then also be unjust of Him to allow that same

---

2. Our Lord obviously knew it. He said to Pilate: *"...if My kingdom were of this world, then would My servants fight..."* (John 18:36).

person to die of cancer, heart failure or whatever, for "it *is* appointed unto men once to die" (Heb. 9:27).

The author sympathizes with those who see only the horrors of war, especially as they are depicted for us on television and in the newspapers and magazines of our day. But he is appalled too as he walks through the corridors of our large hospitals and witnesses the suffering, the discouragement, the heartbreak caused by sin.

But wait! We did not quote the complete statement by the Apostle in Heb. 9:27,28. True, "it *is* appointed unto men once to die," but this is not all he says. Read the whole passage carefully:

"And AS it is appointed unto men once to die, but after this the judgment;

"SO CHRIST WAS ONCE OFFERED TO BEAR THE SINS OF MANY; AND UNTO THEM THAT LOOK FOR HIM SHALL HE APPEAR THE SECOND TIME WITHOUT [APART FROM] SIN UNTO SALVATION."

God graciously offers to *all* who suffer the present consequences of sin, including war, the assurance and joy of eternal life in Christ.

"In whom we have redemption through His blood, the forgiveness of sins according to the riches of His grace" (Eph. 1:7).

It is faith in Christ, who died for our sins, that truly prepares us for sickness, suffering and death—and even for war, if need be, for during "this present evil age" (Gal. 1:4), we are living also under *"the dispensation of the grace of God"* (Eph. 3:2).

ONE EXCEPTION

Since it is *God* who has given the rulers authority over the citizenry, man's *first* responsibility is *to God.* Thus the believer must *disobey* the ruler when the ruler commands him to *disobey* God. We have an example of this obedience to the higher authority in the conduct of Peter and the other apostles in early Acts. The apostles had been sent to preach Christ and the resurrection. When their rulers commanded them to desist, Peter and John rightly replied:

"Whether it be right in the sight of God to hearken unto you more than unto God, judge ye,

"For we cannot but speak the things which we have seen and heard" (Acts 4:19,20).

Even after being further threatened and imprisoned, Peter and the other apostles responded:

"We ought to obey God rather than men" (Acts 5:29).

It may be argued, of course, that the political authority of Israel's rulers was already beginning to fade (Cf. Matt. 21:43), but surely the nation still considered them to be in authority. Moreover, in Acts 23:5 we have Paul apologizing to the High Priest for having spoken disrespectfully to him (Ver. 3).

But in addition we have the case of Paul at Damascus. Rather than submit to the authority of the governor, the Apostle "escaped his hands" and went on preaching Christ (II Cor. 11:32,33).

But the conduct of the twelve apostles and Paul in the above cases is a far cry from the lawlessness which even now prevails in the world, and which both Paul and Peter so categorically forbid.

THE CHRISTIAN, HIS NEIGHBOR AND HIS LORD

"Owe no man anything but to love one another; for he that loveth another hath fulfilled the law.

"For this: Thou shalt not commit adultery, Thou shalt not kill, Thou shalt not steal, Thou shalt not bear false witness, Thou shalt not covet; and if there by any other commandment, it is briefly comprehended in this saying, namely, Thou shalt love thy neighbor as thyself.

"Love worketh no ill to his neighbor; therefore love is the fulfilling of the law.

"And that, knowing the time, that now it is high time to awake out of sleep; for now is our salvation nearer than when we believed.

"The night is far spent, the day is at hand: let us therefore cast off the works of darkness, and let us put on the armor of light.

"Let us walk honestly, as in the day; not in rioting and drunkenness, not in chambering and wantonness, not in strife and envying.

"But put ye on the Lord Jesus Christ, and make not provision for the flesh, to fulfill the lusts thereof."

—Rom. 13:8-14

THE CHRISTIAN AND HIS NEIGHBOR

The Apostle clearly proceeds here from the subject of the believer's relationship toward his government to that of his relationship toward his neighbor. Yet there is a connection. In Ver. 7 he says, *"Render...to all their dues,"* and in Ver. 8, *"Owe no man anything, but to love one another."*

Some have interpreted the words "Owe no man anything" to mean that Christians should not go to the bank for a loan or borrow money to invest in a business. This is not the meaning, for if one borrows, say, $1,000.00 from a bank for one year, he does not *owe* it until it falls due. Indeed in the Greek the word "owe," in Ver. 8 above, is the verb form of the word "dues" in Ver. 7. However, when that note does fall due be sure to *pay* it. This is what these words teach.

The Christian should not get himself involved in unpaid debts, for there is no surer way to ruin friendships, to find one's self always dodging his creditors and to dishonor the Lord than by a failure to meet one's financial obligations.

There is, however, one debt which we can never fully discharge. It is the obligation to love others. If the Lord Jesus Christ, out of love for us, left heaven's glory to bear the shame and penalty for our sins—*and those of others*, are we not indebted to love the others for whom He died? Paul considered himself a "debtor" to others (Rom. 1:14).

But let us finish the verse: *"for he that loveth another hath fulfilled the law."* As we know, the Ten Commandments were divided into two parts, one having to do with Israel's relationship to God, the other with their relationship to man. Our Lord said of the former, *"This is the first and great commandment"* (Matt. 22:38), but Paul, here in Romans, is dealing with man's relationship to his neighbor, thus he quotes the latter (Ver. 9).

But why bring the Law in? Does not Gal. 3:13 declare that *"Christ hath redeemed us from the curse of the law, being made a curse for us"*? Yes, but Rom. 8:4 explains that He has done this *"that the righteousness of the law might be fulfilled in us who walk not after the flesh, but after the Spirit."* In Gal. 5:14, again referring to the manward side of the Law, the Apostle says:

"All the law is fulfilled in one word, even in this, Thou shalt love thy neighbor as thyself."

Thus he concludes in Rom. 13:10:

"Love worketh no ill to his neighbor; therefore love is the fulfilling of the law."

How true! The Law is a testimony to human depravity (I Tim. 1:9,10). If all men loved each other what need would there be for laws? It is a blessed reality, then, that as we are saved and disciplined by grace:

"...the love of God is shed abroad in our hearts by the Holy Ghost which is given unto us" (Rom. 5:5).

While not under the covenant of the Law then, the believer under grace may nevertheless fulfill all the statutes of the Law regarding man's behavior to his neighbor by simply letting the love of God motivate him.

TIME TO WAKE UP

Vers. 11, 12 deserve careful scrutiny. Some able Bible teachers hold that the "day" and the "night" in this passage must be viewed in a dispensational light. The world's night, they suggest, came with the fall of man. Then, when our Lord appeared on earth, the day dawned, for He was "the Light of the world" (John 8:12). But the world and "His own" rejected Him, so that night fell again as He left this earth and ascended to heaven. Nor, they say, will the world see the light of day again until He returns to reign.

This interpretation seems, at first sight, to make sense, but it does not stand the Berean test. As we search the Scriptures we do indeed find our Lord saying, *"I am the Light of the world,"* but He adds, *"he that followeth Me shall not walk in darkness, but shall have the light of life"* (John 8:12). It was only His true followers, then, that did not walk in darkness. They had "the light *of life.*" This corresponds with the Spirit-inspired testimony of the Apostle John:

"In Him was life, and the life was the light of men" (John 1:4).

As to the multitudes who did not partake of this life, John goes on to describe how deep was the darkness of their night:

"And the light shineth in the darkness, and the darkness comprehended it not" (Ver. 5).

The light shone forth but did not penetrate the dense darkness; the darkness was not diffused by it. Indeed, so deep was the night when our Lord was on earth that God sent John the Baptist to point men to Christ, the Light.

"There was a man sent from God, whose name was John.

"The same came for a witness, *to bear witness of the Light*, that all men through Him might believe" (Vers. 6,7).

It is evident, therefore, that our Lord did not dispel the world's darkness at His first coming and that, dispensationally, it was not day while He was on earth. We believe, rather, that the world's night began with the fall of man and that the darkness will not be dissipated until the second coming of Christ to judge and reign. Then the wicked will be judged and "burned up" as stubble (Mal. 4:1), but for those who fear His name:

"...the Sun of righteousness [shall] arise with healing in His wings..." (Ver. 2).

This is why He is called "the Morning Star" in those Scriptures which apply primarily to the Great Tribulation (Rev. 22:16; cf. II Pet. 1:19). [3]

But what, then, does the Apostle Paul mean in Rom. 13:12, where he says that "the night is far spent" and "the day is at hand"?

---

3. In II Pet. 1:19 the words "in your hearts" actually follow the words "take heed." All between is a parenthesis.

OUR NIGHT AND DAY

We believe that the answer to this question is that the Apostle is *not* speaking dispensationally in Rom. 13:11,12. Certainly, if the "night" of this present dispensation followed the supposed "day" of our Lord's earthly ministry, Paul could not have written that the night was "far spent." When he wrote it had barely begun.

Rather, Rom. 13:11,12 should be compared with such passages as II Cor. 4:6:

"For God, who commanded the light to shine out of darkness, hath shined in our hearts, to give the light of the knowledge of the glory of God in the face of Jesus Christ."

Thank God, the day has dawned for the believer in Christ though the night be dark about him. And because the day has dawned, *"it is high time to awake out of sleep*; for now is our salvation nearer than when we believed" (Rom. 13:11).

Our salvation, as believers in Christ, is of course *secure*, but it is not yet *complete*, and one day the dawning of the light which has brought us so much blessing and joy will suddenly burst into full-orbed day as our Beloved comes to catch us away to Himself.

LET US NOT SLEEP

Mark well, it is not the dawn that we are waiting for. For us the night is "*far* spent" (the Greek is in the aorist); the day *has* dawned and it is *the full-orbed day* that is at hand. Could the Apostle advance a better argument why we should "awake out of sleep"?

We find the same challenge forcefully presented in I Thes. 5. After explaining in I Thes. 4:16-18 how we shall be caught up to meet the Lord and be forever with Him, the Apostle goes on in Chapter 5 to say that "the day of the Lord" will come upon this world as "a thief in the night":

"For when THEY shall say, peace and safety, then sudden destruction cometh upon THEM, as travail upon a woman with child; and THEY shall not escape" (Ver. 3).

But the Apostle hastens to explain:

"But YE, brethren, are not in darkness, that that day should overtake YOU as a thief.

"YE are all the children of light, and the children of the day: WE are not of the night, nor of darkness.

"THEREFORE let us not sleep as do others, but let us watch and be sober" (Vers. 4-6).

This is the sole argument upon which he bases his appeal to be awake and alert. He does not urge us to be awake to defend ourselves against the thief, for before our Lord comes as a thief we will have been caught away. He rather says: The thief will come in the night, but *"ye are all the children of...the day: we are not of the night, nor of darkness. THEREFORE let us not sleep as do others, but let us watch and be sober"* (Vers. 5,6).

HIGH TIME TO AWAKEN

We should not fail to observe the urgency of the Apostle's inspired appeal in Rom. 13:11,12.

"It is HIGH TIME to awake out of sleep....The night is FAR SPENT [all but dissipated]; the [full-orbed] day is at hand."

What a disgrace to be sleeping at so late an hour, especially when there are battles to be fought and victories to be won! Thus the urgency of his appeal to *"cast off"* the night clothes of indolence and irresponsibility and to "put on the *armor* of light."

What is "the armor of light"? It is a *person*, the Lord Jesus Christ. In Eph. 5:8 the Apostle says of believers:

"For ye were sometime [at one time] darkness, but now are ye light *in the Lord:* walk as children of light."[4]

The man in Christ is a light to those about him as he *walks* in the light, and this light is an armor against sin, Satan and the allurements of the world. Thus, as Ver. 12

---

4. What a light in this world is a godly, wholesome Christian life! This is the nearest thing to Christ's own presence here. II Cor. 5:20 says that we believers are here "in Christ's stead" to beseech men to be reconciled to God.

says *"put on the armor of light,"* Ver. 14 adds, *"put ye on the Lord Jesus Christ."* [5]

AWAKE AND ARISE

While Rom. 13:11 bids us "awake out of sleep," Eph. 5:14 bids us "awake...*and arise* from [among] the dead." Believers have already been raised *from the dead* with Christ by grace (Eph. 2:4-6), but many, alas, are fast asleep—asleep to their responsibilities and opportunities, asleep to the need and challenge of the hour, asleep to the fact that a war is going on! Such are of no more *use to God* than are those who are still "dead in trespasses and sins." Thus in Rom. 13:11,12 he says, *"awake out of sleep...put on the armor,"* and in Eph. 5:14-17:

"Awake thou that sleepest, and arise from [among] the dead, and Christ shall give thee light.

"SEE THEN THAT YE WALK CIRCUMSPECTLY, NOT AS FOOLS BUT AS WISE,

"REDEEMING THE TIME, BECAUSE THE DAYS ARE EVIL.

"WHEREFORE BE YE NOT UNWISE, BUT UNDERSTANDING WHAT THE WILL OF THE LORD IS."

The Apostle does not refer here to God's will *for our lives*, but to the plan and purpose of God as revealed in the Epistles of Paul. God has *"made known unto us the mystery of His will"* (Eph. 1:9), and He would have us be *"filled with the knowledge of His will in all wisdom and spiritual understanding"* (Col. 1:9).

Paul closes this important passage in his *Epistle to the Romans* with the words:

"Let us walk honestly, as in the day; not in rioting and drunkenness, not in chambering and wantonness, not in strife and envying.

"But put ye on the Lord Jesus Christ, and make not provision for the flesh, to fulfil the lusts thereof" (Vers. 13,14).

---

5. According to Col. 3:10 we *"have* put on the new man," and God now sees us *in Christ.* However, the Apostle *exhorts* us to *"put on* the new man" experientially (Eph. 4:24), as he does here in Rom. 13:14.

"Honestly" here has the sense of "becomingly," as in the daytime, and "chambering and wantonness" refer respectively to the various forms of sexual sin and abandoned sensuality. The believer should "put...on the Lord Jesus Christ" and make no provision for gratifying the flesh.

> When I survey the wondrous cross,
>   On which the Prince of glory died,
> My richest gain I count but loss,
>   And pour contempt on all my pride.
>
> Forbid it, Lord, that I should boast,
>   Save in the death of Christ, my God;
> All the vain things that charm me most,
>   I sacrifice them to His blood.
>
> Were the whole realm of nature mine,
>   That were a present far too small.
> Love so amazing, so divine,
>   Demands my soul, my life, my all.
>
> —Isaac Watts

Chapter XIV — Romans 14:1—15:7

THE CHRISTIAN
AND MATTERS OF CONSCIENCE

DIETS AND DAYS

"Him that is weak in the faith receive ye, but not to doubtful disputations.

"For one believeth that he may eat all things: another, who is weak, eateth herbs.

"Let not him that eateth despise him that eateth not; and let not him which eateth not judge him that eateth, for God hath received him.

"Who art thou that judgest another man's servant? to his own master he standeth or falleth. Yea, he shall be holden up: for God is able to make him stand.

"One man esteemeth one day above another: another esteemeth every day alike. Let every man be fully persuaded in his own mind.

"He that regardeth the day, regardeth it unto the Lord; and he that regardeth not the day, to the Lord he doth not regard it. He that eateth, eateth to the Lord, for he giveth God thanks; and he that eateth not, to the Lord he eateth not, and giveth God thanks.

"For none of us liveth to himself, and no man dieth to himself.

"For whether we live, we live unto the Lord: and whether we die, we die unto the Lord: whether we live therefore, or die, we are the Lord's.

"For to this end Christ both died, and rose, and revived, that He might be Lord both of the dead and living.

"But why dost thou judge thy brother? or why dost thou set at naught thy brother? for we shall all stand before the judgment seat of Christ.

"For it is written, As I live, saith the Lord, every knee shall bow to Me, and every tongue shall confess to God.

"So then every one of us shall give account of himself to God."

—Rom. 14:1-12

EACH ONE TO GIVE AN ACCOUNT OF HIMSELF TO GOD

Romans 14 presents a strong plea for grace and understanding among believers in matters of conduct not specifically dealt with in the Word of God.

The word "receive" (Gr., *proslambano*), in Ver. 1, does not mean merely to accept or admit into the assembly. The brother who is weak *in the faith* is doubtless already a member of the assembly. *Proslambano* is a warmer word, meaning to receive *to one's self*, to embrace. Vine says it "signifies a special interest on the part of the receiver."

But having thus warmly received this brother to yourself, do not then begin to legislate as to questions that may be debatable. Backgrounds, customs, etc., exert great influence upon our thinking and conduct, but these are not to take the place of the Word of God. Thus it is a mistake to judge others in matters not spelled out in the Scriptures.

Romans 14 centers around two phrases: "one believeth" and "another believeth," i.e., "one believeth" one thing, and "another believeth" another. This has led some to suppose that faith matters little in the Christian life; that love and good will are the essential ingredients. Nothing could be farther from the truth. It is "through faith" that we are saved in the first place and it is faith that molds our character and regulates our conduct. In the truest sense, we *are* what we *believe*.

But here in Rom. 14 the Apostle refers to differences of opinion, or even of conviction, regarding practices *not directly discussed in the Scriptures*, and since it is the holy Scriptures that are of plenary authority in matters of faith and conduct, we must exercise great consideration in matters not dealt with therein.

As to the difference between the brother who "believeth that he may eat all things" and the "weak" brother, who believes that to please the Lord he must be a vegetarian, eating only "herbs," the Apostle states plainly:

1. "Let not him that eateth *despise* him that eateth not."

2. "Let not him which eateth not *judge* him that eateth, for God hath received him."

Christian liberty is a priceless possession. Legitimately used it is an ever-flowing source of spiritual joy and power. But it can be used "as an occasion to the flesh" (Gal. 5:13), with pride taking the place of the love it should generate. Thus the Apostle admonishes the brother who eats all things not to despise the brother who does not—the brother who refuses to partake of certain foods because he feels that this will displease God.

On the other hand, the brother who does *not* feel at liberty to eat all things may consider himself more scrupulous in his Christian conduct than the brother who *does* feel at liberty to do so and *he* may pride himself for *this* and tend to judge his brother for his "irresponsibility." This can soon become phariseeism. Hence for him the Apostle has an even stronger admonition:

". . .let not him which eateth not judge him that eateth: for God hath received him.

"Who art thou that judgest another man's servant? to his own master he standeth or falleth. Yea, he shall be holden up: for God is able to make him stand" (Ver. 3,4).

Proceeding now to the question of days, the Apostle says:

"One man esteemeth one day above another; [1] another esteemeth every day alike. Let every man be fully persuaded in his own mind" (Ver. 5).

It is clear that Paul's epistles, containing God's program for the Body of Christ, set no day above any other. The sabbath of the Old Testament was never given to the Gentiles or to the Body of Christ. It was a sign *between God and Israel alone* (Ex. 31:13,17). Thus the Apostle wrote to the Galatian Christians who "desired" to be under the Law:

"Ye observe days, and months, and times, and years.

---

1. It is doubtful that *Jewish* feast days are referred to here.

"I am afraid of [about] you, lest I have bestowed upon you labor in vain" (Gal. 4:10,11).

"I desire to be present with you now, and to change my voice [Lit., my tone]; for I stand in doubt of you" (Ver. 20).

Yet it is true that we may *learn* from the Law that it is good to take one day off each week from our daily labors and devote it more wholly to Christian fellowship and service. Surely there is nothing *wrong* with taking one day each week to meet together for worship and Bible study. Indeed it was a sad day for our land when many Christians began "going places" and "doing things" on Sundays and "forsaking the assembling of ourselves together" (See Heb. 10:25).

The trouble with the Galatian believers was that they observed the Sabbath and other days and seasons in *a desire to go back under the Law* (Gal. 4:9,21). For this Paul rebuked them sternly and bade them:

"Stand fast therefore in the liberty wherewith Christ hath made us free, and be not entangled again with the yoke of bondage" (Gal. 5:1).

This was evidently not the case with those whom he addresses in Rom. 14, however. They rather "esteemed" one day above another, or "esteemed" them all alike, the former making much of some special day or days, the latter holding that all of our days should be dedicated to the Lord and that it would therefore be wrong to "esteem" any day above another. To these the Apostle says:

"....Let every man be fully persuaded in his own mind" (Ver. 5).

Then, summing the whole matter up, he declares:

"He that regardeth the day, regardeth it unto the Lord; and he that regardeth not the day, to the Lord he doth not regard it. He that eateth, eateth to the Lord, for he giveth God thanks; and he that eateth not, to the Lord he eateth not, and giveth God thanks" (Ver. 6).

Let every man search the Scriptures and ask for the Spirit's guidance and thus be "fully persuaded in his own mind," both where "meats" and "days" are concerned, for in each case the sincere believer will surely want to do what he believes to be most pleasing to the Lord. This puts all disputants on the same level.

"For none of us liveth to himself, and no man dieth to himself.

"For whether we live, we live unto the Lord; and whether we die, we die unto the Lord: whether we live therefore, or die, we are the Lord's.

"For to this end Christ both died, and rose, and revived, THAT HE MIGHT BE LORD both of the dead and living" (Vers. 7-9).

Mark well, the words "none of us liveth to himself," etc., here, do *not* mean that our lives influence those of others, though this is also true. Rather the preceding and the following verses clearly reveal that Ver. 7 refers to our living and dying *in our relationship to the Lord*. Thus Ver. 9: *"For to this end Christ both died, and rose, and revived, that HE might be Lord* [the One over all] *both of the dead and living"* (Cf. Eph. 1:22). Seeing, then, that we live *and die* "unto the Lord," Vers. 10-12 follow naturally.

Searching questions are those of Ver. 10—for those on *both* sides of the subject of Christian liberty. *"Why do you judge your brother?"* he asks the one, and *"Why do you set your brother at naught?"* he asks the other—and *both* in the light of the fact that "we shall *all* stand before the judgment seat of Christ."[2]

Some erroneously teach that believers will not be called upon to give an account of themselves before God since, they argue, "there is...no more condemnation to them which are in Christ Jesus." The Apostle refutes this teaching in Vers. 11,12 with the words *"every knee...every tongue"* and *"every one of us."* Rom. 8:1 has to do with judgment *for sin* (which our Lord bore for us). From this believers are blessedly exempt. But we *shall* give an account of our service and conduct *as Christians*. Thus Paul exhorts us in I Cor. 4:5:

---

2. He does not here refer to the judgment of the Great White Throne, for only the unsaved will be judged there. This passage refers rather to the *bema*, or *dais*, at which *believers* will appear to have their service and conduct *as Christians* reviewed, and at which they will either "receive a reward" or "suffer loss" (I Cor. 3:9-15; II Cor. 5:10). This subject is discussed at length in the author's *Man, His Nature and Destiny*, Chapter VIII.

"Therefore judge nothing before the time, until the Lord come, who both will bring to light the hidden things of darkness, and will make manifest the counsels of the hearts: and then shall every man have praise of God."

The thought in the last phrase of this verse is not that the Lord will simply praise all who appear before Him. I Cor. 3:15 alone would deny this. The thought is rather that each will then receive his due praise, or whatever praise is due him.

WALKING IN LOVE

"Let us not therefore judge one another any more; but judge this rather, that no man put a stumblingblock or an occasion to fall in his brother's way.

"I know, and am persuaded by the Lord Jesus, that there is nothing unclean of itself; but to him that esteemeth anything to be unclean, to him it is unclean.

"But if thy brother be grieved with thy meat, now walkest thou not charitably. Destroy not him with thy meat, for whom Christ died.

"Let not then your good be evil spoken of:

"For the kingdom of God is not meat and drink; but righteousness, and peace, and joy in the Holy Ghost.

"For he that in these things serveth Christ is acceptable to God, and approved of men.

"Let us therefore follow after the things which make for peace, and things wherewith one may edify another.

"For meat destroy not the work of God. All things indeed are pure; but it is evil for that man who eateth with offense.

"It is good neither to eat flesh, nor to drink wine, nor anything whereby thy brother stumbleth, or is offended, or is made weak.

"Hast thou faith? have it to thyself before God. Happy is he that condemneth not himself in that thing which he alloweth.

"And he that doubteth is damned [condemned] if he eat, because he eateth not of faith, for whatsoever is not of faith is sin."

—Rom. 14:13-23

The words "any more," in Ver. 13, show how prone we are

to criticize each other, for they have the sense of "let us not keep criticizing," or "let us stop criticizing." *"But judge this rather,"* says the Apostle, *"that no man put a stumblingblock or an occasion to fall in his brother's way."* We *can* cause offense *by having our own way*, but we may avoid this by being thoughtful of our brethren.

Speaking for himself, the Apostle declares that he knows and has been persuaded by the Lord Jesus that nothing is unclean of itself, but he hastens again to add: "But to him that esteemeth anything to be unclean, to him *it is unclean*" (Ver. 14). We believe that he says this, not only in defense of the weaker brother, but also *as a warning* to the brother who *thinks* he is strong, lest he indulge in practices which in his heart he considers wrong, and so stand condemned. And then, still reasoning with the "stronger" brother, he says:

"But if thy brother be grieved with thy meat, now walkest thou not charitably [i.e., in eating it]. Destroy not him with thy meat, for whom Christ died."

It is a solemn thought that things in which I may indulge may "destroy" a brother so far as his spiritual experience is concerned,[3] and Paul indicates how reprehensible such unthoughtfulness is as he uses the words, *"thy meat,"* over against the words, *"Christ died."* Where the welfare of your brother is concerned, he says, do not value *your food* more than Christ valued *His life*. What a disgrace to God if the liberty in which you rejoice is "evil spoken of" (Gr., *blasphemeo*, to blaspheme) because of some small pleasure in which you insist on indulging yourself! "The kingdom of God,"[4] he declares, "is not meat and drink" (almost contemptuously!), *"but righteousness* [rightness], *and peace* [How this would be enhanced if we were all thoughtful of each other!], *and joy in the Holy Ghost* [the natural result of the peace that results from thoughtfulness of each other!]"

---

3. He cannot be destroyed, of course, as far as his life in Christ is concerned (John 3:36; 5:24; Rom. 8:1; Eph. 2:4-7).

4. He uses the broader term here, i.e., of the reign of God over our hearts, not the narrower term, "kingdom of heaven," which has to do with the future reign of Christ on earth.

(Ver. 17). This is indeed a beautiful verse to consider in the light of its context. How naturally Vers. 18,19 follow:

"For he that in these things serveth Christ is acceptable to God, and approved of men.

"Let us therefore follow after the things which make for peace, and things wherewith one may edify another."

Do not misunderstand. The Apostle is still referring to *the proper use of Christian liberty among each other as believers.* Surely such as Paul would not exhort us to "follow after," or pursue, "the things which make for peace," in our stand for the Word of God or our testimony for Christ. Rather he urges us to *"put on the whole armor of God"* and to stand our ground as *"good soldiers of Jesus Christ"* where these are concerned (Eph. 6:10-20; II Tim. 2:3). Too many disloyal Christian leaders have excused their unfaithfulness with the words: "Follow after the things which make for peace"—*taken out of their context!* Thank God it is not so easy to pervert the second part of this verse! It is not by "exercising *my rights*," but by "*yielding* my rights" that God will use me to "edify," or build up, my weaker brother.

Where *doctrine* is concerned, Paul's Spirit-inspired words are clear:

"Let no man therefore judge you in meat, or in drink, or in respect of an holy day, or of the new moon, or of the sabbath days:

"Which are a shadow of things to come; but the body [i.e., the substance] is of Christ" (Col. 2:16,17).

But with respect to our liberty in matters *not* specifically dealt with in Scripture it must be said that the Apostle urges self-denial rather than a refusal to be "judged." Dr. Harry Bultema, a generation ago, declared: "We have no right to give up our dearly-bought liberty, but we do have the liberty to give up our rights."

But there is something even more reprehensible than to "destroy" my brother by insisting on having my own way. In Ver. 15 the Apostle says, "Destroy not *him*," but in Ver. 20 he says, *"Destroy not the work of God,"* and it is possible to do this with a little self-indulgence and self-will. Thus he says again, almost impatiently, *"All things indeed are pure; but it is evil for that man who eateth with offence."* In a similar forceful manner he writes to the carnal Corinthian believers:

"But take heed lest by any means this liberty of yours become a stumblingblock to them that are weak" (I Cor. 8:9).

Ver. 21 introduces us to *one* reason why some Christians of Paul's day, converted from paganism, became vegetarians. For the first time we come to the word "flesh" (Gr., *kreas*). The word "meat," used in the earlier part of the chapter, is an old English word for solid food of any kind (See Luke 3:11; 9:13). We now use the word *meat* for animal flesh.

Much of the meat sold at the "shambles," or meat markets, of Paul's day was first offered in sacrifice to idols. Quite naturally, therefore, some believers felt it would be dishonoring to God to partake of it.

In I Cor. 8:4 Paul declares that *"an idol is nothing,"* since *"there is none other God but one."* However, in Ver. 7 he qualifies this with a "Howbeit": "Howbeit there is not in every man that knowledge: for some with conscience of the idol unto this hour *eat it as a thing offered unto an idol*; and their conscience being weak is defiled." It is not difficult to appreciate their feelings in this matter.

Thus the Apostle rightly says in Rom. 14:21:

"It is good neither to eat flesh, nor to drink wine, [5] nor anything whereby thy brother stumbleth, or is offended, or is made weak."

Note the words *"whereby...stumbleth,"* i.e., by his following me against his conscience, thus impeding his progress; *"offended,"* i.e., embarrassed, or put into a difficult position; *"made weak,"* shaken, and rendered less stable in his opinions or conduct. From these we can see how easy it is to disrupt the spiritual life of a young or weak believer, even by our *example*. Thus the Apostle declares in I Cor. 8:13:

"Wherefore if meat make my brother to offend, I will eat no flesh [6] while the world standeth, lest I make my brother to offend."

---

5. Used as libations in pagan sacrifices.
6. Rom. 14:21 and I Cor. 8:13 are the only two passages where this word "flesh" (Gr., *kreas*) occurs.

Believers have been graciously delivered from the bondage of *childhood* and given the liberty of fullgrown *sons* (Gal. 3:24; 4:1-7), but this advance from infancy to maturity in itself implies the acquisition of a sense of *responsibility*. Hence the Apostle's repeated exhortations to stronger saints to feel responsible for the welfare of their weaker brethren.

In Vers. 22,23 he goes even farther in defense of those who cannot conscientiously partake of certain foods: *"Hast thou faith?"* he asks the "stronger" brother: *"have it to thyself before God."* Don't flaunt your "strong" faith before others and—can you pass this test?—"Have it...*before God.*" Strangely we confess far more on our knees before God than we do standing before our brethren. How strong, then, is our faith *in His sight?* And, probing even deeper, he says:

"Happy is he that condemneth not himself in that thing which he alloweth.

"And he that doubteth is damned [condemned] if he eat, because he eateth not of faith: for whatsoever is not of faith is sin" (Vers. 22,23).

Obviously this is *not* directed to the weaker brother, but to the brother who feels himself to be the stronger. The Apostle warns against confusing liberty with license for, he says, if we *condemn ourselves* in that which we allow, we also *stand condemned in it before God* because we have not acted in faith but in self-will. Christian liberty does not consist in merely being permitted to do what we wish. It is more objective than this. Thus Paul's exhortation to the Galatian believers—and to us:

"For, brethren, ye have been called unto liberty; only use not liberty for an occasion to the flesh, but BY LOVE SERVE ONE ANOTHER" (Gal. 5:13).

CLOSING APPEAL

"We then that are strong ought to bear the infirmities of the weak, and not to please ourselves.

"Let every one of us please his neighbor for his good to edification.

"For even Christ pleased not Himself; but, as it is written, The reproaches of them that reproached Thee fell on Me.

"For whatsoever things were written aforetime were written for our learning, that we through patience and comfort of the Scriptures might have hope.

"Now the God of patience and consolation grant you to be likeminded one toward another according to Christ Jesus:

"That ye may with one mind and one mouth glorify God, even the Father of our Lord Jesus Christ.

"Wherefore receive ye one another, as Christ also received us to the glory of God."

—Rom. 15:1-7

In the first seven verses of Romans 15 we have a forceful summary of the great truths taught us in Chapter 14.

Mark well the words *"ought to"*: it is only reasonable and right that we do this. Also, he does not say that we "ought to" bear *with* the infirmities of the weak; he says we "ought to *bear the infirmities* of the weak, and *not to please ourselves*," i.e., we should not merely *tolerate* the weaker brother but *help* him.

This reminds us of the Apostle's words in I Cor. 13:5, where he says that love *"seeketh not her own,"* and I Cor. 10:24: *"Let no man seek his own, but every man another's wealth [or welfare]."*

Again, always bearing in mind the context, *"Let every one of us please his neighbor for his good to edification,"*—not only to *his edification, or building up, but to the edification of the assembly*, for such thoughtfulness on the part of all is bound to build up *the work of the Lord* as well as the individuals in it. To break down is generally much easier than to build up, but the latter is more commendable. Pride vaunts its liberty and makes a case of its rights, but love thinks of its neighbor and does all it can to help him.

Even Christ, who *alone* had the *right* to please Himself, did not do so, but willingly bore, not merely the *infirmities* of His *friends*, but the *reproaches* of His *enemies* (Ver. 3). Surely, then, the "strong" believer *"ought to"* bear the *infirmities* of his best and closest friends, his brethren in

Christ, even if they seem to him to be weaker in the faith than he.

"FOR whatsoever things were written aforetime," i.e., in the Scriptures—and Paul had quoted many such passages—"were written for our learning *that we through patience and comfort of the Scriptures might have hope*" (Ver. 4). The word "comfort" here appears in such passages as John 14:16,26, where the Holy Spirit is called the "Comforter," i.e., one called to one's side or to one's aid. The New Testament has several words for "comfort," but this one (Gr., *paraklesis*) appears most frequently and has the sense of *consolation* or *encouragement*. The name *Barnabas* meant *"the son of consolation"* (Acts 4:36; same word), one who consoles, or encourages those who are down in spirit. Probably he was well named (Ver. 37). In the Greek the words *"patience and comfort"* (Rom. 15:4) are precisely the same as *"patience and consolation"* (Ver. 5). Obviously so, for it is the *"God of patience and consolation"* (Ver. 5), who gives us the *"patience and consolation of the Scriptures"* (Ver. 4)—which He wrote—*that by these we "might have hope."*

"The God of patience"! Think of it! "Important" people are apt to be *im*patient, but *God* is *"the God of patience."* What patience He showed in His dealings with the patriarchs, with Israel, and now with us! And what *little* patience *we* often exercise toward others! Are *we*, then, more important than *He*? And with His patience God has repeatedly hastened, as it were, to give us *encouragement* in any small matter in which we might have pleased Him! Let us then pray with Paul that "the God of patience and consolation" may grant *us* to be *"like-minded one toward another according to Christ Jesus."*

It is important to note carefully the words, *"according to Christ Jesus"* in Ver. 5 if we would understand clearly what he means by being *"likeminded one toward another."* He does *not* mean that a particular believer should have the same mind toward his brother as his brother has toward him. The thought is rather that in their relationship toward each other *both* should have *the mind of Christ* toward each other

(Ver. 3), and thus should be *"likeminded* one *toward* another." The Apostle, pleading for mutual consideration among believers, says in Phil. 2:4,5:

"Look not every man on his own things, but every man also on the things of others.

"Let this mind be in you, which was also in Christ Jesus:"

And following these words in Phil. 2 the Apostle lists the seven great downward steps by which our Lord voluntarily descended from His glory in heaven to "the death of the cross" (Vers. 6-8). How little consideration, in the light of this passage, do the best of us show toward our brethren in Christ!

That the Apostle has the edification of the assembly in view is evident again from Ver. 6: "That ye may *with one mind and one mouth* glorify God, even the Father of our Lord Jesus Christ."

How important to God is the unity of the Spirit in the Body of Christ! To the Philippian believers Paul wrote:

"Only let your conversation be as it becometh the gospel of Christ: that whether I come and see you, or else be absent, I may hear of your affairs, *that ye stand fast in one spirit, with one mind striving together for the faith of the gospel;*

"And in nothing terrified by your adversaries..." (Phil. 1:27,28).

Such oneness is bound to glorify God (Rom. 15:6).

God—and God alone—*deserves* all the glory of our minds and mouths—and hearts. He is not a monster, whom we must look upon as cruel and vindictive. He is *"the Father of our Lord Jesus Christ,"* that beloved and only Son whom He gave up to judgment and wrath that "whosoever believeth in Him should not perish but have everlasting life" (John 3:16).

And the Son, being one with the Father, was of the same mind, giving Himself up to suffering, shame and death "that we might live through Him." How appropriate, then, are the closing words of this searching exhortation:

"Wherefore receive[7] ye one another, as Christ also received[8] us, to the glory of God" (Ver. 7).

May God, in His grace, enable us to sing in truth those beloved verses:

> Blest be the tie that binds
>   Our hearts in Christian love;
> The fellowship of kindred minds
>   Is like to that above.
>
> Before our Father's throne
>   We pour our ardent prayers;
> Our fears, our hopes, our aims are one,
>   Our comforts and our cares.
>
> We share our mutual woes,
>   Our mutual burdens bear;
> And often for each other flows
>   The sympathizing tear.

—John Fawcett

7,8. Again, to receive *to one's self*; to *embrace*.

Chapter XV — Romans 15:8-33

PAUL'S MINISTRY TO THE GENTILES AND TO THE JEWS

TWO "MINISTERS"

"Now I say that Jesus Christ was a minister of the circumcision for the truth of God, to confirm the promises made unto the fathers:

"And that the Gentiles might glorify God for His mercy; as it is written, For this cause I will confess to Thee among the Gentiles, and sing unto Thy name.

"And again He saith, Rejoice ye Gentiles, with His people.

"And again, Praise the Lord all ye Gentiles; and laud Him all ye people.

"And again, Esaias saith, There shall be a root of Jesse, and He that shall rise to reign over the Gentiles; in Him shall the Gentiles trust.

"Now the God of hope fill you with all joy and peace in believing, that ye may abound in hope, through the power of the Holy Ghost.

"And I myself also am persuaded of you, my brethren, that ye also are full of goodness, filled with all knowledge, able also to admonish one another.

"Nevertheless, brethren, I have written the more boldly unto you in some sort, as putting you in mind, because of the grace that is given to me of God,

"That I should be the minister of Jesus Christ to the Gentiles, ministering the gospel of God, that the offering up of the Gentiles might be acceptable, being sanctified by the Holy Ghost."

—Rom. 15:8-16

THE MINISTRY OF CHRIST TO ISRAEL AND THE MINISTRY OF PAUL TO THE GENTILES

We have come now to a most important passage in the *Epistle to the Romans*, a passage in which Paul, by divine inspiration, calls our Lord Jesus Christ "a minister of *the Circumcision [the Jew]*"[1] (Ver. 8), and calls *himself* "the minister of Jesus Christ to *the Gentiles*"[2] (Ver. 16).

It should be carefully observed that Paul declares here that *"Jesus Christ WAS a minister of the Circumcision"* (Ver. 8). This not only places the ministry referred to in the past, but implies that a change has since taken place. When our Lord was on earth He Himself stated that He had been sent to none *"but unto the lost sheep of the house of Israel"* (Matt. 15:24), and when He first sent His twelve apostles forth, He commanded them: *"Go not into the way of the Gentiles...but go rather to the lost sheep of the house of Israel"* (Matt. 10:5,6). It was not until *after* His ascension to heaven, indeed *after* Pentecost that He raised up *another* apostle, Paul, to go to the Gentiles.

Next it should be noted that our Lord was sent to Israel *"for the truth of God,"* i.e., to demonstrate His veracity, *"to confirm the promises made unto the fathers."*

While our Lord was on earth He said not one word about the "joint Body" of today, or of its "one baptism," or of "no difference" between Jews and Gentiles, or of a heavenly calling and position or of salvation by grace through faith apart from religion or works. All this was part of the great "mystery," or secret, later revealed to and through Paul.

Our Lord, during His earthly ministry was, from beginning to end, *"confirming the promises made unto the fathers." This* was His calling as Israel's Messiah:

---

1. The author uses the words *Jew* and *Israelite* interchangeably. See *Anglo-Israelism, Will it Stand the Berean Test?*, by Richard Jordan (Published by Berean Bible Society).

2. A word should be said here with regard to the term *Gentiles*. The Hebrew *goy* and the Greek *ethnos* are the "Old Testament" and "New Testament" words most often rendered *Gentile* in the *King James Version*, both meaning, basically, *nation*. However, at least eight times in the "Old Testament" and several times in the "New," Israel herself is so named. Perhaps the most important fact to recognize, however, is that in the "New Testament" especially, the word *"Gentiles"* is *mostly* used of *non- Israelitish* people *as such*, distinguishing them from Israel as those who did *not* possess the covenants, the Law, circumcision, the divine worship, etc. We believe therefore that *Gentile*, the usual KJV rendering for *goy* and *ethnos*, is generally to be preferred.

When He was born in Bethlehem (Matt. 2:4-6),

When He was taken into Egypt (Matt. 2:15),

When He was brought up in Nazareth (Matt. 2:23),

When He preached good news and healed the sick (Luke 4:17-21),

When He died on the cross (I Cor. 15:3),

When He was buried (I Cor. 15:4),

When He arose from the dead (I Cor. 15:4),

When He ascended to heaven (Acts 2:34-36),

When He sent the Holy Spirit at Pentecost (Luke 24:49);

In all these, from His birth at Bethlehem *through* the sending of the Holy Spirit at Pentecost, He faithfully discharged His God-given ministry *"to confirm the promises made unto the fathers."*

Some hold that the present dispensation began at Pentecost, or at the resurrection, or at the Cross—or even with John the Baptist, but *all* these are *grossly mistaken* in the light of the above. Even Pentecost did not mark the beginning of a *new dispensation*, rather it confirmed *old promises* made to Israel.

Those who hold that the present dispensation of grace began at Pentecost or before fail to note that at that time the twelve apostles,[3] like their Master, kept *"confirming the promises made unto the fathers"* and did *not* preach salvation by grace, through faith in the finished work of Christ (See Acts 1:16,20-22; 2:14-21,29-31,34-39; 3:19-25; 4:11,25-28, etc.). Thus Paul continues:

"*And* that the Gentiles might glorify God for His *mercy*; as it is written..." (Ver. 9). Mark it well, *"promises"* to the

---

3. Matthias was rightly chosen to fill the place of Judas and was then *"filled with the Holy Spirit"* (Acts 1:24—2:4). See the author's comments on this in *Acts, Dispensationally Considered*, Vol. I. *Then*, when the ministry of the twelve was rejected, God raised up Paul, that *other* apostle, to proclaim *"the gospel of the grace of God"* to all men.

fathers, but *"mercy"* to the Gentiles (Vers. 8,9). No promises had been made to the Gentiles. It was only *because of* "the promises made unto the fathers" that the Gentiles were to find mercy. Thus, in the original promise to Abraham, God said, *"in thee* shall all families of the earth be blessed" (Gen. 12:3).

This was no "mystery," no secret, and it is impressive to observe Paul's insistence on this as he points out that *"again...and again...and again"* this blessing of the Gentiles was predicted by the prophets:

"As it is written...I will confess to Thee among the Gentiles.

"And again...Rejoice ye Gentiles, with His people.

"And again, Praise the Lord all ye Gentiles; and laud Him, all ye people.

"And again...There shall be a root of Jesse...in Him shall the Gentiles trust" (Vers. 9-12).

Thus our Lord's ministry was in confirmation[4] of the promises made to Israel, so that the Gentiles might glorify God for His mercy. This is a millennial picture. Our Lord "confirmed the promises" made to Israel, and those not self-blinded recognized Him as their long-promised Messiah. However, these promises will not be *fulfilled* until He returns to earth to reign. Then, and not until then, the Gentiles will "rejoice...with His people" Israel. As Isa. 60:3 says, with reference to Israel's rise: *"...the Gentiles shall come to thy light, and kings to the brightness of thy rising."*

It is a pity that the *New Scofield Reference Bible*, which claims to follow the *Authorized Version*, has changed the word "people" in Ver. 11 to "peoples" and has even changed the passage quoted (Psa. 117:1) to make *that* read "peoples." In both cases it should read "people," referring to the nation Israel, as in *"His people"* (Rom. 15:10). See Acts 4:25-27 for the distinction.

The Gentiles, or nations, are most assuredly *not* rejoicing

---

4. Not in *fulfillment,* for they were *not yet fulfilled.*

with Israel today, nor will they do so until Christ returns to reign over Israel and the world.

But now we come to a strange and wonderful verse.

"Now the God of hope fill you with all joy and peace in believing, that ye may abound in hope through the power of the Holy Ghost" (Ver. 13).

"Joy and peace in believing"—*believing what?* Believing the promises made in Vers. 9-12? In the first place, these were not made to the Gentiles, and in the second, they were not being fulfilled. The Lord Jesus had *confirmed* them, to be sure, but Israel rejected both Him and them.

What was a spiritually hungry Gentile now to do? Ah, Paul cast them upon "the *God* of hope" who had *made* the promises through which Israel would prove a blessing to the Gentiles. He would find a way—He *had* found a way, long kept secret, but now to be revealed. If there was a "bottleneck," because Israel refused to be the channel of blessing to the Gentiles, He would break the "neck," and let the blessing flow to the Gentiles directly from His heart of love. And this is exactly what He did, sending the blessing to the Gentiles, not through Israel's *rise*, but through her *fall*, as we saw in studying Rom. 11:11-15. Thus He now saves Gentiles apart from the covenants, apart from prophecy, apart from Israel's instrumentality, just by grace, *on the basis of the finished work of Christ at Calvary.*

This is why He raised up Paul, the chief of sinners, saved by grace, to engage in *"the preaching of the cross,"* to proclaim *"redemption through His blood, the forgiveness of sins according to the riches of His grace"* (Eph. 1:7), offering reconciliation to even His bitterest enemies (II Cor. 5:14-21).

Little wonder Paul here writes to these Gentiles, left in such a seemingly impossible position by Israel's rejection of Christ: *"Now the God of hope fill you with all joy and peace in believing"* (Ver. 13).

And then the Apostle proceeds to show *how* God worked out the problem (as we now know—before it ever developed!)

But why, in this context, does the Apostle insert a paragraph about his readers' "goodness" and "knowledge," and their ability to "admonish one another" (Ver. 14)? We believe that the *"Nevertheless"* of Ver. 15 explains. He says, as it were, "This is no reflection on you, but I have something to tell you that you probably do not yet know, or haven't fully appreciated."

"Nevertheless, brethren, I have written the more boldly unto you in some sort, [5] as putting you in mind, because of the grace that is given to me of God,

"That I should be the minister of Jesus Christ to the Gentiles..." (Vers. 15,16).

At the great Jerusalem council, Peter and the other leaders of the Judaean church had recognized *the special grace given to Paul as the Apostle of the Gentiles* (Gal. 2:7,9). Indeed, James, Peter and John had shaken hands with him in *a public, official agreement*, recognizing Paul as the Apostle of God to the Gentiles, while *they* were henceforth to confine their ministry to "the Circumcision" (Gal. 2:9). Here the "great commission" to the twelve to go "into all the world" gave way, by the Spirit's direction, to the greater commission to Paul (II Cor. 5:18,19). How regrettable that most of our great theologians have not yet seen this simple fact, and that many even resist it!

The Apostle now reminds his readers of *"the grace ... given to me of God, that I should be the minister of Jesus Christ to the Gentiles"* (Rom. 15:15,16).

As "Jesus Christ *was a minister of the Circumcision"* Paul, by grace, had now been appointed *"the minister of Jesus Christ to the Gentiles"* and this was *a self-evident fact* (Vers. 16-19).

"The offering up of the Gentiles" to God in this way was certainly not the fulfillment of prophecy concerning the Gentiles; it was rather what Paul calls *"this mystery among the Gentiles"* (Col. 1:27) and not only was this "offering... *acceptable*, being sanctified by the Holy Spirit," but God says

---

5. Lit., in a way, in a sense.

that He would have His saints know *"what is the riches of the glory of this mystery."* How disappointing that most of the leaders of Christendom themselves have little knowledge or understanding of this great truth, so precious to the heart of God and to those of His children who have entered into it!

Before leaving this section let us go back to Ver. 13, to Paul's benediction: *"Now the God of hope fill you with all joy and peace in believing...."* If this applied to these Gentiles, who were seemingly placed in an utterly hopeless position by Israel's rejection of Christ, then how much more does it apply to us who have seen His plan for *them* unfold so beautifully in the raising up of Paul! When the situation seems hopeless, then, trust in *"the God of hope"* and *He* will *"fill you with all joy and peace,"* and cause you to *"abound in hope, through the power of the Holy Spirit."*

PAUL'S APOSTOLIC OBJECTIVE

"I have therefore whereof I may glory through Jesus Christ in those things which pertain to God.

"For I will not dare to speak of any of those things which Christ hath not wrought by me, to make the Gentiles obedient, by word and deed.

"Through mighty signs and wonders, by the power of the Spirit of God; so that from Jerusalem, and round about unto Illyricum, I have fully preached the gospel of Christ.

"Yea, so have I strived to preach the gospel, not where Christ was named, lest I should build upon another man's foundation:

"But as it is written, To whom He was not spoken of, they shall see; and they that have not heard shall understand.

"For which cause also I have been much hindered from coming to you.

"But now having no more place in these parts, and having a great desire these many years to come unto you;

"Whensoever I take my journey into Spain, I will come to you: for I trust to see you in my journey, and to be brought on my way thitherward by you, if first I be somewhat filled with your company."

—Rom. 15:17-24

"In those things which pertain to God," Paul did indeed

have much to boast about, *"through Jesus Christ,"* as he says in Ver. 17. Would that we all were enthused enough with the wonders of "the mystery" to *boast* about it! Would that we, like Paul, could find reason to boast only in *the accomplishments of Christ at Calvary!* (Cf. Gal. 6:14).

Note the striking statement: "I will not dare to speak of any of those things which Christ hath *not* wrought by me . . ." (Ver. 18).

Paul's example in this is a rebuke to most of us. How prone many of us are to accept credit that is not justly our due, and to exaggerate what God *has* done through us! It should be our earnest prayer to be delivered from this sin.

As we read Paul's statement more carefully, however, we feel that he may have had a special situation in mind, *not* wrought by him. He had indeed been used "to make the Gentiles obedient, by word and deed" (Ver. 18). Before him, however, the twelve apostles of the kingdom had been mightily used in Judaea, and the Church there had multiplied greatly in numbers. It was not his desire to cast their mighty ministry into the shade. His purpose was rather to magnify *the grace of God* in saving Gentiles even apart from Israel's instrumentality or any promise previously made.

It was to authenticate this ministry of Paul that God gave him "mighty signs and wonders" and the evident "power of the Spirit of God" (Ver. 19). Indeed, the miracles of Paul's early ministry were such as to be widely recognized. According to the record of Acts, the signs wrought by Peter were more than matched by Paul. Thus Acts 19:11 declares that *"God wrought special miracles by the hands of Paul."* Had we the space it would be interesting to compare the individual miracles wrought by Peter with those wrought by Paul and see how exceeding mighty were "the signs of an apostle" wrought by Paul.

Think of this Spirit-empowered man, used of God to fully proclaim the gospel in widening circles all the way from Jerusalem to Illyricum, far to the north and west, above Macedonia. We know from the Acts record that this included Syria, Cyprus, Galatia, Cilicia, Pisidia, Phrygia, Mysia, Greece, Macedonia and most of the populous area that lay between, including numerous great cities. In our day of fast and easy travel it is hard to visualize all that the Apostle must have endured in his unremitting efforts to reach the Gentiles with "the gospel of the grace of God." We know that by this time he had already suffered stripes and imprisonment, beatings, stonings and shipwreck, perils of all kinds, weariness and pain, hunger and thirst, cold and nakedness—and much more (See II Cor. 11:21-30). We, Christian believers today, should ask God for the heart of love that motivated the Apostle Paul to accomplish all this.

Surely he does not mean to imply, in Ver. 20, that it would be wrong to preach Christ where He has previously been proclaimed. Else why all the churches he established? Surely he expected his co-workers to build upon the foundation *he* laid at Corinth (I Cor. 3:10). Besides laying the foundations of local churches, however, he had also laid the foundation for the Church of this present dispensation, so that it was his desire to reach as many as possible *first*, in the spirit of Isa. 52:15 (Ver. 21).

All this was what had so long hindered him much from reaching Rome.

"But now," having thoroughly covered this territory, and having had a "great desire these many years" to see the saints at Rome (Ver. 23; cf. 1:11), he planned to go to Spain and stop at Rome on the way (Ver. 24) to minister to them and enjoy their fellowship for a season.

Note the words *"somewhat filled with your company"* (Ver. 24). The *"somewhat"* indicates that he feels responsible to go on to Spain without too much delay, yet the following words, *"filled with your company,"* show how he will dislike leaving the Roman believers! What a volume could be written on *The Heart of the Apostle Paul!*

THE POOR SAINTS AT JERUSALEM

"But now I go unto Jerusalem to minister unto the saints.

"For it hath pleased them of Macedonia and Achaia to make a certain contribution for the poor saints which are at Jerusalem.

"It hath pleased them verily; and their debtors they are. For if the Gentiles have been made partakers of their spiritual things, their duty is also to minister unto them in carnal things.

"When therefore I have performed this, and have sealed to them this fruit, I will come by you into Spain.

"And I am sure that, when I come unto you, I shall come in the fulness of the blessing of the gospel of Christ.

"Now I beseech you, brethren, for the Lord Jesus Christ's sake, and for the love of the Spirit, that ye strive together with me in your prayers to God for me;

"That I may be delivered from them that do not believe in Judaea; and that my service which I have for Jerusalem may be accepted of the saints;

"That I may come unto you with joy by the will of God, and may with you be refreshed.

"Now the God of peace be with you all. Amen."

—Rom. 15:25-33

"The poor saints which are at Jerusalem"! This is strange in view of the great prosperity which these saints had enjoyed after Pentecost. Of that time we read, *"Neither was there any among them that lacked"* (Acts 4:34); not one poor person among them. What has happened that Paul must now go and minister to the "poor saints" there, indeed, that far-away Gentile churches must take up collections for their relief?

It is important here to consider the background of this situation so that we may get the whole picture in proper perspective.

When on earth our Lord had taught His disciples to "take no thought" for their food or clothing (Luke 12:22-24). His instructions were: *"Rather seek ye the kingdom of God, and all these things shall be added unto you,"* assuring them, *"Fear not, little flock, for it is your Father's good pleasure to give you the kingdom"* (Vers. 31,32).

Could anything be clearer to the believing reader? The

kingdom, to be *taken from* the chief priests and Pharisees (Matt. 21:43) was to be *given to* the "little flock," of His followers. Indeed, our Lord had already appointed the rulers who were to reign with Him in that kingdom (Matt. 19:28). Thus the disciples were not to "take thought" about the trivial needs of the present, but were to "seek the kingdom," assured that "all these things" would be provided them. [6]

Many who apply the Sermon on the Mount to our day interpret the words *"seek...the kingdom of God"* to mean: seek the *things* of God, and the words *"give you the kingdom"* to mean: give you victory, or give you some spiritual blessing. But all of them stop short at the next verse (Ver. 33), which says, *"Sell that ye have, and give alms"!* It appears that they would rather not discuss this passage, for *none* of them obey it, and to misinterpret this would be too obvious. Yet our Lord included all this in His *Sermon on the Mount* and even sent His apostles forth to preach, with the instructions: *"Provide neither gold, nor silver, nor brass in your purses"* (Matt. 10:9). How would *our* missionaries fare if we sent them forth without providing a dollar, a dime, or even a cent for traveling expenses? Yet this was to be one of the basic requirements of life in the kingdom. The *Sermon on the Mount*, rightly called "the charter of the kingdom," taught communal living [7] with every one concerned about the welfare of his brother.

Human nature does not readily turn over its wealth to those in need, nor would this be in order in "this present evil age" (See I Tim. 5:8), but at Pentecost, when "they were all filled with the Holy Spirit" (Acts 2:4), the thousands of Messianic believers *did* spontaneously live for one another, *"neither said any of them that aught of the things which he possessed was his own,"* with the result that none of them lacked anything (Acts 4:32,34).

---

6. Just before the crucifixion, this program was briefly interrupted (Luke 22:35-37). It was resumed again with the coming of the Holy Spirit (Acts 2:44,45).

7. Not to be confused with modern Communism. Communism says: "You've got plenty; I'll take some," but our Lord's Sermon on the Mount taught the opposite: "I've got plenty; you take some."

As we know, however, Israel rejected the King and His kingdom, thus it was not long before this program passed away and a serious economic problem developed. Now *many* of them were poor. [8]

Some years previous, at the great Jerusalem Council, the Judaean leaders had requested Paul to remember their poor, "which," says Paul, "I also was forward to do" (Gal. 2:10). It was in fulfillment of this promise that Paul had now promoted a vast love-offering from the Gentile churches [9] for the "poor saints" at Jerusalem.

How simple to reconcile Acts 4:34 (where none lacked) with Rom. 15:25,26 (the poor saints) when we rightly divide the Word of truth! The happy, prosperous way of life which the Pentecostal believers enjoyed for a time was a foretaste of the coming kingdom, when all will again be "filled with the Holy Spirit" (Joel 2:28,29; cf. Acts 2:4,17). But, as we say, this program passed from the scene with Israel's rejection of Christ and the raising up of Paul to proclaim grace to the Gentiles.

Thus the Apostle explains that these Gentile believers were truly pleased to be able to help the Judaean saints and, indeed, were their debtors (Ver. 27). And with this he

---

8. It is a serious error, then, to teach, as a popular Fundamentalist of the past generation did: "God has given us in the book of Acts a pattern of Christian testimony, missionary effort, world evangelism and building of Christian churches—a pattern which we would do well to follow . . . .the closer we come to ordering all things according to this holy pattern, the greater blessing will attend our efforts" (Dr. H. A. Ironside, in *Lectures on the Book of Acts*, P. 10). If this still-popular interpretation of Acts is correct, why does no one consistently follow this "holy pattern"? Acts presents *a changing program*; it is a book of *transition* from the old dispensation to the new. If we follow this "pattern," shall we preach repentance and baptism for remission, with Peter (Acts 2:38), or "the gospel of the grace of God," with Paul (Acts 20:24)? Shall we go to the *Jew only* as did the disciples in early Acts (Acts 11:19), or shall we say, *"Your blood be upon your own heads . . .I will go unto the Gentiles,"* as did Paul (18:6)? Shall we dispose of all our investments and have *"all things common"* (Acts 2 and 4), or shall we retain our private possessions and give to the Lord's work *"every man according to his ability"* (11:29)? If we follow this pattern, may we be assured that none of *us* will lack (4:34), or will we end up with *"the poor saints at Jerusalem"* (Rom. 15:26)? For an in-depth discussion of this question see the Author's *Acts, Dispensationally Considered*, Introduction.

9. It appears, however, that the church at Rome was not included in this offering, perhaps because of the distance involved.

teaches a lesson that should be taken to heart by those who have been unfaithful as stewards of their God-given wealth:

> "For if the Gentiles have been made partakers of their spiritual things, their duty is also to minister unto them in carnal [material] things" (Ver. 27).

How many believers there are who rejoice in the riches of God's grace, but *contribute* little toward the expenses involved in proclaiming it to others! How many receive light and blessing from those called of God to proclaim the Word, but fail to fulfil their "duty" to "minister unto them in material things"! This is doubtless why the Apostle has so much to say about the importance of Christian generosity—almost two whole chapters in II Corinthians alone. One thing is certain: that "the churches of Macedonia" who, if Paul had permitted it, would have given "beyond their power," received as an ingredient of that very generosity, an "abundance of joy" (II Cor. 8:2,3). Little wonder! They had first *given themselves* to the Lord and to Paul (Ver. 5). God grant that such "generosity of love" might abound in us all (Ver. 7).

As the Apostle writes of going to Jerusalem and Rome, however, he has firm assurance about one matter, but grave misgivings about another. As to his ministry in Rome, he says:

> "And I am sure that, when I come unto you, I shall come in the fulness of the blessing of the gospel of Christ" (Rom. 15:29).

Paul was not a spiritual pauper, as are so many clergymen who stand in the pulpit but have no real, vital message for their hearers. He could scarcely wait, as it were, to proclaim to the Romans the glorious message he had been commissioned to preach. This message filled his heart to overflowing.

From Vers. 30,31, however, it is evident that he entertained serious misgivings as to his visit to Jerusalem. The unregenerate Jews still considered him the great traitor to their nation, while it appears that the leaders of the church there did not entertain the most cordial feelings toward Paul now that he, rather than they, had been appointed to go to the Gentiles.

As it turned out, Paul's fears were not unfounded, for not only was the gift from the Gentile churches *not* heartily received by the Jewish brethren, but it was here at Jerusalem that Paul was formally charged with blasphemy and finally sent to Rome in chains. Here we quote from *Acts, Dispensationally Considered*:

"As Paul saluted James and the elders there was a superficial show of harmony, but the elements of suspicion and discord lurked beneath. It had not been James who had opened his home to Paul. He had not been among those who had gathered to welcome the great apostle on the previous night. And his party had not made things easy for Paul in late years.

"But now perhaps the atmosphere would be cleared as Paul related to them 'particularly,' i.e., *in detail*, 'what things *God* had wrought among the Gentiles by his ministry.' It must have been thrilling to hear the great apostle tell of idols cast away, sinful books burned, wicked practices abandoned and Christ received and glorified in city after city, the delegates from the various churches doubtless presenting their gifts at this time; an immense amount, and a sacrificial proof of their affection toward their brethren in Judaea.

"The response? 'They glorified the Lord, and said'—quickly changing the subject to a matter that could only embarrass the Apostle. The record does not say one word about their agreeing to help the Judaean believers understand Paul and his God-given ministry, nor one word about their inviting *him* to tell them what God had wrought through him, nor even one word about their thanking him and the Gentile churches for so generously keeping their promise of some years back (Gal. 2:10)—and nothing would have fallen more naturally within the scope of Luke's account, had it taken place." (Pp. 15,16).

It was on the very next day that Paul was seized in the temple and charged with blasphemy, finally to be sent to Rome in chains to be tried before the wicked Nero.

It must not be overlooked here that Paul had earnestly besought his Roman brethren *"for the Lord Jesus Christ's sake,"* and *"for the love of the Spirit,"* to join him in *"striving together"* in their prayers for him, that he might be delivered from those who did not believe in Judaea, and that his efforts in behalf of the saints there might be well received, so that he might arrive at Rome with joy and be refreshed by their fellowship. As we know, none of these prayers were answered in the affirmative; clear evidence that the dispensation of the "whatsoever" prayer promises (Matt. 21:22) had passed away.[10] They were, however, replaced with something infinitely better (Rom. 8:26,28; Eph. 3:20,21). God worked everything out for Paul's good, so that he could write from his Roman prison: *"...the things which happened unto me have fallen out rather unto the furtherance of the gospel"* (Phil. 1:12), and it was from his bondage in Rome that God used him to write those epistles that take the believer to the very highest place of blessing, *"in heavenly places in Christ Jesus"* (Eph. 2:6).

How appropriate that the Apostle should close this section of his epistle with the benediction:

"Now the God of peace be with you all. Amen" (Ver. 33).

> God holds the key to all unknown,
>   And I am glad.
> If other hands should hold the key,
>   Or if He trusted it to me,
>   I might be sad.
>
> The very dimness of my sight,
>   Makes me secure,
> For groping in my misty way,
>   I feel His hand, I hear Him say,
>   My help is sure.
>
> —John Parker

---

10. For a comprehensive discussion on *Unanswered Prayer* see the author's booklet by that title.

Chapter XVI — Romans 16:1-27
THE THREE POSTSCRIPTS
AFFECTIONATE GREETINGS

"I commend unto you Phebe our sister, which is a servant of the church which is at Cenchrea:

"That ye receive her in the Lord, as becometh saints, and that ye assist her in whatsoever business she hath need of you: for she hath been a succorer of many, and of myself also.

"Greet Priscilla and Aquila, my helpers in Christ Jesus:

"Who have for my life laid down their own necks: unto whom not only I give thanks, but also all the churches of the Gentiles.

"Likewise greet the church that is in their house. Salute my well-beloved Epaenetus, who is the firstfruits of Achaia unto Christ.

"Greet Mary, who bestowed much labor on us.

"Salute Andronicus and Junia, my kinsmen, and my fellowprisoners, who are of note among the apostles, who also were in Christ before me.

"Greet Amplias, my beloved in the Lord.

"Salute Urbane, our helper in Christ, and Stachys my beloved.

"Salute Apelles, approved in Christ. Salute them which are of Aristobulus' household.

"Salute Herodion my kinsman. Greet them that be of the household of Narcissus, which are in the Lord.

"Salute Tryphena and Tryphosa, who labor in the Lord. Salute the beloved Persis, which labored much in the Lord.

"Salute Rufus, chosen in the Lord, and his mother and mine.

"Salute Asyncritus, Phlegon, Hermas, Patrobas, Hermes, and the brethren which are with them.

"Salute Philologus, and Julia, Nereus, and his sister, and Olympas, and all the saints which are with them."

—Rom. 16:1-15

The *Epistle to the Romans* contains no less than *three* postscripts! The body of the Epistle closes with the benediction of 15:33. Then in a postscript, the Apostle sends greetings to a long list of his fellow saints at Rome, closing with the benediction of 16:20. Then the *second* postscript, containing greetings from those *with him* at Corinth, and closing with the benediction of 16:24. And finally a *third* postscript, one of profound importance, and a benediction in itself, but closing with the benediction of 16:27.

It is amazing that though Paul had never yet been to Rome, he knew so many of the saints there personally. In his salutations he *names* 27 persons and refers to many others. At least 9 of those named, and one specifically designated, are women, and the first named is a woman.

While the Scriptures give the woman a very special place of honor, the claim that Christianity has "liberated" the woman from her place of subjection to the man is false. No Bible writer speaks so emphatically on this subject as does Paul, nor does any other explain in such depth the divine reasons for the man-woman and the husband-wife relationship. Yet here, in his closing greetings to the Roman saints, at least 9 women are mentioned *by name*, and evidently Paul was on good terms with them all. We believe this confirms what this writer has observed through many years of Christian service: that spiritual Christian women have no desire to wrest from the man his God-given authority—*and responsibility*. They want *him* to take the lead. This is a refreshing fact, surrounded as we are by the demands of many worldly women for "equal rights."

It appears that there were probably *three* local churches at Rome. Priscilla and Aquila had a church in their home (Vers. 3-5). The five brethren of Ver. 14 are mentioned in connection with *"the brethren which are with them."* And finally, in Ver. 15 the Apostle salutes another group of five, three men and two women, *"and all the saints that are with them."*

At least six of those named were Paul's own relatives (Vers. 7,11,21). It is possible that Rufus (Ver. 13) was the son of the Simon who carried our Lord's cross when He fell beneath it (Mark 15:21), but there is no proof of this.

Interestingly, the Apostle Peter is not mentioned—and could Paul possibly have failed to mention him if he had founded the church at Rome as some claim? Indeed, some of the Scriptures were written by John as late as, probably, 95 A.D., and none of these even mention Peter, much less his alleged presence at Rome. We do not mention these facts to belittle Peter in any way, but the fact that he is *not* thus mentioned presents another strong argument against the traditional claims of the Roman Catholic Church as to Rome and the papacy.

Phebe, as we have seen, was doubtless the bearer of the *Epistle to the Romans* (Vers. 1,2). She was evidently a businesswoman of some wealth from Cenchrea, the harbor of Corinth, and a deaconness [1] of the church there (Ver. 1). The Apostle exhorts the Roman Christians not only to *"receive"* her, but to *"assist her"* in whatever business she had there, since she had been a "succorer" [2] of many, including himself (Ver. 2).

It is natural that Priscilla and Aquila should appear next in the list of those to whom the Apostle sends greetings. What blessed memories must have crowded his mind as he mentioned their names! Since the time he had first gained employment with them at Corinth (Acts 18:1-3) they had been devoted to the message of grace and to Paul personally. They had even been used of God to lead the great and eloquent Apollos, a man already "mighty in the Scriptures," into an understanding of the higher truths which Paul had taught them (Acts 18:24-26). It was probably they who had hid Paul during the violent uproar at Ephesus (Acts 19:23,31; 20:1). Thus Paul, writing now to the Roman

---

1. The word "servant" (Ver. 1) is *diakonon* in the Greek. The local churches had deaconnesses as well as deacons to serve the assemblies in various ways: visiting the sick, helping those in need, caring for the church's physical properties, etc.

2. Lit., *protectress*, i.e., she had taken upon herself the responsibility of seeing to their physical and material welfare. Vine says of this word, *prostatis*, that "it is a word of dignity, evidently chosen [to indicate] the high esteem with which she was regarded."

believers, speaks of Priscilla and Aquila as those *"who have for my life laid down their own necks"* (Rom. 16:4); i.e., they had exposed themselves to the gravest personal danger to protect him; "unto whom," he says, *"not only I give thanks, but also all the churches of the Gentiles"* (Ver. 4), including those at Rome—for protecting the life of one so signally used of God for their salvation.

The Apostle does not fail to send greetings also to *"the church that is in their house"* (Ver. 5). These dear people had opened their home to assemblies of believers in Corinth (I Cor. 16:19), now at Rome (Rom. 16:5) and doubtless at Ephesus and elsewhere. What a ministry! How many local churches have begun with gatherings in homes! (Cf. Col. 4:15; Phile. 2).

How well also Paul would remember the first convert to Christ in Achaia (the province of Asia)! He calls him "my well-beloved Epaenetus" (Ver. 5), now residing at Rome.

To which *Mary* does Ver. 6 refer? We know not. All we know is that she "bestowed *much* labor" on Paul and his helpers. But it should touch our hearts that now, after more than 1900 years, Christian believers all over the world are still being reminded of her "much labor" bestowed on Paul for Christ's sake.

It is significant to find that Andronicus and Junia, two of Paul's relatives, were also his fellowprisoners. They too had suffered imprisonment for Christ's sake, though it is questionable whether or not they as yet fully understood the significance of Paul's apostleship and message. They were "in Christ" (he does not say "in the Body of Christ") before him, and evidently highly regarded by the Apostles at Jerusalem. We do not believe that Paul here refers to those whom some have called "the apostles of the Body," for any beside Paul would have been apostles only in a secondary sense.

Why does the Apostle have no complimentary word for Amplias and Stachys (Vers. 8,9)? Doubtless *they* could answer this question better than we. In any case, he mentions them most affectionately which, if they had failed him or had been unfaithful, must have greatly encouraged them. Urbane is at least called *"our helper in Christ,"* but even here there appears to be a note of restraint.

As to Apelles (Ver. 10), was there some shadow over his record that Paul should say that he was "approved in Christ"? As to those of Aristobulus' household, he would hardly be expected to know them all personally. He merely sends them his greeting.

In Ver. 11 the Apostle salutes Herodion, another relative, but evidently cannot say of *him* that he had suffered for Christ. Perhaps this is why he does not mention him along with the others, but waits until later on to mention him. It may be that the same is true of the household of Narcissus, who evidently attended the church services but cannot have done anything to gain the Apostle's special commendation.

At this point we should ask ourselves: Are we among those who attend our local churches, sing songs of praise, rejoice in the truths of the Word of God, but do precious little to *further* the cause of Christ? How would *we* have been mentioned in such a list as that of Romans 16?

Tryphena and Tryphosa are thought to be sisters laboring for the Lord at Rome, but special greetings are sent to "the beloved Persis [a woman] which labored much in the Lord" (Ver. 12). With the word "labored" in the past tense it appears that she evidently had a record of faithful service for the Lord. She was surely not particularly *Paul's* "beloved," but beloved by the church.

There is a tender and delicate touch to Ver. 13. Nothing is said about Rufus except that he was "chosen in the Lord," but Rufus' mother had been a mother to Paul as well, and he was grateful. If Rufus' father was indeed the Simon who carried our Lord's cross when He fell beneath it, he had a famous father too.

In Vers. 14,15 the Apostle sends greetings to two groups of five people each, who appear to have been closely associated with the two other local assemblies at Rome. These groups were perhaps organized or/and entertained by them.

THE HOLY KISS
AND DIVISIVE BRETHREN

"Salute one another with an holy kiss. The churches of Christ salute you.

"Now I beseech you, brethren, mark them which cause divisions and offenses contrary to the doctrine which ye have learned; and avoid them.

"For they that are such serve not our Lord Jesus Christ, but their own belly; and by good words and fair speeches deceive the hearts of the simple.

"For your obedience is come abroad unto all men. I am glad therefore on your behalf: but yet I would have you wise unto that which is good, and simple concerning evil.

"And the God of peace shall bruise Satan under your feet shortly. The grace of our Lord Jesus Christ be with you. Amen."

—Rom. 16:16-20

Before conveying the greetings of his co-workers at Corinth to the saints at Rome, the Apostle exhorts the Roman believers:

"Salute one another with an holy kiss" (Ver. 16).

There is a reason for this. Evidently some were already seeking to cause divisions among the believers at Rome, so that there were undercurrents of ill feeling among some of them.

Bible commentators have written at length on Rom. 16:16 and its kindred passages and, in general, have come to two basic conclusions:

1. Since greeting one another with a kiss was evidently a custom of that time and place—as it is in some lands today, e.g., in France, the passage does not bind us to greet each other precisely in this way. Its parallel in America today would doubtless be a hearty handshake.

2. In any case, the passage is written directly to the "brethren" and does *not* teach, or sanction, promiscuous kissing between men and women.

We believe, however, that in the light of the context this

passage teaches much more than technicalities about a mode of greeting.

Paul had sent his warm greetings to many among them; now he hoped they would feel as warmly toward each other. He had recalled many complimentary facts about those mentioned; now he hoped that they too would take each other's virtues into consideration and not become cool toward each other.

Has the reader ever attended a church where the atmosphere was cold and forbidding? No one said, "Good morning; I'm glad to see you," or gave you a friendly handshake? After the service they all filed out, barely speaking to each other or to you. Did you feel like ever again attending that church?

There was a danger of such a problem developing among the believers at Rome. Thus the Apostle says in effect: "greet one another *heartily*."

How this should speak to assemblies where true brotherly love has vanished! "Greet one another with a warm, hearty handshake," he would doubtless say to us today.

In many a church the members greet each other with a word, or a nod, but this alone can even *increase* the coldness of the atmosphere. As Jim enters the door he sees Joe, whom he cannot abide! "Morning Joe," he says, and Joe responds as coolly, as both go their ways, saying to themselves, *"That was a cold greeting!"*

It might have been quite different had Jim given Joe a warm word and a hearty handshake along with a "Good morning." Then Joe would doubtless have responded warmly and both would have felt better about each other.

This, in the light of the context, is what the Holy Spirit would teach us by the exhortation, *"Salute one another with an holy kiss"* (Ver. 16), i.e., Greet one another warmly and heartily. And he "tops" this by sending greetings from other Gentile churches who had said: "Be sure to greet the saints at Rome for us when you write to them."

Ver. 17 has good advice for dealing with divisive, or contentious brethren: *"Mark them"* and *"avoid them."*

The unity of the Body of Christ is a precious thing and we are to *"endeavor to keep*[3] *the unity of the Spirit in the bond of peace"* (Eph. 4:3). Thus the Apostle writes to the Corinthian believers:

> "Now I beseech you, brethren, by the name of our Lord Jesus Christ, that ye all speak the same thing, and that there be no divisions among you; but that ye be perfectly joined together in the same mind and in the same judgment" (I Cor. 1:10).

This is a high standard to maintain, but sincere believers should earnestly seek to quell dissension and division in the assembly over personal matters. Paul himself had battled hard *for the truth*, and when the Judaizers would have bound his Gentile converts with circumcision and the Law, he and Barnabas had had *"no small dissension and disputation with them"* (Acts 15:2), and Paul would have done the same at the time he wrote the Roman believers about those who would cause division among them. The context explains the difference. Paul, in Rom. 16, writes to the Roman believers about certain of their number whom he knew, expressing his love and esteem for them, and urging them all to show the same love toward each other. It is *in this context* that he advises them to "avoid" those who would cause division among them *"contrary to the doctrine which ye have learned,"* i.e., the doctrine of the one Body; the doctrine of the oneness of believers in Christ (12:5). Nor does he go on to say that differences as to doctrine matter little; he rather refers to the divisive persons as serving not the Lord, but "their own belly," i.e., they live only for their own gratification, and do not hesitate to "deceive the hearts of the simple" by "good words and fair speeches" (16:18). It is important, for the sake of the assembly and of the Body of Christ as a whole that such should be *noted* and *avoided*. A misguided "love" may tend to pamper such troublemakers, but true, Scriptural love for the saints and for the Lord will see the necessity of leaving such a man severely to himself. Indeed,

---

3. Gr., *terein*, to preserve, watch over.

the case here referred to is not unlike that concerning which Paul writes in II Thes. 3:14:

"And if any man obey not our word by this epistle, *note that man and have no company with him, that he may be ashamed.*"

Such discipline is necessary for the preservation of the work of God, which Satan would fain destroy.

In Ver. 19 the Apostle commends the Roman believers for their faithfulness to the truth, but he would have them *"wise unto that which is good, and simple concerning evil."* He would have them be objective in their attitude. Thus the encouraging word:

"And *the God of peace* shall bruise Satan under your feet shortly. The grace of our Lord Jesus Christ be with you. Amen" (Ver. 20).

He is not referring here to the coming of Christ for his saints. Rather he continues with the same subject. Note the phrase *"the God of peace."* Peace is what the divisive brother sought to destroy, but "the God of peace" would soon crush this work of Satan.

MORE GREETINGS!
—FROM THE CORINTHIAN SAINTS!

"Timotheus, my workfellow, and Lucius, and Jason, and Sosipater, my kinsmen, salute you.

"I Tertius, who wrote this epistle, salute you in the Lord.

"Gaius mine host, and of the whole church, saluteth you. Erastus the chamberlain of the city saluteth you, and Quartus a brother.

"The grace of our Lord Jesus Christ be with you all. Amen."

—Rom. 16:21-24

Now those *with Paul* say, "Don't forget to give them our greetings"! There is Timotheus, Paul's faithful "workfellow" ever since those early days when Timotheus had witnessed the cruel and unjust beating Paul received at the hands of the magistrates at Philippi, when they tore the clothes from his back, *"cast"* him into prison and had the jailor *"thrust"* him into a dungeon and fasten his feet in stocks (Acts 16:22-24).

Then there were three more of Paul's own kinsmen: Lucius, Jason, and Sosipater (Ver. 21). It is remarkable that so many of his own relatives had come to know Christ!

And here his secretary, Tertius, slips in his own greeting! Evidently Paul often dictated his letters to others[4] but signed them himself (II Thes. 2:2; 3:17).

Finally, Paul sends greetings from Gaius, his generous host and that of so many other fellow-saints, and from Erastus, the city treasurer. Also from "Quartus, a brother"! They evidently did not know him, but *he* wanted to greet them! Such is the love that should prevail between the members of the One Body. Just think! All these believers greeting each other across the miles as members of the only *true* Church, the Body of Christ! And it is with the prayer: *"The grace of our Lord Jesus Christ be with you all"* that he closes his second postscript.

THE FINAL POSTSCRIPT

And now we come to the third and final postscript to the *Epistle to the Romans*. What will it contain? What is the most important thing he can say in closing? With what benediction can he leave them? The answer has brought blessing to untold thousands of sincere believers.

"Now to Him that is of power to stablish you according to my gospel, and the preaching of Jesus Christ, according to the revelation of the mystery, which was kept secret since the world began.

"But now is made manifest, and by the Scriptures of the prophets, according to the commandment of the everlasting God, made known to all nations for the obedience of faith:

"To God, only wise, be glory through Jesus Christ forever. Amen."

—Rom. 16:25-27

Postscripts are proverbially important. A postscript does not necessarily indicate that some matter of questionable importance has been overlooked and is now added as an afterthought. On the contrary, this writer frequently uses

---

4. Perhaps due to an eye affliction (See Gal. 4:15; 6:11; *"with what large letters...with mine own hand"*).

postscripts to call special and final attention to matters of pressing importance.

We believe that this was the case with Paul's final postscript to the Romans epistle. Certainly this postscript is of profound significance, for it concerns that which establishes believers in the faith, and which God has *"made known to all nations for the obedience of faith"* (Ver. 26).

But what is it that God uses above all to establish His people in the faith, and has made known to all nations for the obedience of faith?

Some say *the whole Bible*. They hold that according to the above passage believers are established by:

1. That message which Paul calls "my gospel," i.e., "the preaching of the cross" and "the gospel of the grace of God" (Ver. 25).

2. *"and* the preaching of Jesus Christ according to the revelation of the mystery" (Ver. 25).

3. *"and*...the Scriptures of the prophets" (Ver. 26).

Agreeing, of course, that *"all Scripture is given by inspiration of God, and is profitable,"* we believe, however, that a closer examination of Paul's final postscript to this epistle will reveal that the Apostle did not have the whole Bible in mind here, but rather *that particular body of truth revealed to and through him.*

THE DISTINCTIVENESS OF PAUL'S MESSAGE

In the first place Paul's gospel and the mystery which he proclaimed, together with the writings of the prophets, do *not* make up the complete Word of God. What about the Pentateuch, the historical books of the Old Testament, the four "gospels," the epistles of James, Peter, John and Jude, the book of Revelation and those epistles which he himself had not yet written, are not these also "profitable" according to II Tim. 3:16?

Second, "the preaching of Jesus Christ according to the revelation of the mystery" *was* Paul's gospel—*"the gospel of the grace of God."* This could hardly be stated more plainly than it is in Eph. 3:1-3:

> "For this cause I Paul, the prisoner of Jesus Christ for you Gentiles,
>
> "If ye have heard of THE DISPENSATION OF THE GRACE OF GOD, WHICH IS GIVEN ME TO YOU-WARD;
>
> "HOW THAT BY REVELATION HE MADE KNOWN UNTO ME THE MYSTERY."

The dispensation of God's grace committed to Paul, then, *was* the mystery.

Third, "the Scriptures of the [Old Testament] prophets" are *not* now to be "made known to all nations for the obedience of faith."

Fourth, the word *and* (Gr., *kai*) in the New Testament Scriptures, by no means always indicates mere addition. Often it is used by way of emphasis, explanation, or elaboration. Sometimes this word is rendered *"even"* in our *Authorized Version*. Thus the phrase *"the preaching of Jesus Christ according to the revelation of the mystery"* is an *elaboration* of the term *"my gospel."*

Fifth, the word rendered "prophets," in Ver. 26, is actually an adjective, not a noun,[5] so that the phrase actually reads *"prophetic* Scriptures," and since Paul himself was a prophet, or spokesman for God, it evidently refers to his own writings, by which his message was "made known to all nations for the obedience of faith" (Ver. 26).

Thus, in his final postscript to the Romans the Apostle declares that "his gospel" and "the preaching of Jesus Christ according to the revelation of the mystery" had been "kept secret since the world began," but was "now made manifest and by prophetic Scriptures [his own]...made known to all nations for the obedience of faith."

That this "mystery," revealed to and through Paul, is the particular revelation which establishes God's people and illuminates the whole Bible for them, must be clear to those who even begin to study his epistles with an open mind.

---

5. The KJV translators departed from the *Received Text* here.

How many sincere believers there are who still fail to recognize the distinctive character of Paul's apostleship and message! Result: the Church has been gripped by the most appalling confusion. They have erroneously concluded that "the gospel" is one and the same, no matter where we find the term. Misreading Gal. 1:8,9 they say: "The gospel is the gospel. There is only one gospel, not two." They suppose that "the gospel" which the twelve were sent to proclaim in Luke 9:1-6 must have been the same gospel as that which Paul later proclaimed.

But how can this be? After having preached their "gospel"[6] (or good news) for some two years the twelve did not even know that Christ would die and rise again (Luke 18:31-34). Moreover, "the gospel" which the twelve were sent to proclaim under their "great commission," required water baptism *"for the remission of sins"* (Acts 2:38; cf., Mark 16:16). Sadly, many Christian leaders simply alter Mark 16:16 and Acts 2:38 to fit their theological systems, and when we point out that Gal. 2:2-9 explicitly deals with *two* different gospels, the one proclaimed by the Circumcision apostles to the Circumcision, and the other proclaimed by Paul to the Gentiles, they generally alter that too, making the terms *"gospel of the uncircumcision"* and *"gospel of the circumcision"* refer to *one* gospel, to be sent to both Gentiles and Jews, only by two different instruments. But IF this were possible—and it is not—would this passage not still teach a dispensational change since the giving of the "great commission"? For in Galatians 2:1-9 one fact is made crystal clear: Whereas the twelve had at first been sent to *"all nations," "all the world,"* and *"every creature,"* Paul was now recognized as God's apostle to the nations while they, the twelve, agreed to confine their ministry to Israel.

If the various gospels in the New Testament are all the same, why does God label them differently: *"The gospel of the kingdom," "the gospel of the circumcision," "the gospel of the uncircumcision," "the gospel of the grace of God,"* etc.? Clearly He has done this to *distinguish* between them.

---

6. I.e., "the gospel of the kingdom."

Women do not label their jars of preserves differently because they all contain the same thing! Nor would it be very palatable to partake of peaches, pickles, strawberries, tomatoes and corn, all mixed together! Yet this is exactly what most Fundamentalist believers—and their leaders—have done with the various gospels referred to in Scripture.

The word "gospel," of course, simply means *good news*. Thus we must always determine *what* good news is referred to, either by noting how it is designated or by considering the context.

If "the gospel," wherever we find the term, is the same, why should Paul write, by divine inspiration, about:

"my gospel"—three times.

"our gospel"—three times.

"that gospel which I preached unto you" (I Cor. 15:1).

"the gospel which was preached of me" (Gal. 1:11).

"that gospel which I preach among the Gentiles" (Gal. 2:2).

"that [gospel] which we have preached unto you" (Gal. 1:8).

Surely such phraseology *distinguishes* the "gospel" which he and his associates proclaimed from that which others had previously proclaimed.

If we do not distinguish Paul's good news about the cross and his preaching of Jesus Christ according to the revelation of the mystery from the the good news which the twelve had proclaimed, we will most assuredly *never* be established in *the faith*. Paul's inspired postscript to the *Epistle to the Romans* makes this abundantly clear, and many pastors and Bible teachers and their followers are proving it every day. Too preoccupied with their own affairs to take another look at the divine Road Map, they continue down the wrong theological road, with its labyrinth of dead end streets. May God convict these brethren of this sin and bring them still into the knowledge and joy of *"the preaching of Jesus Christ according to the revelation of the mystery."*

THE UNITY OF PAUL'S MESSAGE

One more word should be said about the *unity* of Paul's message, for some have gone to the other extreme, recognizing the distinctive character of his ministry, but failing to observe its *unity*. Result: confusion fully as great as that among Fundamentalists in general.

These people, many of them sincerely in earnest, argue that Paul had *two* messages and ministries, that at first, before Acts 28:28, he had a kingdom ministry like the twelve, practically working under their commission and offering the kingdom to Israel. These hold that "the mystery" was not revealed to Paul or proclaimed by him until at or after Acts 28.

Noting the Apostle's references to the Body of Christ in the epistles he wrote *before* Acts 28, however, these brethren have concluded that there must be *two* "Bodies" in Paul's epistles. They have further concluded that what Paul wrote about the Lord's supper, the Rapture, our Lord's High Priestly work etc., does not apply directly to us since all this is found in his early epistles when he still had "a kingdom ministry."

But Paul himself never says he had *two* messages or ministries. On his last journey to Jerusalem, he expresses his desire:

"That I might FINISH MY COURSE with joy, and THE MINISTRY [singular] which I have received of the Lord Jesus, to testify THE GOSPEL [singular] of the grace of God" (Acts 20:24).

And in Eph. 3:1-3 he clearly associates this *"dispensation of the grace of God"* with the *"mystery"* which was *"made known"* to him *"by revelation."*

But did he ever proclaim the mystery before Acts 28? He most certainly did. Besides several instances where he discusses these truths using the very word "mystery," he deals with many of the component parts of the mystery in *all* of his earlier epistles. Take the Romans epistle alone as an example: There he deals with his unique apostleship to the

Gentiles (11:13), his unique message, "my gospel" (2:16; 16:25), our baptism into Christ (6:3), the blessing of the Gentiles through the *fall* of Israel (11:11), "no difference" between Jew and Gentile as far as grace is concerned (10:12), the "one body" (12:5), the temporary and parenthetical character of this present Gentile dispensation (11:25,26), etc. All of these truths were *in fact* kept secret until revealed to and through Paul, and all are directly associated with, or identical to, the great truths of his prison epistles.

As to Paul's alleged offers of the kingdom to Israel, there is not a single instance of such an offer either in the Acts record or in his epistles. Indeed, how could he have offered the kingdom *to Israel* (the nation) as the twelve did? To do this he would at least have had to *begin* at Jerusalem, but he was summarily commanded to *leave* Jerusalem *with haste* before he even had an opportunity to begin a ministry there (Acts 22:18,21).

But did he not, in his early ministry, go always to the Jew first? Yes, to present *Christ* to them, so that the nation, all the way out to Rome, might be without excuse as God began dealing with the Gentiles apart from their instrumentality.

But did he not consistently prove to the Jews that "Jesus is the *Christ*," the *Messiah*? To be sure, and wouldn't any Christian believer do the same today in dealing with a Jew? If a Jew, even today, refused to believe that the crucified Jesus was the Christ, how could he trust Him as his Savior?

But didn't Paul consistently confirm Peter's kingdom message during his early ministry? Of course, and so do we today.

But to say that all this was part of a separate early message and ministry, committed to Paul before he received the revelation of the mystery, is a grave mistake. He confirmed Peter's message and proved that Jesus was the Christ, just as we do this, to lead his hearers up to that which he was specially sent to proclaim: "the gospel of the grace of God" and all the rich blessings that go with it.

We have a good example of this as early as Acts 13 where

we have his *first recorded address* delivered in a *Jewish synagogue* some twenty years before his imprisonment at Rome. After the reading of the law and the prophets the ruler of the synagogue asked Paul and Barnabas whether they might have some "word of exhortation" for the people. Paul then responded by speaking about Israel's history, about John the Baptist and the Christ whom Israel's rulers had rejected, but whom God had raised from the dead. But was this the *theme* of his message? No, it was only the point of contact, the natural approach—the same approach we might use today were we to address a company of Jews in a synagogue. The *theme* of his message, that which he especially wished to press home upon their hearts, is found in Verses 38,39:

"BE IT KNOWN UNTO YOU THEREFORE, MEN AND BRETHREN, THAT THROUGH THIS MAN IS PREACHED UNTO YOU THE FORGIVENESS OF SINS:

"AND BY HIM ALL THAT BELIEVE ARE JUSTIFIED FROM ALL THINGS, FROM WHICH YE COULD NOT BE JUSTIFIED BY THE LAW OF MOSES."

This is certainly *not* the gospel of the kingdom. It is the gospel of the grace of God which no one before Paul had preached or could have preached: the good news of salvation by grace, through faith, *without the law*.

But do we not find higher, more blessed truths in Paul's prison epistles than we find in his earlier writings? Yes, this is true, but it is not due to a *change* in his message, but rather to *a fuller development* of it as he received revelation after revelation.

Let us not forget that when our Lord first appeared to Paul He sent him forth to be *"a witness both of these things which thou hast seen, and of those things in the which I will appear unto thee"* (Acts 26:16).

We can trace from the record many of these revelations in which the Lord appeared to him, from the first day, when the stricken Saul saw Him as the glorified Lord, far above all (as the twelve never had seen Him) to the closing revelations in prison at Rome. Gradually we see the glorious message unfolded as the old dispensation passes completely away. Those who do not see *the progress, the sweep, the development* in the unfolding of this great "mystery" miss a great deal of enjoyment as well as a great deal of light in their study of the Scriptures.

One more comment about extreme dispensationalism. Some of those who hold that Paul had two ministries have been driven to the odd conclusion that the final postscript to the Roman Epistle must have been added by Paul after his imprisonment in Rome, where he is alleged to have received the revelation of the mystery. But why add it then? He himself was *among* them. Also, why add to a letter which (extremists allege) does not contain the mystery, a declaration that it is through the mystery that men are established? Some, seeing this inconsistency, have concluded that some *other* person added the postscript at a later date. To all this we reply: if another added this postscript to Paul's letter he was a forger; if Paul wrote it he surely added it to the wrong epistle—*if* Romans does not contain the truth of the mystery.

FINIS

As we view the sublime harmony of God's Word and wonder at His grace in dealing with sinful men who will receive that grace, we bring this book to a close as the Apostle did his:

"To God, only wise, be glory through Jesus Christ forever. Amen."

> Great God, my eyes with pleasure look
>   On the dear volume of Thy Book.
> There my Redeemer's face I see,
>   And read His name who died for me.
>
> Let the false raptures of the mind
>   Be lost and vanish in the wind;
> Here I can fix my hopes secure;
>   This is *Thy Word* and *must* endure.
>
> —Isaac Watts

Appendix No. 1

A CONSIDERATION OF ROMANS 8:1b
AS FOUND IN THE AUTHORIZED VERSION

We believe that the English *Authorized*, or *King James Version* of the Bible stands head and shoulders above the *Revised Version* and all the modern translations that have followed in RV's train.

We do not, however, subscribe to the merely philosophical argument that "surely God would have" preserved His revelation *word-for-word* for all the generations that followed the disappearance of the original writings, and that today this "perfectly preserved" Bible *is* the English *Authorized Version*. We believe this argument virtually answers itself, for:

(1) To *preserve* the Scriptures word-for-word, *the original documents* would have had to be kept safe *for us* intact up to the present time, and it is evident that God has *not* seen fit to do this. Actually God *has* preserved the Scriptures intact, but not in one translation into one language (Psa. 119:89). (2) It is *impossible* to translate any extended passage from one language into another word-for-word, for the simple reason that each language contains words and expressions which others do not. (3) Probably no extensive copies of any early manuscript, text or translation of the Bible have ever been *perfectly identical*.

We believe that God in His wisdom has been pleased to withhold the original manuscripts from the succeeding generations, perhaps because man is so prone to idolatry (consider the brazen serpent and Elijah's altar, both of which were destroyed).

We believe, however, that God has graciously overruled human infirmity and sin so that we have in our hands, in the *Authorized Version*, a Bible so remarkably free from error that we can say of even this *translation*, "This is the Bible," with *greater* confidence than we could say of an English translation of, say, *Luther's Galatians*, "This is Luther's Galatians."

We believe that theological integrity as well as linguistic ability has ever been important in the translation of the Bible from the original tongues (I Cor. 2:11,14).

While *Textus Receptus* (the Received Text of the Reformation, mainly followed by AV) is aptly called the *majority text*, it does not follow from this that *every single* rendering in AV is *necessarily* correct or best. The translators of AV, though great and godly men, *were not inspired by the Holy Spirit*, as were the original writers (though they were signally *aided* by the Holy Spirit in their work), and must often have had to weigh the validity of one set of evidence against another. All this bears witness that the Bible is more than paper and ink; it is the *living* Word of God.

Textual evidence as to which MSS, etc., include the latter part of Rom. 8:1 and which omit it, can hardly be *wholly conclusive*, for if indeed this clause is a gloss added by some copyist, this was probably done to an earlier MS than any we possess.

Let us turn, then, to some of the theological considerations involved.

1. Rom. 8:1b can hardly be *a statement of fact*, for many, indeed most believers do *not* consistently walk "after the Spirit" but rather walk all too consistently "after the flesh." Even Paul, in Rom. 7, acknowledges this problem with respect to himself, though *he* walked "after the Spirit" to a remarkable degree. Also, if 8:1b is a statement of fact, i.e., that all those "in Christ Jesus" *do* "walk after the Spirit" and not "after the flesh," then why all of Paul's *exhortations* to believers to walk after the Spirit rather than after the flesh? This is not to deny, of course, that *in exercising faith in Christ* in the first place, one does in fact follow the dictates of the Spirit rather than those of the flesh.

2. If, on the other hand, 8:1b is *a qualifying clause*, our security in Christ is made to depend upon our walk. This clause is also found in Ver. 4, where it fits in naturally with the context, but the moral state of those not condemned does *not* fit in with the truth of 8:1a. Furthermore, 8:1a *does* fit in perfectly with 8:2,3, which follow immediately if 8:1b is omitted.

3. Considering the fact that the exact same phrase is found in Rom. 8:4 (within a *different* context, where it fits perfectly), would it be strange if a copyist added these words to 8:1a, fearing that this unqualified declaration might produce harmful effects? Many in our day fear that the proclamation of pure grace might produce lax conduct among believers, and this has been a common problem through the centuries. Indeed, it was a problem even in Paul's day, as is evident from the fact that he deals with it so fully in Rom. 6 and 7.

4. The bold declaration of 8:1a, following immediately after the climactic cry, *"Who shall deliver me"!* of 7:24,25, does not appear to justify the addition of the clause "who walk not," etc., after 8:1a, for the believer is set free from condemnation *simply because he is "in Christ Jesus,"* not because he succeeds in walking after the Spirit (See Rom. 6 and 7).

5. It has been suggested that self-condemnation is in view here as

in Rom. 14:22,23, but this is not consistent with the words of 8:1*a*, for there *is self*-condemnation to "them that are in Christ Jesus" (See 7:15-25). Furthermore this would militate against the whole sweep of this part of Romans and most especially against the immediate context of 7:24,25 and 8:2-4.

If Rom. 8:1*b* is to be considered *in any sense* a statement of fact, as in the last sentence of No. 1 above, then surely it belongs in parentheses so that the force of Rom. 8:1*a* with 8:2,3 is not destroyed and may rather be fully appreciated. Read Rom. 8:1-4 without the latter part of Ver. 1, and rejoice in the power of the Apostle's declaration.

APPENDIX NO. II

A BRIEF CONSIDERATION OF DIVINE ELECTION AND HUMAN RESPONSIBILITY

It is an interesting fact that the three great points of contact between God and man are shrouded in mystery. We refer to *the Lord Jesus Christ, the Bible and Redemption*, in each of which God and man, the Infinite and the finite, come together as one.

In the teachings of the Word of God as to all three of these subjects declarations are made which are *antinomous*, or at least *paradoxical*. They seem to be contradictory, yet each is in fact—sometimes very obviously—true. Thus it is our purpose in this Appendix to induce the reader to simply *believe what God has said*, even when He makes two statements that *seem* logically to contradict each other, remembering that while our poor intellects cannot yet reconcile such statements, it does not follow from this that they are indeed irreconcilable.

Let us then consider the above subjects in order.

THE LORD JESUS CHRIST

Some suppose that Christ was *only* a *man*, but *they are wrong*.

The whole "Gospel According to John" was written to prove that our Lord was—and is—*God*, and His deity is insisted upon in many individual passages of Scripture (Matt. 1:23; John 1:1-5; 8:58; 20:28; Tit. 2:13; Heb. 1:8,10; *et al*).

Others suppose that Christ was *only God*, but *they too are wrong*.

The "Gospel According to Luke" was written to prove that He was —and is—*true Man*, and His humanity is likewise insisted upon in many individual passages of Scripture (Matt. 20:28; Luke 2:11; John 1:14; Gal. 4:4; I Tim. 2:5; I John 4:2,3; II John 7; *et al*).

Still others hold that our Lord was *partly* God and *partly* man, but *they too are wrong*.

For one thing, if He were but *partly* God He would not be *God* at all, for in the nature of the case there cannot be a non-infinite God!

The Bible teaches that our Lord is *wholly God*, and at the same time *wholly Man* (though without sin). We are doubtless unable to comprehend this at present, but these are Scriptural facts, and to hold any of the other three positions one must ignore plain passages of Scripture, or distort them to make them conform to his own doctrinal views.

Do we thus place God and man on the same level? In no wise, for our Lord's humanity was always subordinate to His deity, even though He was equally God and Man.

THE BIBLE

As with Christ, the living Word, so with the Bible, the written Word:

Some hold that it was written *only* by *man*, but *they are wrong*. Everywhere this Book abounds with evidence that *God* is its divine Author. Its fulfilled prophecies, its sublime harmony, its power to regenerate and transform lives, the authority with which it speaks, never deigning to defend its divine authorship, but rather *assuming* it—all this stamps it as *the Book of God*. In addition its divine authorship is declared in many individual passages (Rom. 3:1,2; Eph. 6:17; II Tim. 3:16; Heb. 4:12; 5:12; II Pet. 1:21 *et al*).

Others hold that the Bible is *only* the Word of *God*, but *these too are wrong*.

It is significant that God chose *Matthew*, the publican, to portray Christ as *King*; *Luke*, the physician, to portray Him as *Man*; *Mark*, Paul's attendant, to portray Him as *Servant*; and *John*, the disciple who was closest to Him, to present Him as *God*. These men, individually, were the very ones to present Him as they did.

Often this human authorship is shown to be important. Our Lord frequently reminded His hearers of what *Moses* had said to them in the Scriptures, knowing their great respect for Moses (Matt. 19:8; *et al*). Luke says, "I had a complete understanding of these things from the beginning" (Luke 1:3), implying that he was *qualified* to write about our Lord's earthly ministry. Paul says: "Behold, *I Paul* say unto you..." (Gal. 5:2), implying that *his* saying it should bear weight with his readers. The freedom with which these men wrote is manifest on every hand, as for example, in the closing paragraphs of Paul's last epistle, where he sends greetings to individuals, includes small news items, asks for the cloak he had left at Troas, etc. Surely he had no idea at the time that he was writing *the Word of God*. He wrote as one human being to another.

To solve this problem still others have concluded that the Bible is *partly* the Word of God and *partly* the word of man, but *these too are wrong*. If they were right we would still be without an authoritative revelation from God, for none of us could ascertain what was written by man and what by God.

The truth is that the Bible is *wholly* the Word of God, yet at the same time, *wholly* the word of man, and to hold any of the other three positions one must ignore plain passages of Scripture, or distort them to make them conform to his own doctrinal views. It is the miracle of divine inspiration that a man could sit down and write, in one mood or another, with complete freedom to express himself and lo, what he writes is also, every word, the Word of God! We cannot comprehend this—*yet!*—but the regenerate heart bows in faith to the Book and says, *"I believe."*

Do we then place God and man on the same level? By no means, for the human writers in every case were subordinate to the divine Author, even though this Book was written *wholly* by man and at the same time *wholly* by God.

PERSONAL SALVATION

Now let us consider the subject of personal salvation in this light. Generalizing for a moment, we may correctly state:

Some hold that salvation is dependent *only* on the will of man, the offer having been made to all alike. *They are wrong*, for the Scriptures indicate all too clearly that believers are *"God's elect."*

Others hold that salvation is dependent *only* on the will of God. *These too are wrong*, for the Scriptures also teach that men who do not themselves *will* to be saved *are not* saved and *cannot* justly be saved.

Still others seek to solve the problem by rationalizing that salvation is *partly* dependent upon God's will and *partly* on man's; that God has an overall plan, as it were, but that man decides on the details. *These too are wrong*, as we shall see.

Now to particularize:

THE DOCTRINE OF ELECTION

The Arminian view of election is not election at all. According to this school of thought election is made to be dependent upon *foreseen human faith*, and is merely the consequent recognition of that faith. Consistently Arminians teach that man must continue in faith (and its fruits) to remain saved.

This doctrine does violence to a whole volume of important passages of Scripture, some of which follow:

"There is *none that seeketh* after God" (Rom. 3:11).

"No man can come to me, *except the Father which hath sent Me draw him*" (John 6:44).

"...God hath from the beginning *chosen you to salvation* through sanctification of the Spirit and belief of the truth" (II Thes. 2:13).

"According as He hath chosen us in Him *before the foundation of the world*, that we should be holy and without blame before Him, in love,

"Having predestinated us unto the adoption of children [sons] . . .

"To the praise of the glory of His grace, wherein HE hath made us accepted in the Beloved . . . .

"In whom also we have obtained an inheritance, *being predestinated according to the purpose of Him who worketh all things after the counsel of His own will*:

"That we should be to the praise of His glory, who first trusted in Christ" (Eph. 1:4-6,11,12).[1]

Thus believers are said to be *"God's elect"* (Rom. 8:33), *"chosen in the Lord"* (Rom. 16:13), etc.

The doctrine of election, rightly taught, should not discourage the fearful sinner. II Thes. 2:13 and other passages link election inseparably with *faith*. Thus the anxious sinner may be assured that since *some* are saved, and salvation is received by faith, *he* will be saved if he believes.

Or, to put it in another way: Is a sinner anxious that he may not be included among the elect? Then let him call upon God to save him through Christ and see if he is rejected! Rom. 10:13 and many other passages assure him that he will be gladly received and gloriously saved.

ELECTION AND FOREKNOWLEDGE

I Pet. 1:2 states that believers are "elect *according to the foreknowledge of God."*

We have already dealt with the Arminian view of the foreknowledge of God, which represents it as merely knowing beforehand who will believe and be saved. This view is completely unacceptable since the saved are said to have been *"chosen"* in Christ *"before the foundation of the world"* (Eph. 1:4).

But neither can we accept the view which makes God's foreknowledge "that which He Himself purposes to bring to pass" (Dr. Lewis Sperry Chafer in *Systematic Theology*, Vol. VII, P. 158, Dallas Seminary Press). If God's foreknowledge *is* His eternal purpose, then words have no meaning.

If I Pet. 1:2 means anything, it means that election is *based upon* the foreknowledge of God. Therefore we believe that this passage refers to God's foreknowledge of *all things*—of all that is involved in the salvation of any sinner. Why limit the foreknowledge of *God* to His merely knowing beforehand who would be saved, on the one hand, or to His purpose to save, on the other?

---

1. We realize that predestination has special reference to that *to which* the elect have been predestinated, but this automatically *involves* election itself.

Salvation is the result of God's *love* for sinners. Therefore the Scriptures would teach us that He did not *arbitrarily* elect some and pass others by, without regard to moral principles and only on the ground of volition or caprice. Rather, knowing all things (as no judge on earth ever can) He could and did elect justly. We may not *now* understand why He elected some and passed others by, and we know assuredly that *none* of us deserved to be elected, but one day we shall witness the truth of the Scripture: *"Shall not the Judge of all the earth do right?"*

THE QUESTION OF LIMITED REDEMPTION

Some have concluded from what the Bible says about election that God loves *only* the elect and that Christ died for *only* the elect. Such, however, have adopted this view as a "logical" conclusion drawn from their own set of Scripture passages, apparently ignoring all that the Scriptures say to the contrary. Certainly there is no Scripture which *says* that Christ died for *the elect only*.

One commentator has written: "*Paul* never writes that God loved the world." But what does this prove? *Our Lord did say* that God loved the world and in this matter dispensationalism is no factor. Paul *does* declare again and again that God loved, and that Christ died for "all men," "every man," etc. The following are some passages that teach unequivocally that God does love, and that Christ did die for, all men:

John 3:16: "For God so LOVED THE WORLD, that He gave His only begotten Son, that whosoever believeth in Him should not perish but have everlasting life."

Some have interpreted the word "world" here to refer to "the world of the elect," but how can this be so when the very next verse shows that the reference is to *the world into which Christ came*, the world of men, the world of sinners, whom He did not wish to condemn? In any case *"world"* would be a strange word to use to refer to *the elect*, would it not?

II Cor. 5:14,15: "For the love of Christ constraineth us, because we thus judge: that if ONE DIED FOR ALL, then were all dead,

"And that HE DIED FOR ALL, that they which live should not henceforth live unto themselves, but unto Him which died for them and rose again."

If the "all" here refers only to the elect, as some teach, should not the passage rather read that Christ "died for all, that ALL might live unto Him," instead of distinguishing *those who live* as being part of the "all" for whom Christ died? Further, in Ver. 14 the Apostle declares that *"the love of Christ"* constrained him to preach this gospel. Did Paul then proclaim this love, or this gospel, only to the elect?

I Tim. 2:4-6: "Who will have ALL MEN to be saved and to come unto the knowledge of the truth.

"For there is one God and one Mediator between God and MEN, the Man Christ Jesus:

"Who gave Himself A RANSOM FOR ALL, to be testified in due time."

If the "all men" of Ver. 4 refers only to the elect, why does Ver. 5 add that Christ is the "Mediator between God *and men*," rather than "certain men" or "the elect"?

I Tim. 4:10: *"...we trust in the living God, who is THE SAVIOR OF ALL MEN, SPECIALLY OF THOSE THAT BELIEVE."*

Here is a *qualified* statement against the background of an *unqualified* one (as in Rom. 3:22). If, as some teach, the "all men" are the elect, who are "those that believe"?

Heb. 2:9: *"...that He by the grace of God should TASTE DEATH FOR EVERY MAN."*

How could "*every* man" here possibly refer only to the elect? The argument that the word "man" does not appear in the Greek is a subterfuge, for obviously the Greek uses the word "every" here as it does the word "all" in II Cor. 5:14,15, meaning "all men." Surely the Apostle could not have meant to refer to every *angel* or every *thing* in this passage, as the rest of Hebrews 2 clearly shows.

II Pet. 2:1: *"...false prophets...false teachers...who privily shall bring in damnable heresies, even denying THE LORD THAT BOUGHT THEM."*

Could the Holy Spirit have stated more clearly that our Lord "bought" even false teachers, who *denied Him*?

II Pet. 3:9: *"The Lord...is longsuffering to us-ward, NOT WILLING THAT ANY SHOULD PERISH, BUT THAT ALL SHOULD COME TO REPENTANCE."*

Here we have a negative testimony to the effect that it is *not* God's will that *any* should perish, and a positive one to the effect that He would have *all* come to repentance. What could be clearer?

I John 2:2: *"And He is the propitiation [satisfaction] for our sins, and not for ours only, but ALSO FOR THE SINS OF THE WHOLE WORLD."*

Clearly the word "our" here refers to the elect: "He is the satisfaction for *our* sins." Then how can it be argued that the words "*also* for the sins of *the whole world*" likewise refer to the elect, or to "*all* the elect"? Obviously the passage means *just what it says*.

More such passages could be cited, but this is not a volume on Election!

HUMAN RESPONSIBILITY

Extreme Calvinists appear to have overlooked the fact that originally God created man not as a machine which He might manipulate, but a rational being, made in His own image and after His likeness, with a mind and a will with which to contemplate and choose and plan. This image was *de*faced by the fall, but not *e*ffaced, for Paul declares in I Cor. 11:7 that man is still *"the image and glory of God."* Certainly there is a vast gulf between man and the highest creature of the animal kingdom, a greater gulf than that which exists between man and the angels. Any man trusting Christ as his Savior does so voluntarily, never conscious of being forced or made to do so. Thus man is a responsible moral agent and God holds him accountable for what he does—especially for what he does with the gospel and with Christ, His beloved Son.

John 3:36 declares that God's "wrath" abides upon those who reject Christ, and Rom. 1:18 states that His "wrath" is revealed against those who suppress the truth in unrighteousness. How could a just, not to say a gracious God, be *angry* with men for rejecting what was not provided for them in the first place, or for suppressing the truth when they were given over to the lie to begin with?

Rom. 1:24-28 clearly states that God "gave up" the Gentiles because *they* gave *Him* up. Likewise we learn from II Thes. 2:8-12 that God will give the world up to Antichrist "BECAUSE THEY RECEIVED NOT THE LOVE OF THE TRUTH, THAT THEY MIGHT BE SAVED. And FOR THIS CAUSE God shall send them strong delusion . . . ."

CONCLUSION

From all this it is clear that God's Word teaches both His own complete sovereignty in election *and* man's responsibility to accept or reject His provision for salvation. Let us bow our hearts in faith and believe *both* these doctrines, though our poor intellects cannot yet reconcile them.

Indeed, strangely, we *do* believe them both in spite of ourselves. All believers acknowledge that no man in heaven will ever be able to boast. Each one will freely acknowledge: "It was all of God." Yet, at the same time, no man in hell will be able to complain. Each one will have to acknowledge: "It was my own fault."

Years ago the Reformed Church won an argument over the Methodists. They proved that God was sovereign in election. But in doing so they sought to *disprove* the Methodists' beliefs as to man's free and responsible moral agency. The Methodists too won a victory by proving from Scripture that man *is* a free and responsible moral agent, but in doing so *they* practically denied the Scriptural doctrine of election. *Both* erred in trying to *disprove* Scriptural doctrines which they had "logically" concluded to be inconsistent with the views they championed. The result is that both denominations lost out spiritually.

In these matters the true preacher is *both* Reformed and Methodist! Before the service he prays: "Lord, work in their hearts. If Thou dost not work, nothing will be accomplished." Yet to his congregation he says: "*You* are responsible. It's up to *you*. Believe and you will be saved; reject and the wrath of God will abide upon you." Not only is such a preacher Scriptural in both these attitudes, but *it is only in this way that he can experience the power of the Holy Spirit in his ministry*. If, indeed, we rationalize the one or the other of these doctrines away, we dishonor God and rob ourselves of the power of the Spirit.

A homely illustration may prove helpful here. Consider a young lad who knows virtually nothing about electricity, beginning his first day's work at a machine shop. "Take this wire," says his employer, "attach it to that motor and plug it in so that we can get the motor running."

Upon inspection the lad notices that the wire is really *two* wires, one white and the other black. Asking his employer about this he is told that the white is *positive*, the black *negative*.

Since he has been told to get the motor *running*, he attaches the *positive* wire, first to one terminal, then to the other, but nothing happens. Assuming that he has attached the wrong one, he now attaches the other—but still to no effect.

Going again to his employer about this he is told to attach them *both*. "But how can the motor run, then?" asks the lad. "One wire is positive and the other negative." "Nevertheless attach them *both*," replies the employer. So the lad attaches them both and, lo, the motor runs!

Sir Robert Anderson wrote with regard to the doctrines of election and free moral agency: "Doubtless they may appear to be incompatible, but to maintain that therefore they are so in fact, is to put reason above revelation, or in other words to place man above God" (*The Gospel and Its Ministry*, P. 74, A. C. Gaebelein, publisher).

These two great doctrines give us the two aspects of the message of grace committed to our trust: the one, that God in His love chose believers in Christ before the world began: the other, that God gave Christ to die for all without distinction and makes *a bona fide offer* to all to receive salvation through faith in Him. The former truth is proclaimed to the saved so that they may revel in the goodness of God to them. The latter is proclaimed to the unsaved for their acceptance. It is not without significance that the Word of God closes with the offer: "And *whosoever will*, let him take of the water of life freely" (Rev. 22:17).

In thus challenging those who stand, or try to stand, only on one side or the other of this great subject, we do not, however, overlook the importance of a statement made in this connection by the late Dr. Lewis Sperry Chafer:

> "The disagreement now under discussion is not between orthodox and heterodox men; it is within the fellowship of those who have most in common and who need the support and encouragement of each other's confidence. Few themes have drawn out more sincere and scholarly investigation" (*Systematic Theology*, Vol. III, P. 184, Dallas Seminary Press).

It is in this spirit that we have written the foregoing lines, and it is in this spirit that we pray they will be considered by our readers.

Do you receive
THE BEREAN SEARCHLIGHT
our monthly Bible study magazine?

Other Books by the Same Author

Many of the subjects touched upon in this volume are dealt with more comprehensively in the following books by the author:

Things That Differ
 The Fundamentals of Dispensationalism

Acts, Dispensationally Considered (Four Volumes)

The Twofold Purpose of God
 Prophecy and the Mystery

Satan in Derision
 The Heart of the Mystery

Moses and Paul
 The Dispensers of Law and Grace

Our Great Commission
 What Is It?

The Present Peril
 The New Evangelicalism

No Other Doctrine

Man, His Nature and Destiny

True Spirituality

Two Minutes with the Bible
 A Daily Bible Study Devotional

A COMPLETE PRICE LIST
...is available free of charge. Address your request to:
BEREAN BIBLE SOCIETY
7609 W. Belmont Avenue
Chicago, IL 60635

Can You Answer These Questions?

What is a dispensation?

If it is impossible for the blood of beasts to take away sins (Heb. 10:4), why did God once require blood sacrifices for the remission of sins (Heb. 9:22)?

In what sense, if any, did works ever save?

Would it be merely unnecessary, or would it be *wrong* to offer blood sacrifices today?

Why did God tell Moses to put the law in a coffin?

What solemn agreement did the leaders of the twelve make with Paul as to the evangelization of the Gentiles?

How did this affect the so-called "great commission"?

What is the difference between "the gospel of the kingdom" and "the gospel of the grace of God"?

Were Old Testament saints saved by looking in faith to Calvary? Can you prove this by Scripture?

What is "the preaching of Jesus Christ according to the revelation of the mystery" (Rom. 16:25)?

These questions and many more
are answered in

THINGS THAT DIFFER
THE FUNDAMENTALS OF DISPENSATIONALISM
By CORNELIUS R. STAM

Mrs. Malone
Bel-Air Rd.
Hollidaysburg, Pa.
16648

St. 6/21/81